extbooks

Betw   through a
series   l rebellion.
This   who lived
throu   , peasants,
town   w they ob-
taine   idence for
their   d. Did the
aristc   e peasants
really   ortunes of
differ   ntury, the
crises   e fifteenth.
Dr D   of weather
and (social and
econc   sequence a
book   s of social
ment

Int   er's study
will p   economic
histo   nt general
contr   f medieval
socie

rary

Cambridge Medieval Textbooks

This is a series of specially commissioned textbooks for teachers and students, designed to complement the monograph series Cambridge Studies in Medieval Life and Thought by providing introductions to a range of topics in medieval history. This series combines both chronological and thematic approaches, and will deal with British and European topics. All volumes in the series will be published in hard covers and in paperback.

For a list of titles in the series, see end of book.

STANDARDS OF LIVING

IN THE

LATER MIDDLE AGES

Social change in England c. 1200–1520

REVISED EDITION

CHRISTOPHER DYER

Professor of Medieval Social History
University of Birmingham

CAMBRIDGE
UNIVERSITY PRESS

PUBLISHED BY THE PRESS SYNDICATE OF THE UNIVERSITY OF CAMBRIDGE
The Pitt Building, Trumpington Street, Cambridge CB2 1RP, United Kingdom
CAMBRIDGE UNIVERSITY PRESS
40 West 20th Street, New York, NY 10011–4211, USA
10 Stamford Road, Oakleigh, Melbourne 3166, Australia

First published 1989
Reprinted 1990, 1993, 1994, Revised edition, 1998

Typeset in Bembo 11/11.5

British Library cataloguing in publication data

Dyer, C (Christopher), 1944–
Standards of living in the later Middle Ages: social change in England c. 1200–1520. –
(Cambridge medieval textbooks).
1. England. Social life 1154–1485.
I. Title
942.03

Library of Congress cataloguing in publication data

Dyer, Christopher, 1944–
Standards of living in the later Middle Ages: social change in England, c. 1200–1520 /
Christopher Dyer.
p. cm. – (Cambridge medieval textbooks)
Bibliography.
Includes index.
ISBN 0 521 25127 3 ISBN 0 521 27215 7 (pbk.)
1. Cost and standard of living – England – History. 2. England – Social conditions –
Medieval period, 1066–1485. 3 England – Social conditions – 16th century. I. Title.
II. Series.
HD7024.D94 1989
339.4'7'0942–dc19 88–21087 CIP

ISBN 0 521 25127 3 hard covers
ISBN 0 521 27215 7 paperback

Transferred to digital printing 2002

CONTENTS

ILLUSTRATIONS

FIGURES

MAPS

TABLES

PREFACE

This book has been written in the belief that the everyday lives of ordinary medieval people are of interest to a modern readership. The fact that the lives that are here chronicled ended more than five centuries ago does not diminish their significance. They were as important and their experiences as valuable as those of their modern successors, or indeed as our own, and they are worthy of rescue from the condescension of posterity. In addition, past societies should be relevant to our own because our foundations are built on their achievements. To know of them is to understand ourselves.

Parts of this work are written directly from my own research, and much depends on others, because its aim is to offer an overview of a whole society. My debts to published works will be appreciated from the footnotes. I cannot acknowledge all my obligations because a high proportion of my conversations with dozens of colleagues and students over the last twenty years has contributed to my understanding of the subject; I cannot remember all of my creditors, and a partial list would offend those who have been omitted. I will indicate here the most substantial debts. The unpublished works of Simon Penn and Yang Jei helped my understanding of wage-earning for chapter 8. I was given research leads and general guidance for chapters 4 and 5 by three unpublished theses, by K. Mertes, J. Thurgood and Christopher Woolgar. The latter talked and corresponded with me on a number of occasions on the subject of household accounts and lent me transcripts from manuscripts. Chapters 5 and 6 were much assisted by the generosity of colleagues in allowing me to use their transcripts, especially from court rolls: these were Jean Birrell, Rodney Hilton, Graham Platts, Richard Smith, Jan Titow and Janet Williamson. Rodney Hilton's advice has influenced every chapter, but especially chapter 7. David Aldred helped me to prepare map 2 from his detailed local knowledge. Librarians and archivists gave information and help beyond the call of duty, notably in the British Library, the Chancery Lane section of the Public Record Office and Cambridge University Library. The materials used in chapters 3 and 4 (and scattered throughout the rest of the book) were collected with financial support from the British Academy. Travel costs and research time in study leaves were provided by the University of Birmingham. Authors usually thank their families for tolerance at being neglected. In my case the neglect is habitual, whether or not a book is being written, and they find themselves drawn in to the work. Jenny Dyer criticized drafts, and Thomas Dyer calculated the statistics in table 19. Josephine Dyer helped with proof-reading. Susan Wright and Sally Howard turned my primitive typing and illegible scrawl into a word-processed typescript with remarkable patience.

I hope that this book marks the beginning of a new set of enquiries by others that will inevitably modify its conclusions and correct its errors.

ACKNOWLEDGEMENTS

The author wishes to thank the earl of Berkeley's will trust for permission to use documents in the Berkeley Castle muniment room, and the Fellows of St John's College, Cambridge, for allowing him to use their archives.

The author and publishers are grateful to the following who gave permission for the use of figures based on their drawings: J. M. Dent; Royal Commission on Ancient and Historical Monuments in Wales; Royal Commission on the Historical Monuments of England; G. Beresford; Society of Medieval Archaeology; Economic History Society.

ABBREVIATIONS

Ag.H.R.	*Agricultural History Review*
Annales E.S.C.	*Annales, Economies, Sociétés, Civilisations*
B.L.	British Library
C.B.A.	Council for British Archaeology
E.H.R.	*English Historical Review*
Ec.H.R.	*Economic History Review*
Med. Arch.	*Medieval Archaeology*
P. and P.	*Past and Present*
P.R.O.	Public Record Office
R.O.	Record Office
T.R.H.S.	*Transactions of the Royal Historical Society*
U.L.	University Library
V.C.H.	*Victoria County History*

WEIGHTS, MEASURES AND PLACES

Weights and measures are given in the units used in the middle ages, and which in essentials remained in use in England until the late twentieth century. The monetary system, by which 12 pence (d.) made one shilling and 20 shillings (s.) a pound cannot be given modern equivalents without misleading the modern reader. An approximation to current values can be obtained by remembering that a skilled building worker earned 2d. per day in 1250, 4d. in 1400 and 6d. in 1500.

Those readers more familiar with the metric than the traditional system of weights and measures should note that an acre is about 0.4 hectare, or alternatively a hectare is equivalent to about 2.5 acres. Grain was measured by volume, in bushels (b) (36 litres) and quarters (qr) (290 litres). 4 pecks made a bushel, and 8 bushels a quarter. One problem discussed in this book is the size of grain yields, measured sometimes in bushels per acre. The metric equivalent of 10 bushels per acre would be 900 litres per hectare.

Ale and wine were measured by the gallon (4.5 litres), which contained 8 pints (0.57 litre), and dry goods such as fruits and spices by the pound (0.45 kilogramme). We will need to calculate weights by the ounce (28 grammes), which was a sixteenth of a pound. Cheese and wool were weighed by the stone of 14 pounds (6.4 kilogrammes).

Linear measures for cloth were the yard (3 feet, or 0.9 metre) or the ell, which was often as long as 45 inches (1.1 metre). The dimensions of buildings, which are measured by modern archaeologists in metres, but which were planned and built in feet, are given here in feet (0.3 metre). Longer distances are given in miles (1.6 kilometre).

Places are identified by their historic counties (before 1974).

INTRODUCTION

This book is concerned with standards of living and patterns of consumption in England between the thirteenth and the early sixteenth century. It is the first work to treat the period wholly in this way, but the approach has many antecedents in historical writing going back for more than a century, and owes much to a growing tide of research in the last twenty years.

Perhaps the first modern interest in the subject can be seen among nineteenth-century antiquarians in search of curiosities and specifically of material to illustrate the social background to medieval literature. They produced works of lasting value in editions of aristocratic household accounts, which have not been used by historians until recently.[1] The first scholar to employ modern methods of analysis to the history of living standards was J. E. Thorold Rogers, a professor of economics in the universities of London and Oxford who, with remarkable energy and persistence, collected a mass of information on prices and wages from 1259 to 1793, published in seven fat volumes between 1866 and 1902.[2] His interpretation of these figures, *Six centuries of work and wages*, first appeared in 1884 and went through many reprintings and editions. Thorold

---

1 For example, T. H. Turner (ed.), *Manners and household expenses of the thirteenth and fifteenth centuries* (Roxburgh Club, 1841).

2 J. E. Thorold Rogers, *A history of agriculture and prices in England* (7 vols., Oxford, 1866–1902).

Rogers was a radical social reformer, for a time serving as a Liberal MP, for whom historical research was linked directly with a concern for the condition of the working class in his day. He argued that agricultural workers had suffered a continuous fall in their living standards since the middle ages. We would not share in Thorold Rogers's optimistic view of all medieval wage-earners, but his identification of the fifteenth century as the 'golden age of the English labourer' is a valuable insight that still forms part of our interpretation of the period. By providing evidence for the relatively high level of real wages in the later middle ages, Thorold Rogers gave scientific support to a widespread belief in progressive circles in the late nineteenth century that modern industrialization had destroyed an admirable traditional way of life. Their imagined 'Merrie England' of upright yeomen, honest craftsmen and village maypoles as presented in such works as William Morris's *Dream of John Ball* was, of course, a world of fantasy.[3] For us the myth is important as an expression of the outlook and attitudes of the nineteenth-century critics of expanding capitalism.

Most of the founders of the new discipline of economic history in the early twentieth century had little sympathy either with Thorold Rogers's approach, or with the socialists who had idealized medieval society. Such writers of textbooks as Lipson and Clapham were more interested in the growth and decline of economic and social institutions than in the experience of individuals.[4] Their accounts of the middle ages concentrated on the organization of economic life in the manor, the borough and the guild. They viewed society from above, especially in their preoccupation with government policies. Commerce was emphasized because it was believed that the growth of the market changed the medieval economy profoundly, and led progressively to the emergence of modern capitalism.

Thorold Rogers's work was not forgotten, and in the inter-war years William (later Lord) Beveridge continued the tradition of combining historical enquiry with a concern for current social problems; Beveridge's accumulation of statistical material has regrettably

3 W. Morris, *A dream of John Ball. A king's lesson* (Berlin, 1958), pp. 11–13, imagines rebels in 1381: 'they were merry and good tempered enough'. 'Their . . . buckles and belts and the finishing and hems of their garments were all what we should now call beautiful'. 'The houses were almost all built of oak framework . . . with their windows and doors of well moulded free-stone', and much more.
4 E. Lipson, *The economic history of England* (3 vols., London, 1915–31), vol. 1; J. Clapham, *A concise economic history of Britain* (Cambridge, 1949).

only partially been published.[5] In the post-war period, and in particular since the 1960s, interest in standards of living has grown with stimuli from at least four different directions. Firstly the study of peasants, workers, women and other underprivileged sections of society has now been widely accepted as a legitimate area of historical investigation. A notable example of this concern was the controversy over working-class living standards in the period of industrialization of the eighteenth and nineteenth centuries, which originally centred on questions of real wages and earnings, but which extended over such related problems as working-class housing conditions, and the quality of life under factory work-disciplines.[6] Such preoccupations are not confined to the period after 1750. The French school of historians associated with the journal *Annales* has had a slow but strong influence on English-speaking historians, and provides a second source of inspiration for their study of living standards. The *Annalistes* have pioneered the scientific investigation of the totality of human experience. Largely because of their work, such subjects as population, the family, diet and popular mentality are regarded as proper fields of enquiry. The most influential practitioner of this elevation of the ordinary to become an area of academic concern was Fernand Braudel, who began research with a monumental regional study of the Mediterranean, and then turned to the growth of the capitalist economy with an emphasis on consumption.[7] Braudel's work has been admired more than it has been imitated partly because of its formidable bulk and detail. A third, and quite different impetus for the investigation of living standards has come from the great expansion in archaeology since the late 1960s. The archaeologists have accumulated a mass of information, almost embarrassing in its sheer quantity, for the physical conditions of the past – called 'material culture' on the continent. This refers not just to pottery, objects of bone, stone and metal, and to the remains of houses, but also to human bones (which yield valuable information about the age of death and disease) and to animal bones and plant remains. The interpretation of this wealth of new evidence is still

---

5 W. Beveridge, *Prices and wages in England, from the twelfth to the nineteenth century* (London, 1939), vol. 1.

6 A. J. Taylor (ed.), *The standard of living in Britain in the industrial revolution* (London, 1975); E. P. Thompson, *The making of the English working class* (London 1965).

7 F. Braudel, *The Mediterranean and the Mediterranean world in the age of Philip II* (2 vols., London, 1972–3); F. Braudel, *Capitalism and material life* (London, 1973); F. Braudel, *Civilization and capitalism* (3 vols., London, 1981–4).

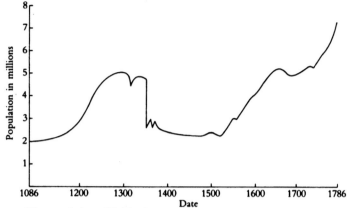

Fig. 1 The population of England, 1086–1786
For 1086 to 1525 much conjecture has been used, based on J. Hatcher, *Plague, population and the English economy, 1348–1530* (London, 1977); from 1541 the graph follows the more secure calculations in E. A. Wrigley and R. S. Schofield, *The population history of England, 1541–1871: a reconstruction* (London, 1981), pp. 528–9.

continuing and already, in the light of preliminary findings, historians have had to think again about some of their assumptions.[8]

A fourth influence has come from our growing awareness of contemporary 'underdeveloped', 'developing', or 'third world' economies. Here famines, poverty and technical backwardness superficially similar to the problems of medieval Europe are still causing human misery. To explain the plight of the third world is a matter of pressing importance – should we emphasize the imbalance between population and resources? Or can we point to the difficulties caused by greedy local élites? Or does the root of the problem lie in the exploitation of people and resources for the benefit of the developed countries?[9]

Pre-industrial Europe experienced fluctuations in levels of population and economic activity. In the case of England we now know in detail about population history from 1540 onward, and can with some confidence project a graph of demographic change back to the eleventh century.[10] Between the Norman Conquest and the Indus-

8 For example, C. Platt, *Medieval England* (London, 1978); H. Clarke, *The archaeology of medieval England* (London, 1984).

9 For example, S. Amin, *Unequal development* (Hassocks, Sussex, 1976); E. R. Wolf, *Europe and the people without history* (Berkeley and Los Angeles, 1982).

10 E. A. Wrigley and R. S. Schofield, *The population history of England, 1541–1871: a reconstruction* (London, 1981).

trial Revolution there were three phases of expansion: in the century or two before 1300, in the sixteenth century, and in the eighteenth. In between these periods of increase were two lengthy episodes of decline or stagnation, from *c.*1300 to *c.*1520, and in the seventeenth century (see fig. 1). To describe these trends is relatively easy; to explain them presents many more difficulties. There must have been a relationship between living standards and movements in population, but the two interacted in very complicated ways. After 1540, it is argued that acute misery was avoided because if living standards declined, the age of marriage rose because couples could not afford to set up new households, and many people were unable to marry. There followed a fall in the birth-rate. If earnings and profits of farming, manufacture and trade increased, earlier and more frequent marriage led to a rising population. Such a regulatory system may have prevailed before 1540, but it is also likely that mortality from starvation and disease also acted as a check on population growth in hard times, so that low standards of living produced demographic catastrophes. On the other hand, the level of population could have changed independently, either upwards by natural increase, or downwards because of the effects of epidemic diseases. Living standards would tend to decline if the population rose to too high a level, through the shortage of productive land and the depressed level of wages; epidemics would bring in their wake cheap land and high wages.[11] A further level of interaction between population and prosperity relates to the market, because an increased number of people may have caused some impoverishment, but it could also stimulate demand through the multiplication of consumers.

These related problems of underdevelopment, demography and economic fluctuations were brought to the forefront of medieval historical studies by Professor Sir Michael Postan. He applied to the study of medieval England both a grasp of economic theory and personal experience of life in a peasant society in pre-revolutionary Russia. Having cast doubts on the prevailing notion of the economic historians of the 1920s and 1930s that there had been a linear growth of the market and the use of money in the middle ages, Postan developed the idea that population expansion in the thirteenth century created an excess of people, and that nature punished man for his prodigal use of resources by reducing numbers drastically in the

11 These issues are discussed in J. Hatcher, *Plague, population and the English economy, 1348–1530* (London, 1977); and R. M. Smith, 'Hypothèses sur la nuptialité en Angleterre aux XIII*e*–XIV*e* siècles', *Annales E.S.C.*, 38(1983), 107–36.

fourteenth century. The argument rested on the assumption that in a peasant society, the crucial determinant of all other changes was the relationship between people and land, peasants being holders of 'family farms', which provided the subsistence needs of the household, using mainly family labour. Too many people led not just to a reduction in the amount of land per head, and a diminution in the size of holdings, but also to damage to the earth itself: the area of pasture and the numbers of animals were reduced by the extension of arable land, and there was consequently a shortage of manure. Standards of living played an important part in Postan's reasoning, because in his view the crisis of *c.*1300 was brought about by growing impoverishment, while the relaxation of population pressure after 1350 created a 'golden age' for peasants as well as labourers.[12] Although Postan's arguments have been received with respect, and have won a good deal of acceptance, much of the reasoning is based on assumptions and logical deduction rather than detailed empirical research, not least in the case of standards of living.

A criticism that can be made of historians such as Postan, who stress the interaction of population and land, is their tendency to underestimate the importance of social structures. Impersonal factors, such as climate, or soil exhaustion, or the spread of microbes are placed in the forefront of the stage, and inequality and the mechanisms of social exploitation are pushed into a subsidiary rôle. Yet anyone examining demand or consumption needs to devote a great deal of attention to the enormous disparities between rich and poor. There is more to this social dimension of the study of living standards than simply assessing the varying quantity and quality of goods consumed at different social levels, though this can be a worthwhile exercise in itself. The inequalities of the middle ages were not an incidental by-product of economic activity but an inherent feature of society. The great wealth of the aristocracy derived from their military, political and judicial domination of the subordinate peasantry. Services, goods and cash flowed upwards from the peasants to the lords. At an early stage of its development the pervading feudal principle had been that tenure of land was dependent on the performance of service, whether military or administrative service in the case of the aristocracy, or labour for the peasants. In the later middle ages the services were turned into money rents, but this did not lead to any sudden transformation in the power structures of society. The manor, the administrative

---

12 M. M. Postan, *The medieval economy and society* (London, 1972).

organization through which lords collected rents, continued to function, and indeed was given a new lease of life in the thirteenth
century when the growth of the market enabled the lord's own
reserve of land, the demesne, to be run for profit, and the peasants
were expected to produce a flow of cash payments. In exploring the
consumption patterns of the aristocracy, often at a level of considerable luxury, we are revealing the *raison d'être* of a feudal society. The
whole purpose of manors and estates was to concentrate wealth into
the hands of a few, who were then expected not to hoard or save, but
to redistribute the goods among their followers and supporters in
acts of generous giving. We may also be exposing one of the great
weaknesses of the feudal economy, and one of the sources of its
backwardness, because the rest of society was deprived of resources
by the constant demands of the lords. It is scarcely surprising to find
that such a consumption-oriented society lacked investment
capital.[13]

A simple view of the late medieval economy would depict the
thirteenth century as a period of strong and wealthy lords and
relatively poor peasants, with the balance being weighted in the
opposite direction in the fourteenth and fifteenth centuries because
of peasant tenants' scarcity value, and their resistance to the lords.
However, the medieval economy was complicated by the market.
The wealthy aristocratic consumers put some of their wealth back
into circulation by buying goods and services, so townsmen and
rural craftsmen gained some indirect benefit from the riches of lords.
The peasants did not forfeit all of their surplus income, and they too
generated a demand for manufactures. The towns that had grown up
initially to serve the needs of these rural consumers became sufficiently complex to generate an internal market, so that urban
traders and craftsmen made much of their living by selling to their
fellow townsmen. The commercial economy had to some extent
developed a life of its own, and was subject to booms and slumps,
which caused fluctuations in urban living standards quite distinct
from the rise and fall in demand from the countryside.

The emphasis in historical writing has always been on the forces of
production. Medieval historians have enquired into such subjects as
field systems, the efficiency of corn-growing, the organization of
cloth-making and the techniques of trade. It is in no way the aim of
this book to detract from the importance of production, but I intend

---

13 R. H. Hilton, 'Rent and capital formation in feudal society' in R. H. Hilton, *The
English peasantry in the later middle ages* (Oxford, 1975), pp. 174–214.

to show that the study of consumption can help our understanding of medieval society in many ways. Indeed, some notable contributions to this type of enquiry have already been made. R. H. Hilton was able to demonstrate that a small monastery, which consumed much of its own agricultural produce, was better able to survive the economic problems of the fifteenth century than a large estate. This observation had implications for small landowners in general in the period.[14] E. Veale, by paying attention to the fickle demands of fashion, was able to explain some of the changes in the late medieval fur trade.[15] E. Carus-Wilson suggested that the Devon cloth industry boomed at the end of the middle ages because its products were bought by a large, prospering, relatively lower-class group of consumers.[16] Such interpretations based on consideration of consumption are, however, somewhat exceptional. All too often agriculture is seen as a matter of cultivation and productivity, and the end products of bread, porridge, ale and fodder are forgotten. Trade is seen in terms of sellers rather than buyers. Market places and towns were indeed inhabited by merchants, shopkeepers and hucksters, but their presence would have been futile without customers. Weavers, cutlers and potters could only make their living if their cloth, knives and jugs were bought and used.

This neglect can be partly attributed to the fact that sources ideal for the study of consumption are by no means plentiful. Thousands of manorial accounts can give us a mass of information about production of aristocratic estates while accounts detailing expenditure in upper-class households survive in much smaller numbers, and then often contain fragmentary evidence. At the lower end of the social scale, hard information is not acquired easily, especially because the written sources were compiled by the upper classes for their own administrative purposes. We find ourselves involved in some guesswork, using every variety of evidence and still feeling uncertain of the results. We must venture into such elusive areas as social psychology, used with much success by Thrupp in her study of consumption patterns of London merchants, but treacherous ground for the unwary.[17]

14 R. H. Hilton, *The economic development of some Leicestershire estates in the fourteenth and fifteenth centuries* (Oxford, 1947), pp. 117–38.
15 E. Veale, *The English fur trade in the later middle ages* (Oxford, 1966), especially chapter 7.
16 E. M. Carus-Wilson, *The expansion of Exeter at the close of the middle ages* (Exeter, 1963).
17 S. Thrupp, *The merchant class of medieval London* (Chicago, 1948).

Despite the difficulties and dangers involved in the study of living standards, it is a subject in need of investigation. Many others have researched parts of the subject. My purpose is to define the different levels of living standards in late medieval society, and to explore changes over three centuries. Before the enquiry can proceed, however, it is necessary to examine the stratification of society.

I

LATE MEDIEVAL SOCIETY

To state that standards of living varied with social rank is a truism; to define the groups that can be used in our analysis presents us with a hard task. There is no lack of information, as the medieval sources contain a bewildering plenty of titles and social labels. Because of England's linguistic peculiarities, the names of social groups appear in our documents in three languages – Latin, French and English. They varied from region to region, and they changed over time. To look at the main developments, let us take three samples, slices of evidence compiled at roughly 100-year intervals, in 1279, 1379 and the late fifteenth century.

The Hundred Rolls of 1279–80 provide our first cross-section through English society. They survive in their most detailed form as surveys of villages from six counties, a fragment of an ambitious attempt to carry out a nationwide survey of land-holding in much more detail than the earlier Domesday Book. Let us take a single example, the survey of the Oxfordshire village of Ducklington.[1] Here was a lord (*dominus*) called Richard de Carbroc, who held about 300 acres of arable land in demesne, that is under his direct control. His subordinates were listed under three headings: 'free tenants' (*liberi tenentes*), who were sixteen in number, 'serfs' (*servi*), of whom there were twelve, and five 'cottars' (*cottarii*). Thus tenure is used as

---

1 E. Stone (ed.), *Oxfordshire hundred rolls of 1279.1: the hundred of Bampton* (Oxford-shire Record Soc., 46, 1969), pp. 59–60; *Rotuli hundredorum* (2 vols., Record Commission 1812–18), vol. 2, pp. 700–1.

the basis of classification. This was common to other thirteenth-century writings, and of course words such as *dominus* and *servus* derive from a need also to define social and legal status. The most important distinction lay between lords and tenants, in a ratio of 1:33 at Ducklington, which was probably quite near to the national average. The free tenants were distinguished from the others by their low rents. William le Honte, for example, paid a penny and a half-pound of pepper (worth 6d.) for a half-yardland of about 10 acres of arable land, with common rights in a meadow, pasture and wood. The serfs, most of whom each held a full yardland of 20 acres (with common rights), owed an annual cash rent of 3s. 4d. and labour services valued at 9s. 2¹/₂d. 'Free' and 'serf' refer also to the personal status of the tenants. The Hundred Rolls do not spell out the implications, but we can take it that the serfs of Ducklington, like those elsewhere, had to obtain the lord's permission for the marriage of their daughters or the migration of their sons, and were expected to pay entry fines on taking up their holdings, fines when their daughters married, and other occasional dues. The free could in theory plead in the royal courts, from which the serfs were excluded. The term 'cottars' introduced an economic as well as tenurial basis for assigning people into social categories, because the defining characteristic of this group lay in the relatively small size of their holdings, mostly between 2 and 10 acres, compared with the majority of their neighbours who held 20 acres. Judging from their rents, the cottars were as heavily, or more heavily burdened in proportion to their holdings as the serfs, one paying as much as 1s. per acre.

The complexities of thirteenth-century society may be glimpsed beneath the orderly lists of free tenants, serfs and cottars in the Ducklington survey. The group of tenants was by no means homogeneous. Heading the free-holders appears Godfrey the Franklin, whose standard yardland may have been supplemented with other assets to support his status, because franklins usually formed the highest rank of village society.[2] Other Ducklington tenants included three millers and a smith. Their wealth may therefore have been greater than their land-holdings alone suggest, and they occupied a special position within village society by virtue of their occupations. The presence of other craftsmen and traders may be hidden from us; the survey did not intend to give occupational descriptions.

2 N. Saul, 'The social status of Chaucer's Franklin: a reconsideration', *Medium Aevum*, 52 (1983), 10–23.

Status was not always determined by tenure. Richard de Carbroc held the manor of Ducklington by knight service, that is for the obligation to serve as a knight for his overlord, Hugh de Plessetis, and ultimately for Hugh's lord, the king. But although many thousands of people held land by knight service, only a thousand or so at any time were dubbed knights.[3] Those who were dubbed tended to be drawn from the wealthier of the small landowners, and the choice involved some complex assessments by contemporaries as to the candidate's 'knightly' qualities, and an element of choice by the man himself, who might decline the honour on the grounds that it involved too much responsibility and expense. Knights or not, men like Carbroc were important leaders of society, collectively holding a great deal of land, and forming a group of resident worthies from whom local administrators were recruited. Carbroc's overlord was a baron, which meant that he held a large estate directly from the Crown. The exact qualification for a barony is not certain, except that it had a *caput* or headquarters, usually a castle.[4] When he died twelve years after the making of the Hundred Rolls Hugh de Plessetis held three manors in Buckinghamshire and Oxfordshire, an unusually modest endowment for a barony.[5] The top rank of aristocracy at the time of the Hundred Rolls was that of earl, like William de Valence, earl of Pembroke, who had rights of jurisdiction over Ducklington because he held the Hundred of Bampton, the unit of local government, for his private profit, among many other lands and rights scattered widely over England, Wales and Ireland. Many of the lords listed in the Hundred Rolls were churchmen, like the abbot of Eynsham, a leading Oxfordshire magnate, who held a small hamlet in Ducklington called *Estwelde*. The position of such ecclesiastics, apart from the fact that they held land on behalf of an institution rather than in a personal capacity, was clearly closely analogous to that of the secular lords. Churches often exercised strong lordship, and typically the abbot's yardlanders paid 2s. 5^1/2d. more in rent than did Carbroc's tenants.

Finally, the Hundred Rolls cover towns such as Witney (near to Ducklington), which lay under the lordship of the bishopric of Winchester, and the much larger royal town of Oxford.[6] Again, our

3 N. Denholm-Young, 'Feudal society in the thirteenth century: the knights' in N. Denholm-Young, *Collected papers on mediaeval subjects* (Oxford, 1946), pp. 56–67.
4 S. Painter, *Studies in the history of the English feudal barony* (Baltimore, 1943), pp. 14–17.
5 *Calendar of the inquisitions post mortem*, vol. 3, p. 41.
6 *Rotuli hundredorum*, vol. 2, pp. 788–811.

source is concerned with tenure. The burgesses are simply listed by name as the holders of burgages, messuages or cottages for cash rents. The main hint of the special character of the settlements comes from the diversity of occupational surnames, like the four smiths, two dyers, two bakers, ironmonger, cobbler, weaver and tailor at Witney.

The terms for lords – knights, barons and earls – were used fairly uniformly throughout thirteenth-century England. The words describing tenants were much more diverse: free-holders were often called sokemen in eastern England, and the unfree were listed as villeins, bondmen and naifs (*nativi*). Tenants of intermediate status appeared as molmen in the east of England, and various kinds of leaseholders were called *terminarii* and (in Cornwall) conventionaries.[7] Whatever the local customs and nomenclature, however, in the minds of officials tenure provided an important means of categorizing people.

Moving forward a century to our second survey of society, in 1379 a description of the social hierarchy was set out in a parliamentary schedule that gave the rates of contributions to the experimental graduated poll tax.[8] A relatively new title, that of duke, headed the list. This title was conferred at that time only on members of the royal family. Earls and barons followed; their exclusiveness had been reinforced during the fourteenth century by the stricter definition of the secular peerage as those who received a personal summons to attend the house of lords in parliament. There was some overlap in wealth between the barons and the next rank, the knights, and the schedule refers to the possibility that some knights would be 'able to spend as much as a baron'. Such statements show that, appropriate to a document compiled for purposes of taxation, income was being given more prominence than status. A new group appears below the knights, the esquires, who clearly were the successors of the sometimes wealthy non-dubbed landowners of the thirteenth century, because a better-off esquire 'ought . . . to be a knight'. Below the esquires lay a miscellaneous collection of 'farmers of manors', sergeants and franklins, no doubt including the people described as 'gentle' in the sumptuary law of 1363, but who had not yet been accepted as a definite group of 'gentlemen'.[9]

7 E. Miller and J. Hatcher, *Medieval England: rural society and economic change, 1086–1348* (London, 1978), pp. 111–20.
8 R. B. Dobson, *Peasants' revolt of 1381*, 2nd edn (London, 1983), pp. 105–111.
9 *Statutes of the realm* (11 vols., Record Commission, 1810–28), vol. 1, p. 380.

The 1379 schedule is explicit in making equations between the ranks of landed, ecclesiastical and urban society. Archbishops, bishops and the richest abbots are put on the same level as dukes and earls; abbots, priors and archdeacons are equated with barons and knights; and prosperous merchants are assumed to be equivalent to knights and esquires. Such assumptions of the existence of parallels between both urban and rural society are found in other formal statements of hierarchy, like the sumptuary law which states that 'merchants, citizens and burgesses, who have goods and chattels to the value of £1,000 . . . may . . . wear [clothing] in the same manner as esquires and gentlemen who have land and rent to the value of £200 a year'.[10] A later courtesy book, setting out an order of precedence for a hypothetical feast, begins at the rarefied level of pope and emperor, and with more realism puts together at the lower tables 'parsons and vicars that are of dignity' (that is, superior beneficed clergy), merchants and gentlemen.[11]

The 1379 scheme is a very useful source for the higher social echelons, but as the masses were all expected to contribute 4d. each, no details are given of their ranks. However, the records of the collection of the next (and last) poll tax, of 1380–1, contain plentiful information on the non-aristocratic tax-payers. The assessors and collectors used inconsistent terminology from one county to another. Some poll tax lists are reminiscent of the Hundred Rolls in their emphasis on tenures and legal status, and divide rural society into free and servile tenants, though recognizing the existence of 'franklins'. Other assessors and collectors used economic criteria to classify the tax-payers as *cultores* (cultivators) or *agricolae* (farmers), and *laboratores* (labourers), *servientes* (servants) and *famuli* (also servants, especially those who belonged to their employer's household). These distinctions were based on the amount of land held and the extent of wage-earning, the *cultor* or *agricola* having enough land to achieve self-sufficiency, in some cases needing to employ labour, and the labourers and servants being partly or wholly dependent on wages. In both types of tax-list, craftsmen and traders in town and country alike were identified by their occupations, as smiths, weavers, drapers and so on, with an occasional payment at a higher rate to distinguish the wealthy merchant or

10 *Ibid.*
11 F. J. Furnivall (ed.), *The babees book* (Early English Text Soc., O.S., 32, 1868), p. 187.

entrepreneur from the normal run of artisans and small traders.[12] For our third social survey, no single source for 1479 can be compared with the Hundred Rolls or the poll taxes. Almost any set of legal records, however, can provide a sample of social descriptions, because of the insistence of the Statute of Additions in 1413 that anyone coming before the courts must always be identified by his or her 'estate, mystery or degree'; other information can be gleaned from the sumptuary law of 1463, and the growing literature of instruction and exhortation on social themes, teaching good manners in the case of the courtesy books, or extolling the virtues of gentility and chivalry.[13] These show important developments in the language used to describe social groups.

Firstly it is apparent that the title 'lord' had changed. Although it was still used as a means of address, and to describe the lords of manors and clergymen, it had developed another, more exclusive meaning, reserved for the peerage, the members of the house of lords. A second extension of the social vocabulary had produced the word 'gentleman' to describe those of some standing who fell below the knights and esquires.[14] Henceforth the 'gentry' or lesser aristocracy consisted of the three ranks of knights, esquires and gentlemen. Thirdly, at the lower end of rural society, vestiges remained of the old free/unfree vocabulary, but these were obsolescent. Instead, the economic classification that had begun to develop at the time of the poll taxes had achieved universal acceptance with the adoption of the triple terminology of 'yeomen', 'husbandmen' and 'labourers'. Again, the individual was assigned to one category or another depending on the amount of land held. A yeoman's lands were extensive (not necessarily freehold, though this had been one of the yeoman's characteristics); the husbandman had sufficient land to support himself; the labourer had a few acres, or just a cottage, and lived mainly on wages. There was also a category of servants, distinct from the labourers.

Craftsmen and traders, both in town and country tended to be known by their occupations (or 'mystery', to use the language of the 1413 statute). Some occupations, such as that of 'merchant', could imply higher status than others, and membership of the upper strata

---

12 C. C. Fenwick, 'The English poll taxes of 1377, 1379 and 1381' (University of London Ph.D. thesis, 1983), pp. 145–9.

13 *Statutes of the realm*, vol. 2, pp. 399–402; Furnivall (ed.), *Babees book, passim*.

14 G. R. Sitwell, 'The English gentleman', *The Ancestor*, 1 (1902), 58–103; D. A. L. Morgan, 'The individual style of the English gentleman' in M. Jones (ed.), *Gentry and lesser nobility in late medieval Europe* (Gloucester, 1986), pp. 15–35.

of London society was indicated by such a title as 'citizen and draper'. A single occupational description could cover both wealthy wholesalers and relatively poor retailers. Labourers and servants are commonly found in towns – as also are occasional yeomen and husbandmen. The jurors who supplied identifications had to acknowledge the complicated nature of society by using 'aliases' to cover every aspect of a person's life and activities: thus Hugh Calcote of Gloucestershire in 1459 could be called 'chapman, *alias* merchant, *alias* mercer, *alias* yeoman'. He evidently traded in a variety of goods, and also held some land.[15]

Now in this brief outline of changing terminology about forty titles or occupations have been mentioned, and restraint has been necessary to exclude dozens more. To consider the living standards of each group would be a wearying task, and in any case it seems unlikely that people's status would necessarily have much bearing on their material conditions – we have already seen that knights and barons, or knights and abbots, might enjoy the same income. Perhaps broader and simpler social divisions can be discerned behind the highly fragmented and complicated society that legal and taxation documents seem to portray?

Many influential contemporaries believed that their society could be divided into three orders or estates. This was an old notion going back at least to the early middle ages and was revived in the fourteenth century.[16] The three orders, those who prayed (the clergy), those who fought (the secular aristocracy) and those who worked (the rest of society, but especially the peasants) were held to have mutual rights and obligations – the clergy prayed on behalf of the other two orders, and in exchange could expect to be protected by the aristocrats and to be supported by the labour of the peasants. In theory this made for an harmonious and cohesive society, in which everyone had a rôle. Contemporaries were fully aware of the imperfections of the reality around them, which they blamed on human sin. After all, they believed that the estates were ordained by god, so that anyone failing in his social duty was offending against the divine order. There were also practical problems in knowing where to fit anomalous groups. The ordinary townsmen, for example, could be

15 E. Power, 'The wool trade in the fifteenth century' in E. Power and M. M. Postan (eds.), *Studies in English trade in the fifteenth century* (London, 1933), p. 53.
16 R. Mohl, *The three estates in medieval and renaissance literature* (New York, 1933); G. Duby, *The three orders: feudal society imagined* (Chicago, 1980); J. le Goff, 'A note on the tripartite society' in J. le Goff, *Time, work and culture in the middle ages* (Chicago, 1980), pp. 43–52.

accommodated in the third estate with the peasants and servants, but surely grand merchants would belong in the aristocracy? And what to do with those laymen who had broken the church's monopoly of learning and become lawyers?

A sophisticated writer like Geoffrey Chaucer, in his prologue to the *Canterbury tales*, acknowledged the existence of the three orders idea by depicting a model knight, parson and ploughman. Their virtues shone out from a much more numerous group of characters who did not accord with the ideal because they pursued a variety of (mainly urban) trades and professions, or, like the cheating reeve or hunting monk, because they belonged firmly to one of the orders but their behaviour was not calculated to aid the harmony and mutual benefit of an organic society.[17] From the vantage point of a sophisticated London civil servant, having close connections with aristocratic, mercantile and clerical society, Chaucer was gently criticizing this simple notion, and demonstrating that it was an unworkable model in a complex and sinful world. The notion had, of course, been a myth from its inception, because the burdens and benefits were so unequal. The workers in particular were parties to a very one-sided social contract. The repetition of the idea of three orders, especially its revival in the fourteenth century, points to the disquiet felt by some clerical and aristocratic writers. As their world seemed to be going wrong, they advocated a formula which recalled an old and stable system of values. The idea had a practical consequence, as it guided the thinking of governments when they devised the representative machinery which gave consent to taxation in the late thirteenth century. The three estates in continental Europe consisted of clergy, nobles and townsmen. In England the clergy met separately in convocation, and some of the higher clergy also attended parliament as lords. The house of lords therefore consisted of the highest members of the aristocracy, both ecclesiastical and lay. And the commons contained knights and esquires from the shires and the burgesses and citizens from the towns, representing not the common people as such, but their local communities.[18]

To advance *our* understanding of medieval society we must explain the divisions and groups in terms that have a meaning for *us*.

17 F. N. Robinson (ed.), *The works of Geoffrey Chaucer*, 2nd edn (London, 1957), pp. 17–25; J. Mann, *Chaucer and estates satire* (Cambridge, 1973).
18 A. R. Myers, *Parliaments and estates in Europe to 1789* (London, 1975); R. H. Hilton, 'Popular movements in England at the end of the fourteenth century' in L. S. Olshki, *Il tumulto dei ciompi* (Florence, 1981), p. 226.

We must not neglect the medieval vocabulary, because it gives us an insight into their outlook, but to make sense of it all we must also use modern words and modern ideas. To begin with the upper ranks of society, the most useful term for us is 'aristocracy'. 'Nobility', which was used in medieval England and is often applied to the landed classes both in England and on the continent, leads to confusion and ambiguity in England because of its frequent restriction to the peerage or some other small grouping at the very apex of society, unlike the much wider spectrum covered by a continental *noblesse*.[19] In the thirteenth century there was a distinction between those holding land directly of the Crown (the tenants-in-chief, mainly barons and earls), and their inferiors who held their lands of other lords, often in relatively small quantities such as a single manor (like Richard de Carbroc). In the fourteenth and fifteenth centuries the notion of peerage emphasized the gulf between seventy or so important families and the rest. In each case contemporaries were drawing a line beneath the barons. We are bound to see that in any normal sense the aristocracy included those both above and below the base of the peerage. Much more united the earls, barons, knights and potential knights than divided them. Their incomes were very varied, from as little as £10 per annum to as much as £10,000, or, excluding a handful of exceptional magnates, between £10 and £2,000. But for most people £10 represented a great fortune, and we are justified in regarding anyone receiving such a sum regularly as being wealthy. The important characteristic of the aristocracy in any case was not the size of the income but the means by which it was obtained, that is by lordship. The bulk of their regular revenues came from land, most often rents and other payments enforced through rights of jurisdiction that were exercised in manorial courts. Many lords also held the view of frankpledge (that is, they held private courts dealing with petty crime in the king's name). The social domination of the aristocracy was essential to their income: they took rents from their subordinates, and judged them. It is true that some of their income might consist of annuities or fees, but these cash payments were often collected directly and regularly from manors assigned for the purpose, so cannot be readily distinguished from normal manorial revenues.

The aristocracy at all levels also had a common function of providing military and administrative services. Even when the formal

---

19 K. B. McFarlane, *The nobility of later medieval England* (Oxford, 1973) argued for a wider definition of the nobility, but then wrote mainly about the peerage.

obligations to do knight service lapsed in the thirteenth and fourteenth centuries, aristocrats still made up a high proportion of royal armies because of their continued sense of the pleasures and duties of waging war. They also played a major rôle in both national and local government, and served each other in private administration. In their own day, the aristocracy would have been recognized by their style of life: their clothing and horses, their houses surrounded by at least token fortifications, and above all their leisure, which enabled them to avoid both physical labour and retail trade, and to indulge in such pastimes as hunting. The aristocrats themselves were acutely conscious of their special qualities. They hoped that their hallmark was their gentle behaviour, expressed by their generous and courteous treatment of others. Outsiders were aware of the aristocratic vices, notably the pride criticized in contemporary sermons. The common characteristics of incomes derived from rents, of the possession of jurisdictional rights, of military and government functions, of a distinctive life-style and a self-conscious adherence to a set of courtly and chivalric values could be found in each tier of the aristocracy. An earl and an esquire, say, were divided by the size of their income, the number of their manors, the grandeur of their offices and the scale of their hospitality, but they had a great deal in common. The differences were in matters of quantity, not quality. Judged by their economic rôle as lords, and their consciousness of their social position, the aristocracy can be regarded as a social class.

Defining a class in terms of its middle layers poses no problems; the difficulties are encountered in locating its upper and lower limits. In the case of the aristocracy the top needs no debate, except to note that the monarch can be regarded, not as a separate figure, but as a super-magnate. What were the lower limits of aristocracy? The knights lie in some sense at the core of the class, because of the universal admiration of the chivalric (knightly) way of life. The esquires must be swept up along with the knights, because an esquire could be a trainee or aspirant knight; often esquires had every quality and attribute necessary to acquire the title, but exercised a personal choice against it. However, the gentlemen of the fifteenth century cause problems because although they enjoyed considerable incomes (a minimum of £10, often much more), and their very name demonstrates their involvement with the value system of the aristocracy, they sometimes lacked the lordship of a manor and lived on leasehold land, or even the rents of urban property, or entirely on fees and payments for administrative or legal services. In 1436, lawyers disputing a man's status agreed that a gentleman might work with his

Table 1. *The social hierarchy in late medieval England*

Late thirteenth century		Late fifteenth century		
Laity Landed/rural		Urban	Laity Landed/rural	
Laity	*Clergy*		*Laity*	*Clergy*
	Archbishops		Dukes	Archbishops
Earls	Bishops		Earls	Bishops
	Abbots			Abbots
Barons			Barons	
Knights	Rectors	Merchants	Knights	
			Esquires	Rectors
			Gentlemen	
'Lesser				
gentry'	Vicars			Vicars
Franklins	Lesser clergy	Master craftsmen	Yeomen	Lesser clergy
Free			Husbandmen	
Cottars		Journeymen Labourers	Labourers	
Unfree				
Servants		Servants	Servants	
Marginals		Marginals	Marginals	

hands, though it is in practice unlikely that many did so.[20] If the gentlemen seem socially ambiguous, their predecessors are even more shadowy figures, lacking as they did any convenient identifying label. In 1344 in Gloucestershire, a list of landowners made by the government gives a total of 177 with incomes of £5 per annum or more. Almost a half of these had incomes assessed at £5 or £6 13s. 4d., presumably a substantial underassessment, so we can guess that

20 R. L. Storey, 'Gentleman-bureaucrats' in C. H. Clough (ed.), *Profession, vocation and culture in later medieval England* (Liverpool, 1982), pp. 90–129, especially p. 91.

most had in reality £10 or more. [21] These people were neither knights nor esquires, yet they held the lordship of manors and filled minor administrative posts. The convenient term for them is 'lesser gentry', though this is a modern phrase.

In spite of these uncertainties, it is proposed for the purposes of this study to regard the gentlemen and their predecessors as part of the aristocracy, and to put the knights, esquires and gentlemen into the category of 'gentry' or lower aristocracy (see table 1).

The three orders idea made a sharp distinction between the clergy and the warriors. This was a proper separation to make, especially after the church reformers of the eleventh and twelfth centuries had made such a commotion about the strict demarcation of the sacred from the profane. Yet, when the government levied taxes or when a household official drew up a seating plan, or when the king summoned both the lay and ecclesiastical magnates to deliberate in the house of lords, an equivalence of rank was assumed between the church hierarchy and that of laymen. To us, in terms of a sociological analysis, the better-off churchmen seem almost indistinguishable from lay lords. Their incomes were comparable; they derived their revenue from manors of similar type; they held courts; they eschewed manual labour; and many enjoyed the relaxations of the chase and the songs of minstrels. They came from the same families, as the sons of the earls and barons often gained preferment as bishops, and the gentry presented their relatives to local benefices. Many rectories resembled small manors, because they were endowed with glebes and tenant holdings, and tithes were analogous to rents. This cannot be taken too far; the clergy were set apart by their spiritual functions, and by their celibacy. Also monastic houses and other religious corporations, such as colleges, though collectively resembling any other landlord, had a distinct ethos and style of life that cannot allow us to equate their inmates exactly with a specific rank of laymen. Toward the end of the middle ages, the greater privacy of monks and the general relaxation of the stricter discipline of the monastic rules meant that many of the religious came to resemble members of the gentry more closely. [22] By no means all clergy can be equated with the aristocracy, because in addition to the relatively wealthy beneficed rectors and vicars, the parish clergy and

21 N. Saul, *Knights and esquires. The Gloucestershire gentry in the fourteenth century* (Oxford, 1981), pp. 33-4.
22 D. M. Knowles, *The religious orders in England* (3 vols., Cambridge, 1948-59), vol. 2, pp. 240-7.

chaplains included many with poor benefices, worth £5 per annum or even lower sums, and much clerical work was carried out by stipendiaries who were in effect skilled wage-earners.

The third estate was defined by the manual work of its members, by which the other two estates were supported. This contemporary view fits with our conception of their social function, though we would stress the mechanism by which labour, goods and cash for the use of the aristocracy were levied from the lower orders. It has become customary to use the term 'peasant' to describe the rural lower classes. There are those who argue that just as the word was scarcely mentioned in the middle ages, so the whole notion is alien to English society. Such sceptics believe that the essential characteristic of a peasantry is the prominence of the family as a collective group, sharing in the tenure, work and produce of a holding, as found in, say, nineteenth-century Russia or twentieth-century Asia. As (they argue) English countrymen lacked this strong attachment to the family and family land, they cannot be regarded as peasants.[23] In fact the absence of 'family holdings' is still a matter of debate, and even if the case against them was conclusive, the existence of the English peasantry would not be disproved. 'Peasant' is a convenient, if rather elastic term to describe many types of small-scale cultivators. The amount of land at their disposal led them to produce crops mainly with their own labour resources, and for the consumption needs of their household. The limited scale of their activities often drew them into cooperation with neighbours in village communities, whose members shared common assets such as pastures. They were subordinated to lords through the institutions of serfdom and the manor. Contemporaries rarely needed to discuss these people *en masse*, and when they did so in writing often used the Latin word *rustici* (countrymen). Usually, as we have seen, they were either classified in terms of their legal status or form of tenure, or later in the period by the size of their holdings. The great majority of the people mentioned above under the names of serfs, villeins, free tenants, cottars, *cultores*, labourers, husbandmen and yeomen would fall within the peasantry as normally understood. Many wage-earners and rural craftsmen could also be included because they gained a substantial part of their living from a holding of land. Poll-tax collectors and fifteenth-century jurors called on to label a peasant-craftsman must often have been faced with the choice of using either the size of his holding or his trade as his identifying feature. Doubts arise in our minds in the case of the wealthiest tenants, often free-

23 A. Macfarlane, *The origins of English individualism* (Oxford, 1978), pp. 7–33.

holders in the earlier part of our period, 'farmers' (meaning tenants of substantial amounts of leasehold land) and yeomen. Not many of them held more than 80 acres of land, but those that did begin to slip outside the characterization of the peasantry given above. The scale of their land-holding caused them to sublet land and so live at least partly on rents, or to work the land with a good deal of wage labour and to sell most of the produce. In the first case the 'peasant' might come to resemble a member of the lesser gentry, and in the second he was *en route* to becoming a capitalist farmer. The landless labourers or the 'servants in husbandry' pose problems at the base of the peasantry. As will be seen, permanent full-time wage-earning was a minority activity, and at least a proportion of rural servants were young people from peasant households intending to obtain a holding of their own in later life.

We usually envisage the peasantry in three layers, of rich, middling and poor, by reference to the amount of land held, showing that modern historians are as besotted with the number three as were medieval clerks. All of them, however, were involved in agricultural production, and had a stake in the common fields of their village. All belonged to village communities which in limited ways governed themselves. All paid rents or owed services, and were subject to the jurisdiction of a lord. Their involvement in acts of rebellion and resistance suggests a recognition of a common interest in the removal of restrictions and irksome dues. For these reasons the peasantry can be regarded as a social class.[24]

Townsmen accounted for about one in seven of the third estate. Because urban societies still exist, historians have sometimes regarded medieval towns as islands of modernity surrounded by a feudal countryside, and have claimed the prominence in the later middle ages of capitalist employers and wage-earners. More recent interpretations stress the integration of the town into an aristocratically dominated society, in which the leading townsmen had much in common with the rural gentry. Their wealth was on a comparable scale, and although much of it derived from the profits of trade, they often received rent income from rural as well as urban property. They intermarried with the gentry, and shared their tastes and values. Merchants often trained the sons of gentry as apprentices, who themselves became merchants. Successful townsmen would often buy up enough land to become country landowners.[25] Urban society was no less dominated by matters of tenure and status than

24 R. H. Hilton, *The English peasantry in the later middle ages* (Oxford, 1975), pp. 3–19.
25 S. Thrupp, *The merchant class of medieval London* (Chicago, 1948), pp. 234–319.

that of the countryside. A superior group within towns early in our period, and in smaller towns throughout, were those who held houses and land by burgage tenure, that special form of free tenure which obliged them to pay no more than a modest and fixed cash rent, and enabled tenants to divide, sell, or bequeath land as they wished. A more important distinction in the larger towns was that of the possession of freedom (meaning privilege), which gave a sizeable minority of the population (through birth, apprenticeship or purchase), including many master-craftsmen, the right to trade without toll-payment in the town's market. The wage-earners were numerous, but unlike a modern work-force they were often employed by craftsmen and small traders working from their houses with the help of their own families and apprentices, similar to the family unit of production found on peasant holdings.[26]

Given these links and similarities between town and country, urban society is best regarded as fully part of the medieval scene rather than as some precocious forerunner of the modern world. The upper rank in the larger towns is often called a mercantile élite. Merchants are emphasized because their trade on a large scale, over long distances, often involving highly valued commodities like wine or cloth, gave them high profits. However, in many towns there were also important and wealthy individuals whose incomes derived from office-holding, legal practice, and rents on property.[27] The élite's position as a governing group came from their tendency to occupy such influential offices as the mayoralty, and to serve as aldermen of guilds and as jurors in the borough courts. They could exercise some control over the craftsmen and small traders by virtue of their economic superiority – for example, they traded the cloth which had been made by the weavers, fullers and dyers. In addition they could issue rules and regulations for the working practices of the craftsmen through the town's government. Below the mercantile élite were the master craftsmen who in turn employed journeymen (trained workers in crafts), and unskilled labourers and servants. The depth of the hierarchy depended very much on the nature of the town's economy. A developed merchant class was confined to thirty or so of the larger towns, both ports and important regional centres of trade. In the more numerous small towns (per-

26 Hilton, 'Popular movements in England', p. 230.
27 S. Reynolds, *An introduction to the history of English medieval towns* (Oxford, 1977), pp. 76–80; R. H. Britnell, *Growth and decline in Colchester, 1300–1525* (Cambridge, 1986), pp. 32–3.

haps 500 places with a population in the region of 500 to 2,000) there was no real mercantile element, and leading offices were taken by traders in foodstuffs, the wealthier craftsmen and the retailers.[28]

In towns in particular, but also in the countryside, lived an unknown number of people who cannot be accommodated into any system of social analysis based on considerations of either status or class. These were the vagabonds, beggars, street-entertainers, prostitutes and professional criminals, who are usually described as marginals. They may not have contributed much to the economy, but contemporaries were fully aware of them, occasionally valuing them (friars, who were clerical beggars, attracted much admiration), and more often being alarmed by their numbers. Their failure to fit into any neat social pigeon-hole should not lead us to ignore them.[29]

Finally, by stressing the use of status groups and classes as means of understanding medieval society, other divisions have necessarily been neglected. As in any period, sex and age influenced social and economic opportunities and hence living standards. Women tended to derive their social status from that of their fathers or husbands, and enjoyed most independence as young servants, or as widows, when they might continue with the cultivation of their husband's holding or follow his craft or trade.[30] Both women and children were socially disadvantaged, but for male children at least, their position often improved progressively, from beginning full-time work or training at the age of twelve to fourteen, and certainly with their acceptance into the adult world in their twenties.

To sum up, contemporaries tended to describe their own society in terms of many subtle gradations of status, emphasizing vertical divisions, such as that between clergy and laity, or between free and unfree. They also recognized the importance of horizontal stratification, as can be seen from their use of economic function (such as that of the workers in the three orders theory), and of levels of income, to define social groups. We naturally use modern notions of class to explain the medieval social order, and therefore stress the horizontal layers and the rôle of each group in the economy. We can argue that the primary social categories in the countryside were the aristocracy and the peasantry. Each of these was in turn subdivided by wealth and status, into an upper and lower aristocracy, the latter

28 R. H. Hilton, 'Lords, burgesses and hucksters', *P. and P.*, 97 (1982), 3–15.
29 B. Geremek, *The margins of society in late medieval Paris* (Cambridge, 1987).
30 For example, B. A. Hanawalt (ed.), *Women and work in pre-industrial Europe* (Bloomington, Indiana, 1986).

conveniently known as the gentry, and the peasantry into at least three layers. Urban society is marked by less clear-cut social categories, particularly in view of the variety of urban economies. A merchant group is identifiable in the larger towns, and a layer of small traders and craftsmen in all towns. Wage-earners are found everywhere – journeymen, labourers and servants in the towns; labourers (who were often smallholding peasants) and servants in the country; stipendiary priests among the clergy. It is doubtful if these groups earning wages, dispersed as they were among many employers, and consisting of so many potential masters or peasants, can be regarded as a separate class, except perhaps in the largest towns.

We are concerned to identify social change, which can be approached in many different ways. It can be defined in extreme terms, of the overthrow of one class and its replacement by another, but there is little chance of discovering such a successful revolutionary upheaval in our period. Still, the later middle ages were stirring times, of plague, war and rebellion. The air was full of crises, with many violent actions against governments and lords, and much questioning of orthodox values in both the religious and secular worlds. Did these merely accelerate social mobility, that is, cause the ruin of some individuals, and create the opportunities for the advancement of others? Or did the whole balance of society shift? Did the material conditions of individuals or social classes decline or improve? Our concern in the coming chapters is to use the evidence for living standards to explore these problems, bearing in mind that despite the historical convenience of visualizing past societies in groups and classes, we must never lose sight of the experiences of individual people, which cumulatively created social change.

2

ARISTOCRATIC INCOMES

___ • ___

Late medieval aristocrats lived in constant anxiety about their incomes. This state of mind was to some extent justified throughout the period but they had especially good cause for concern after about 1320, when revenues from their estates began to decline for the first time in the known history of the class. They faced an economic crisis in the early fifteenth century, as land values became more deeply depressed.

The sources that historians can use to investigate aristocratic incomes are themselves the product of worried men. When incomes were steady and the class felt secure in the twelfth century, no-one bothered to keep accounts. When their complacency was shaken by rising prices in the period 1180–1220, they took demesnes that had previously been let out to farmers into direct management, and they then needed to keep more careful records.[1] 'Extents' or 'valors' contained detailed descriptions of demesne lands and lists of tenants, ending with a cash sum for the value, the estimated annual income. Even more numerous were the manorial accounts, the first series beginning in 1208 for the estates of the bishopric of Winchester, with more from large estates by the middle of the thirteenth century.

1 P. D. A. Harvey, 'The English inflation of 1180–1220' in R. H. Hilton (ed.), *Peasants, knights and heretics* (Cambridge, 1976), pp. 57–84; P. D. A. Harvey, 'The pipe rolls and the adoption of demesne farming in England', *Ec.H.R.*, 2nd ser., 27 (1974), 345–59; P. D. A. Harvey, *Manorial records* (British Records Association, Archives and the User, no. 5, 1984).

Large numbers of accounts were compiled for landlords of all kinds from the 1270s onwards. Such documents were the product of a laborious administrative process. First, the reeve or bailiff who looked after each manor kept records of payments, sales and purchases, in the form of tallies (receipts made from pieces of wood notched with the appropriate sum) or pieces of parchment containing bills or short-term records of accounts. At Michaelmas (29 September), the end of the agricultural year, he had the annual account written out by a clerk in a conventional sequence, receipts first, followed by expenses, for the cash, grain, stock, and sometimes the tenants' labour services. Then the estate auditors came to check the account, using their experience and training to question the reeve's claims, looking back to the last extent to see if the totals were the same, and also comparing the current account with those for previous years. They enquired about the prices in the local market, and listened sceptically to stories of storms, robbers and other explanations of poor returns and extra expenditure. The resulting document with its audited totals provided the lord with an assurance that his estates were being run with reasonable efficiency, and that local officials were not making large illicit profits at his expense. Lords were concerned about slackness in management and cheating. One textbook for training estate officials warned that threshers might be walking out of the barn at the end of a day's work with their boots full of grain.[2]

The Crown also suffered from financial anxieties. Record-keeping improved in the thirteenth century in order to ensure that the king's subjects did not hold back too much money, and this can tell us a great deal about aristocratic incomes. For example, the *Inquisitions post mortem*, which valued the manors of recently dead tenants of the Crown, are especially useful in the late thirteenth and early fourteenth century as sources of information about lay landlords whose own records are less well preserved than those of church estates. There were also periodic enquiries into the incomes of aristocrats connected with military service (in the early fourteenth century) or taxation (in the early fifteenth). The most thorough royal enquiry of all, the *Valor ecclesiasticus* of 1535, revealed the wealth of the clergy on the eve of its wholesale confiscation. Contemporaries, especially those connected with government, showed an awareness of incomes by expressing views on, for example, the

---

2 D. Oschinsky (ed.), *Walter of Henley* (Oxford, 1971), pp. 276–7.

minimum amount needed to be a knight. Any calculation of income deriving from a government source, especially one made in order to collect taxes, must be treated with suspicion, because subjects who supplied information would naturally protect their interests by underestimation.

All this concern might seem unnecessary when we examine the actual incomes, because of the enormous sums involved. Around the year 1300, when the evidence is especially abundant, six earls received annual incomes in excess of £3,000, including the earls of Cornwall and Gloucester each with about £6,000.[3] In 1311 Thomas, earl of Lancaster was enjoying one of the highest landed incomes recorded for the period, about £11,000 per annum.[4] Another half-dozen earls managed on incomes below £3,000, going down to as little as £400, according to a treatise of the 1320s.[5] The same source tells us that a barony could be worth as little as £266, but examples are known worth half of that sum. Most of the barons in the decades around 1300 were receiving annual revenues in the range of £200 to £500. Their numbers are impossible to calculate exactly, but in 1300 there were seventy-six complete baronies and at least another sixty fractions of baronies (the result of splitting inheritances between daughters).[6] To put these sums in perspective, at that time a labourer could earn in a year a maximum of £2, and the Crown in a peace-time year received revenues totalling £30,000. By these standards of comparison the higher aristocrats resembled in their wealth modern multi-millionaires. Such equations are misleading because of the enormous gulf in social structure and in the use of money that separates their world from ours, but they help us to appreciate the scale of incomes.

The lesser aristocracy with their revenues measured in tens rather than hundreds of pounds were still very wealthy individuals, and collectively disposed of a larger total of income than the barons and

3 N. Denholm-Young, *Seignorial administration in England* (Oxford, 1937), pp. 22–3; N. Denholm-Young, *Richard of Cornwall* (Oxford, 1947), p. 163; G. A. Holmes, *The estates of the higher nobility in fourteenth-century England* (Cambridge, 1957), pp. 35–6.
4 J. R. Maddicott, *Thomas of Lancaster 1307–1322* (Oxford, 1970), pp. 22–3.
5 S. Painter, *Studies in the history of the English feudal barony* (Baltimore, 1943), pp. 170–90; N. Pronay and J. Taylor (eds.), *Parliamentary texts of the later middle ages* (Oxford, 1980), p. 68.
6 Painter, *English feudal barony*, pp. 173–5; I. J. Sanders, *English baronies* (Oxford, 1960).

earls. In 1300 there were about 1,100 knights, a few of whom received more than some barons. The minimum income for a knight was fixed by the royal government when it implemented 'distraint of knighthood' (that is, ordered all those with appropriate landed incomes to be dubbed knights). Under these measures the lowest knightly income was often set at £20 or £30 per annum until 1292, and increased to £40 thereafter.[7] As the distraint measures show, many who were not dubbed knights had landed incomes in excess of £40. The government seemed to attach some importance to an annual income of £5 as marking a significant social bench-mark, and lists of those with £5 or more were compiled for purposes of taxation or military service in the early fourteenth century. Extrapolating from these documents, it seems reasonable to estimate that about 10,000 families were in receipt of incomes between £5 and £40. In reality most of them received considerably more than £5, because of the usual evasions and underassessments. A high proportion of the 10,000 can be regarded as 'lesser gentry'. Much uncertainty surrounds this calculation, and some writers have suggested a figure as high as 18,000 to 20,000.[8] An element of guesswork is necessary because this section of the aristocracy rarely kept records of their own, and only occasionally attracted the attention of the government. A few individuals are revealed in the records of magnates because, by feudal custom, their lands came temporarily into the hands of an overlord. An example would be Robert de Aula (Robert Hall), who in the late thirteenth century held a quarter of a knight's fee (the fief or landed endowment once regarded as sufficient to support a knight) at Over (Cambridgeshire) and a similar holding and 40 acres in two other nearby villages. His income was 'not much over £5 a year', yet he could claim considerable powers of jurisdiction because he held the view of frankpledge over his tenants in Over.[9]

---

7 N. Denholm-Young, 'Feudal Society in the thirteenth century: the knights' in N. Denholm-Young, *Collected papers on mediaeval subjects* (Oxford, 1946), pp. 56–67; M. Powicke, *Military obligation in medieval England* (Oxford, 1962), pp. 72–81, 105–9.

8 N. Saul, *Knights and esquires. The Gloucestershire gentry in the fourteenth century* (Oxford, 1981), pp. 33–4; R. H. Hilton, 'Lord and peasant in Staffordshire in the middle ages' in R. H. Hilton, *The English peasantry in the later middle ages* (Oxford, 1975), pp. 215–18; N. Denholm-Young. *The country gentry in the fourteenth century* (Oxford, 1969), p. 16.

9 E. Miller, *The abbey and bishopric of Ely* (Cambridge, 1951), pp. 183, 189, 212.

Another opportunity to survey the incomes of the secular aristocracy is provided by records around the 1430s. Then the very wealthiest magnate fortunes had gone, either absorbed into the royal estates, in the case of the duchy of Lancaster, or broken up by partitions between heiresses, as had happened to the earldom of Gloucester. There were still estates worth £3,500 to £4,000 a year, in the hands of the earls of Warwick and the dukes of Buckingham and York. In the second rank of the peerage the barons were less numerous than in the late thirteenth century, but they had higher average incomes, suggesting that landed wealth had been concentrated into fewer hands. Using the income tax of 1436 as the basis of our calculations, and adding information from private records to correct some of its many flaws, it seems that about seventy families received between £300 and £2,500, most of them with less than £1,000.[10]

The knights in the early fifteenth century were somewhat reduced in number. Less than a thousand of them disposed of annual incomes that ranged between £40 and £400. For the 'lesser gentry', now called esquires and gentlemen, there is more information than in the thirteenth century. The income tax of 1436 netted 6,200 landowners worth £5 to £39. Many of them were not gentry, but yeomen and merchants, and an unknown number of gentlemen evaded the tax by claiming that their incomes fell below the £5 limit. Local studies of Lancashire in the late fourteenth century and Derbyshire and Warwickshire in the fifteenth have identified totals of gentry families of 240, 125 and 125–153 respectively. If these were extended to the whole country the national total would be 6,000 or more. All of these would be in receipt of at least £10 a year, the minimum regarded as necessary to support a gentleman, and esquires would have received at least £20. The £5 income on which some gentry

10 H. L. Gray, 'Incomes from land in England in 1436', *E.H.R.*, 49 (1934), 607–39; T. B. Pugh and C. D. Ross, 'The English baronage and the income tax of 1436', *Bulletin of the Institute of Historical Research*, 26 (1953), 1–28; T. B. Pugh and C. D. Ross, 'Some materials for the study of baronial incomes in the fifteenth century', *Ec.H.R.*, 2nd ser., 6 (1953), 185–94; C. Rawcliffe, *The Staffords, earls of Stafford and dukes of Buckingham 1394–1521* (Cambridge, 1978), pp. 110–15; K. B. McFarlane, *The nobility of later medieval England* (Oxford, 1973), pp. 197–9; C. D. Ross, 'The estates and finances of Richard duke of York', *Welsh History Review*, 2 (1966–7), 299–302.

were assessed in 1436 was certainly an understatement, because that was a very inferior sum, 'a fair living for a yeoman' as Sir John Fortescue put it, and a fully employed carpenter could have earned as much.[11]

Finally in our survey of aristocratic wealth, the church hierarchy must be included. The fullest guide, the *Valor ecclesiasticus*, though compiled in 1535, reflects the broad pattern of churchmen's incomes going back into the middle years of the fifteenth century. Seventeen archbishops and bishops were worth £400 to £3,500 per annum, very much in line with the wealthier end of the secular peerage. The revenues of monastic houses, because they belonged to communities rather than individuals, are not strictly comparable with either lay aristocrats or bishops, yet it is still worth noting that 126 monasteries with £300 or more were sufficiently wealthy to enable their inmates to live in a similar style to the members of a baronial household, and many abbots, who usually enjoyed a separate endowment and lived in their own households, functioned as landed aristocrats in every sense. To pursue the analogy, the remaining 700 or so religious houses with incomes below £300 were on a par with knights and esquires. The beneficed parish clergy, the rectors and vicars, lived on revenues similar to those of the gentry: less than a tenth of the 8,000 to 9,000 parish clergy were worth £40 or more, and the bulk had incomes assessed at between £5 and £20 with a high proportion in the region of £10.[12]

To put the figures for the laity and the clergy together, in the fifteenth century a total of 200 households (comital, baronial, episcopal and monastic) received £300 or more; another 12,000 clerical and gentry households lived on £10 to £300, of whom about 2,000 belonged at the knightly end of that group, with £40 or more per annum. The lay aristocracy and their families, assuming five per family, together with 20,000 monks, nuns and beneficed clergy,

11 M. J. Bennett, *Community, class and careerism. Cheshire and Lancashire society in the age of Sir Gawain and the Green Knight* (Cambridge, 1983), pp. 67–89; S. M. Wright, *The Derbyshire gentry in the fifteenth century* (Derbyshire Record Soc., 8, 1983), pp. 1–11, 196–202; C. Carpenter, 'Political society in Warwickshire *c.*1401–72' (University of Cambridge Ph.D. thesis, 1976); D. A. L. Morgan, 'The individual style of the English gentleman' in M. Jones (ed.), *Gentry and lesser nobility in late medieval Europe* (Gloucester, 1986), pp. 16–19.

12 D. Knowles and R. N. Hadcock, *Medieval religious houses: England and Wales*, 2nd edn (London, 1971); A. Savine, *English monasteries on the eve of the dissolution* (Oxford, 1909); P. Heath, *The English parish clergy on the eve of the Reformation* (London, 1969), p. 173; J. C. Russell, 'The clerical population of medieval England', *Traditio*, 2 (1944), 179.

make a total of 50,000 people, or about 2 per cent of the English population.[13] Their total annual landed revenues must have come near to half a million pounds.

This picture of aristocratic incomes would not seem to justify the disquiet evidently felt by many aristocrats about their financial situation. As the comparison between the distribution of incomes in *c.*1300 and the 1430s has shown, the class maintained a good deal of stability. Indeed, if we look forward into subsequent centuries the continuity of aristocratic wealth is a striking feature of the English social scene. In the 1690s, for example, Chamberlayne could calculate that the peers, baronets, knights, esquires and gentlemen received a total of £5,690,800, or 57 per cent of the 'rent of land'.[14]

Nonetheless, a closer examination of the changes in the aristocracy between *c.*1300 and the 1430s does suggest a degree of retrenchment. The upper ranks had been reduced in numbers by replacing the rather amorphous concept of the baronage by the stricter notion of peerage, and evidently this change was accompanied by a tendency for more land to be held in fewer estates. A similar development may have occurred among the lesser aristocracy. The vaguely defined but numerous group of small landholders, the 'country gentry' or 'lesser gentry', had in the early fifteenth century been given a name by contemporaries – gentlemen – and had perhaps also been reduced in number. Closer definition had evidently been accompanied by a degree of shrinkage, helping to preserve the standing of those left within the class. The same process had affected the knights in earlier generations. There were evidently 6,000 or more *milites* (knights) in the twelfth century, some of them prestigious warriors and administrators well-endowed with land, others with only small manors or living in noble households, and called 'rustic knights' and 'common knights'.[15] By the end of the thirteenth century a new process of definition had whittled down the numbers of dubbed knights to little more than a thousand. The process continued in the

---

13 This assumes a population of about 2.5 million, which may be a little too high: J. Hatcher, *Plague, population and the English economy, 1348–1530* (London, 1977), pp. 68–71.

14 J. P. Cooper, 'The social distribution of land and men in England', *Ec.H.R.*, 2nd ser., 20 (1967), 432.

15 A. L. Poole, *Obligations of society in the XII and XIII centuries* (Oxford, 1946), pp. 35–56; S. P. J. Harvey, 'The knight and the knight's fee in England' in Hilton (ed.), *Peasants, knights and heretics*, pp. 133–73.

later middle ages, until there were only about five hundred knights in the sixteenth century.[16]

These calculations are surrounded by uncertainties. Titles reflected status and social perceptions, which were influenced but not controlled by economic considerations. The records of estate administration give us the best guide to landed incomes and the various influences on them. Most of the documents – accounts, surveys and rentals – come from individual manors. They are valuable because they show the relative importance of different sources of revenue – rents as compared with the sale of produce, for example – and they allow us to calculate trends in income. The main purpose of the account was to ensure that the lord's affairs were being properly managed, so that the reeve or bailiff was required firstly to list all money and goods that came into his hands, including the backlog that he should have paid over from the previous year (arrears), and then to explain how the money and goods had been used, both in the expenses of the manor (mending ploughs and carts, for example) and in the money sent to the lord's receiver or treasurer. So in an ideal world the expenses and payments would have equalled the arrears and income, and the reeve would have discharged all of his obligations. At the end of the account the clerk wrote, in a perfect account: 'And he [the reeve] withdrew quit', that is with nothing owing to the lord. In reality the conclusion was usually a statement of debt 'And he owes . . .', the smaller the sum the better for the lord. Medieval administrators understood very well the notion of profit, and this could be calculated from the account, but as it was not the primary purpose of the document, the 'profit' or 'valor' total was often added as an afterthought.[17] These addenda were so brief that the principle behind the calculation often cannot be discovered. Modern historians prefer to estimate the profits of manors in terms of the income that the lord actually gained from them, by adding the 'cash liveries' (money sent to the receiver) to the value of any goods used in the lord's household.

The whole of a lord's income can be known, not from manorial records, but from either the receivers' accounts, which contain the total of all of the money sent in from the manors, or estate 'valors'. These used cryptic methods of calculation, and sometimes are fic-

16 W. G. Hoskins, *The age of plunder* (London, 1976), pp. 54–5.

17 E. Stone, 'Profit-and-loss accountancy at Norwich Cathedral Priory', *T.R.H.S.*, 5th ser., 12 (1962), 25–48; D. Postles, 'The perception of profit before the leasing of demesnes', *Ag.H.R.*, 34 (1986), 12–28.

tional in the sense that they include debts as well as money actually received; sometimes they are usefully based on the 'cash liveries' of each manor. [18] These sources are not easy to use; they pose problems like the notion of 'gross' and 'net' income which cannot easily be applied to medieval estates. For example, many lords paid, often out of the profits of individual manors, fees and annuities to officials and supporters. If the money was a reward for professional services to a steward or bailiff, then it can be counted as an administrative expense and deducted from the income total to give net income, that is revenues received after the payment of costs. Most fees went to the lord's retinue, who, under the system of 'bastard feudalism', supported the lord's interest in government and even in civil war. These payments were surely not necessary for the running of the estates? They represent a sort of consumption, almost an indulgence, like the lord's purchase of cloth and wine. Yet the retinue contributed indirectly to the landed estate, by preventing the loss of lands to rivals, and by strengthening the lord's influence in the law courts. They even allowed the lord to acquire manors if he came out on the winning side of factional rivalries, or impressed the king or other lords with his strength. There is no certain answer to such problems, and this means that any calculation of net income must be qualified by the statement that a different method would produce a figure higher or lower by 10 or 15 per cent. As a statistician would put it, there is a sizeable margin of error.

Armed with these figures, which are imperfect, but the best that are available to us, we can generalize about trends in lords' incomes. Table 2 gives some examples. They demonstrate a widespread upward movement in the thirteenth century. Surely this then was a period when lords were sitting on the crest of an economic wave, when they could enjoy the fruits of a doubled or tripled income? Many economic ingredients made this increase possible. There was a redistribution of manors through the land market and marriage, both of which allowed the Clares, for example, to increase their revenues with particular rapidity. All lords were able to increase the profits of manors by the direct management of their demesnes, which enabled them to sell grain, livestock, wool and dairy produce at prices that increased through the century. Production could be improved by marling or drainage, and by investment in buildings.

---

18 R. R. Davies, 'Baronial accounts, incomes and arrears in the later middle ages', *Ec.H.R.*, 2nd ser., 21 (1968), 213–18; I. Jack (ed.), *The Grey of Ruthin valor* (Bedfordshire Record Soc., 46, 1965).

Table 2. *Some examples of aristocratic incomes*
(net, per annum, unless stated otherwise)

Bishopric of Ely[a]		Battle Abbey[d]		Earls and dukes of Lancaster[h]	
1171–2	£920	1211	£340–£488		
1256–7	£1,930	1291	£591†	1311	£11,000
1298–9	£2,550	1346	£1,568	1330–1	£6,000–£6,877
1454	£2,224	1383	£1,145	1361	£8,380 (gross)
1535	£2,281	1535	£900–£1,100	1394–5	£12,474

Bishopric of Worcester[b]		Westminster Abbey[e]	
1185–6	£330	*c.*1175	£739
1211–12	£345	*c.*1300	£1,641
1299	£1,192	*c.*1400	£2,407
1312–13	£1,307	1535	£2,827
1453–4	£949		
1535	£986		

Percies, earls of
Northumberland[i]

1455	£3,100 (gross)
1489	£4,044 (gross)
	£2,161 (net)
1523	£3,900

Bolton Priory[f]

	Cash	Estimated value
1280s	*c.*£243	
1305–15	*c.*£460	*c.*£960
1538–9	£397†	*c.*£450

Canterbury Cathedral Priory[c]	
c. 1200	£1,406
1292	£2,063
1331	£2,540
1411	£4,100*
1437	£2,382
1456	£2,060
1468	£1,828
1473	£2,841
1535	£2,349

Clares, earls of
Gloucester[g]

1266–7	£3,700 (gross)
1317	£6,000

Staffords, earls of
Stafford
and dukes of
Buckingham[j]

1372	£3,000
1400–1	£1,987
1447–8	£3,700
1521	£4,906

* Unusual year   † Underassessment

Source notes:
a. E. Miller, *The abbey and bishopric of Ely* (Cambridge, 1951), p. 94; F. Heal, 'The Tudors and church lands: economic problems of the bishopric of Ely during the sixteenth century', *Ec.H.R.*, 2nd ser., 26 (1973), 208
b. C. Dyer, *Lords and peasants in a changing society. The estates of the bishopric of Worcester, 680–1540* (Cambridge, 1980), pp. 53–5, 176–8
c. R. A. L. Smith, *Canterbury Cathedral Priory* (Cambridge, 1943), pp. 12–13
d. E. Searle, *Lordship and community. Battle Abbey and its banlieu 1066–1538* (Toronto, 1974), pp. 134–40
e. B. Harvey, *Westminster Abbey and its estates in the middle ages* (Oxford, 1977), p. 63
f. I. Kershaw, *Bolton Priory. The economy of a northern monastery, 1286–1325* (Oxford, 1973), pp. 161–90; I. Kershaw (ed.), *Bolton Priory rentals and ministers' accounts, 1473–1539* (Yorks. Arch. Soc. Record Ser., 132,1970), pp. xxiii–xxiv
g. M. Altschul, *A baronial family in medieval England. The Clares, 1217–1314* (Baltimore, 1965), pp. 203–6
h. J. R. Maddicott, *Thomas of Lancaster 1307–1322* (Oxford, 1970), pp. 22–3; K. B. McFarlane, *The nobility of later medieval England* (Oxford 1973), p. 179; K. Fowler, *The King's Lieutenant. Henry of Grosmont 1st duke of Lancaster* (London, 1969), pp. 225–6
i. J. M. W. Bean, *The estates of the Percy family, 1416–1537* (Oxford, 1958), pp. 81–2, 128–30, 140
j. C. Rawcliffe, *The Staffords, earls of Stafford and dukes of Buckingham 1394–1521* (Cambridge, 1978), pp. 10, 107, 115, 133

An age of especially successful management or 'high farming' has been recognized on some monastic estates in the period 1280–1315, under the vigorous lordship of such monks as Henry of Eastry at Canterbury Cathedral Priory and John of Laund at Bolton in west Yorkshire. Increases in rents made a major contribution to rising incomes, and they often accounted for more than a half of manorial profits. There were new tenants, settled on land colonized from woods, moors and marshes, or occupying the burgage plots of new towns. Holdings were increased in numbers because the rules governing peasant inheritance were adjusted to allow divisions. Old tenements were expected to yield higher rents, and to produce higher occasional dues such as entry fines. Labour services and payments in kind were being converted to cash.

Contemporaries were acutely aware of the drawbacks to this apparent boom in aristocratic revenues. The adoption of direct management, with the necessary new army of administrators, was not decided spontaneously, but was forced on landed society by adverse circumstances in 1180–1220. A combination of bad harvests, sustained upward movements in prices, and the financial demands of the Crown drove the aristocracy into changing their economic methods, and with them their whole way of life. Henceforth lords would have to devote more of their time to mundane chores of administration, because not all decisions could be left to the officials. And lords were kept alert through the thirteenth century by new surges of prices, for example in the 1270s and 1290s. To some extent these contributed to estate profits if they led to a rise in the price of produce sold from the demesnes, but lords bought as well as sold, and although we are not sure of the changes in the cost of luxuries, they are likely to have joined in the general price trend. For example, the prices of high-quality horses cannot be organized into a statistical series, but ordinary cart-horses cost twice as much in *c.* 1310 as they had done in *c.* 1210.[19] The impact of rising prices should not be exaggerated, because wages, which played a major part in aristocratic spending, increased very little, and it would be misleading in consequence to think that incomes were merely keeping pace with expenditure – the real incomes of the higher aristocracy were certainly increasing, albeit at a rather slower pace than incomes measured in cash.

All of the figures in table 2 show movements in the income of large

19 D. L. Farmer, 'Some livestock price movements in thirteenth-century England', *Ec.H.R.*, 2nd ser., 22 (1969), 4–5.

estates. The smaller landholders are omitted because their records are too fragmentary, and it is possible that they had different experiences. The financial problems of a sizeable minority of gentry are revealed in the cartularies of monastic houses and other wealthy lords, in which sales of land are recorded, said to have been occasioned by 'urgent need'. Jewish money lenders were often involved because debtors who had borrowed too much found themselves unable to repay loans, and so were forced to sell land to a monastery, which in turn paid off the Jew. In particularly acute cases the debtors' downfall was complete. In a final transaction they surrendered all of their remaining lands, in exchange for a promise that they could spend the rest of their days in the monastery as pensioners or corrodians, entitled to draw a fixed allowance of food and drink. A fully documented example comes from the Gloucestershire village of Pitchcombe. Here Walter le Bret sold parcels of land continuously in the years 1295–1303, in forty separate transactions, for sums of money varying between £3 and £20. The buyers were often local people, perhaps Bret's neighbours and social peers. Two names recur often, those of John de Standish, clerk, and Gilbert de Masynton, who were probably acting as the agents of the local ecclesiastical magnate, Gloucester Abbey. Certainly the bulk of the land, and the collection of charters recording the sales, eventually came into the hands of the abbey.[20] In explanation of the gentry's difficulties at this time it has been suggested that their changing perception of their own status tempted them into extravagant expenditure. It also seems that they could not profit as much as the magnates from the increase in the prices of demesne produce, because of the small size of their manors. For example, we can estimate that the 300-acre demesne at the gentry manor of Ducklington should have produced 200 quarters of grain, of which the bulk would have been used internally, as seed for the next year, to feed servants and animals on the manor, and to supply the lord's household with bread, ale and horse-fodder. Still, there would have been a saleable surplus of perhaps 50 quarters of grain, which would have given the lord a high proportion of his cash income. But many gentry demesnes amounted to less than 150 acres, and most of their produce would have been absorbed by the consumption of the

20 H. G. Richardson, *The English Jewry under Angevin kings* (London, 1960), pp. 83–108; J. Melland Hall, 'Pychenecumbe-abstracts of original documents in the register of St Peter's Gloucester', *Transactions of the Bristol and Gloucestershire Archaeological Soc.*, 14 (1889–90), 141–62.

manor and household. On gentry manors the free tenants often outnumbered the tenants in villeinage (serfs), so that rents made only a modest contribution to the revenues of the manor. The scale of the gentry's land-holding made them vulnerable to misfortune. Sheep disease, which reached epidemic proportions in the 1270s and 1280s, or a run of bad harvests, could reduce the profits of demesnes with especially serious results on manors where rents provided no financial cushion. Also, small estates could be ruined by risky divisions of income or property, as when fathers sought to make some provision for younger sons and daughters out of limited resources. The laws of inheritance, which led to the division of property between daughters in the absence of male heirs, broke into two, three or more parts estates that were already dangerously small. Finally many small landowners, perhaps partly motivated by the harsh economic climate, supported the losing side in political agitations in the 1260s and 1320s, leading to sales of land after the collapse of the rebellions and the disgrace of the 'disinherited' or 'contrariant' gentry.[21]

These problems seem to have affected only a minority of the gentry. Some had large demesnes which yielded increasing profits in a favourable market. A few gentry manors were provided with exploitable customary tenants, or were well placed to take advantage of the assarting movement. Above all, in an age of growing demand for administrators and lawyers, the gentry provided both the higher aristocracy and the Crown with expert services, receiving in return fees and the profits of office.[22] We do not know whether the failures among the gentry outnumbered the successes. On the basis of the small sample studied so far they appear to have been equally balanced, while many others kept their heads above water and neither rose nor fell.[23] The thirteenth century seems to have been a testing time, in which a form of natural selection purged the gentry of its less able (or less fortunate) members, and the fittest survived and even flourished. The beneficiaries of the financial problems of the weak-

21 E. A. Kosminsky, *Studies in the agrarian history of England in the thirteenth century* (Oxford, 1956), pp. 273–8; M. M. Postan (ed.), *The Cambridge economic history of Europe*, 2nd edn, vol. 1 (Cambridge, 1966), pp. 592–5.
22 R. H. Britnell, 'Minor landlords in England and medieval agrarian capitalism', *P. and P.*, 89 (1980), 3–22; S. L. Waugh, 'Tenure to contract: lordship and clientage in thirteenth-century England', *E.H.R.*, 101 (1986), 811–39.
23 E. King, *Peterborough Abbey 1086–1310* (Cambridge, 1973), pp. 35–54; D. Carpenter, 'Was there a crisis of the knightly class in the thirteenth century? The Oxfordshire evidence', *E.H.R.*, 95 (1980), 721–52.

lings were not just rich monasteries, but also included rising members of the lesser aristocracy, like the Braybrookes, a Northamptonshire family who held local offices, or Sir Geoffrey de Langley, an administrator and justice who benefited from the patronage of the Crown, and Adam de Stratton, from a Wiltshire gentry family, who did well from work of a dubious kind in the Exchequer.[24]

The generalization that the aristocracy prospered in the thirteenth century might be met by a further qualification. Lay magnates and large monasteries, like members of the gentry, fell into debt. The richest man in England in the 1290s, Gilbert de Clare, earl of Gloucester, borrowed £1,800 from a Sienese banking company, and his son owed the Frescobaldi of Florence £933 in 1308. A wealthy ecclesiastical magnate, Canterbury Cathedral Priory, was in debt to Italian bankers for more than £1,300 in 1285. However, these loans should not be seen as evidence of serious financial problems. Even a magnate with a high income would be unable to cope with the extra expenditure of war or a new building project, and the necessary cash could be readily obtained from lenders who knew of the steady income from which repayments could be made. The loans demonstrated the fundamentally healthy financial state of the borrowers. No major estates were ruined by accumulated debt at this time. And on the other side, the Italian companies or monasteries could act as deposit bankers, where landlords wealthy enough to save could send their cash surpluses.[25]

Finally, the most important reservation that must be made about the expansion of the thirteenth century lies in its failure to continue in the early fourteenth. External circumstances helped to call a halt to growth, notably the sheep scab, the disastrous run of bad harvests in 1315–18, the cattle plague that followed, and the strains of both external and civil wars that continued intermittently from the 1290s. Investigations of the internal economy of the great estates suggests

24 Richardson, *English Jewry*, pp. 100–2; P. R. Coss, 'Sir Geoffrey de Langley and the crisis of the knightly class in thirteenth-century England', *P. and P.*, 68 (1975), 3–37; M. W. Farr (ed.), *Accounts and surveys of the Wiltshire lands of Adam de Stratton* (Wiltshire Archaeological and Natural History Soc. Records Branch, 14, 1958), pp. xiv–xxiii.

25 T. H. Lloyd, *Alien merchants in England in the high middle ages* (Brighton, 1982), pp. 196–8; Staffordshire R.O., D641/1/3/1; M. Mate, 'The indebtedness of Canterbury Cathedral Priory 1215–95', *Ec.H.R.*, 2nd ser., 26 (1973), 183–97; I. Kershaw, *Bolton Priory. The economy of a northern monastery, 1286–1325* (Oxford, 1973), pp. 168–78.

certain structural weaknesses, which would have had their effect even without the misfortunes of the period. The low levels of productivity in arable farming meant that on many estates, like that of the bishopric of Winchester, wheat yielded 10 bushels per acre. This can be compared with the vastly higher twentieth-century English figures, such as 58 bushels per acre in the 1960s and 1970s, and is low even by the contemporary standard of the yields that were achieved in the late thirteenth and early fourteenth century by lords using superior methods in Norfolk or in northern France.[26] The poor results may be connected with low levels of investment, insufficient manure, and poorly motivated management and labour. The solution on the Winchester estates in the fourteenth century, and many others, was to lease out a proportion of the arable demesnes to peasant tenants.

Income from rents also reached a ceiling on many estates in the decades around 1300. Holdings began to fall vacant, variable payments like entry fines levelled out, and new lettings of assarted land decreased. This was partly because tenants could pay no more, and partly because of actual or anticipated peasant resistance, the period seeing notable battles against the demands of some lords. More difficult to describe with precision was a general economic malaise, which has been called 'stagflation' (a combination of rising prices and economic stagnation) in early fourteenth-century France.[27] An explanation could lie in the tendency of any economic system to produce diminishing returns after a long period of growth. In the case of a feudal society, the principal weakness lay in the tenants' desire to escape from their dependence and avoid their obligations. Such a change occurred in the twelfth and thirteenth centuries when the lesser aristocracy ceased to perform military and administrative services in return for their lands. In the fourteenth century it was the turn of the peasantry to attempt to follow suit.

The generalization that many aristocrats increased their incomes in the thirteenth century remains valid, even after so many qualifications. The fourteenth century was a period of divergent move-

---

26 J. Z. Titow, *Winchester yields* (Cambridge, 1972); B. M. S. Campbell, 'Agricultural progress in medieval England; some evidence from eastern Norfolk', *Ec.H.R.*, 2nd ser., 36 (1983), 26–46; G. Duby, *L'économie rurale et la vie des campagnes dans l'occident médiéval* (2 vols., Paris, 1962), vol. 1, p. 186.

27 These issues are discussed by some of the contributors to the 'Brenner debate': T. H. Aston and C. H. E. Philpin (eds.), *The Brenner debate* (Cambridge, 1985), pp. 111–13, 129–32; G. Bois, *The crisis of feudalism. Economy and society in eastern Normandy c. 1300–1550* (Cambridge, 1984), pp. 263–76.

ments. Many lords, especially those still involved in a campaign of 'high farming', saw their incomes continue to grow in the first decade. After the disruptions of the famine and the cattle plague, large estates seem commonly to have entered into a period of slow decline. The quarter-century after the Black Death of 1348–9 has been characterized either as an 'Indian Summer' or a false dawn for many landlords, as cereal prices and rents held up against all expectations. After 1375 some lords continued to enjoy incomes perhaps 10 per cent below those prevailing before the epidemics. Increasing numbers of them sought to stabilize their positions by leasing out their demesnes to farmers who would take over the headaches of low grain prices and high wages, while paying a fixed cash farm.[28]

In the fifteenth century the general trends are again unmistakable. Landlords who had been in any doubt as to the unfavourable times now faced diminishing returns. The majority of demesnes on large estates not already in the hands of farmers were soon leased. And through the century, as leases came up for renewal, farmers more often than not were able to resist any increases or to negotiate for a lower rent. They were justified in their hard bargaining by the continued sluggish market for agricultural produce. The customary tenants now paid rents almost entirely in cash. They secured reductions, refusing payment if the lord showed reluctance to concede. The revolt of 1381, though a failure, still haunted landlords as a dreadful lesson.[29]

The pattern was general, but not without some contrary tendencies. Some short-term movements ran against the trend, especially after the period of decline in revenues in the early part of the century and the trough of the 1440s and 1450s, when some incomes rose. The good management of estates, it has been claimed, could prevent the worst effects of decline by careful supervision of the leasing arrangements, but it is difficult to see how such methods could do more than moderate the effects of an economic tide.[30] A few enterprising gentry broke the mould of traditional mixed farming, converted their land

---

28 A. R. Bridbury, 'The Black Death', *Ec.H.R.*, 2nd ser., 26 (1973), 577–92; Holmes, *Higher nobility*, pp. 114–20; C. Dyer, 'Social and economic background to the rural revolt of 1381' in R. H. Hilton and T. H. Aston (eds.), *The English rising of 1381* (Cambridge, 1984), pp. 19–36.

29 C Dyer, *Lords and peasants, in a changing society. The estates of the bishopric of Worcester, 680–1540* (Cambridge, 1980), pp. 153–92, 264–97; Hilton, *English peasantry*, pp. 54–73.

30 A. J. Pollard, 'Estate management in the later middle ages; the Talbots and Whitchurch, 1383–1525', *Ec.H.R.*, 25 (1972), 553–66.

to pasture, and by producing beef and wool for the market with a relatively small labour force, increased the profits from individual manors threefold. The experience of the gentry differed in general from that of the magnates, because they tended to keep more of their lands in direct management, partly to supply their own domestic needs, and partly for sale. They acted as farmers, taking over the demesnes of the higher aristocracy and making a profit from them. Perhaps they were aided in this by their personal management. John Hopton of Suffolk, like other gentry, slipped in and out of direct management, as need required. They ventured into such diverse activities as mining, quarrying and tile-making.[31] There were also gentry who showed none of this enterprise, kept their lands out on lease, and suffered the same slide in incomes as their social superiors. Some are found to have become seriously indebted, though there is less evidence of ruin than two centuries earlier.

The location of estates, both large and small, counted for a good deal in terms of profit and income. The lordships on the Welsh marches, so long a valuable source of revenues for the lay magnates, and which often held their value in the fourteenth century, collapsed financially in the aftermath of the Glyn Dwr revolt of 1400–6.[32] Estates in the far north were badly damaged by the Scottish incursions in the 1320s and by continued border troubles. The most favourable economic climate was enjoyed by those landlords with lands in the vicinity of still prosperous London. Kent's landowners apparently declined in prosperity less than in most counties (see table 2). Lords in districts with a high proportion of woodland and pasture seem to have fared better than those whose estates were confined to specialized corn-growing areas, with little prospect of diversifying their agriculture.

Most lords experienced a pronounced but not a catastrophic fall in manorial income in the adversities of the later middle ages, often by no more than 25 per cent over a lengthy time span. Radical changes in income could be achieved not by economic means, such as reforms in management or new agricultural initiatives, but by

---

31 C. Dyer, *Warwickshire farming, 1349–c.1520* (Dugdale Soc. Occasional Paper, 27, 1981), pp. 16–21; C. Richmond, *John Hopton. A fifteenth-century Suffolk gentleman* (Cambridge, 1981), pp. 31–99; C. Carpenter, 'The fifteenth-century English gentry and their estates' in Jones (ed.), *Gentry and lesser nobility*, pp. 36–60; Wright, *Derbyshire gentry*, pp. 12–28.
32 R. R. Davies, *Lordship and society in the march of Wales, 1282–1400* (Oxford, 1978), pp. 176–98; T. B. Pugh (ed.), *The marcher lordships of south Wales, 1415–1536* (Cardiff, 1963), pp. 145–53.

additions or subtractions to the total amount of land held by an aristocratic family. The fourteenth and fifteenth centuries saw important changes in the tenure and transmission of land which helped to secure family control over inheritance and to some extent avoided fragmentation of holdings. Enfeoffment to uses was a legal device that put land, on the death of a lord, into the care of hand-picked trustees rather than the crown or an overlord. If the heir was a child the estates would be run in the best interests of the family, and then passed on to the heir when he came of age. This arrangement also gave the family more control over the marriage of heirs and heiresses. In the absence of a son, the head of a family could dictate the inheritance of land, for example by providing that the land would descend in 'tail male', so that it would go to a male relative such as a nephew intact, rather than being divided among female heirs. This growing control over inheritance tempted some lords to look after younger sons and daughters by dividing lands, but opinion generally favoured keeping inheritances intact. In addition, demographic reality reduced the temptation to split inheritances, because fewer lords in the later part of our period were survived by large numbers of children. Legal developments also strengthened the rights of women, especially through the jointure, by which they kept for their lifetime all or part of their husband's estates. This could result in a long-lived dowager preventing her son acquiring the full inheritance for many years. It could, however, also help to maintain the continuity of an estate through a minority.[33]

Demographic accidents left a proportion of inheritances in each generation in the hands of female heirs, and they provided the main avenue for advancement for other aristocratic families. With limited amounts of land coming onto the market, marriage offered the best opportunity for adding to estates. The lay families whose incomes increased substantially in the period (such as the Staffords and the Percies, see table 2) were plagued by falling income from individual manors like most other aristocrats, but more than compensated for these difficulties by good marriages. The king's patronage could extend the resources of the aristocracy, either directly by gifts of manors, or because royal influence could be decisive in settling

---

33 J. M. W. Bean, *The decline of English feudalism, 1215–1540* (Manchester, 1968); Holmes, *Higher nobility*, pp. 41–57; R. E. Archer, 'Rich old ladies: the problem of late medieval dowagers' in A. J. Pollard (ed.), *Property and politics; essays in later medieval English history* (Gloucester, 1984), pp. 15–35; P. Jeffries, 'The medieval use as family law and custom: the Berkshire gentry in the fourteenth and fifteenth centuries', *Southern History*, 1 (1979), 45–69.

disputes in favour of allies. The interest of the Crown also helped some church landlords, like Westminster Abbey, the royal monastery, which alone among Benedictine houses continued to receive substantial new endowments (see table 2). Both the king and other landowners were creating a new generation of religious communities by founding colleges. They received the former possessions of 'alien priories' (religious houses once attached to French monasteries in the period after the Norman Conquest, and confiscated when the Hundred Years War made such an arrangement untenable), or rectories which were appropriated, so transferring much of the income formerly enjoyed by the rector to the college, and leaving a smaller sum to pay a substitute clergyman, the vicar. All of these transfers of property added nothing to the collective wealth of the aristocracy, and meant that some families or institutions lost land while others were gaining it. These changes contributed to a general redistribution of aristocratic income by enabling the accumulation of manors in larger estates. The paradoxical conclusion is that in an age when aristocrats were troubled by a substantial drop in the value of manors, the income of many landlords increased.

Although land provided the basis of their incomes, aristocrats had many opportunities to gain wealth in cash. In the period 1340–1453 the war with France gave a chance of profit, directly from plunder or ransoms, in the long term from the revenues of captured French estates, and from the pay attached to military commands or administrative posts made necessary by the war. Contemporaries believed that fortunes could be made, and this helps to explain aristocratic support for the war, even in the 1370s when the campaigns went in the French favour. A famous soldier like Sir John Fastolf rose from modest origins in the service of Henry V and VI, and was able to salt away enough cash to buy lands worth £1,000 a year. The more chequered career of Sir John Talbot, a commander in the last phases of the war from 1427 to 1450 offers a less impressive but more typical example of both gains and losses. He received pay in his various offices which totalled about £700 per annum at the peak of his campaigning. His share of the plunder, including that from the sack of Le Mans, must have been worth some hundreds, and he acquired lands and offices in France worth some hundreds again. So in theory in most years of his active military career he doubled his landed income (assessed at £1,200 in the tax of 1436). Like Fastolf he was able to use money from the war to buy land – eight Shropshire manors – to extend his estates. On the debit side it must be remembered that the crown was an inefficient employer and still owed him £7,000 at his death. Also, the Norman lordships that he gained produced very little revenue because of the devastated condition of the land and the truculent attitude of the French peasants. Both Talbot and his two sons were captured by the French on separate occasions, and had to pay ransoms to secure their release. Talbot did make a profit from the war, but not a fortune, and for the aristocracy in general the war provided no more than an episodic compensation for the loss of landed revenue.[34] It should be added that researches into war profits, which were often transferred to England by merchants, have revealed another source of cash income for the aristocracy, the financing of overseas trade. Unfortunately the general scale of such activities is not known.

In peace as well as war a high proportion of the lay aristocracy, and especially the gentry, received the fees or annuities associated with 'bastard feudalism' (see p. 35). The system originated before the thirteenth century, but the documents recording payments are more numerous in the fifteenth. By the reign of Edward IV, 600–800 people were on the pay roll of the royal household, because the king had the largest retinue of all, and a politically active magnate like Henry Percy, third earl of Northumberland, was spending in 1461 as much as a third or a half of his income (c. £3,000) on fees and annuities to supporters.[35] The individual fees of £2 to £10 were not large in relation to a magnate's income, but for the recipients who normally obtained less than £40 per annum from land, they gave a welcome supplement. Historians usually discuss bastard feudalism in political or legal terms, but from the point of view of economics it provided a means by which wealth was redistributed from the upper to the lower tiers of the aristocracy.

Finally, an important group in receipt of these fees were the gentry who provided services as administrators and above all as lawyers.

34 M. M. Postan, 'Some social consequences of the Hundred Years War'; and 'The costs of the Hundred Years War' in M. M. Postan, *Essays on medieval agriculture and general problems of the medieval economy* (Cambridge, 1973), pp. 49–80; K. B. McFarlane, 'War, the economy and social change: England and the Hundred Years War'; and 'The investment of Sir John Fastolf's profits of war' in K. B. McFarlane, *England in the fifteenth century* (London, 1981), pp. 139–49; 175–97; C. T. Allmand, *Lancastrian Normandy, 1415–1450* (Oxford, 1983), pp. 50–80; A. J. Pollard, *John Talbot and the war in France, 1427–1453* (London, 1983), pp. 102–21.

35 D. A. L. Morgan, 'The king's affinity in the polity of Yorkist England', *T.R.H.S.*, 5th ser., 23 (1973), 1–22; J. M. W. Bean, *The estates of the Percy family 1416–1537* (Oxford, 1958), p. 91.

A growing professionalization of the law, needing lengthy training, is apparent from the twelfth century onwards. By the late fifteenth century the legal élite of judges, sergeants and apprentices amounted to about 120 men, and below them were many hundreds of attorneys and others 'learned in the law' working in the local as well as the central courts. A complaint of 1455 reported that eighty lawyers were practising in the Norfolk and Suffolk courts alone. A lawyer at the top of his profession, a sergeant-at-law, earned £300 annually, enough to fund the purchase of a landed fortune. A part-time local lawyer could pick up a useful £26 per annum without difficulty.[36]

The upper class had experienced a difficult period over the last two centuries of the middle ages, and especially in the first half of the fifteenth century. The effects of their falling landed incomes were to some extent countered by new administrative methods, by the tendency of the size of landed estates to increase, and by the addition of cash incomes to their resources in land. Cash income, however, reflected the vagaries of royal and magnate favour, and the fortunes of war, and so provided an unstable and intermittent source of revenue. The aristocracy preferred the security of landed resources, and so used the occasional windfalls or the profits of office and legal practice to buy land. And yet, even when an inheritance was increased by purchase, grant or marriage, the recipients often found, especially in the first two-thirds of the fifteenth century, that their income from the new acquisition was diminishing.

The aristocracy were a remarkably resilient and flexible class, able to adapt to new circumstances and thus to maintain their social position. One of their strengths lay in their toleration of changes in personnel, which allowed them to receive recruits to replace old families that died out. Of the 136 barons who attended the house of lords at the end of the thirteenth century, the direct descendants of only 16 still survived in 1500, and only about a fifth of the gentry of 1500 can be traced back to the landed families of their counties in 1300.[37] Many of the recruits were the younger sons of the aristocracy, but there was still a gradual acceptance of newcomers, showing that the class was no exclusive caste. In this the aristocracy resembled

---

36 E. W. Ives, *The common lawyers of pre-Reformation England* (Cambridge, 1983), pp. 322–9.
37 McFarlane, *Nobility*, pp. 144–5; Wright, *Derbyshire gentry*, pp. 196–202.

their continental contemporaries, and may have been more open to outsiders than their modern successors.[38]

38 E. Perroy, 'Social mobility among the French *noblesse* in the later middle ages', *P. and P.*, 21 (1962), 25–38; L. Stone and J. C. Fawtier Stone, *An open élite? England 1540–1880* (Oxford, 1984).

3

THE ARISTOCRACY AS CONSUMERS

As the calculations of aristocratic incomes have shown, the class disposed of a great quantity of money and goods, amounting in a year to about a half-million pounds, or more than ten times the budget of the state in peace-time. The getting and spending of the aristocracy account for a sizeable share of the total economic activity of the country, and a very high proportion of the cash transactions, given that for much of the period the value of the coinage in circulation amounted to less than one million pounds. How was their wealth spent? And on what was it spent?

Aristocrats functioned within the social and administrative unit of the household, and our knowledge of their spending depends on household accounts. These documents took many different forms, including daily or weekly statements of goods bought or used, and annual summaries of expenditure. The earliest known accounts were compiled in the late twelfth century, and they became more elaborate and formalized in the succeeding two centuries. They were written by household stewards or their clerks, and were then audited, often daily. Because they had little lasting administrative utility they were kept on wax tablets that could be reused; if on paper or parchment, the records were destroyed. Relatively small numbers of these documents survive, and then often in isolated examples, so unlike manorial accounts they cannot be studied in long series. They do not cover a complete cross-section of the aristocracy, surviving mainly from the larger, wealthier and more bureaucratic households. Nor do they provide a complete picture of aristocratic expenditure, because lords spent money at every level of the administrative hierarchy of the estate, by payments made by reeves, bailiffs and receivers, as well as through the household, and the lord had his own privy purse for which records were rarely kept. The Latin word for the household, *familia*, meant a group of servants and followers, not a family. Often a great lay lord and his wife led separate lives, she in the 'inner' household, he in the 'riding' household. This allowed him to travel with a relatively small company on the many journeys needed to carry on his own or the king's business.[1] Superior households like the royal court with its assembly of lords of all kinds, and the magnate establishments which entertained and employed the gentry, attracted aristocratic men and thus detached them from their own families. Children, especially boys, were commonly absent from their parents, acquiring an education or training at school, or in another household.[2] Although their effective head was often a woman (either a wife in charge in her husband's absence, or a propertied widow), households were predominantly masculine societies, because with the exception of a few female companions for the lady, and a washerwoman, the officers and servants were always male. For all of the energy expended by the aristocracy in pursuit of the interests of their lineage, in marriage negotiations for example, their domestic arrangements, far from maintaining the unity of nuclear families, helped to fragment them. A thirteenth-century treatise on the management of a magnate household advised against allowing its members (some of them gentry), too frequent or too lengthy visits to their homes: 'And if any of them complain or grumble, say that you intend to be lord or lady, that you intend that they serve you according to your will.'[3]

The size and composition of the household naturally varied with the status and income of the lord. Dukes and earls maintained between 40 and 166 people; bishops and wealthy abbots from 40 to 80. For comparison, the royal household in the late fourteenth century contained about 400.[4] Baronial households could be as small

1 C. D. Ross, 'The household accounts of Elizabeth Berkeley, Countess of Warwick, 1420–1', *Transactions of the Bristol and Gloucestershire Archaeological Soc.*, 70 (1951), 81–105; on the household in general, see D. Starkey, 'The age of the household' in S. Medcalf (ed.), *The later middle ages* (London, 1981), pp. 225–90.

2 N. Orme, 'The education of the courtier' in V. J. Scattergood and J. W. Sherborne (eds.), *English court culture in the later middle ages* (London, 1983), pp. 63–85.

3 D. Oschinsky (ed.), *Walter of Henley* (Oxford, 1971), pp. 402–3.

4 J. W. Sherborne, 'Aspects of English court culture in the later fourteenth century' in Scattergood and Sherborne (eds.), *English court culture*, pp. 1–27.

as twenty, and rich knights had between twelve and thirty. According to a model budget of 1471–2 an esquire on £50 per annum would employ seven servants, and the lowliest documented secular household, that of Thomas Bozoun, a member of the Northamptonshire gentry, contained in 1348 only seven or eight people, both family and servants.[5] In a world dominated by hierarchies, the members of a household, especially the larger ones, were strictly stratified, with the gentry (*generosi*) or free household (*libera familia*) at the top, including relatives of the lord, important retainers and officials, and gentlemen servants, and two or three ranks of servants below them, the yeomen (*valletti*), grooms (*garciones*) and young pages. An example is that of the bishop of Bath and Wells on 9 March 1338, staying at Dogmersfield (Hampshire), when the staff of eighty-nine was divided into sixteen of the free household, seventeen yeomen (called *officiales*) and fifty-six grooms. No doubt the free or gentry element, as the lord was an ecclesiastic, included both clergy and laity, like the eleven clerks and seven esquires in the bishop of Ely's household in 1381.[6] A smaller household, that of Sir Hugh Luttrell of Dunster Castle (Somerset), gave liveries in 1425–6 to four gentlemen, eleven yeomen and four grooms.[7] Neither of these lists mentions guests, who would be treated according to their rank. Guests also added considerably to the household's size, twenty or thirty at any one time for many earls or bishops, in some cases contributing a third of the mouths to be fed.

The household served many purposes. Its primary function was to provide domestic services, through a number of departments, at their most basic the pantry (for bread), buttery (for drink), kitchen (other foods) and marshalsea (for horses). The more elaborate arrangements for a magnate might include a separate saucery (where sauces were prepared), a cellar for wine, a larder, a department supplying poultry, a hall, a chamber, a chapel and an almonry.[8] The

5 A. R. Myers, *The household of Edward IV* (Manchester, 1959), pp. 129–30; G. H. Fowler, 'A household expense roll, 1328', *E.H.R.*, 55 (1940), 630–4. This document has been redated to 1348 by C. M. Woolgar, 'The development of accounts for private households in England to c.1500 A.D.' (University of Durham Ph.D. thesis, 1986), p. 198.

6 J. A. Robinson (ed.), 'The household roll of bishop Ralph of Shrewsbury, 1337–8' in *Collectanea*, vol. 1 (Somerset Record Soc., 39, 1924), p. 156; Cambridge U.L., EDR D5/2.

7 Somerset R.O., DD/L P37/10.

8 B. F. Harvey (ed.), *Documents illustrating the rule of Walter de Wenlok, abbot of Westminster, 1283–1307* (Camden Soc., 4th ser., 2, 1965), p. 6; F. R. H. Du Boulay, *The Lordship of Canterbury* (London, 1966), pp. 254–61.

Map 1   Location of aristocratic households mentioned in chapters 3 and 4

preparation and serving of food occupied a high proportion of the servants' time.

A body of numerous followers demonstrated their lord's standing, and this could justify the employment of men for whom there were no specific useful tasks. They wore badges and liveries which would identify their affiliation, and the constant movements of the household brought the group to the attention of many observers. A visitor to a hall would be impressed by the gentlemen, who could put on a show of ceremony, treat the lord and his guests with appropriate etiquette, and practise such formalities as carving meat in the approved fashion.[9] By surrounding themselves with elegant companions, lords demonstrated their superiority and competed with their peers. The large company would deter thefts and assaults, though a striking comment on the relative security enjoyed by lords was the lack of much household expenditure on weapons, except in the unusual circumstances of the Scottish border, where fifteenth-century bishops of Carlisle supplied their servants with arrows and 'Carlisle axes', and arranged for escorts from the garrison of the royal castle.[10]

The household also provided a venue for practical administrative tasks. In the smaller establishments, like that of Sir William Mountford, a knight based at Kingshurst, Warwickshire, the receiver of the estate revenues would also live in the household and pay for its expenses.[11] When these tasks were performed on a large scale they had to be carried out separately, but the household was still visited by a stream of estate officials on business. A good deal of cash was kept for current use, and carried around from residence to residence; it was replenished by the estate receivers or their messengers. The household might also provide the venue for sessions of the lord's council, and bishops would similarly meet with their diocesan officials. Lords could call on household clerks and chaplains to write letters and other necessary documents.

The lord's wider social and political rôle was achieved through the services of the household. Good lordship meant establishing personal contact with retainers and allies, to reward them and to confirm their loyalty or win over waverers. The wandering household

9 R. W. Chambers (ed.), *A fifteenth-century courtesy book* (Early English Text Soc., O.S., 148, 1914).
10 Cumbria R.O., DRC/2/10, DRC/2/29.
11 Shakespeare's Birthplace Trust R.O., Stratford-upon-Avon, DR37/73.

visited many castles and manor houses, eating the estate produce or using up the accumulated cash from rents. At each venue a new circle of guests would be entertained, some of them travellers regarded as worthy of generous treatment, such as pilgrims, university scholars or merchants, but many were members of the lord's affinity of supporters.[12] Monastic hospitality was practised differently because the household did not move, but the monks were no less selective in their choice of guests. According to the instructions at Beaulieu Abbey, priority should be given in receiving 'noble ecclesiastical persons . . . pilgrims, and the messengers of magnates and other honest travellers'. Monasteries were well integrated into local landed society, and regularly invited the local gentry and leading clergy to dinner.[13] In sociological terms, household entertainment reinforced horizontal solidarities between equals or near equals, typified by the grand meal for 268 people provided by Ralph of Shrewsbury, bishop of Bath and Wells, when he invited Thomas de Berkeley to his palace at Wells on 19 November 1337. Hospitality in the household might also be used to establish vertical loyalties, notably in the Christmas meals given by lords to their tenants. A case would be Lady Alice de Bryene's spread for 300 tenants at Acton (Suffolk) on 1 January 1413.[14] The household could reach further down the social scale and act as a dispenser of charity, even to the point of keeping a group of paupers as part of the permanent establishment.

Medieval society maintained its equilibrium because lords combined dominance with acts of patronage. The household's internal hierarchy formed a microcosm of the whole society, in which in the great hall the lord, gentry and servants sat together and ate as a social unit, while at the same time being arranged on tables in strict ranking order. The household, in receiving guests, acted as a funnel through which the lord's largesse could be distributed more widely, his generosity being reciprocated by feelings of respect, loyalty and deference from his inferiors. There was an element of sham in all this, the harsher reality being indicated by the servants' theft of

---

12 For example, Ross, 'Elizabeth Berkeley', pp. 92–6; V. B. Redstone and M. K. Dale (eds.), *Household book of dame Alice de Bryene* (Suffolk Institute of Archaeology and Natural History, 1931), *passim*.
13 S. F. Hockey (ed.), *The account-book of Beaulieu Abbey* (Camden Soc., 4th ser., 16, 1975), p. 269; R. H. Hilton, *A medieval society*, 2nd edn (Cambridge, 1983), p. 84.
14 Robinson (ed.), 'Ralph of Shrewsbury', p. 102; Redstone and Dale (eds.), *Alice de Bryene*, p. 28.

household goods. The aggressive attitude sometimes adopted by the peasants shows that an occasional Christmas dinner was not sufficient to overcome the inevitable tensions between lords and tenants.

SPENDING ON FOOD

The largest single item in aristocratic budgets was food (which will here include both food and drink). Generally, in accordance with 'Engel's law', the proportion of expenditure devoted to food diminished towards the higher levels of the social scale, so that a small clerical household, that of two chantry priests at Bridport (Dorset), with an income below £20 per annum in the 1450s spent more than half of its money on foodstuffs, and a model budget of an esquire's household with £50 per annum reckoned that almost £25 of this would be spent on food. Food accounted for rather less than half of the expenditure of a rich knight, Sir Hugh Luttrell of Dunster in the 1420s, and earls required no more than a quarter of their spending to cover food.[15] Important exceptions to this rule include some wealthy monasteries, notably Battle Abbey, where food expenditure came to nearly two-thirds of the total, and Thomas de Berkeley (of Berkeley, Gloucestershire), a wealthy baron who devoted 57 per cent of his budget to food, but seems to have been living beyond his means (see table 5).[16]

A correlation can be seen between wealth and the types of foodstuff consumed, with the smaller households spending a larger share of their budgets on bread and ale, and a much smaller percentage on wine and spices (see table 3). A model late fifteenth-century knight was expected to spend only 2 per cent of his £100 income on wine, while a magnate of the same period spent 20 per cent. Not everyone fits into this pattern; for example Hugh Luttrell's wine consumption was unusually high for a knight.

Even in the wealthiest establishments bread was regarded as the basis of the diet, and the pantry that supplied it invariably headed the household account. Wheat bread was always provided for the upper

15 K. L. Wood-Legh (ed.), *A small household of the XVth century* (Manchester, 1956); Myers, *Edward IV*, pp. 129–30; Somerset R.O., DD/L P37/10; J. R. Maddicott, *Thomas of Lancaster 1307–1322* (Oxford, 1970), pp. 22–7.
16 C. Dyer, 'English diet in the later middle ages' in T. H. Aston *et al.* (eds), *Social relations and ideas* (Cambridge, 1983), pp. 191–2; Berkeley Castle muniment room, Select Roll 64.

Table 3. *Expenditure on foodstuffs in late medieval households*

	Chantry priests of Bridport 1456–7*		Katherine de Norwich Sept.– Dec. 1336*		Sir Hugh Luttrell of Dunster 1425–6	
Bread	40	(26%)	111	(23%)	17	(16%)
Ale	41	(27%)	69	(14%)	24	(23%)
Pottage corn	3	(2%)	4	(1%)	not known	
Meat	35	(23%)	158	(33%)	25	(23%)
Fish	28	(18%)	68	(14%)	13	(12%)
Wine	0		25	(5%)	25	(23%)
Spices	2	(1%)	42	(9%)	3	(3%)
Dairy produce	4	(3%)	6	(1%)	not known	
Misc. inc. fruit, vegetables, cider	0		1	(0%)	not known	
Total	153 (£7 13s. od.)	(100%)	484 (£24 4s. od.)	(100%)	£107	(100%)

	Thomas de Berkeley 1345–6		Humphrey Stafford, duke of Buckingham 1452–3	
Bread	130	(18%)	112	(8%)
Ale	130	(18%)	192	(14%)
Pottage corn	39	(5%)	2	(0%)
Meat/Fish	356	(48%)	673	(50%)
Wine	46	(6%)	278	(21%)
Spices	26	(3%)	92	(7%)
Dairy produce	6	(1%)	not known	
Misc. inc. fruit, vegetables, cider	9	(1%)	4	(0%)
Total	£742	(100%)	£1353	(100%)

* Cash total to nearest shilling

Source notes: K. Wood-Legh (ed.), *A small household of the XVth century* (Manchester, 1956), pp. 45–56; B.L., Add. Roll 63207; Somerset R.O., DD/L P37/10; Berkeley Castle muniment room. Select Roll 64; M. Harris (ed.), 'The account of the great household of Humphrey, first duke of Buckingham' in *Camden Miscellany XXVIII* (Camden Soc., 4th ser., 29, 1984), pp. 1–57

strata of the household. In parts of the country where wheat was scarce, or in the case of less wealthy lords, maslin (mixed wheat and rye), rye, barley, peas and beans were used as bread corns, usually for consumption by horses, dogs and paupers. Lower grades of servants were sometimes given bread baked from mixed corn, like the 'gruel' bread containing rye, barley and beans issued at Bolton Priory, in an area where wheat was a decided luxury. The household of a Norfolk knight, Hamon le Strange of Hunstanton, in the early fourteenth century used maslin for trenchers, that is the thick slices of bread on which other foods were served and eaten at table.[17] Most households obtained their wheat as grain (whether by purchase or from their own demesnes), and arranged for the milling themselves. The whitest bread was much admired, so an eighth or a fifth of the grain was milled off, or even as high a proportion as a quarter and a third.[18] The resulting bran was not wasted but fed to the animals, often in the form of specially baked horsebread. Households usually did all of their own baking; in the more highly-organized ones the pantry was required to account for every loaf, which weighed about 2 lbs each, 250 or so being made from each quarter of grain. Baking occurred every few days, sometimes once a week.

Ale, also regarded as a staple, was often brewed in the household from malt purchased on the market or supplied directly from manorial demesnes. Barley malt predominated, but malted wheat, drage (made from a mixture of barley and oats) and oats are all recorded, the latter appearing in such bleak agricultural environments as the uplands of west Yorkshire. Throughout the period, and especially in the fifteenth century, ready-brewed ale was purchased and even households that brewed their own would sometimes supplement their supplies from the market. Both methods of obtaining ale required a great deal of organization, because of the large quantities involved. Home brewing meant that vats, leads and containers had to be made and maintained in the succession of residences used by a wealthy lord. Purchase of ale led to a procession of carts bearing heavy, leaking barrels from the local market town to the lord's castle

17 I. Kershaw, *Bolton Priory. The economy of a northern monastery, 1286–1325* (Oxford, 1973), pp. 72, 145; G. H. Holley, 'The earliest roll of household accounts in the muniment room at Hunstanton for the second year of Edward III (1328)', *Norfolk Archaeology*, 21 (1920–2), 77–96; Norfolk R.O., N.H.8.
18 The high figures: W. B. D. D. Turnbull (ed.), *Compota domestica familiarum de Bukingham et d'Angouleme* (Abbotsford Club, 1836); J. Ridgard (ed.), *Medieval Framlingham* (Suffolk Records Soc., 27, 1985), p. 106.

– the duke of Buckingham's annual 30,000 to 40,000 gallons would have filled 300 carts.[19] The strength of the household brew can be judged from the numbers of gallons obtained from a quarter of malt, which varied from 50 to 96 gallons, the normal figure being in the region of 50 to 75. The price per gallon indicates the quality of purchased ale, which often came in two grades. A wealthy magnate like Hugh Audley in 1320 bought six times as much ale for 1d. as that costing ³/₄d., while a knight, Hugh Luttrell, bought three gallons at 1d. per gallon for every one at 1¹/₄d. in 1423–4 (the difference in prices between the two examples reflects not long-term inflation, but annual fluctuations in the price of barley, from which ale prices were calculated according to a sliding scale fixed by the assize of ale).[20] Households had to brew or buy ale at regular intervals because it deteriorated quite rapidly. Beer, which was a continental invention with a distinctive flavour of hops and better keeping qualities, appeared alongside ale in many fifteenth-century households, but had not overtaken ale in the early sixteenth century.

Cereals were consumed mainly in the form of bread and ale. A little wheat flour went to the kitchens for pastry, and pottage was made from oat-meal and pulses. Pottage was eaten in limited quantities, judging from the small expenditure on the appropriate grains, though it was served regularly to the Bridport chantry priests, the humblest documented household.

The special characteristics of the aristocratic diet was its emphasis on meat and fish, which were served in large quantities, and in great variety. Fish was eaten on Fridays and Saturdays, and commonly on Wednesdays also. Meat was served on the other days, except during the six weeks of Lent and on the vigils of important feasts. Over the whole year, therefore, the consumption of meat and fish was balanced almost equally. Meat came either from 'stock', that is, major supplies laid in well in advance, or from smaller quantities of daily or weekly purchases. Cattle, sheep and pigs were bought for stock in the autumn, the traditional date for their slaughter being 11 November (Martinmas), and this has given rise to the common belief that all food animals were killed and salted then. In fact, many households were able to feed a high proportion of their animals on pastures or

19 M. Harris (ed.), 'The account of the great household of Humphrey, first duke of Buckingham', in *Camden Miscellany XXVIII* (Camden Soc., 4th ser., 29, 1984), p. 37.
20 P.R.O., E101/505/17; Somerset R.O., DD/L P37/10.

Table 4. *Meat consumption in two aristocratic households*

	Alice de Bryene of Acton, Suffolk, 1418–19[a]			John de Vere, earl of Oxford, of Wivenhoe, Essex, 1431–2[b]		
	Number	Weight of meat in pounds	%	Number	Weight of meat in pounds	%
Cattle	46	9,750	48	48½	18,188	56
Sheep	97	2,767	14	140	4,340	14
Pigs	87	5,630	28	62	5,580	17
Poultry	1,584	1,836	9	723	1,902	6
Game:						
Rabbits	102 ⎫			306 ⎫		
Birds	26 ⎬	150	1	164 ⎬	2,362	7
Deer	0 ⎭			36 ⎭		
Total		20,133	100		32,372	100

N.B.: The estimates of weight are related to the age of the animals. For example, Alice de Bryene's household consumed twenty-three calves, sixteen lambs, and forty-four piglets, which are included in the figures listed above. The de Vere records do not include details of these young animals.

Source notes:
a. V. B. Redstone and M. K. Dale (eds.), *Household book of dame Alice de Bryene* (Suffolk Institute of Archaeology and Natural History, 1931), pp. 128–35
b. Essex R.O., D/DPr 137

hay so as to maintain a supply of fresh meat through the winter and spring. They also regularly purchased joints of fresh meat from butchers. The relative importance of preserved meat deriving from the 'autumn slaughter' and fresh meat from animals killed at other times of the year can be judged from the accounts of the household of Alice de Bryene. In 1418–19 we are given the date of slaughter of seventeen cattle, of which ten were killed in October and November, and the rest at other times of the year. Of eighty-one sheep, thirty-one were killed before June, and fifty after shearing in the late summer and autumn. The suggestion has been made that the proportion of fresh meat consumed in aristocratic households increased between the thirteenth and fifteenth century, which would coincide with an increasing availability of pasture and more stable residential patterns (see below, pp. 99–101). A few households bought in meat as preserved carcasses; for special occasions, when the household was near to a town, poultry was bought ready cooked.[21]

21 B.L., Add. Roll 63207.

The proportions of different types of meat can be judged by estimating the weight of carcasses (see table 4). The importance of beef is clear, often exceeding a half of the total of meat consumed, followed by pork and mutton, with game and poultry of least significance. The proportion of beef was even greater in the household of Sir William Skipwith of South Ormsby (Lincolnshire) in 1467–8, where of the larger animals forty-nine cattle were eaten as compared with seventy-four sheep and seventy-two pigs and piglets, so that beef accounted for about three-quarters of the weight of meat. The smallest proportion of beef known, as little as 15 per cent, was consumed at Beaulieu Abbey in 1269–70.[22] Very young animals, calves, lambs and piglets, though clearly regarded as desirable delicacies, contributed only a small quantity to the total amount of meat, and often a half of the cattle were fully grown oxen, cows and bulls, slaughtered after a lifetime's work. Again, Skipwith's household shows a rather unusual pattern because of the forty-nine beasts, thirty-three were relatively youthful steers and heifers. Ewes and wethers were selected from the sheep flocks because of their advancing years. The pigs provided the most consistent source of more delicate meat; they were often slaughtered in their first or second year. Poultry and rabbits contributed to the quality, if not greatly to the quantity, of aristocratic meals.

The real importance of game is difficult to assess because it was rarely bought and sold but was taken from parks or exchanged by gift and consequently scarcely enters the household accounts. When it is recorded, the quantities seem small, compared with the meat of domesticated animals. An ideal earl's household with an income of £2,000, according to an estimate of 1471–2, each year would have consumed 140 deer, amounting to one tenth of the animals eaten. However, a real magnate, John de Vere, earl of Oxford, in 1431–2 made do with only thirty-six deer (about 6 per cent of his meat), and Henry Percy (the earl of Northumberland) expected in 1512 to consume forty-nine deer, representing a smaller percentage of his meat supply.[23] The only case where venison can be shown to have played a major part in provisioning a household was during the bishop of Coventry and Lichfield's stay in south Staffordshire in

22 Lincolnshire Archive Office, M.M.1/3/26; Hockey (ed.), *Beaulieu Abbey*, pp. 186–8.
23 T. Percy (ed.), *The regulations and establishment of the household of Henry Algernon Percy, the 5th earl of Northumberland* (London, 1905), p. 134.

1461.[24] In a four-month summer period, the bishop (John Hales) and his men ate twenty-three deer, and from stock eleven cattle and sheep. However, this was around Cannock Chase, where the bishops enjoyed hunting rights in a large tract of wild countryside. The advance of cultivation and enclosure had left few such habitats, hence the deliberate emparking of land to create artificial environments for deer. Game birds, from swans, herons, pheasants, partridges and plover, down to larks, thrushes and even smaller species, appeared regularly on the aristocratic tables, but again accounted for a limited weight of meat. However, the importance of game cannot be assessed in merely quantitative terms. Game symbolized the aristocratic style of life. It was nurtured in private parks or protected in forests and chases. The fences that separated the game from the non-aristocrats, like moats, castle walls and monastic precincts, gave physical expression to social barriers. Hunting parties provided the aristocracy with their principal diversion, and they accompanied the chase with rituals and ceremonies. If the cost of game is counted in terms of the expense of fencing parks, the loss of rent from land of potential agricultural use, and the labour expended in its capture, every piece of venison would have been very valuable indeed. Venison's status led to its use as a gift, and its consumption at special occasions, and then only at the top table.

The ritual abstinence from meat for two or three days each week and in Lent created a strong demand for fish. A great variety of species came from the English commercial fishing industry, from long-distance trade with Norway and Iceland, and (for fresh-water species), from farming in ponds. The 'stock' of preserved fish maintained by all households consisted of barrels of herring, both white (salted) and red (smoked), and salted or dried white fish, such as 'stockfish' (dried cod), ling, winterfish and haberdens. Salt salmon and salt eels were also laid in as stock. These bulk supplies were supplemented by regular purchases of fresh fish, herrings, white fish, flat-fish, shell-fish of every variety, crustaceans and even marine mammals like porpoises. Fishmongers were ingenious and skilful enough to ensure that supplies of fresh sea fish were available throughout the country, at whatever distance from the coast.

Fresh-water fish, like game, is poorly documented because supplies often came direct from the lord's ponds, or as gifts. When they are recorded they varied markedly in quantity, from the abundance

---

24 Staffordshire R.O., D1734/3/3/264.

enjoyed by the bishop of Ely's household in the 1380s in the fens (2,000 in two sample months in the 1380s), to the modest 215 consumed in a year in the de Vere household in Essex in 1431–2.[25] Eels, dace and other river-caught species were not especially expensive or prestigious, but the larger pond fish such as pike and bream were served, like game, as a luxury for the lord and his honoured guests.

The different scales of wine-drinking help to define the hierarchy of consumption within the aristocracy, as only the magnates were able to afford to lay in the pipes and tuns (barrels containing about 120 and 240 gallons respectively) necessary to maintain regular supplies. At 3d. to 4d. per gallon at its cheapest, rising to 8d. and even 10d., gentry like the le Stranges of Norfolk or the Moultons of Moulton, Lincolnshire, tended to buy a few gallons at a time. The social horizon of wine-drinking in the late thirteenth century is suggested by the instructions to the guest-house at Beaulieu Abbey that abbots and priors and other dignitaries would be given wine, and parsons and knights, 'but not all'; some knights and parish clergy had to be content with good ale.[26] Wines were imported mainly from Gascony, with a little from northern France and the Rhineland. In the fifteenth century, increasing amounts of sweet wines, malmsey and rumney for example, came from the Mediterranean. English vineyards may have been significant sources of wine before the 1260s, but certainly by the end of the thirteenth century only one household, that of the bishop of Hereford (who received seven tuns from his vineyard at Ledbury in 1289–90), is known to have drunk much from demesne supplies.[27]

Spices were also consumed in varying amounts depending on the wealth of the household. The term referred to two types of imported foodstuffs. Firstly, there were the dried fruits (notably currants, dates, figs, prunes and raisins), with almonds and rice, generally priced at 1d. to 4d. per pound, sometimes up to 6d., of which modest households could afford to buy a few pounds, and richer establishments hundreds. Secondly, there were the strongly flavoured spices – cinnamon, cloves, ginger, mace, pepper, sugar and many more – which often cost 1s. to 3s. per pound, occasionally

25 Cambridge U.L., EDR D5/3, D5/5; Essex R.O., D/DPr 137.
26 Norfolk R.O., N.H.8; Magdalen College, Oxford, Moulton Hall 160; Hockey (ed.), *Beaulieu Abbey*, p. 273.
27 J. Webb (ed.), *A roll of the household expenses of Richard de Swinfield, bishop of Hereford* (2 vols., Camden Soc., 59, 62, 1853–4), vol. 1, p. 59.

rising to as much as 6s. Saffron, bought for 12s. to 15s. per pound, was in a luxurious class of its own. The use of expensive condiments tended to be concentrated in the magnate households. A modern mythology has grown up to explain the medieval taste for spices. It is assumed that dishes were flavoured with them habitually, because of the dullness or even the corruption of preserved meat. In fact, as we have seen, not all meat was salted, and there is no reason to think that it was eaten in a decayed state. Spices were used to flavour both salted and fresh meat, so they seem to have been appreciated for their aesthetic rather than their utilitarian properties. The magnates were able to buy enough spices to flavour their food regularly and quite abundantly. The duke of Buckingham in 1452–3, for example, used almost 2 lbs per day. However, below the magnate level the daily quantities were much more modest, such as the ½ oz in the Bryene and Luttrell households. It is unlikely that these amounts were used to provide a light flavouring of spices every day; rather they were saved up for special meals, like the blancmange (among other dishes) served by Katherine de Norwich on the anniversary of her husband's death on 20 January 1337, or the dinner using spices worth 10s. 6½d. provided by Edmund Stonor to celebrate a judicial session in Oxfordshire on 5 August 1378. The use of spices was a common characteristic of the western European aristocratic culinary tradition. To participate in this culture the less wealthy members of the class bought spices for occasional use, and had to be content with cheaper locally produced flavourings – salt, vinegar, mustard, onions and garlic – for their daily meals.[28]

Bread, ale, meat, fish, wine and spices accounted for the bulk of aristocratic food consumption, and dairy produce and fresh fruits and vegetables were of lesser importance. Eggs were bought in large numbers, often to provide an accompaniment for fish. Liquid milk is occasionally mentioned in accounts with the explanations 'for the kitchen', or 'for the children'. Butter seems generally to have been used for frying, as an alternative to animal fats or the more expensive olive-oil or nut-oil. Cheese had a rather low status; it was more prominent in monastic diet than those of secular households, though it is possible sometimes to identify a rather higher level of consumption. For example, Lord Grey of Codnor (Derbyshire) provided

28 C. B. Hieatt and S. Butler (eds.), *Curye on Inglysch* (Early English Text Soc., S.S., 8, 1985), pp. 13–14; S. Mennell, *All manners of food* (Oxford, 1985), pp. 53–4; for the households mentioned see notes 12, 19 and 21; for the Stonors, P.R.O., c47/37/1/25.

4 lbs per day to a household of rather less than a hundred people.[29] Garden produce from a manor's or monastery's kitchen garden would not normally enter into the accounting procedure. Some lords' gardens were very large and productive, like that of Glastonbury Abbey which supplied to the monastery 8,000 heads of garlic and 3 quarters of onions in the year 1333–4. The large gardens just outside London belonging to the town houses of such notables as the archbishop of Canterbury or the earl of Lincoln, tended by expert gardeners, yielded a great variety of fruits and vegetables both for the lord's table and for sale in the markets of the city. However, most manor houses were provided with gardens of limited size which were not tended by specialists. They yielded enough leeks, onions, garlic, apples and pears to supply the lord's kitchen on his visits and to provide ingredients for the pottage given to the farm servants. Vegetables and fresh fruits were used in a number of the dishes described in the recipe books, but they were not regarded as an essential element of diet. Garden produce had a low status and was associated with poverty or penance, hence an increase in purchases of vegetables during Lent. On occasion apples and pears were used to prepare delicacies, especially at Christmas, and households would buy strawberries and peascods when they were in season in the summer.[30]

Our sources give much more information about the total consumption of the household than about the allowances for individuals. Many accounts give apparently helpful figures of the number of *fercula* or 'messes', while occasionally letting us know that a mess was shared by two, three or four people. The most precise documents list the people present, but do not tell us how many meals they each took. Because of these uncertainties it is very hazardous to calculate precise figures for a single person's consumption. However, an individual in a magnate household could well have received an allowance each day as large as 2 lbs of bread, between 6 and 8 pints of ale, and 2 or 3 lbs of meat or fish. Meat-eating was regarded as both pleasurable and a contribution to health and strength. We can conclude that the average member of a household was supplied with a diet of high calorific content and with plenty of animal protein.

29 Nottingham U.L., Mi A1.
30 T. J. Hunt and I. Keil, 'Two medieval gardens', *Proceedings of the Somerset Archae-ological and Natural History Soc.*, 104 (1959–60), 91–101; J. Harvey, 'Vegetables in the middle ages', *Garden History*, 12 (1984), 89–99; C. Dyer, 'Jardins et vergers en Angleterre au moyen âge' in *Jardins et vergers en Europe occidentale* (Centre Culturel de l'Abbaye de Flaran, 9e journées internationales d'histoire, 1989), pp. 145–64.

Modern nutritional fashion would disapprove of its high fat and low fibre content, and the apparently small intake of vitamins A and C, resulting from the often low levels of consumption of dairy produce and fresh fruits and vegetables. The pursuit of an 'average' member of such a sharply stratified organization as an aristocratic household would be futile. The cost of boarding members of the Shropshire le Strange household in 1383 was calculated according to the following daily scale:

the lord	7d.
an esquire	4d.
a yeoman	3d.
a groom	1d.[31]

The expensive elements in the diet – wine, spices, game – were reserved for the lord's family and the gentry. The discrimination practised is occasionally revealed in daily or weekly household accounts when the lord went off with his companions and left the servants to feed themselves. Ralph Shrewsbury, bishop of Bath and Wells, kept twenty-four of his servants at his Somerset manor of Evercreech while he with his *libera familia* visited the rector of Somerton on 13 November 1337. The fresh beef, veal, game and other luxuries which appeared regularly in the account up to that point were replaced by much more solid fare – bread, ale, bacon and mutton were good enough for the servants.[32] Not only was this much cheaper than the diet of the whole household, it also differed in its balance, with two-thirds of the cost deriving from cereal-based foods (bread and ale) as distinct from one-third on normal days when the 'quality' were in residence. At the base of the aristocracy the Woodford (Northamptonshire) household of the modestly-landed Thomas Bozoun bought fresh meat regularly in the local market town of Higham Ferrers when the lord was present. When he went off on business or pleasure to Northampton, London or Windsor, meat purchases stopped and the household lived on 'stock'.[33]

Seasonal changes affected aristocratic consumption. Some foodstuffs became available or plentiful at particular times of the year, like fresh herring in the autumn or milk and eggs in the summer. Most of the changes through the year were man-made rather than

31 B. Ross, 'The accounts of the Talbot household at Blakemere in the county of Shropshire, 1394–1425' (Australian National University M.A. thesis, Canberra, 1970), p. 102.
32 Robinson (ed.), 'Ralph of Shrewsbury', pp. 96–100.
33 Fowler, 'A household expense roll', pp. 633–4.

imposed by nature. Lent marked the most profound break in the normal routine when, after a last fling at which such treats as frumenty (wheat grains boiled in milk with spices) were served, the household settled down to six weeks of abstention from meat; they ate a great variety of fish, accompanied by spices and dried fruits. The observance of such a fast was only relevant to those who normally expected to enjoy plenty, and abstinence was almost as much an aristocratic indulgence as feasting. It highlighted the contrast not just between Lent and the pleasures of the rest of the year, but also between the aristocracy and the masses, who would have regarded the supposed rigours of aristocratic Lent as the height of luxury.[34] The times for feasting were determined by the religious calendar – Easter, Whitsun and Christmas were observed by all. Christmas lasted for the full twelve days, and many households served their largest and most luxurious meals not on 25 December but on 1 January or 6 January (Epiphany). In the rest of the year households would vary in their choice of occasions for grand feasts – some opting for the feast of the Assumption (15 August), others the Nativity of John the Baptist (24 June) or All Saints (1 November). Some of the largest recorded junketings were held for funerals, and for commemorations held on the anniversaries of deaths. The monastic year was punctuated by parties at which the monks consumed spices, wine and other luxuries. However, for all these variations and special occasions, the aristocracy were distinguished by their ability to maintain a high standard of diet throughout the year and from year to year. They had the resources to ensure that meat or fish could be served every day. They could insulate themselves from temporary shortages, and continued to buy some foodstuffs even when prices were high. Wheat bread was eaten, whether wheat cost 3s. 4d. or 13s. 4d. per quarter. Only a very extreme series of bad harvests disrupted the established routines of household life; the famine of 1315–18 caused Bolton Priory to dismiss half of its servants, and in the late 1430s a similar episode of bad weather precipitated changes in the administration of Durham Cathedral Priory.[35]

The consumption patterns of the aristocracy also rose above geographical differences. The aristocracy belonged to an international

---

34 J. Goody, *Cooking, cuisine and class. A study in comparative sociology* (Cambridge, 1982), pp. 144–7.
35 Kershaw, *Bolton Priory, economy*, pp. 52–8; R. B. Dobson, *Durham Priory, 1400–50* (Cambridge, 1973), pp. 266–7.

society, with a common culture of chivalry and christianity that ignored frontiers. Cookery books all over Europe included recipes with supposed local origins, like 'bruet of Almayne' (German broth), which formed part of a cosmopolitan repertoire of dishes. Household accounts from different parts of Europe show the influences of the local agrarian economy, in the ale- and beer-drinking of the north or the use of olive-oil in the south, but we cannot fail to be impressed by their similarities.[36] An esquire of the bishop of Salisbury in the early fifteenth century would have found himself in a familiar environment if he had visited the household of the archbishop of Arles. Similarly, within England the regional variations seem of small significance. From Dover to Cockermouth and from Carlisle to Salisbury wheat bread, Gascon wine, fresh beef, herrings and oriental spices were all available to the higher aristocracy, because they were prepared to pay the price. Some differences in the consumption of game or fresh-water fish have already been noted. The range of fish generally was influenced by local supplies, with salmon being relatively plentiful in the north-east, hake, conger and dogfish in the south-west, and oysters and whiting in the south-east.

There were a few long-term changes in consumption of foodstuffs. The moves towards sweet wines and beer in the fifteenth century represent small but significant changes in fashion. The most important development arose from the leasing of demesnes in the decades around 1400, which had repercussions for food supply. In the early middle ages, lords had apparently been self-sufficient. Monasteries like Ramsey or Ely could organize their manors in a rota, by which each demesne supplied the monastery for a week or two each year, and more mobile lords – kings, bishops and earls – would travel from manor to manor, both their own or those which owed them hospitality, eating the produce as they went. These direct methods of linking production and consumption were probably in decline as early as the tenth century with the development of a market for agricultural produce. The ideal of self-sufficiency still survived in the thirteenth century, when the treatise on estate and household management attributed to Bishop Grosseteste of Lincoln advised a new lord to work out the grain production on the demesnes of the estate, 'and base on it the consumption of your

36 J. L. Flandrin, 'Internationalisme, nationalisme et régionalisme dans la cuisine des XIVᵉ et XVᵉ siècles: le témoinage des livres de cuisine' in D. Menjot (ed.), *Manger et boire au moyen âge* (2 vols., Publications de la faculté des lettres et sciences humaines de Nice, 28, 1984), vol. 2, pp. 75–91.

household in bread and ale'.[37] The account-book of Beaulieu Abbey, which was partly a treatise on management as well as a set of model accounts, also assumed a high level of consumption of estate produce within the monastery. What better lesson in economy could there be than that of the monastic shoe-maker who greased his products with the dripping from herrings collected in the kitchens? However, in some ways Beaulieu departed from the ideal pattern, for example by selling its wool clip for a high price, and making the monks' clothes from cheaper wool bought for the purpose. By the late thirteenth century most estates had gone over to a mixed economy, in which part of their needs came from the estates and part from the market, whichever was most convenient.

An extreme example of a market-dominated system is found at Worcester Cathedral Priory in the 1290s, which sold its demesne grain in large quantities, and bought most of its own supplies.[38] A general transition to a more market-oriented mentality is found in the practice in household accounts of assigning a value to demesne produce, which would also be entered on the accounts of the manor in the form of a fictitious sale. Not all estates show a continuous tendency away from direct demesne supplies to the use of the market – in the fourteenth century both the bishops of Worcester and Westminster Abbey swung back temporarily to the use of demesne produce.[39] The decisive change for many estates came with the leasing of the demesnes. This change of management could give the lord an estate income purely in the form of cash, and all of the household supplies could then be obtained on the market. John Hales, bishop of Coventry and Lichfield, in 1461 bought his bread and ale ready baked and brewed, and only game and fresh-water fish came from his own resources. The retention of parks and ponds when all other demesne assets had been leased is typical of the period. At the other extreme was the household of a near contemporary, Sir William Skipwith, the wealthy Lincolnshire knight, which obtained nine-tenths of its wheat, all of its barley and oats, half of its cattle and most of its sheep from the demesnes of the estate. Smaller land-owners, especially gentry who held a single manor, were most likely to continue to supply their households directly. In between these

---

37 Oschinsky, *Walter of Henley*, pp. 392–3.
38 J. M. Wilson and C. Gordon (eds.), *Early compotus rolls of the priory of Worcester* (Worcestershire Historical Soc., 1908), pp. 15–23; Hilton, *A medieval society*, p. 79.
39 C. Dyer, *Lords and peasants in a changing society. The estates of the bishopric of Worcester, 680–1540* (Cambridge, 1980), p. 133; B. Harvey, *Westminster Abbey and its estates in the middle ages* (Oxford, 1977), pp. 134–40.

extremes were many compromises. Lords of all kinds tended to retain parks, enclosed pastures and meadows in direct management after leasing their arable demesnes. The parks that surrounded many manor houses and castles served as open-air larders, enabling the household to enjoy fresh meat throughout the year. Estates of all sizes kept a manor near the residential centre – Elvethall attached to Durham Priory provides a good example – as a home farm for arable crops.[40] Nor did the transfer of the management of manors to farmers always give the lord a solely cash income. Lords often received part of the rent in kind. On the Coventry Cathedral manors in Warwickshire in the early fifteenth century the farmers paid grain, meat and hay to provision the monks; the estate bore a superficial resemblance to one of the early middle ages.[41] Sometimes a farmer with a contract specifying a cash rent negotiated with the lord to send grain rather than money when the market was especially sluggish in the mid-fifteenth century.

By 1500 most of the higher aristocracy were receiving a largely cash income. The gentry were more likely to supply their own needs, as they had always done, though they were also involved in the market as producers. The aristocracy were clearly moving in the direction of a more commercial economy. Feudal trappings remained: some lords retained rights of pre-emption from their tenants, enabling the Luttrells to buy fish 'at the lord's price' in the early fifteenth century; in 1422–3 salt conger, which fetched 6d. each on the market, were being acquired for the household at Dunster for 4d.[42] Lords were also committed to the ideal of *largesse*, which they practised by sending each other, as a mark of friendship among equals, or in deference to superiors, or as patronage to inferiors, presents of foodstuffs. They were often prestigious items, such as wine, game or fresh-water fish, but almost anything was acceptable, even cartloads of oats for the horses in the recipient's stable.

Did the long-term decline in self-sufficiency lead to a change in a lord's cost of living? In theory the middleman's profit ought to have added to the cost. On the other hand, no matter how strict the accounting methods, there was undoubtedly a good deal of inefficiency and waste, and perhaps some dishonesty, in the system of direct supply from demesnes and processing within the household.

---

40 R. A. Lomas, 'A northern farm at the end of the middle ages: Elvethall Manor, Durham 1443/4–1513/14', *Northern History*, 18 (1982), 26–53.

41 P.R.O., E164/21.

42 Somerset R.O., DD/L P37/10.

Table 5. *Some examples of expenditure by aristocratic and institutional consumers*

Thomas de Berkeley 1345–6[a]		Sir Gilbert Talbot 1417–18[b]	
Food	£742 (57%)	Food	£176 (71%)
Food and bedding of		Food and purchase of	
horses	£148 (11%)	horses	£ 16 (7%)
Horses and falcons	£ 26 (2%)	Wax and candles	£ 1 (0%)
Clothing	£142 (11%)	Fees and wages	£ 22 (9%)
Household cloth and		Cloth	£ 20 (8%)
silver	£ 45 (3%)	Travel	£ 3 (1%)
Wax	£ 22 (2%)	Letters	£ 6 (2%)
Legal expenses	£ 11 (1%)	Miscellaneous	£ 4 (2%)
Pensions & gifts to			
relatives	£ 65 (5%)	Total	£248 (100%)
Building	£ 21 (2%)		
Miscellaneous		St John's Hospital[d] Cambridge	
(including alms, boots,	£86 (6%)	1484–5	
shoes, wages etc.)		Food	£32 (45%)
Total	£1308 (100%)	Wages	£13 (18%)
		Rent	£ 2 (3%)
		Buildings	£12 (17%)
John Catesby 1392–3[c]		Fuel	£ 5 (7%)
Food	£13 (12%)	Clothing	£ 1 (1%)
Horses	£ 1 (1%)	Wax	£ 1 (1%)
Payments to servants	£15 (13%)	Miscellaneous	£ 6 (8%)
Clothing	£18 (16%)		
Building	£14 (13%)	Total	£72 (100%)
Agriculture	£17 (15%)		
Education	£ 2 (2%)	An esquire 1471–2[e]	
Kitchen equipment	£ 2 (2%)	Food and fuel	£24 (48%)
Rents	£23 (21%)	Clothes and alms	£ 4 (8%)
Tithes and taxes	£ 3 (3%)	Buildings	£ 5 (10%)
Miscellaneous		Horses, food for horses	£ 5 (10%)
(including alms and	£ 2 (2%)	Servants' wages	£ 9 (18%)
entertainment)		Robes	£ 3 (6%)
Total	£110 (100%)	Total	£50 (100%)

(N.B.: In no case are these figures comprehensive, so the omission of say, building in Sir Gilbert Talbot's household, is a feature of the source. For John Catesby, cash payments only are given and the bulk of food and fodder came from the estate. These statistics are to give an impression of expenditure only.)

Source notes:
a. Berkeley Castle muniment room, Select Roll 64
b. B. Ross, 'The accounts of the Talbot household at Blakemere in the county of Shropshire, 1394–1425' (Australian National University M.A. thesis, Canberra 1970), pp. 89–127
c. P.R.O., E101/511/15   d. St John's College, Cambridge, MS. 106.9
e. A. R. Myers, *The household of Edward IV* (Manchester, 1959), pp. 129–30

SPENDING ON ITEMS OTHER THAN FOOD

Information on the whole range of goods and services used by any single medieval aristocrat is almost impossible to collect, but we can build up a composite picture if we look at a sufficient range of sources. Some evidence for spending patterns has been assembled in table 5. It includes information about a wealthy baron, the third Thomas de Berkeley, a very rich knight, Sir Gilbert Talbot of Whitchurch in Shropshire, and a wealthy esquire, John Catesby of Ashby St Ledgers (Northamptonshire). To extend our knowledge of the lesser aristocracy, a model budget for an esquire with half of Catesby's income is included, and the analysis of a modestly endowed institution, St John's Hospital in Cambridge, by 1485 already evolving into an academic college. Its income is comparable with that of many minor monastic houses.

That different groups within the aristocracy spent their incomes in dissimilar ways is well illustrated by their transport costs. A large mobile household like Hugh Audley's in 1320 kept between thirty and fifty horses each day, while the sedentary dowager, Alice de Bryene, with half as many people as Audley, fed in 1412–13 only four to eight horses on most days, increasing only when wealthy guests stayed. Small monastic or clerical households did not need to travel very much, so kept no riding horses at all, and hired them when necessary. For most laymen the marshalsea or stable department cost about one tenth of the total annual expenditure. Most of this sum went on feed – hay, oats, bran and horsebread, which was baked from beans, maslin or wheat siftings left over from milling the household bread. Horses had other needs, from the litter of straw, heather or ferns on which they were bedded, to the ironmongery of the stable, shoes, stirrups, spurs and fetterlocks, and the leatherwork of saddles, bridles and harness. Tallow was used to treat their hoofs and medicines were bought for their ailments. The highest grade of horses were better treated than most humans, judging from the cost of keeping the earl of Cornwall's destrier (war-horse) at Mere (Wiltshire) for eighty-two days in the summer of 1297, which at 36s. 9½d. amounted to more than an unskilled worker's annual wage.[43]

Horses were bought only sporadically, so that many of our scattered records for individual years record no purchases at all. The

---

43 L. M. Midgley (ed.), *Ministers' accounts of the earldom of Cornwall 1296–1297* (2 vols., Camden Soc., 3rd ser., 66, 68, 1942, 1945), vol. 1, p. 64.

price of destriers is known to have risen as high as £80 in the thirteenth century, but high-grade riding horses cost about £10, and the majority of any household's horses were ordinary draught animals worth 10s. to 20s. each. So William Moleyns in 1400–1 was able to buy ten horses at prices varying from 10s. to £6 16s. 8d., for a total outlay of £20.[44]

Cart-horses were needed to pull the household's vehicles, which transported the 'harness' (luggage) from one residence to another, and brought in supplies. The 'chariot' was the largest and most costly of the vehicles, a four-wheeled coach drawn by five or six horses, capable of carrying the ladies when necessary, or of bringing a load of fish across country. Epic overland journeys are recorded, of Sir William Mountford's chariot from Stourbridge Fair near Cambridge to Kingshurst in north Warwickshire in 1433, and that of the duke of York from London to south Worcestershire in 1410.[45] A new chariot cost Thomas Arundel, bishop of Ely, in excess of £8 in 1381, and every household with one of these vehicles needed to spend at least a few shillings every year on repairs to axles, wheels and harness, and on the wages of an expert 'charioteer'. Lords well-placed to use them might buy and equip boats, like the barge bought at a cost of £10 by John de Vere, earl of Oxford in 1431–2, to carry goods and people up and down the Thames estuary between the earl's manor of Wivenhoe and the port of Colchester, and down to London. Worcester Priory owned boats for travel on the river Severn, and the monks of Beaulieu maintained a sea-going ship that traded for the abbey's profit.

The mobility of the household required spending on the hire of extra horses and vehicles, and overnight stays for servants *en route*. When the duke of York uprooted his household from Cardiff Castle in October 1409 and sent them to Hanley Castle in Worcestershire, some went with the 'harness' by boat up the Severn and others travelled overland through Monmouth and Ross-on-Wye. Costs included the ferry toll across the Wye and the hire of guides to take them along unfamiliar roads. The scale of the operation can be judged from the forty-two wainloads of goods and supplies that were transported from the boat at the landing stage on the Severn to Hanley. Towards the end of our period households became more sedentary. However, no-one could stay put for ever. Lady Talbot in

44 P.R.O., E101/512/17.
45 Shakespeare's Birthplace Trust R.O., Stratford-upon-Avon, DR37/73; Northamptonshire R.O., Westmorland (Apethorpe), 4xx4.

the 1410s spent most of her time at her manor house of Blakemere (near Whitchurch, Shropshire) but went on a short visit with twenty servants to see the duke of Bedford at Kenilworth Castle, sixty miles away, at a cost of 52s. 8^{1}/2d. Her husband was on the king's service in France at the time, and she spent as much as £6 on sending letters to him. Some of the heaviest recorded travelling expenses were incurred by the new colleges, which had been endowed with widely scattered properties, requiring periodic visits to collect rents and hold courts. So All Souls (Oxford) in 1448–9 spent £108 on travel, or 16 per cent of its total receipts.[46]

Heating and lighting involved a relatively small proportion of total expenditure for some households, usually less than 4 per cent. St John's Cambridge spent more, perhaps because of its unusual need as a town-based institution to buy its fuel. Most estates were provided with at least a small wood or turbary, for which the main cost lay in the labour of cutting firewood or digging peat, and carriage to the household. The types of fuel depended on regional availability. Peat (turf) was used in the north and east, from Carlisle to Cambridge, and supplies were locally available throughout the country; the monks of Beaulieu in the New Forest exploited a local turbary as well as their abundant woodlands. Wood, the main fuel in the midlands and west, was obtained in a variety of sizes, from logs called *astellae* or talwood, to brushwood bundled into faggots. Different fuels had specialized uses, as is shown by the arrangements in Katherine de Norwich's town house in Norwich, where logs heated the hall and chamber, turf was used for cooking in the kitchen, and faggots gave the necessary heat for brewing. Other recorded fuels included sedge in the fenland, and wood charcoal, which was burnt in large quantities in the household of the duke of Buckingham in the mid-fifteenth century, for braziers in rooms without fire-places and for cooking. Mineral coal, or sea coal, as it was called, was often bought for industrial rather than domestic use, for forging iron for the stables or burning lime in building work. Northern households used coal for domestic heating, with some discomfort if they had not abandoned open hearths and invested in efficient chimneys to remove the smoke. The Household Book of Henry Percy advised in 1512 that coal should not be used over Christmas at Alnwick to avoid damage to the arras (fine textile hangings) which were put up to mark the festivities.

The main material for lighting, tallow, was available as a by-

46 Bodleian Library MS. D.D. All Souls, c276.

product of the kitchens, though the standard 'paris candles' made by most households were obtained not entirely without expense, because wick yarn had to be bought and the tallow needed to be processed. Even when tallow candles were purchased, they were still relatively cheap, at about $1^{1}/2$d. per lb. Wax required much greater expense: Richard Mitford, bishop of Salisbury, bought 238 lbs in 1406–7 at $6^{1}/2$d. per lb and then had it made into seven grades of candles, from large torches to the smallest tapers.[47] It was also used to fill cresset lamps, which were open bowls of stone in which the wick floated on liquid wax. In very large households life evidently continued after dark, judging from their use of as much as 100 lbs of wax and tallow in a single winter night. Less wealthy establishments, which burnt more modest amounts, retired early to bed, like the monasteries, at 8.00 p.m. or even earlier.

Purchase and maintenance of equipment for food preparation represent another constant if small source of expenditure. Brewing or baking facilities could cost a good deal, like the £4 spent by the duke of York on a new lead brewing vessel at Hanley Castle in 1410. Metal utensils in general – brass pots and pans, 'garnishes' of pewter plates for use at table, as well as lead vats – were expensive items, but as they were durable new purchases appeared in accounts at widely-spaced intervals. Much kitchen-ware was made of cheap materials, such as the wooden tubs and barrels, turned treen bowls, plates and cups, earthenware pots and jugs, and canvas for wrapping or straining. These, with small iron goods such as knives and hooks, did not normally account for more than 1 or 2 per cent of any household's expenditure.

The aristocracy consumed services as well as goods. Rewards were given to both professional and amateur entertainers visiting the household. As these must often have come from the lord's privy purse, they are ill-recorded, but an apparently full account of such expenditure has survived for the household of Richard Mitford in 1406–7. This bishop of Salisbury is known as a patron of the visual arts, so his household may be assumed to have been more culturally active than most. He saw at least eleven plays or interludes, mostly performed by local people, including tenants from his Wiltshire manors. In addition the household was visited by three musicians and seven minstrels, one of whom was a local, and the others itinerants under the patronage of secular magnates. Most of the performances took place over the Christmas holiday, when the household put on its own play, for which much paper and paint was

47 B.L., Harley MS. 3755.

purchased. All of this cost Mitford £3 out of a total expenditure of £600. He spent rather more on hunting and hawking (£4), and the difference would have been even greater in most households, and overwhelmingly so if the expenditure on parks is taken into account. Most households made their own entertainment, hence the education of young ladies and gentlemen in the courtly arts of music and dancing. The only really expensive indoor pastime, gambling, went largely unnoticed in our dry official records.[48]

Richard Mitford's accounts for 1406–7 are also notable for the information that they give about medical expenses, because the unfortunate bishop suffered from a serious illness from which he died in May 1407. He consulted a number of doctors and bought many medicines, running up a bill of more than £16. Again this seems to have been an exceptionally large sum. Professional services of a less expensive kind were needed to educate aristocratic children. In 1392–3 John Catesby's two sons were at school at the monastery at Warden (Bedfordshire). Their 'doctrine and victuals', or tuition and boarding fees, came to a little more than £2 in the accounting year. More advanced study incurred higher costs, as university students needed a minimum of £2 to £3 per annum, and those of good birth, who had higher expectations of their food and accommodation, required £4 to £10.[49] Attendance at the Inns of Court in London, a more frequent source of education for the aristocracy, cost rather greater sums. This brings us to the most expensive and continuous of the services bought by the aristocracy, those of lawyers. In the late thirteenth century some magnates paid annual retaining fees, up to £5 per annum, to judges. In the late fourteenth and fifteenth centuries this practice was regarded as unacceptable, but lords still commonly retained a group of lawyers for a pound or two each. When specific problems arose lawyers were engaged in the short-term to deal with the case, and actual litigation would produce a crop of bills for travel, entertainment and other incidental expenses as well as the specific legal fees. In normal years legal costs were kept to below 2 per cent of the total expenditure. They rose above this figure most often when a lord acquired property, as did Sir John Fastolf, who had to defend his purchases from rival claimants.[50]

Having examined a number of small, but cumulatively significant

48 K. B. McFarlane, *The nobility of later medieval England* (Oxford, 1973), p. 101.
49 T. H. Aston, G. D. Duncan, T. A. R. Evans, 'The medieval alumni of the University of Cambridge,' *P. and P.*, 86 (1980), 40–51.
50 J. R. Maddicott, *Law and lordship: royal justices as retainers in thirteenth- and four-teenth-century England* (P. and P. Supplement, 4, 1978), pp. 14–17; E. W. Ives, *The common lawyers of pre-Reformation England* (Cambridge, 1983), pp. 285–320.

expenses, we must turn to major items. Inventories of aristocratic chattels give valuations of their possessions and therefore indicate the relative importance of different goods. A Leicestershire knight, Sir Edmund Appleby of Appleby Magna, had his possessions listed in 1374 because of his indebtedness.[51] They were worth a total of £200, of which about a half consisted of grain, animals and agricultural implements. He also had foodstuffs worth £8 in stock. Of the contents of Appleby's house, his most valuable possessions were his armour, worth £16 6s. 8d., and his two horses, together worth £10, reflecting his active military career. His most costly furnishings were the fine textiles of his beds (he owned seven), with curtains, canopies and other trimmings valued at £12 13s. 4d., and a large tapestry in the hall worth £6 13s. 4d. Wooden furniture consisting of beds, chests and tables were not worth much. Appleby's silver (five bowls, three jugs, a ewer, four mazers and fifteen spoons) amounted to £14 in value, and the equipment of the chapel, which apparently included the household's only book, came to £5. The inventory of a different type of knight, Sir Thomas Ursewick of Essex, who died in 1479, suggests that Appleby's money problems had not caused any great distortion in the types of chattels that were listed. Ursewick's goods were worth rather more than Appleby's, about £317. Again a high proportion of the valuation, £130, derived from the farm stock, including 'timber framed for a barn' worth £13 6s. 8d. Beds, hangings, linen and clothing were together valued at £53, and silver plate at another £50. Furniture of modest worth, the accoutrements of a chapel, and pots and pans made up the rest of the total. As befits his rôle as a lawyer rather than a soldier, Ursewick's inventory makes no reference to armour, but does list seven books, worth a little under £5. Other inventories, and the bequests made in gentry wills, confirm that silver plate, bedding and clothes figured among their most valuable possessions, followed by kitchen and farming equipment. Really valuable armour and weapons tended to be owned by a minority.[52]

The goods found in the possession of magnates were similar in kind to those of the gentry, but surpassed them both in quantity and quality. An example is provided by Thomas of Woodstock, duke of Gloucester, whose property was seized by Richard II when he over-

---

51 G. G. Astill, 'An early inventory of a Leicestershire knight', *Midland History*, 2 (1974), 274–83.
52 F. W. Steer, 'A medieval inventory', *Essex Review*, 63 (1954), 4–20; F. W. Weaver (ed.), *Somerset medieval wills* (Somerset Record Soc., 16, 1901).

Table 6. *Inventories of the goods of Thomas of Woodstock, duke of Gloucester, 1397*

	Pleshey Castle		London house	
Arras, tapestries, hangings	£381	(20%)	£16	(6%)
Beds	£295	(16%)	£68	(25%)
Chapel vestments	£684	(36%)	£19	(7%)
Clothes and household linen	£140	(7%)	£20*	(7%)
Silver plate	£192	(10%)	£124	(45%)
Armour	£103	(5%)	None	
Furniture	£2	(0%)	£7	(2%)
Books	£113	(6%)	£11	(4%)
Horses	—†		£7*	(3%)
Kitchen equipment	—†		£4	(1%)
Total	£1910	(100%)	£276	(100%)

* The escheator excluded clothing and two 'chariots' from the valuation
† These items must have been present at Pleshey, but were omitted from the inventory

Source note: Viscount Dillon and W. H. St John Hope, 'Inventory of the goods and chattels belonging to Thomas duke of Gloucester', *Archaeological Journal*, 54 (1897), 275–308; *Calendar of inquisitions miscellaneous*, vol. 6, pp. 223–5

threw his principal opponents in 1397. The inventories analysed in table 6 were taken at two of his main residences, Pleshey Castle in Essex and his London house. The totals are very large, as we would expect of a magnate in receipt of £2,500 per annum since the mid-1380s, a sum which had increased by the time of his disgrace to nearly £4,000.[53] The figures cannot convey the sumptuousness of his goods, which included a bed of cloth of gold with a *celure* (canopy) of blue satin, valued at £182 3s. 0d., and 126 books, an unusually large library, and a great array of silver plate with gilded ornament.

The luxurious items listed in inventories do not appear so often in accounts because of their durability. Plate, jewellery, fine textiles and arms tended to be transmitted by inheritance and gift without appearing on the market. If their income was growing, lords would accumulate plate partly as a convenient means of storing wealth. Sir Hugh Luttrell bought silver plate worth £54 (about a sixth of his

53 A. Goodman, *The loyal conspiracy. The lords appellant under Richard II* (London, 1971), pp. 91–4.

normal annual income) in 1414–15. Bishops bought plate regularly on election to office because, unlike laymen, they did not inherit such movables from their predecessors. Accordingly we find Bishop Bourgchier of Worcester in 1435–6 buying items of precious metal for £131 in his first year of office.[54] The demands of a succession of occupiers of the seventeen bishoprics must have given the London goldsmiths a steady trade.

Both accounts and inventories make plain the high proportion of any household's expenditure that was devoted to the purchase of textiles. A glance at both tables 5 and 6 will help to indicate why the manufacture and sale of cloth played such an important rôle in the medieval economy, as its purchase accounted for about a tenth of aristocratic consumption. The aristocracy bought clothing for themselves and their families, liveries for their servants and followers, fabrics for beds, hangings and other soft furnishings, linen for sheets, table cloths and towels, and sacking and other coarse cloth for storage and wrappings. Clothing was given by the higher aristocracy both to household servants and to a wider circle of retainers. Elizabeth de Burgh, lady of Clare, issued liveries to more than 260 people in 1343, and the earl of Devon gave them to only a few less in 1384–5.[55] Each livery contained 3½ to 5½ yards of woollen cloth, enough to make two or three garments. Naturally the quality of the cloth depended on the wealth of the lord and the status of the servant or retainer. Bishop Swinfield of Hereford in 1289–90 provided his esquires with cloth worth 2s. 11d. per yard, while his yeomen's cloth cost 2s. and that for the lesser servants 1s. 7d.[56] The clothes in some households differed in colour and pattern as well as price, so the status of each member could be identified at a glance. The everyday clothes of the lord and his family were sometimes made from material in the same price range as that supplied to the servants, from 1s. to 3s. per yard, but they also provided themselves with much more expensive textiles. The best woollen cloth could cost 5s. per yard, as bought by the bishop of Ely in 1380, and the Stonor family in 1479–82 were wearing clothes made from tawney and russet cloth which cost 6s. per yard.[57] The highest prices were paid for silks which were imported from the Mediterranean at 10s. or 12s. per yard.

54 Dyer, *Lords and peasants*, p. 200.
55 G. A. Holmes, *The estates of the higher nobility in fourteenth-century England* (Cambridge, 1957), pp. 58–9.
56 Webb (ed.), *Richard de Swinfield*, p. 112.
57 Cambridge U.L., EDR D5/3; C. L. Kingsford (ed.), *The Stonor letters and papers, 1290–1483* (2 vols., Camden Soc., 3rd ser., 30, 1919), vol. 2, p. 75.

A good example of the full range of textile purchases by a gentry family derives from the accounts of the Eyres of Hassop (Derbyshire) in the 1470s, who obtained most of their woollens by contract with local weavers, fullers and dyers, as much as 100 yards in one year. They also bought ready-made a wide range of cheap woollens, cottons, canvas and linens (fustians, kendalls, russets, buckrams and hollands) often 2 or 3 yards at a time, at prices that varied between 2½d. and 1s. 2d. per yard. The very luxurious silks were bought in very small amounts, such as ½ yard of velvet on one occasion and 3 yards of blue taffeta on another. In addition came the other items of dress, shoes at 4d. per pair and boots at 6d., points (clothes fastenings), pins, thread, a few furs for trimming, ribbons, a purse (which cost 1½d.) and hats at 10d. and 1s. 2d.[58] Most gentry families must, like the Eyres, have bought silks very sparingly, and more woollens than linens. The higher aristocracy wore silks in greater quantity, more good quality woollens at 3s. per yard or more, and also large quantities of linens that cost as much as 1s. per yard, imported from the Low Countries, Flanders and Germany. Their clothes were more likely than those of the gentry to be lined with fur. They bought squirrel skins in the thirteenth and fourteenth centuries, changing to marten, sable and budge (black lamb fur) in the fifteenth. Such linings could add £2 or £3 to the cost of a garment, reflecting both the value of the materials, and the amount of skilled labour needed to match and stitch the skins.[59]

The aristocracy spent as much on buildings as on textiles. This is not always apparent (see table 5) because the expenses were often recorded in separate accounts. Much of this activity falls into the category of investment rather than consumption, in the case of buildings such as barns and mills. When demesnes were leased to farmers this type of expenditure ought to have diminished, but lords often continued to pay for some agricultural buildings. A new source of expense arose from the maintenance and even new construction of peasant buildings in an effort to combat widespread decay of the housing stock on estates.[60] Aristocratic buildings could cost a great deal because of the use of high-quality materials and much labour. Constructing a large tiled barn for the bishop of Winchester's manor of Ivinghoe (Buckinghamshire) cost £83 in

58 Bodleian Library, MS. D.D. Per Weld c19/4.
59 E. Veale, *The English fur trade in the later middle ages* (Oxford, 1966), pp. 1–21, 133–55.
60 R. H. Hilton, 'Rent and capital formation in feudal society', in R. H. Hilton, *The English peasantry in the later middle ages* (Oxford, 1975), pp. 188–96.

1309–10. A hall and chamber for a modest Northamptonshire manor house in 1289 cost £12, excluding the stone and timbers. The stonework of a parish church at Catterick (Yorkshire) 125 feet long, without a tower, was contracted to be built for £113, though with all of its fittings the total must have been much more than this. A castle tower, that is, a subsidiary tower in the curtain wall, not the central keep, cost £395 at Warwick in the late fourteenth century, and £333 at Carlisle. A transept of Gloucester Abbey in 1368–73 was built for £781.[61] A complete castle or monastery, if built in a single programme, ran to thousands of pounds.

Buildings for agricultural use, the main form of capital investment, took up less than 5 per cent of manorial profits before 1349, and a rather higher proportion, 10 per cent or more, in the late fourteenth and fifteenth centuries. Major building projects for residences, churches and castles tended to occur in episodes. Lords would avoid a crippling cost by spreading the work over a number of years, as with the transept at Gloucester, mentioned above, which took six years to build, the annual charge of £130 being fairly easily afforded from the monastery's annual income of nearly £2,000. In addition to new building there was a necessity for constant repair and maintenance. Accordingly the lowest possible spending on building would amount to 2 or 3 per cent of total expenditure, as is found at Bolton Priory in the period 1287–1325. The usual minimum was 5 per cent, combining maintenance with a modest amount of new building, and this is the figure found at Durham Cathedral Priory between 1416 and 1446 (about £80 per annum).[62] Higher figures were incurred by laymen involved in castle building. A combination of work on castles and manor houses led the politically active Thomas of Lancaster to commit more than 17 per cent of his income in 1313–14.[63] Another wave of work on castles was a feature of the spending of a group of aristocrats who came into new wealth in the early fifteenth century. Sir Hugh Luttrell in the four years 1419–23 laid out £252 on Dunster Castle, perhaps a fifth or a quarter of his landed income. He was helped by his involvement in the conquest and occupation of Normandy at the time.[64] Ralph, Lord

61 J. Z. Titow, *English rural society* (London, 1969), pp. 203–4; D. Willis (ed.), *The estate book of Henry de Bray* (Camden Soc., 3rd ser., 27, 1916), p. 48; L. F. Salzman, *Building in England, down to 1540*, 2nd edn (Oxford, 1967), pp. 487–90, 456–7, 394; W. Dugdale, *Antiquities of Warwickshire*, 2nd edn (London, 1730), p. 401.
62 Kershaw, *Bolton Priory, economy*, pp. 125–7; Dobson, *Durham Priory*, pp. 292–6.
63 Maddicott, *Thomas of Lancaster*, pp. 25–6.
64 Somerset R.O., DD/L PI/16, 17.

Cromwell provides an unusual example of an apparent spendthrift, building on a grand scale beyond his means. His great project for a new castle and college at Tattershall (Lincolnshire) apparently cost £450 per annum for as many as thirteen years from 1434 to 1446. He embarked on a major programme at South Wingfield (Derbyshire) in 1439, and in the 1440s was also involved in work at Collyweston (Northamptonshire) and apparently at other lesser manor houses, such as Lambley (Nottinghamshire). He must have been spending in excess of £1,000 a year on building in the mid-1440s, yet his annual income was declared at £1,000 in 1436, and had reached a sum of £2,263 in 1450. The explanation lies not in reckless extravagance, but in his profits as Treasurer of England between 1433 and 1443, from which period he still had more than £5,000 on his conscience when he died in 1456. His buildings had a grandiose character – they were intended to impress – but they also accorded with a new trend in the period for improving the privacy and comfort of accommodation (see fig. 2).[65]

Magnates were committed to the building and repair of a whole range of residences, from a major castle or two to a chain of manor houses. They might be used by the household occasionally in their travels, and would regularly accommodate visiting estate officials, court sessions and even workers on the manor. The gentry, who often owned no more than one or two residences, were nonetheless involved in considerable expense in relation to their incomes. A wealthy knight, Sir John de Bishopsdon, in 1313 could build a stone gatehouse measuring 40 feet by 18 for his manor at Lapworth (Warwickshire), at a cost of £16 13s. 4d., for which he was providing the timber and other materials, except the stone. The total expense, taking into account carriage of stone, for which Bishopsdon paid extra, must have been near to £30. Most gentry with incomes below £40 could afford only to build in timber, because the materials came from their estates, and the labour costs were much lower. Sir Thomas Ughtred in 1341 was able to contract for his Yorkshire manor house to be provided with a gatehouse (30 feet long) and a drawbridge and barn, for £5 6s. 8d. and a robe (suit of clothing) for the carpenter. Other costs would have made the total three times this

65 W. Douglas Simpson (ed.), *The building accounts of Tattershall Castle: 1432–1472* (Lincolnshire Record Soc., 55, 1960); M. W. Thompson, 'The construction of the manor at South Wingfield, Derbyshire' in G. de G. Sieveking *et al.* (eds.), *Problems in economic and social archaeology* (London, 1976), pp. 417–38; A. Emery, 'Ralph, Lord Cromwell's manor at Wingfield (1439–c.1450): its construction, design and influence', *Archaeological Journal*, 142 (1985), 276–339.

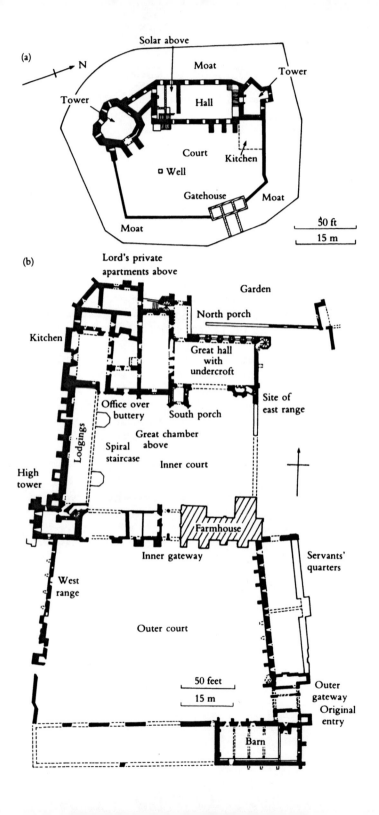

(a)

N

Solar above

Moat

Tower

Tower

Hall

Court

Kitchen

Well

Gatehouse

Moat

Moat

50 ft

15 m

(b)

Lord's private
apartments above

Garden

North porch

Kitchen

Great hall
with
undercroft

Office over
buttery

South porch

Site of
east range

Lodgings

Great chamber
above

Spiral
staircase

Inner court

High
tower

Farmhouse

Inner gateway

Servants'
quarters

West
range

Outer court

50 feet

15 m

Outer
gateway

Original
entry

Barn

sum, but still considerably cheaper than a stone building. Excavations of thirteenth- and fourteenth-century manor houses, often
lying in moated enclosures, show that the gentry commonly built
with no more than small-scale stone foundations, and sometimes
their houses were entirely of timber or cob.[66]

The third major item of expenditure, besides textiles and buildings, was the wages of servants and payments to supporters. These
are difficult to separate from expenditure on food and liveries,
because servants received the bulk of their rewards in kind. Servants'
wages in cash often accounted for about a tenth or more of spending.
The highest proportions, up to 16–20 per cent, are found at the very
top of the scale, such as in the household of the earl of Northumberland in 1511–12, and much lower down, in the model budget
for an esquire in 1471–2, both of which reflect the problems of
keeping up appearances at a time of relatively high labour costs. If all
payments to subordinates, including fees and annuities to retainers,
are included in the calculation, some politically active magnates of
the late fifteenth century are found to have been paying out more
than a third of their revenues, though 15 per cent would have been a
normal maximum.[67]

Finally some references must be made to the many calls on a lord's
income which brought no immediate material benefit. Royal taxation, in the form of subsidies on movable goods, cannot be regarded

66 Salzman, *Building in England*, pp. 421–2, 595; H. E. J. Le Patourel, *The moated sites
of Yorkshire* (Soc. for Med. Arch. Monograph, 5, 1973), pp. 68–70.
67 I. Jack (ed.), *The Grey of Ruthin valor* (Bedfordshire Record Soc., 46, 1965), pp.
53–6.

Fig. 2   Aristocratic houses of the thirteenth and fifteenth centuries
(The black lines indicate medieval walls, the shaded parts are modern buildings, in the
case of (a) probably on the site of a medieval predecessor)
(a)   Stokesay Castle in Shropshire, which was mostly built in 1285–1305 for Law-
rence de Ludlow, a successful merchant who acquired land and established his family
as gentry. Note the prominence of the hall. Chambers and store-rooms were accommodated in the towers. Less substantial structures, such as the kitchen, are no longer
standing.
Sources: J. D. La Touche, 'Stokesay Castle', *Transactions of the Shropshire Archaeological
Society*, 1 (1878), 311–32; R. A. Cordingley, 'Stokesay Castle, Shropshire: the chronology of its building', *Art Bulletin*, 45 (1963), 91–107
(b)   South Wingfield (Derbyshire) was begun in 1439 by Ralph, Lord Cromwell.
Cromwell's wealth and status, superior to Ludlow's, explain the larger scale of the
building. But the symmetrical plan of the later house, with its emphasis on ranges of
rooms rather than the hall, is typical of its period.
Source: M. W. Thompson, *The decline of the castle* (Cambridge, 1988), p. 65

as a major drain on secular lords' resources because of frequent underassessment of the value of goods and the exemption of many luxuries. Few paid as much as 5 per cent of their incomes. The experimental income taxes of the early fifteenth century were supposed to make a levy on landed incomes at rates of 5 to 10 per cent, but again evasions and the exclusion of non-landed incomes spared most payers from too great a burden. High royal demands came in the 1290s, when laymen were hit at a time of bad harvests by a combination of different taxes. The clergy suffered at the same time because their share of taxation was levied at a high rate, and it was assessed on their incomes as declared in a generous but not totally fictitious calculation of 1291. In 1294 some monasteries found themselves paying 20 per cent or more of their actual cash receipts, and were forced to go to money lenders.[68] Other episodes of high taxation which affected aristocratic and especially ecclesiastical tax-payers came in the years around 1340 and at the time of Henry V's French campaigns of 1415–22.[69] The clergy also had commitments to pay taxation to the Papacy.

The costs of religion were spread throughout society, mainly through tithe payments which do not enter into our calculations of expenditure because the produce was taken at source. Extra expenditure on religion by laymen included the maintenance, fittings and staffing of private chapels, and any contributions that they might make to the building of parish churches. Much larger sums were committed in the patronage of monastic houses, and the funding of new chantry foundations and collegiate churches. Everyday acts of piety involved the payment of small sums in oblations and acts of charity, or the purchase of beads (rosaries).

Families also required the outlay of cash, whether in the form of pensions or annuities to relatives lacking landed resources, or the payments associated with the marriage of daughters, which could involve magnates in sums of £1,000 or above, and esquires as much as £66 13s. 4d. Mercifully for the budgets of families with many daughters, such contributions were normally spread over a number of years.[70]

---

68 M. Mate, 'The indebtedness of Canterbury Cathedral Priory 1215–95', *Ec.H.R.* 2nd ser., 26 (1973), 192; E. Miller, 'War, taxation and the English economy in the late thirteenth and early fourteenth centuries' in J. M. Winter (ed.), *War and economic development* (Cambridge, 1975), pp. 11–31.

69 L. J. Redstone (ed.), *The cellarers' accounts for Bromholm Priory* (Norfolk Record Soc., 17, 1944), pp. 74–5.

70 McFarlane, *Nobility*, pp. 84–7; S. M. Wright, *The Derbyshire gentry in the fifteenth century* (Derbyshire Record Soc., 8, 1983), p. 45.

In death the aristocracy expected to spend large amounts, both to ensure that their funeral ceremonies adequately reflected their standing, and to leave permanent memorials. A relatively cheap gentlewoman's burial in 1497 cost her executors £7, for such items as clergy's fees, bell ringing, and the feeding of guests. A simple monument appropriate for a lesser aristocrat – a brass incised with a figure set in a marble slab – could be obtained in the early fourteenth century for about £8. Perhaps a year's income was needed to cover the costs of death, and the magnates' expenses rose *pro rata*. The incomplete accounts for Bishop Mitford's funeral in 1407, including food and drink for 1,450 guests, and great quantities of cloth to dress his household in mourning, total £130. The memorial chapel built at Warwick over the tomb of Richard Beauchamp, earl of Warwick, who died in 1439, was not completed until 1463, when it was reckoned that £2,481 had been spent. This includes the sum in excess of £400 that was devoted to the splendid bronze effigy of the earl on an ornate tomb of marble and gilded metal.[71]

These many and varied pleasures and obligations together depict the ways in which the aristocracy disposed of their wealth. The time has now come for us to carry out the exercise that they so often had to do – to match their expenditure to their incomes.

71 P.R.O., PROB 2 / 132; J. Blair, 'English monumental brasses before 1350: types, patterns and workshops', in J. Coales (ed.), *The earliest English brasses* (London, 1987), p. 144; B.L., Harley MS. 3755; Dugdale, *Antiquities of Warwickshire*, vol. I, pp.405–7.

4

ARISTOCRATIC EXPENDITURE: MAKING ENDS MEET

—————— • ——————

Medieval aristocrats did not live in a consumer society like our own, but they were still tempted into over-spending by the prevailing ethics which encouraged such economically dangerous virtues as generosity. The need for balance, for a combination of magnanimity and prudence, runs as a theme through medieval thinking on economic subjects. Grosseteste's *Rules*, written in the 1240s supposedly for the instruction of a countess, advise making a survey of the manors, to find out how much produce and cash was available. The household would therefore be run on a scale appropriate to the estate's resources. The need to achieve balance and moderation continues through the instructions on management. The aim was to live economically but not cheaply. There must be many servants and they should be well-dressed and of good character: 'faithful, diligent, chaste, honest and useful'; discipline among them should be maintained, and theft and waste avoided. The treatise assumes that honour accrues from generosity and hospitality. The lord or lady must attend meals, sitting in the middle of the high table, 'that your presence . . . is made manifest to all', handing out morsels personally to guests in a courteous fashion, while at the same time two officers were set to supervise the staff, which would 'earn you great fear and reverence'. The object seemed to be to present a superficial sociability to the outside world, while behind the scenes a constant coercion kept underlings in control.[1]

1 D. Oschinsky (ed.), *Walter of Henley* (Oxford, 1971), pp. 388–407.

The poem *Winner and waster* is dated conventionally to 1352–3, though it may have been written a little later. It can be seen as a product of the uncertainty that followed the Black Death, as well as a reassertion of older ideas. It takes the form of a debate, evenly matched and apparently without decisive result. Winner acts as herald for an army of foreigners, merchants, lawyers, friars and the Pope. Waster is the spokesman for men-at-arms and esquires. In fact both seem to be debating in the context of landed society, the poem evidently having been aimed at an audience of west midlands gentry. Winner deplores the neglect of the land resulting from Waster's extravagance. He spends his time drinking without concern for estate management; he eats luxuriously, and will destroy his inheritance. Waster's series of replies advocate the circulation of wealth for the benefit of the poor. He argues that Winner uselessly hoards his own wealth, and profits from other people's misfortunes in bad harvest years by selling his grain dear. Winner's frugal life style is a threat to the social order, because if lords do not live well, they will be indistinguishable from their servants. His accumulated wealth will end up in the hands of those stock medieval villains, the dishonest executors of wills.[2]

Sir Isaac Gollancz, who edited this poem in the 1920s, reacted to it in a typically modern way. He felt that Winner, as a prototype for a capitalist, was in the right, but that the poet had missed his opportunity by failing to give him the best arguments! In fact the poem is not a debate between a new model capitalist and an old-fashioned representative of feudalism, but expresses the inner dilemmas and ambiguities of a feudal economy. The subject-matter is what we would call economics, but the themes are essentially moralistic. Waster is accused of the sins of pride and gluttony (with hints of sloth and lechery too), while Winner in Waster's view is guilty of avarice. At the end of the poem, which is incomplete, the king seems in his judgement to be accepting that each side has a rôle to play, and indeed we can recognize that both were criticizing forms of economic behaviour that were combined in the life of every aristocrat.

Winner and waster is a unique work in every respect. It is the only piece of literature surviving to pursue this theme in detail, and it is known in only one manuscript. However its ideas are echoed in many other comments on social matters. The dangers of hoarding

2 I. Gollancz (ed.), *Winner and waster* (Oxford, 1921); T. Turville-Petre, *The alliterative revival* (Cambridge, 1977), pp. 1–4; E. Salter, 'The timeliness of *Wynnere and Wastoure*', *Medium Aevum*, 47 (1978), 40–65.

wealth and the need to give alms appear as common themes in sermons. There were numerous complaints about extravagance, particularly provoked by new styles of dress which in the mid-fourteenth century seemed to threaten sexual as well as economic morality.[3] The sumptuary law of 1363, which was designed to prevent members of the lower orders from dressing above their customary standard, echoes Waster's comment on the dangers to the social hierarchy if lords and servants were to become too similar in their outward appearance. The law stated that grooms, servants and the employees of urban craftsmen should eat meat or fish for only one meal of the day, that they should wear clothes made from woollens costing no more than 1s. 1d. per yard, and that they should not wear any silks or luxurious textiles.

The commons in parliament (gentry and leading townsmen), who petitioned for the 1363 legislation, seem to have been agitated in this particular year over problems of rising prices. The sumptuary law was a product of that concern, and a typical symptom of the 'moral panic' that moved the propertied classes after the Black Death. They believed that the increased demand from the wage-earners and other new rich for goods formerly bought only by the élite had pushed up prices. They only partially understood the changes that were going on around them, and their counter-measures were ineffective, judging from the fact that the statute (or ordinance as it should more strictly be called) was repealed in the next year.[4] The chief historical interest of the 1363 law is that it reveals the economic psychology of the upper classes, who believed that in a well-ordered society, consumption patterns would reflect strictly the hierarchy of status. As has been argued for the city states of late medieval Italy, clothes were such an important expression of social rank that they constituted 'a way of ordering human relations'.[5] Although the sumptuary law was primarily designed to prevent the lower orders from wearing

3 G. R. Owst, *Literature and pulpit in medieval England* (Oxford, 1966), p. 401; S. M. Newton, *Fashion in the age of the Black Prince* (Woodbridge, 1980), pp. 6–13.
4 *Statutes of the realm* (11 vols., Record Commission, 1810–28), vol. 1, pp. 380–3; *Rotuli parliamentorum* (6 vols., Record Commission, no date), vol. 2, pp. 276–9; F. E. Baldwin, *Sumptuary legislation and personal regulation in England* (Baltimore, 1926); N. B. Harte, 'State control of dress and social change in pre-industrial England' in D. C. Coleman and A. H. John (eds.), *Trade, government and economy in pre-industrial England* (London, 1976), pp. 132–5, 141–8.
5 D. O. Hughes, 'Sumptuary law and social relations in renaissance Italy' in J. Bossy (ed.), *Disputes and settlements. Law and human relations in the west* (Cambridge, 1983), pp. 69–99.

'outrageous and excessive apparel', the thinking behind such notions of consumption and the social order had implications for the upper ranks too. By seeking to prevent the gentry from wearing high-quality woollens, silks, expensive furs or luxurious jewellery the legislators were indicating their assumption that the higher aristocracy *ought* to wear such things. They would not dream of enforcing this by law, but unwritten conventions and social norms would be a more powerful pressure on the aristocracy to spend heavily, and perhaps overspend, than any unenforceable ordinance.

The social morality of medieval people provides insights into their economic behaviour. Because of our modern prejudices, we tend to agree, like Gollancz, with Winner's arguments, and therefore to denounce the whole aristocratic way of life as extravagant and destructive. A phrase that is often used in discussion of this subject is Thorstein Veblen's 'conspicuous consumption', which he coined in a satire on the new rich of the United States in the nineteenth century, and which may not be the most appropriate description of the medieval aristocracy's spending habits.[6] We must beware of criticism based on ignorance, like the ridicule to which chivalry, the central ideology of the medieval lay aristocracy, was once subjected. It was mocked as hypocritical and anachronistic, but now we appreciate that chivalric ideas were genuinely held, and served useful functions, both for the training and motivation of warriors, and as a source of social cohesion.[7] Such an understanding should not lead us into an uncritical admiration of these ideas, nor into advocating their survival in the modern world, but it prevents us from ignorant dismissal of unfamiliar attitudes and behaviour.

The high living and hospitality practised by the aristocracy are easily scorned as demonstrating their greed and selfishness, but their life-style had a real purpose. N. Elias has shown that prestigious display was an essential part of the maintenance of social distinctions, and that social competition, both with other groups and among the aristocrats, played an important part in their motivation.[8]

6 T. Veblen, *The theory of the leisure class*, Mentor edn (New York, 1953), pp. 60–80; for a more sensitive historical view, P. Burke, 'Investment and culture in three seventeenth-century cities: Rome, Amsterdam, Paris', *Journal of European Economic History*, 7 (1978), 311–36.

7 M. G. A. Vale, *War and chivalry* (London, 1981); J. Vale, *Edward III and chivalry* (Woodbridge, 1983); M. Keen, *Chivalry* (New Haven and London, 1984).

8 N. Elias, *The court society* (Oxford, 1983); see also A. J. Gurevich, *Categories of medieval culture* (London, 1985), pp. 246–58.

We can add that the aristocratic life-style helped to reinforce bonds of loyalty and the mutual transfer of favours. The lord, his retainers and his guests enjoyed companionship within the household. The lord's hospitality and liberality were freely given, but belonged to a system of gift exchange, in which some reciprocal act was expected. It is true that lords often failed to invest large sums in demesne production, but in the terms of their own society the distribution of liveries, the maintenance of a large household, and the payment of fees and annuities represented an investment in human resources. A lord who impressed his fellow aristocrats with his numerous following and good connections would be more likely to contract advantageous marriages or receive royal patronage, and thereby increase his family's income. The clerical aristocracy were not involved in social competition in quite the same way, but they were drawn into a similar network of patronage and reciprocal favours.

Nor should we exaggerate aristocratic luxury. Our impression of the lavishness of their lives is based on comments by contemporaries who were observing as outsiders, like the poet who wrote *Gawain and the green knight* at the end of the fourteenth century, probably for an audience of provincial gentry who looked to a royal or magnate court with admiration and perhaps a little envy:

> Ay two had dishes twelve,
> Good ber and bright wyn bothe.[9]

Or we can take the similar description of Waster's feastings in which the same ratio of diners to dishes is mentioned, together with long lists of delicacies, swans, pheasants, kids and tarts 10 inches wide. Here the poet distances himself from the luxuries he describes with his tone of moral disapproval. The theme has been taken up by modern writers, who seek to impress their readers with the statistics of medieval indulgence, a favourite example being the enthrone-ment feast for Archbishop Neville of York in 1467, a quite excep-tional occasion.[10] As we have seen, even among the magnates, households were served a modest everyday diet of bread, ale and mutton. The lesser gentry, living in timber-framed manor houses with only three or four servants, and drinking wine only on special

9 I. Gollancz (ed.), *Sir Gawain and the green knight* (Early English Text Soc., O.S., 210, 1940), p. 5.
10 For example, W. A. Mead, *The English medieval feast* (London, 1931), p. 33.

occasions, were clearly much better off than the peasantry; but they can scarcely be accused of reckless consumption. Even the highest aristocracy, who lived very well indeed, practised some prudent economies, like selling off the fats from the kitchens and making sausages from the entrails of animals. In order to avoid the unnecessary purchase of beds or pewter dishes, extra supplies would be hired temporarily to cope with an unexpected influx of guests. They were very cost-conscious in their purchases, often obtaining imported goods, such as wines, spices, wax and fish in bulk, direct from the merchants in London, the great fairs or the major ports, at considerable savings. Any tendency towards extravagance was balanced by common-sense moderation. Perhaps the ascetic tradition, though in retreat in the monasteries, still had a fitful influence on the secular world, expressed for example in admiration for the privations suffered in war and travel by real and imaginary knights.

The aristocracy seem then to have been influenced by ideas about consumption that put emphasis on largesse, tempered always by a practical restraint and occasional moral qualms. The ideal was a lord who used his wealth, neither running foolishly into debt, nor hoarding in a miserly fashion. In modern economic terms, they were expected to live up to their income. It is against this background that we must examine the experiences of the aristocracy in the changing circumstances of the later middle ages. Did their standards of living improve in the thirteenth century? Did they deteriorate with the subsequent decline in land values? Or were the experiences of individuals or groups within the class so divergent that generalization is impossible? In particular it is worth examining the argument that because there is little evidence of belt-tightening among the lay lords after 1350, the decline of landed revenues must have been relatively unimportant, and that incomes must have been adequately supplemented from other sources.[11]

At the outset it must be said that there were individuals in every generation who were able to keep expenditure well below their income, and who therefore accumulated cash. Walter de Merton, a successful civil servant who derived income from a number of church benefices, even though in his lifetime he had spent a great deal in founding a college, left a sum of £1,232 3s. od. in cash on his death in 1277. When that old soldier Sir John Fastolf died in 1459, he was in possession of £2,643 10s. od. in cash besides a hoard of plate,

---

11 K. B. McFarlane, *The nobility of later medieval England* (Oxford, 1973), pp. 57–60, 83–101.

jewels and other valuables. Perhaps the greatest collector of coin of all was Richard Fitzalan, earl of Arundel, who benefited from the union of two great inheritances, and had also been active in Edward III's wars. He was wealthy enough to lend money to the Crown, and on his death in 1376 his coffers and money bags were found to contain £60,000 in cash.[12] These examples should not be regarded as anything but exceptions, often reflecting the advantages of unusual royal patronage. The majority of the aristocracy lived mainly on their landed income, and normally there was an approximate equality between their income and expenditure. This was by no means easy to achieve, and it is worth turning to the administrative systems which enabled them to balance their budgets.

Household accounts, for all of their faults, provide us with a good deal of evidence for changes in expenditure in the later middle ages, especially for the greater lords. The patchiness of their survival throws some light on changing aristocratic consumption. They have not come down to us dispersed evenly over the whole period, but are concentrated in certain decades. This surely points to a link between the making of household accounts and times of financial uncertainty. The first household accounts date from the time when lords were feeling the stress of inflation in the years around 1200.[13] An unusual number have survived from the 1340s, at the time when lords' incomes were beginning to decline, and the years between 1380 and 1420, when they were having to make hard decisions about direct management and leasing. The aristocracy were simultaneously concerned with estate management and household economy, as is evident from the survival along with household accounts of documents showing a concern for the generation of income. So Walter de Wenlok, abbot of Westminster (1283–1307) acted as a new broom in reforming the finances of both his estates and his household. Elizabeth de Burgh in the 1320s and 1330s had valors, central accounts and household accounts compiled in an interlocking system of financial records. John Catesby in the 1380s and 1390s was one of the earliest gentry landlords known to have compiled a document surveying the 'state of the manors', as well as making an unusually

---

12 J. R. L. Highfield (ed.), *The early rolls of Merton College, Oxford* (Oxford Historical Soc., 18, 1964), pp. 90, 96; N. Davis (ed.), *The Paston letters and papers of the fifteenth century* (Oxford, 1971), p. 107; McFarlane, *Nobility*, pp. 88–91.

13 C. M. Woolgar, 'The development of accounts for private households in England to *c.* 1500 A.D.' (University of Durham Ph.D. thesis, 1986), pp. 32–55, has revealed for the first time this early phase of household accounting.

detailed (if somewhat jumbled) record of household expenditure.[14] Sir Hugh Luttrell kept valors and household accounts simultaneously. The failure to survive of most household accounts does not mean that financial anarchy normally prevailed, and that only a few exceptional lords took the trouble to keep accounts. The usual routine would either be for the account to be presented orally, with the steward of the household or the lord himself interviewing the staff, or for the accounts to be written down and treated as ephemera. The unusual characteristic of our more conscientious lords was their careful preservation of household accounts, presumably for consultation and comparison in future years.

Sometimes the accounts reveal serious financial problems, like those of William Moleyns in 1400–1, who received cash totalling £357 (including £15 in loans), and spent £539, in which moneys for horses, clothes, wine and other luxuries figure prominently. He still owed £149 at the end of the accounting year, much of it to London tradesmen.[15] The successive accounts of the first duke of Buckingham in the mid-fifteenth century reveal, as we will see, a household apparently living consistently beyond its means. Smaller monasteries were especially vulnerable to problems of expenditure outrunning income, as is shown by the records of visitations by bishops from the late thirteenth century onwards. Monastic indebtedness or mismanagement were apparently more frequently reported after 1350. Stories of shocking poverty were told, of church roofs so neglected that they let in the rain, of nuns reduced to drinking water because their house could not afford ale, and of sisters provided with new clothes only once every three years.[16] One of these crises affected Southwick Priory (Hampshire) in the 1390s, as a result of which a financial statement was compiled, showing that annual income totalled £242, and expenditure £480.[17] A good deal of the deficit had been caused by debt repayments and a heavy building

14 B. F. Harvey (ed.), *Documents illustrating the rule of Walter de Wenlok, abbot of Westminster* (Camden Soc., 4th ser., 2, 1965), pp. 6–17; G. A. Holmes, *The estates of the higher nobility in fourteenth-century England* (Cambridge, 1957), pp. 109–10; J. R. Birrell (ed.), 'The *status maneriorum* of John Catesby, 1385 and 1386' in R. Bearman (ed.), *Miscellany I* (Dugdale Soc., 31, 1977), pp. 15–28; P.R.O., E101/511/15; 512/5.

15 P.R.O., E101/512/17.

16 D. M. Knowles, *The religious orders in England* (3 vols., Cambridge, 1948–59), vol. 1, pp. 85–112; vol. 2, pp. 204–18; E. Power, *Medieval English nunneries* (Cambridge, 1922), chapters 2 and 5.

17 Hampshire R.O., 5 M50/47.

programme. When monasteries were subjected to visitations the bishops recommended reforms and economies, including the reduction of expenditure on non-necessities such as clothing, ale, meat and buildings. They often enjoined improvements in administration, primarily better systems of account-keeping and auditing. Most surviving examples show that in households of all kinds the accounting system worked, and problems were avoided or contained. Accounts were audited, a process that has left its mark on the documents in the form of comments such as 'seen up to here', or '*probata*' (proved or checked). Some lords read the accounts personally, and signed them, both in a relatively small knightly household, that of Elizabeth Stonor in 1478, and in the earl of Oxford's in 1507.[18] By that date the king had taken up the practice of personal auditing, presumably following the example of the aristocracy. Such a mundane activity was in no way regarded as unworthy of a great lord. In the late fourteenth century the chronicler Froissart, who was always sensitive to any inappropriate behaviour by his chivalric heroes, reported with approval that the count of Foix read his accounts regularly.[19] Auditing had a number of functions. Firstly, corruption or mismanagement were detected, unlikely claims being struck out and the offending household official being made to pay. Secondly, the knowledge that auditing would happen deterred servants from detectable theft or carelessness. Thirdly, the auditors could play a rôle in future budgeting by calculating average costs, or setting targets and quotas for specific items of expenditure. Such devices occasionally appear in the fourteenth century. The cellarer's account of Durham Priory in 1334 ends with the calculation:

> Sum of all the expenses in the kitchen, £416 3s. 2d.
> Of which exonerated because of various things remaining in the kitchen, £6 2s. 4d.
> And thus the clear sum is £410 0s. 10d. Which divided by the month, namely £31 10s. 10d per month.
> And thus each week £7 17s. 8^1/2d.[20]

This was a sensible measure to enable the officials in following

18 P.R.O., c47/37/7; Longleat MS., vol. 11.
19 J. A. C. Buchon (ed.), *Les chroniques de sire Jean Froissart* (2 vols., Paris, 1840), vol. 2, p. 399.
20 J. T. Fowler (ed.), *Extracts from the account rolls of the Abbey of Durham* (3 vols., Surtees Soc., 99, 100, 103, 1898–1900), vol. 1, p. 31 (a month of four weeks is meant).

years to check from week to week that they were not overrunning their budget. A well-audited lay account of 1385–6, that of the countess of Norfolk, contains auditor's notes looking forward to comparison with future records ('Remember for the next account' was written a number of times in the margin). The auditor discovered a case of apparent mismanagement in the Framlingham (Suffolk) household, because the baker and brewer, John Stebbing, could not explain the absence of 20 quarters of malt, for which he was asked to pay £4 3s. 0d. The lady, however, forgave him. The auditor also calculated an average day's expenditure, 'one with another' at 52s. 1d.[21]

Some examples show how lords could use the accounting system, not just as a routine precaution against overspending, but as a means of taking actions that would solve financial problems.

(1) The third Thomas de Berkeley's political fortunes changed after his restoration to royal favour in 1326–7. John Smyth, the seventeenth-century historian of the family, made statements which have been taken to imply that the estate's income rose from £452 to £1,151 per annum between 1328 and 1347, but the figures could refer to cash left in the receivers' hands at the end of the year. Berkeley was certainly very rich by the late 1340s, but at the same time seems to have felt the need for a control on spending, because in 1346 an unusual financial statement was made, recording his outgoings at £1,310. As food accounted for most of the sum, the official responsible for the statement noted changes in consumption since the previous year. The household had made less use of drage malt for brewing, and had substituted cheaper malt made from oats. Also less beef and pork had been eaten, with only a slight increase in mutton consumption to compensate. In all almost £22 had been saved, a modest economy indeed, but a move in the right direction. Perhaps the problem lay in the sheer size of the establishment. Berkeley was employing too many servants, and entertaining too many guests. It was certainly the belief of John Smyth that Berkeley was a leader of local society on a grand scale, and the 1346 account reveals that an average of forty-two horses were being fed every night. As the family survived in considerable prosperity after the 1340s, presumably the sensible precautions revealed in 1346 had a beneficial effect.

---

21 J. Ridgard (ed.), *Medieval Framlingham* (Suffolk Records Soc., 27, 1985), pp. 104, 108, 109, 113.

The interest of the document lies in its revelation that written accounts could be used to define a problem and to find a solution.[22]

(2) Sir Hugh Luttrell came into the estate centred on the Somerset castle of Dunster in 1405, having purchased the reversion from Lady Mohun twenty years earlier. In his first year the household cost £238, out of a total income of about £300, so there was little money for anything else. The shortfall may have arisen from the difficulties of adjusting to a new estate, and because the lord himself was preoccupied with military service in Wales, where he assisted in the suppression of the Glyn Dwr revolt. The overspending was such that the servants' wages were not paid, including those of the steward of the household, John Bacwell. As an aid to understanding the problem Bacwell calculated at the end of the accounts the cost of food: £170 per annum, £42 11s. 9d. per quarter, 65s. 6¹/₄d. per week, and 9s. 4¹/₄d. per day. By contemporary standards, 2s. 7d. per week on average to feed each member of the household was somewhat excessive, and the price was brought down in later years. In 1422, the feeding of a similarly sized household cost £60 less. In the 'teens and twenties of the fifteenth century Luttrell not only ran his household in moderate fashion, he also gained extra income as a soldier and administrator in Normandy, and was able to rebuild his castle. The Luttrell family's silver plate illustrates well how the acquisition of luxury goods could be a form of saving. It was noted earlier that Sir Hugh bought plate for £54 in 1414–15. This was added to an existing collection, which according to an inventory of 1420–1 contained more than a hundred items, including four chargers, twenty-four dishes and seven ewers. As well as helping to impress guests, this hoard of precious metal had a practical purpose. After the death of both Hugh Luttrell and his son John, Margaret, John's wife, had financial obligations in 1430–2 to her mother-in-law, Katherine. Lacking ready cash, she sold at least £32 worth of the silver. Buying and selling plate could thus even out the differences between good times and bad.[23]

(3) The Talbot family of Whitchurch, Shropshire, faced some serious problems of declining landed income in the years around

22 Berkeley Castle muniment room, Select Roll 64; J. Maclean (ed.), *The lives of the Berkeleys by John Smythe* (3 vols., Gloucester, 1883), vol. I, pp. 304–6.
23 Somerset R.O., DD/L P37/7, P1/16, 17; H. Maxwell-Lyte, *A history of Dunster* (London, 1909), pp. 93–5, 117.

1400. No administrative measures could save them from the downward movement in rents and other revenues. Their household accounts show the family coping with the expenditure side in a realistic fashion. They reduced the cost of the household from about £300 in 1391–2 to £163 in 1417–18. At the latter date the lord was absent in France so the household was a little smaller, but the averaging done in the household accounts shows a reduction in the expenditure on food, from 2^1/2d. per *ferculum* (mess) in 1391–2 to 2^1/8d. in 1417–18, a cut of 15 per cent. Some careful budgeting was needed to secure this fall in costs, because food prices were rather higher at the second date. One economy had been to buy a higher proportion of 'second' ale at ^{1}/2d. per gallon. Notes on the account reveal a general vigilance in checking on possible danger areas, such as the numbers of guests and the high price of wine.[24]

(4) The dukes of Buckingham were more wealthy on paper than in reality, because although they had accumulated a large estate through good marriages, they suffered from falling rents and a growing arrears total, especially from their Welsh lands. So an estate which in theory in 1447–8 was worth £5,000 actually produced £3,700. The first duke's household account reveals debts of £729 in 1453, most of which were owed to suppliers of goods going back over a number of years. The sum of £40 had been unpaid for thirteen years. In a sense this slow payment of debts posed no serious problem, because the dukes were very wealthy and powerful, and therefore 'creditworthy'. They owed some money to tenants and supporters whose frustrated feelings about their unpaid bills would be mingled with deferential respect for their 'good lord'. As long as the suppliers were prepared to wait, the dukes could go on living beyond their means. That the dukes did recognize that the situation was not entirely satisfactory is indicated by their measures to prevent waste or corruption among the household staff. Accounts were strictly audited and unexplained losses were charged to officials. For example, in 1453 the pantry was found to be deficient by 5,000 loaves over a five-year period, for which the baker was charged £4 6s. 2^1/2d. The third duke actively pursued his servants through the

24 Bodleian Library, MS. Rolls Herefs., 40; B. Ross, 'The accounts of the Talbot household at Blakemere in the county of Shropshire, 1394–1425' (Australian National University M.A. thesis, Canberra, 1970), pp. 89–127.

courts to make them pay debts which had been incurred in this way.[25]

(5) The monks of Bury maintained a remarkable archive of documents from which they were able to take a historical perspective of their plight in 1434–5. Abbot William Curteys in his concern for the house's finances looked back over the previous century of cellarers' accounts. They revealed that in a majority of years the cellarer had shown a deficit, with a cumulative total of £5,822, an average 'loss' of £58 per year. Then, in a pointed calculation of the burden of taxation since 1399, Curteys was able to show that together the abbot and convent had paid in excess of £6,000 to the crown. Nothing could be done about this burden. The answer lay in an *'economia'* (budget), in which the monastery was to be fed for £480 11s. 4d. per annum, in the usual hierarchy, with the prior's table costing 5s. per week, each monk being fed for 2s. 6d. per week, each gentleman servant for 1s. 8d., each yeoman for 1s. 2d. and each groom for 10d.[26]

These examples show that lords of varied kinds used their accounting system to match their expenditure to their incomes. They made changes, sometimes simply tightening up financial discipline, but on occasion setting ceilings on living standards, and sometimes reducing them.

One method of making economies involved a reduction in the size of the household. This is most easily documented in the case of the monasteries. At the time of Curteys's reforms, there were fifty-two monks at Bury. He did not mention the fact in his calculations, but there had been eighty in the late thirteenth century. A decline on this scale affected most religious houses, from a national total of 17,000 to 18,000 monks, canons, friars and nuns in *c.* 1300, to 11,000 or 12,000 two hundred years later. Although the trend has been linked with a decline in the spiritual attractions of the monastic life, an equally likely explanation is that recruitment was restricted in order to keep the numbers of the religious within affordable limits. The beginning of this discouragement of novices has been identified in the first phase of declining landed incomes, in the period 1329–48.[27]

---

25 C. Rawcliffe, *The Staffords, earls of Stafford and dukes of Buckingham 1394–1521* (Cambridge, 1978), pp. 109–15, 164–81.

26 B.L., Add. MS. 14848, fols. 32–5.

27 D. Knowles and R. N. Hadcock, *Medieval religious houses: England and Wales*, 2nd edn (London, 1971), p. 494; R. H. Snape, *English monastic finances in the later middle ages* (Cambridge, 1926), pp. 21–2.

We cannot trace long-term changes in the size of secular house-holds. It is possible, however, to detect a new stringency in attitudes towards guests and hospitality. The open-handed treatment of visitors had always been something of a myth (see p. 54). A more restrictive attitude is apparent in the household accounts of the early fourteenth century which counted guests and listed them by name. In the early fifteenth century, the Talbot household actually cut its number of visitors so that the proportion of meals consumed by strangers was reduced from about a third of the total (in 1391–2) to only 14 per cent. And households charged visitors for their keep: when Lady Harington stayed with the Luttrells for eight months in 1423–4 she gave Sir Hugh Luttrell £32. Nor does the custom of keeping paupers in the household seem to have been continued after 1350.

The most radical change in aristocratic domestic life involved the lords' patterns of residence. From early times households had been peripatetic, partly for reasons of practical politics and administration, to allow a lord to show himself in the areas of his rule, and partly as an efficient way of consuming manorial food surpluses. The growth of a market for agricultural produce in the thirteenth century gave the aristocracy the opportunity to buy foodstuffs and cease their wanderings, though under direct management lords wished to keep a personal eye on manors. The itineraries of a great lord, such as those of Thomas, earl of Lancaster, or of bishops, shows that the traditional pattern persisted into the decades around 1300. The countess of Pembroke stayed at a dozen houses, mostly her own manors, in the nine months between September 1295 and June 1296.[28] Many households travelled more rapidly than this. Great lords during the thirteenth century made visits to London a regular part of their routine, using town houses in the London suburbs, and manor houses on the road between their provincial estates and the capital. The arrival of a household was a great event in the life of a manor, and preparations included minor building repairs, the cleaning of rooms, and the cutting of fuel. These, however, presented minor problems and expense compared with the building programme to which lords were committed by their itinerant existence. If a manor was to accommodate a large household it needed many chambers, a well-equipped kitchen, bake-house and brew-house, and a large stable.

With the leasing of demesnes in the late fourteenth and early

28 P.R.O., E101/505/25.

fifteenth century, lords no longer had the option of consuming produce on their manors, and the surrender of management to farmers removed another reason for regular visits. Most important, they could save on building costs by concentrating their efforts on a few favoured dwellings. Between the fourteenth and early sixteenth century the bishops of Worcester reduced the number of their houses used as residences from fifteen to six. Great secular magnates spent more of their time at a few houses, or at least left their wives and main household in almost permanent occupation while they moved around with a relatively small band of servants and companions. In the mid-fifteenth century the first duke of Buckingham's household travelled between three places, Maxstoke Castle in Warwickshire, the manor of Writtle in Essex and his London house. The third duke in the early years of the sixteenth century turned to Thornbury in Gloucestershire as his main seat.[29] The new pattern of living bears a strong resemblance to that of modern landed aristocrats, who would occupy one or two major country houses and a town house. One advantage of this lay in the superior buildings that could be had for less money. Many of the manor houses of even wealthy magnates of the thirteenth and fourteenth centuries were built with timber framing, and were not greatly superior in their construction to those of the gentry. In the fifteenth century, aristocrats concentrated on quality rather than quantity. They experimented with brick, a new material in some regions. They favoured aesthetically pleasing symmetrical designs, with less emphasis on defensibility. The multiplication of chambers and of fireplaces, and the increasing size of the windows suggests a greater desire for privacy and comfort. The new residences did not come cheap, but they cost less than thirteenth-century castles with their massive volumes of stone and elaborate defensive earthworks. Historians have admired these showy new country houses-cum-castles, like Maxstoke, Thornbury, Tattershall, Sudeley and Farleigh Hungerford, and have remarked that the late medieval aristocracy cannot have been so badly-off if they could afford to build so well. However, they forget the houses that we cannot see, or rather which are now visible as grassed-over mounds or as foundations uncovered by excavation. Hundreds of manor houses (and not a few redundant castles) fell into ruin in the later middle ages, as is shown by the frequent references in documents to valueless 'capital messuages' in decay, and archaeological evidence for a cessation of occupation, or a change in its character, at this

---

29 C. Dyer, *Lords and peasants in a changing society. The estates of the bishopric of Worcester, 680–1540* (Cambridge, 1980), p. 202; Rawcliffe, *The Staffords*, pp. 86–7.

period. A side-effect was the appearance of large inns in many towns, especially on main roads. Notable examples survive, such as the New Inn at Gloucester, and many more are recorded in such sources as building contracts.[30] These establishments had to be large enough to shelter a travelling household, or at least a substantial part of it, which sought accommodation previously available on the far-flung manors of an estate.

The decline in the quantity of major ecclesiastical buildings has been demonstrated from a sample of cathedrals and monasteries, using the evidence of the buildings themselves. According to Morris's figures (see fig. 3) the peak of building lay between 1210 and 1350. A profound slump, beginning before the Black Death, reached a low point in the mid-fifteenth century. Many complex factors influenced the pace of the building of major churches. A general decline in religious devotion cannot be invoked because of the apparent vigour of smaller church building after the Black Death, though a shift in spiritual fashion away from the main religious orders may have been a contributory factor. However, the monks were going out of favour long before 1340, and this seems to have had no effect on building campaigns then. It therefore seems likely that many monasteries and cathedrals were no longer being rebuilt and extended after the mid-fourteenth century because bishops, monasteries, cathedral chapters and aristocratic patrons were suffering losses in their disposable incomes. Evidently the same pressures were not felt in other sections of society, hence the continued rebuilding of parish churches.

The late medieval aristocracy had problems with the level of their cash incomes, and as consumers were caught in the 'price scissors'.[31] In the thirteenth century, estate revenues rose partly because of the increase in the prices of agricultural produce. Wheat, for example, was sold for 3s. per quarter in the early thirteenth century and 6s. in the years around 1300 (the figures are approximate, because of the rapid movements from year to year). At the same time oxen rose in price from 5s. to 10s.[32] These movements had beneficial effects on lords' incomes because they profited from the sale of grain and

30 W. A. Pantin, 'Medieval inns' in E. M. Jope (ed.), *Studies in building history* (London, 1961), pp. 166–91; L. F. Salzman, *Building in England, down to 1540*, 2nd edn (Oxford, 1967), pp. 517–19.

31 G. Fourquin, *Les campagnes de la région parisienne à la fin du moyen âge* (Paris, 1964), pp. 192–202.

32 D. L. Farmer, 'Some grain price movements in thirteenth-century England', *Ec.H.R.*, 2nd ser., 10 (1957), 207–20; D. L. Farmer, 'Some livestock price movements in thirteenth-century England', *Ec.H.R.*, 2nd ser., 22 (1969), 1–16.

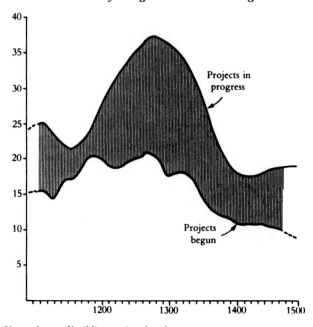

Fig. 3 Chronology of building major churches, 1100–1500
The lower curve (Projects begun) represents the average trend of major building projects begun at cathedrals and abbeys, by decade, based on a sample of eighty-five buildings. The upper curve represents the average trend of building projects in progress in each decade, based on a sample of forty buildings.
Source: Taken from R. Morris, *Cathedrals and abbeys of England and Wales* (London, 1979), p. 180

animals from their demesnes, and their better-off tenants could pay higher rents. At the same time, the price of manufactured goods purchased by the aristocracy, and above all the price of labour, increased by a much smaller amount. The prices of building materials, such as wooden shingles, solder and nails went up by less than 50 per cent between the 1220s and the early fourteenth century, and threshing and winnowing a quarter of grain increased from 1d. at the beginning of the thirteenth century to 1½d. at its end. From the 1320s these tendencies were reversed. Grain prices declined, and after some important upward surges in the third quarter of the fourteenth century, a quarter of wheat was sold for about 5s. for most of the fifteenth century. Manufactured goods became much more expensive; ceramic tiles, much used in aristocratic buildings, cost 2s. to 3s. per thousand in the early fourteenth century and 5s. to

6s. in the late fifteenth.[33] The price of manufactured goods reflected closely the increased wages that went to make them. The price scissors refer to the divergent lines on the graphs of goods sold and goods bought, and the aristocracy were caught (metaphorically) between the blades of the scissors after 1320. Real income, that is the income expressed in terms of its power to purchase the goods that were habitually needed, declined more steeply than cash income.

Some manufactured and imported goods were bought mainly by the aristocracy, and a study of these commodities can help us to appreciate some of the general trends in their consumption. Lead is a useful example, because it was a metal used mainly for roofs, gutters and water pipes in major buildings such as castles and churches, with less important functions as the material from which brewing vessels were made, and as a minor ingredient in pewter. Though cheap when reckoned per pound ($^1/_4$d.–$^1/_2$d. for much of the period) it was used in such large quantities that it was often bought by the fother of 2,184 lbs. The trends in production are known from one of the main mining areas, the Derbyshire Peak District. Levels of output were very high around 1200 and 1300, with a puzzling dip in the 1230s and 1240s. After the Black Death, the price of lead increased in line with the extra cost of the labour for digging and smelting the ore, and of the carriage of the finished product. Production declined in the fourteenth century, but recovered towards 1400, and then fell in the early fifteenth century, showing no sustained recovery until the 1480s. This would suggest that aristocratic builders were discouraged in the long run by the combination of reduced incomes and high cost of materials, and so demand for lead fell. However, it is important to note that the deepest decline came in the early fifteenth century.[34]

Tin was consumed mainly, though not exclusively, by the rich, in the form of pewter plate, and less importantly for solder in plumbing, for plating iron articles (spurs, for example) as a rust preventive, and for such specialized uses as organ pipes. Many non-aristocrats bought the occasional pewter plate or spoon, and cumulatively they

---

33 H. M. Colvin (ed.), *Building accounts of king Henry III* (Oxford, 1971); J. E. Thorold Rogers, *A history of agriculture and prices in England* (7 vols., Oxford, 1866–1902), vols. 1–4; D. L. Farmer, 'Prices and wages' in H. Hallam (ed.), *Agrarian history of England and Wales*, vol. 2 (Cambridge, 1988), pp. 716–817.

34 I. S. W. Blanchard, 'Derbyshire lead production, 1195–1505', *Derbyshire Archaeological Journal*, 91 (1971), 119–40.

may have had an effect on gross demand. However, the aristocracy bought very large quantities of pewter, which was used every day instead of silver, hence its common name of 'counterfeit'. A further complication in interpreting tin production as an index of English consumption is the European-wide market served by the Devon and Cornwall mines. Tin seems to have behaved in a very similar way to lead, with an early-thirteenth-century peak, a slackening which continued after 1300, but then, with a surge in fashion for pewter table-ware, the all-time peak of medieval production (1,644 thousand weights, or 1.6 million pounds) was reached in 1332. Output rose after a mid-fourteenth century slump, and was then plunged into a deep depression in the fifteenth century, until in the 1450s only about half of the weight of metal was being sold as in the 1340s. Again a doubling of the price in the fourteenth century from 1½d.–2d. to 2½d.–3d. per pound helped to suppress demand from already hard-pressed consumers, but not immediately after the price rise; the trough was delayed until the fifteenth century. Output expanded from 1465 and in 1515 surpassed the peak of 1400.[35] With both lead and tin we need to make the reservation that our statistics for production depend on payments made to lords or the Crown, such as the toll on lead ore called 'lot and cope' and the coinage payment made on tin after smelting, and corruption and evasion may have influenced the figures.

Wine imports from Gascony, which rose in the thirteenth century to a level of 20,000 tuns (4–5 million gallons), in the early fourteenth century declined to as little as 6,000–8,000 tuns after the Black Death. Imports then revived to reach another peak in 1403–20, and fell below 10,000 tuns for the rest of the fifteenth century, dipping to 5,000 or less in the 1450s and 1460s, with no sustained recovery until the 1490s. This is customarily explained solely in terms of political factors – the Gascon trade developed after 1204 when Gascony was the Crown's main continental possession, and was disrupted by the Hundred Years War and the eventual loss of the province to the French in 1453. It is true that the war diminished supplies, but it also added to the costs of transport, hence the steep price rise from the pre-war 3d.–4d. per gallon to 8d. and more afterwards.[36] The fact that alternative sources did not replace the lost Gascon wine – the

35 J. Hatcher, *English tin production and trade before 1550* (Oxford, 1973), pp. 89–91, 152–63; J. Hatcher and T. C. Barker, *A history of British pewter* (London, 1974), pp. 24–80.
36 M. K. James, *Studies in the medieval wine trade* (Oxford, 1971), pp. 1–69.

sweet wines fashionable in the fifteenth century were very expensive and were bought in small volume – suggests that the wine-drinking aristocracy were cutting back their consumption, either by reducing daily allowances, or, in the case of the gentry, dropping out of regular wine-drinking altogether.

Finally, the fur trade illustrates well the complex non-economic factors that could influence consumer behaviour. In the thirteenth and fourteenth centuries hundreds of thousands of squirrel furs were imported from the Baltic to be made up into linings for high-quality clothes worn by the rich. The trade declined in the fifteenth century, but unlike other goods did not recover towards 1500. This was apparently because fashion had decreed that smaller numbers of more expensive furs should be worn, such as marten and budge (see page 79), which were better suited to accompany the rich fabrics that were also coming into vogue. In addition, the increased spending power of urban craftsmen and other decidedly non-aristocratic types allowed them to wear cheap squirrel fur, so the aristocracy had to move to a more rarified plane of luxury to maintain their social distance.[37]

A number of trends suggest a differentiation in aristocratic consumption towards the end of the middle ages. Contemporaries complained that lords were becoming more private and exclusive in their domestic lives. They no longer ate in the hall with the household, but in private rooms. Now this was to some extent an age-old grumble, exposing a constant tension between public and private life that was an inherent problem when a lord cohabited with a group of servants and followers. However, it really was happening in the fifteenth century, to judge from the architectural evidence of the scaling-down of the hall and the multiplication of chambers, evident in a comparison between a house like Stokesay (Shropshire) of the thirteenth century and one of the new fifteenth-century mansions like South Wingfield (see fig. 2). The consumption of small quantities of special luxury items, such as sweet wines and marten fur, can be linked with the same tendency. Closed off from his household, the lord could concentrate his limited resources on special refinements for himself and his intimates, while leaving the household with a plainer style of life. As a Venetian observer remarked in *c.* 1500:

Besides which the English being great epicures, and very avaricious by

---

37 E. Veale, *The English fur trade in the later middle ages* (Oxford, 1966), *passim*.

nature, indulge in the most delicate fare themselves and give their households the coarsest bread, and beer, and cold meat . . .[38]

Much of the evidence for consumption concerns products bought by the higher aristocracy rather than the gentry. No certainty can be achieved in analysing the expenditure of the thinly-documented lesser gentry. In the thirteenth century, developments in housing suggest that their living standards were rising. The construction of buildings was improved by replacing earthfast foundations (the upright posts being set in holes in the ground) by timber framing based on low stone walls, or at least pad-stones. This change in the foundations went with high-quality timber work and roofs, which can be appreciated in a scatter of thirteenth and early fourteenth-century manor houses still standing and inhabited in midland and southern England.[39] However, similar changes affected urban and peasant houses, and more striking as an aristocratic innovation was the proliferation of moats. More than 5,000 of these wide ditches surrounding houses are known in England. From the sample of sites that have been excavated, most were constructed between 1200 and 1325. They are distributed most densely in the regions where clay soil made a water-retaining ditch technically feasible, such as Essex and Suffolk, and in the west midlands. Every type of landlord built moats, even kings, earls and bishops for their minor residences. The great majority seem to have been constructed for the gentry. It is sometimes alleged that they are so numerous (twelve in one parish at Tanworth-in-Arden, in Warwickshire, for example) that some must have belonged to the upper ranks of the peasantry, but this assertion may be based on too narrow a definition of the gentry.[40] They represent a considerable outlay for a minor lord. Digging even a small moat would have involved moving 3,000 cubic yards of earth, and all of this work would have been carried out by wage labour, as few gentry would have commanded enough tenant labour services

·

38 C. A. Sneyd (ed.), *A relation, or rather a true account of the island of England* (Camden Soc., 37, 1847), p. 25; on the general problem, P. Ariès and G. Duby (eds.), *Histoire de la vie privée*, vol. 2 (Paris, 1985), pp. 49–95.
39 For example, F. W. B. Charles, 'Rectory Farm, Grafton Flyford, Worcestershire' in *Miscellany I* (Worcestershire Historical Soc., 1960), pp. 92–8; K. Sandall, 'Aisled halls in England and Wales', *Vernacular Architecture*, 6 (1975), 19–27.
40 F. A. Aberg (ed.), *Medieval moated sites* (C.B.A. Research Report, 17, 1978); B. K. Roberts, 'The historical geography of moated homesteads in the forest of Arden', *Transactions of the Birmingham and Warwickshire Archaeological Soc.*, 88 (1976–7), 61–70.

for such a task.[41] They served a useful defensive function against minor assaults, and also demonstrated the aristocratic status of the owner. If a lord was unable to afford a castle, a moat was the next best thing. Perhaps moat building, as well as buying fine horses or other luxuries, tempted a minority of thirteenth-century gentry into debt? (See pp. 38–9.)

Did the gentry's consumption continue to expand in the fourteenth and fifteenth centuries? The arguments are as evenly balanced as the debate over their incomes. In their favour was the ratio between food and non-food items in their expenditure. The higher aristocracy were caught much more sharply in the price scissors because two-thirds of their budgets went on goods other than food. The scale of the gentry's expenditure on houses (of which most had only one) was so much smaller that they did not feel the same pinch of increased costs. Those upper gentry with a number of manors seem to have concentrated their spending on one or two houses in a move parallel to that of their magnate superiors.[42] Certainly the standing buildings with elements of stone known to have been built by fifteenth-century gentry, such as Baddesley Clinton (Warwickshire) or Ightham Mote (Kent) show much the same tendencies, aesthetic, military and domestic, that are apparent in the new castles of the magnates. There are in addition some remarkably well-built and comfortable houses of parish and chantry priests, often of stone, surviving in the west of England from this same period.[43] Neither the large numbers of fifteenth-century timber-framed manor houses still surviving, nor the foundations from excavated sites, would suggest that gentry building standards had deteriorated in any way; rather the opposite would be true, because the period saw the dissemination of refinements such as fireplaces, chimneys and glazed windows.[44]

On the other hand, whereas the higher aristocracy could easily economize on the cost of meals, or by cutting down on their servants and visitors, or abandoning surplus manor houses to fall into ruin, an

---

41 The example is from A. Dornier, 'Kent's Moat, Sheldon, Birmingham', *Transactions of the Birmingham and Warwickshire Archaeological Soc.*, 82 (1967), 45–57.

42 J. Le Patourel, 'Fortified and semi-fortified manor houses in eastern and northern England in the later middle ages' in M. Bur (ed.), *La maison forte au moyen âge* (Paris, 1986), p. 25.

43 W. A. Pantin, 'Medieval priests' houses in south-west England', *Med. Arch.*, 1 (1957), 118–46; W. A. Pantin, 'Chantry priests' houses and other medieval lodgings', *Med. Arch.*, 3 (1959), 216–43.

44 M. Wood, *The English medieval house* (London, 1965), pp. 265–72, 286–91, 358.

esquire or gentleman on £20 or £10 a year who was employing only three servants and living in one house, and whose meals were devoid of much luxury in the way of wine or spices, had little room for manœuvre. They must have cut back, or even cut out completely, their occasional wine-bibbings, and avoided travel where possible, but too many economies of this kind might force them to drop out of the aristocracy, and accept yeoman status. Perhaps the answer to the problem of the gentry's social survival as consumers and in many cases, their expansion, lies in their eligibility for sources of income unavailable to the higher aristocracy, such as their profits from direct agricultural management and earnings from legal practice, so they did not so often have to make such hard decisions about spending cuts.

To sum up, the aristocracy as a whole expanded their consumption in the thirteenth century; they drank more wine, rebuilt their monasteries, cathedrals and castles, and surrounded their houses with moats. In the fourteenth and fifteenth centuries they experienced greater or lesser degrees of financial embarrassment. Some families were able to expand their incomes by marriage, patronage or the profits of war. Churchmen, and a good number of laymen, did not have such opportunities. Even those skilful and fortunate families who did add to their estates still had to cope with the fact that their newly acquired assets were deteriorating in value. Cash incomes declined, and real incomes declined still further because of the operation of the price scissors. The problem was first felt in the twenty or thirty years before the Black Death. After that catastrophe the aristocracy felt vulnerable but did not suffer drastic drops in income. The most serious decline came after 1400, and the worst was over by the 1470s or 1480s. The aristocracy showed remarkable resilience and ingenuity in adapting their consumption to new circumstances. They used their accounting system to adjust their spending to fit their incomes; they reduced the size of their households and the number of their residences; they bought less of the most expensive luxuries, such as wine and furs. The new stratification within the class, and even inside individual households, helped to preserve social distinctions which were felt to be under threat. The English aristocracy looked into an abyss of social ruin, but pulled back, survived, and flourished once more.

——— 5 ———

PEASANT LIVING STANDARDS:
MODELLING THE PEASANT ECONOMY

——— • ———

1200–1350

Peasants have left no accounts: they were often illiterate, and such documents had no place in a domestic economy in which most of the produce was consumed within the household. The peasantry *used* goods, rather than making profits, so that a calculation of surplus in purely financial terms would have been foreign to their outlook. The evidence for the living standards of the peasants comes from documents compiled by lords or by the state, whose main interest lay in squeezing money and services from them. There are two approaches to research into peasant living standards. One is to attempt to build models of peasant income and expenditure. The other is to seek more direct evidence of peasant material conditions, such as housing, clothing and food. This chapter is devoted to the first method, and chapter 6 to the second.

Modelling the peasant economy can be attempted on a grand, theoretical scale. Lunden, for example, who is concerned with the medieval peasantry of Norway, argues that the variable factors were the peasants' diet, the number of people, the area of land in agricultural use, rents and taxes, climate and technology.[1] He assumes that diet did not change (being close to the minimum necessary to sustain life), and that technology was static. Accordingly, if the number of

---

1 K. Lunden, 'Some causes of change in a peasant economy: interactions between cultivated area, farming population, climate, taxation and technology', *Scandinavian Ec.H.R.*, 22 (1974), 117–35.

people rose, or the taxes increased, or the climate deteriorated, the area of agricultural land would have grown. In the opposite circumstances the cultivated area shrank. English historians rarely express themselves in such abstract terms, but they acknowledge (sometimes unconsciously) the existence of such a framework of variables. Professor Postan assumed that technology developed very little in the later middle ages, and believed that by the thirteenth century all of the productive arable land in England was being exploited. Accordingly a growth in population (as occurred in the thirteenth century) could only be accommodated by reducing the diet, and any short-term fluctuations in the weather caused hardship and higher mortality, culminating in the famine of 1315–18. Postan's critics would disagree with his assumption that the land had been used up, and that technology was unchanging. Others would give more emphasis to the increased rents and taxes. In other words, attempts to simplify the problem by reducing the numbers of variable factors may not be valid – everything, including the standard of living, was in a state of flux! Such theorizing is helpful in putting our thinking into order, but the model-building in this chapter will be of a more specific kind.

Our example is Bishop's Cleeve in Gloucestershire, as described in a survey of 1299 made for its lord, the bishop of Worcester.[2] The manor contained almost a hundred tenants living in two villages, Cleeve and Woodmancote, and two hamlets, Wick and Wontley. The first peasant to be investigated is Robert le Kyng, who held a yardland by customary (servile) tenure, which made him one of a minority of better-off tenants on the manor. His house lay in the main village of Cleeve, and his lands were scattered in narrow strips over the common fields, mostly on the lowlands surrounding the village, and on the slopes of the Cotswold escarpment to the east (see map 2). The soil tended to be a heavy clay, of average quality and suitable for cereal cultivation. Possession of a yardland gave Kyng rights to pasture animals on the fields after the harvest and when they lay fallow, and on the grassland at the top of the hill overlooking the village. He was entitled to a share in the not-so-plentiful meadowland along the edges of the small streams running through Cleeve, and he could take firewood from woodland on the hill.

The first step in calculating Robert le Kyng's budget must be to work out his produce from cultivation. Let us assume that his

2 M. Hollings (ed.), *The Red Book of Worcester* (Worcestershire Historical Soc., 1934–50), pp. 327–48.

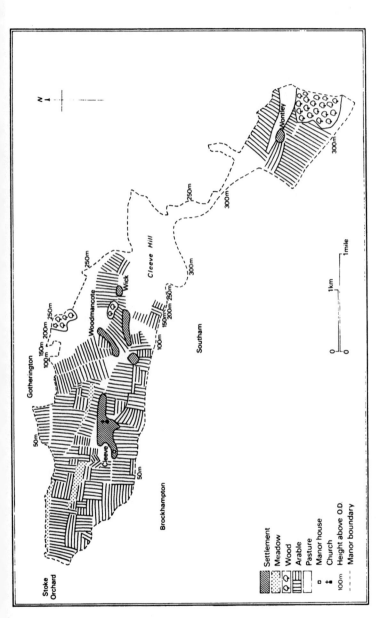

Map 2 The manor of Bishop's Cleeve, Gloucestershire, in 1299

The distribution of arable land is based mainly on the evidence of air photographs, but is partly conjectural. There are many difficulties in reducing the complexities of a manor's rights and connections to a form which can be mapped. It should be remembered that Cleeve, Brockhampton and Southam shared the same fields, so the map should include individual strips extending to Gotherington the south. Similarly, the manor included some tenants and lands in Gotherington to the north. Part of the meadow at Bredon, Worcestershire, at a distance of 6 miles to the north-west, was attached to the Bishop's Cleeve demesne. And pasture rights on Cleeve Hill were probably shared with neighbouring villages, so the sheep from Cleeve and Woodmancote grazed beyond the boundaries shown here. Gotherington, Stoke Orchard, Brockhampton and Southam all lay within Cleeve parish, having once been part of an early medieval estate.

yardland contained about 30 acres of arable land. Not all of this would have been cultivated each year. The survey of 1299 implies that a two-course rotation prevailed at Cleeve; later sources state that a three-course system was in use.[3] The difference is important, because the first, in which a half of the land was planted each year while the rest lay fallow, would give Kyng the ability to plant each year 15 acres, and the second, by which two-thirds of the land was planted and a third lay fallow, would allow him to plant 20 acres. In reality peasants commonly departed from any rigid system of rotation, sowing a different acreage each year. At nearby villages in south-east Worcestershire, for example, two-field systems were modified by *inhoks* (the modern equivalent would be intakes), which were pieces of land from the fallow field that were cropped for two years in succession.[4] Because of the uncertainties about the methods of management of Kyng's land, two calculations, for both a two- and three-course régime, will be made. The proportions of the different crops are not known for Cleeve in 1299, but they are recorded in the very similar nearby village of Bourton-on-the-Hill for peasant holdings which came into their lord's hands in 1349 after the Black Death, and the tithe receipts for Cleeve parish are known from the 1390s.[5] The two sets of figures are in close agreement, and allow the confident assumption that about half of Kyng's land was planted with barley, rather more than a third with wheat, and the rest with small quantities of peas and oats (see table 7). The amount of grain that would have been harvested in 1299 can be calculated by assuming that corn would have been sown, and that it would yield, at rates similar to those found on demesnes of comparable manors. In fact the yields would have been higher, because the rector took a tenth of the crop as tithe, but this subtraction need not be made by us because our yield ratios were calculated after tithe payment. Similarly, some of the corn would have been wasted and spoilt before threshing, and again the yields were calculated after this had happened to the demesne crops. Kyng's holding can be estimated to have produced 23 1/2 quarters on a two-course rotation, or 28 quarters 3 bushels on a three-course. After the deduction of seed for the next year Kyng would have been left with a surplus of 17 quarters 5 bushels or 20 quarters 4 bushels.

3 C. Dyer, *Lords and peasants in a changing society. The estates of the bishopric of Worcester, 680–1540* (Cambridge, 1980), p. 322; *V.C.H. Gloucestershire*, vol. 8, p. 15.

4 The villages were Elmley Castle and its neighbours; Hereford and Worcester R.O., ref. 899: 95, BA989/1.

5 Westminster Abbey Muniments, 8282; Corpus Christi College, Oxford, B/14/2/3/6.

Table 7. *Reconstruction of the arable contribution to the budget of Robert le Kyng of Bishop's Cleeve, Gloucestershire, 1299–1300*

(A and B represent alternative reconstructions, depending on the use of a two- or three-course rotation on the Cleeve fields)

	A. Two-course rotation (15 sown acres)					B. Three-course rotation (20 sown acres)				
	Wheat	Barley	Peas	Oats	Total	Wheat	Barley	Peas	Oats	Total
Production										
Acreage of crops	5ac	7½ac	2ac	½ac	15ac	7ac	10ac	2ac	1ac	20ac
Sowing rate per acre	2b	4b	3b	3b		2b	4b	3b	3b	
Total of seed	1qr 2b	3qr 6b	6b	1½b	5qr 7½b	1qr 6b	5qr	6b	3b	7qr 7b
Yield ratio (seed:crop, tithe deducted)	3.6	4.4	2.6	3.0		3.2	4.0	2.3	2.7	
Crop harvested (tithe deducted)	4qr 4b	16qr 4b	2qr	4½b	23qr 4½b	5qr 5b	20qr	1qr 6b	1qr	28qr 3b
Consumption										
Seed deducted for next year	1qr 2b	3qr 6b	6b	1½b	5qr 7½b	1qr 6b	5qr	6b	3b	7qr 7b
Remaining	3qr 2b	12qr 6b	1qr 2b	3b	17qr 5b	3qr 7b	15qr	1qr	5b	20qr 4b
Food corn deducted	2qr 2b	4qr	0	3b	6qr 5b	2qr 2b	4qr	0	3b	6qr 5b
Remaining	1qr	8qr 6b	1qr 2b	0	11qr	1qr 5b	11qr	1qr	2b	13qr 7b
Drink corn deducted		3qr			3qr		3qr			3qr
Remaining	1qr	5qr 6b	1qr 2b		8qr	1qr 5b	8qr	1qr	2b	10qr 7b
Mill tolls deducted	1b	2b			3b	1b	2b			3b
Remaining	7b	5qr 4b	1qr 2b		7qr 5b	1qr 4b	7qr 6b	1qr	2b	10qr 4b
Price per qr	6s. 0d.	4s. 4d.	2s. 8d.			6s. 0d.	4s. 4d.	2s. 8d.	2s. 9d.	
Cash from sales	5s. 3d.	23s. 10d.	3s. 4d.		32s. 5d.	9s. 0d.	33s. 7d.	2s. 8d.	8d.	45s. 11d.

Having gathered in his corn, Kyng's first concern would have been to feed his family. If we assign to him a typical late thirteenth-century yardlander's wife and three children, ranging in age from five to twelve years, their food needs in bread and pottage could have been met by 6 quarters 5 bushels of wheat, barley and oats, and another 3 quarters of barley could have been malted and brewed to give the household a regular supply of ale. Grinding this grain and malt required payment of a mill toll of $^1/_{24}$, and in our calculation 3 bushels have been deducted (for arithmetic convenience, only from the wheat and barley). Kyng was thus left with 7 quarters 5 bushels or 10 quarters 4 bushels of grain, depending still on the rotational system. This could have been sold at current prices for about 32s. or 46s. At this point it might be thought that Kyng would have been foolish to continue with a two-course rotation in view of the higher returns of the three-course alternative. The disadvantage of planting two-thirds of the fields every year lay in the less frequent manuring and fallowing which in the long run may have reduced productivity. Because we do not know the precise difference in yields, the assumption has been made here that corn returned 10 per cent less under the three-course system. This could be an underestimate.[6] So the two columns of table 7 present possible alternatives, and the most realistic estimate may well lie somewhere between the two figures.

Kyng would also have obtained a cash income from his animals, which can be supposed to have consisted of two cows and their offspring, thirty adult sheep and a pig. The sheep's wool, weighing 3–4 stone, could have been sold for 20s., but three of the fleeces would have been paid in tithe, leaving Kyng with 18s. The two cows between them would have produced 160 lbs of cheese, of which a half would have been consumed in Kyng's household, and the remainder sold for 3s. 4d. The pig provided the family with bacon, lard and offal. The calves and lambs bred on the holding replaced older stock, and some were sold, together with culled animals. The annual income from this source is estimated at about 12s., allowing some money to buy animals, such as a young pig each year for fattening. The draught animals, at least two oxen and a horse or two,

---

6 H. S. A. Fox, 'The alleged transformation from two-field to three-field systems in medieval England', *Ec.H.R.*, 2nd ser., 39 (1986), 526–48; D. L. Farmer, 'Grain yields on Westminster Abbey manors, 1271–1410', *Canadian Journal of History*, 18 (1983), 345–6.

were vital to the running of the holding, but contributed little directly to Kyng's cash income.

Our yardlander could therefore have received each year from his main farming activities about £3 6s. od. or £3 19s. od. in money. The first call on this sum was the payment of rent, which, if he paid in cash as some Cleeve yardlanders did, would have entailed an annual rent of assize of 22s., with an additional 4s. for Kyng's contribution to collective payments of aid (called tallage elsewhere) and extra dues like pannage for feeding his pig in the lord's wood, and amercements (judicial fines) in the manorial court. Tithes on hay and cheese were paid in cash, and together with semi-compulsory church dues would have added at least another 2s. Kyng would therefore have had to pay 28s., so reducing his surplus to about £1 18s. od. or £2 11s. od.

Many more additions and subtractions must be made to complete these calculations. No allowance has been made for the petty profits of the garden, bee-hives and poultry. We are not entirely ignorant of these because tithe accounts from Cleeve from the late fourteenth century show that the most valuable garden crops, flax and hemp, were worth each year (multiplying the tithe by ten) 10s. to 30s. The tithe on vegetables was not sold or valued because it was given to the rector's servants. This, and figures from elsewhere, suggest that they would have been of less value than the flax and hemp. In one year, total egg production in the parish reached 10,800, and the numbers of tithe geese varied between 12 and 30, implying broods of 120 to 300. As these products came from the huge Cleeve parish, which was much larger than the manor of Cleeve, they were distributed over 150 households living in six villages, so each household was profiting by perhaps a shilling from gardening and poultry-keeping (eggs were sold for about 4d. per hundred, and geese at 4d. each). Garden produce, together with hay and straw, were used on the holding and in the household and brought in no cash income. A source of cash that must not be neglected, though it is difficult to put a figure on its profits, derived from Kyng's wife, who apart from assisting on the holding and managing the household, might have brewed ale for sale, or spun yarn. Other sources of potential income, ewes' milk and the skins of sheep that died, were worth at least a few pence each year.

On the debit side the costs of farming would include some hired labour, to help at hay-making or harvest, and to repair buildings, ploughs and carts. Kyng would have needed to buy each year tools, horse-shoes and tar (to treat diseased sheep). Some of the grain, the peas in particular, would have been fed to working horses and to sheep in winter. This practice alone could have reduced the size of the surplus by 10s. each year. Similarly, the profit on animal husbandry has been based on the assumption that the peasant family consumed from their holding only cereals, dairy produce and bacon. There is every likelihood that they ate more than this, some meat for example, and they would have bought foods that were not locally available, such as salt (for the dairy and for preserving meat as well as direct consumption) and herrings. The assumption that rents were paid solely in cash is convenient for purposes of calculation, but Kyng may well have been required to do some labour services. This would not have led to a financial saving, because he might have needed to hire a substitute. These expenses might leave a pound of the cash surplus to be spent on clothing, housing and other items.

The budget calculation has been deliberately focussed on a man in middle life functioning in a normal year. Different circumstances could have important effects on the size of the surplus. In a bad harvest year, as occurred earlier in the 1290s, yields could have fallen by 20 per cent, cutting the saleable surplus to between 3 and 5 quarters. This grain would have fetched a better price in a year of general scarcity, but not enough to compensate for the loss of quantity. Years of sheep scab would have made similar inroads into the cash surplus. In many years in the 1290s Kyng would have been expected to contribute 4s. or so for lay subsidies, and to pay money for foot soldiers levied for service in Wales and Scotland. The death of a tenant and the subsequent need to pay a heriot to the lord (in Kyng's case, probably an ox worth 10s.), a mortuary to the rector (another ox) and a burial fee, as well as the lord's entry fine of a few pounds, would leave the heir in debt for at least a year or two. The need to replace an ox absorbed a substantial part of the surplus, and all of it would have been used if a barn or house had to be rebuilt. A few years later in his life, Kyng would have saved on hired labour because his children would have contributed to work on the holding. They might have gone out to work and added their earnings to the family's income, or saved on costs by accepting a position as a living-in servant in another household. Less advantageous times in the life of the holding would have been those when the tenant was incapacitated by illness or old age. Then hired labour would have to be employed in some quantity, or the peasant would hand over to a new tenant, so that temporarily the holding had to support the retired couple and their successors. Equally disadvantaged was a tenant at an early stage of his life-cycle who had produced six children. Our conclusion must be that an average yardlander in a normal year was in a good position to make a cash surplus, but adverse circumstances could eat into that surplus.

The calculation of the customary half-yardlander's budget leads to much less confident conclusions. A peasant like Henry Benet of Cleeve, with a surplus (after allowing for seed) of 8 quarters 7½ bushels to 10 quarters 2 bushels (depending again on the rotational system), with the same sized family as Robert le Kyng, fed to the same standard, and paying the same rate of mill toll, would have had either no surplus of grain to sell, or no more than a modest 2 bushels. If he kept half as much stock, the profit from cheese, wool and animals would have covered his rent and tithe payments of 14s. and left him with a surplus of two or three shillings. However, half-yardlanders often kept considerably less animals than did full yard-landers, so the size of the cash surplus must be in doubt, in which case the shilling or two that could have come from the garden and poultry, or the earnings of wife and family became very much more important to the income of the household. Men like Benet would be seeking to economize, and it is doubtful if he would really have brewed 3 quarters of barley except in good years. How he paid for clothing, cooking pots or furnishings is not at all clear. In bad harvest years he would have slipped into debt, and Benet himself might have looked for employment. In 1299 at Cleeve there were eleven half-yardlanders like Benet and only four yardlanders, so peasants with a small surplus outnumbered those with relatively comfortable margins. And below Benet were twenty-seven cotlanders with 12 acres of land, who would only have broken even in normal years. Kyng belonged to a small prosperous minority; in the context of his village his surname (originating as a nickname) aptly indicates his economic position.

Finally we turn to a customary tenant with a smallholding, John le Gavisare. He was one of the thirteen Cleeve tenants holding 3 acres. With two of his acres planted each year he could have produced enough grain (3 quarters to be optimistic) to provide a part of the food needs of his family of a wife and three children. His single cow gave a supplement of cheese for a mainly cereal diet. In order to pay his rent of 4s., and to buy another 3 quarters of barley he would have had to earn some 17s., which at 1½d. per day required 130 days of work. He could have spared that time, because his holding would have detained him for only a few weeks in the year, but would so much paid employment have been available? The lord of the manor and the wealthy rector of Cleeve hired some agricultural labour, and so did the better-off tenants like Kyng, but Gavisare and his kind were numerous. Bad harvest years, when barley reached 5s. per quarter, would send Gavisare in search of even more work, when potential employers were anxious to cut down on labour costs. The earnings of his wife and children must have played a crucial rôle in making up the family income.

All of these budgets have been reconstructed for customary tenants, and a third of the Cleeve tenants were freeholders. They held land in the same fields as the servile tenants and used identical farming methods, but paid much lower rents. Richard Bury lived in the adjacent village of Gotherington though he held his half-yardland from Cleeve manor. An enterprising predecessor had bargained with the lord to pay a lump sum in return for a single cash rent, without labour services, and on very advantageous terms, namely 3s. 4d. per annum. He was thus almost 10s. a year better-off than a customary half-yardlander, and would have made a surplus every year without having to scratch around for extra sources of income. However Bury was Cleeve's only free half-yardlander. As on many manors, most of the free tenants had small parcels which compelled them to lead a precarious existence relying on wages because of the small contribution that their land made to their income.

Reconstructing peasant budgets is such a risky exercise that some justification and explanation is required for the assumptions made and the figures used. We need to know if the examples can be applied to the rest of the country, and how the year 1299 stands in the long-term changes of the thirteenth and early fourteenth century. We will look at six variable elements: the size of holdings, the productivity of agriculture, income from other sources, the size of the family, food consumption and rents and taxes.

The size of peasant holdings

Accurate calculations of holding size are made difficult by the different acres used: some surveys counted the strips in a holding and called them acres (field acres), while others measured acres but did not necessarily use the standard rod or perch of 5½ yards to do so.[7]

---

7 A. Jones, 'Land measurement in England, 1150–1350', *Ag.H.R.*, 27 (1979), 10–18.

Table 8. *Size of tenant holdings in the Hundred Rolls of 1279–80*

	Free		Villein	
Over 1 yardland	521	(8%)	173	(1%)
1 yardland	904	(15%)	3,940	(25%)
½ yardland	1,083	(18%)	5,724	(36%)
¼ yardland	775	(12%)	1,378	(9%)
small	2,251	(47%)	4,687	(29%)
Total	5,534	(100%)	15,902	(100%)

Source note: E. A. Kosminsky, *Studies in the agrarian history of England in the thirteenth century* (Oxford, 1956), pp. 216–23

Holdings were often assessed as shares in the assets of a village, and consequently varied in size. In the south and midlands the shares were called yardlands or virgates (English and Latin terms for land measured with a rod or yard); in the north they were known as oxgangs or bovates.[8] Fortunately such units tend to average around 30 acres for a yardland or 15 acres for an oxgang, so in large-scale comparisons the local differences are reduced in importance.

The most extensive survey of holding sizes is provided by the Hundred Rolls of 1279–80 (see table 8). Together with other surveys of the type used at Cleeve, they suggest that in much of midland and southern England yardlanders were in a distinct minority, and nearly a half of all holdings were smaller than a half-yardland. Very few tenants held more than a yardland. In the east of the country, from Lincolnshire to Kent, holdings were much smaller and it is not uncommon to find manors where the majority of tenants held 5 acres or less. Individual manors or groups of manors with high proportions of smallholders are found everywhere, and their location suggests various factors that favoured the fragmentation of holdings. A system of partible inheritance, by which a dead tenant's lands were divided among his sons, could have played some part in this. Assarting of woodland or the drainage of marshes often produced small-holdings, partly because of the limited quantity of land that anyone could clear. Smallholders were also concentrated in areas of commercial development, such as the outskirts of large towns,

8 P. D. A. Harvey (ed.), *The peasant land market in medieval England* (Oxford, 1984), pp. 7–19.

where there were more opportunities for employment. Strong lordship tended to perpetuate the standard yardland and oxgang units, so holdings were more prone to division among heirs, or to be split by sales, if they were held by free tenure (see table 8).[9]

Lords kept standard holdings because they had an interest in the preservation of the units from which rents and services were levied. We must ask, though, whether the surveys which list these holdings reflect the land worked by the tenants named, or an administrative fiction. Surveys were 'accurate' documents in the sense that the information was collected thoroughly by inquest, that is from a sworn jury. But surveys were compiled for the use of lords, not for the benefit of later historians. Does the statement that 'Robert le Kyng holds a yardland' mean no more than that Kyng was responsible for the rents and services of a yardland? The 1299 survey for Cleeve, like most others of its type, raises our suspicions. Fourteen of the tenants named, one in seven of the total, were women, probably widows holding their former husbands' land. Some no doubt were active and hardy people who worked the land with the help of hired labour or a son. It seems likely that many elderly women would come to some arrangement by which other tenants worked the land for rent. The existence of another type of subletting is revealed by two unusually explicit notes at the end of the Cleeve survey: 'There are there many male cottars who do nothing for the lord except one day's *bedrip* [harvest work]', and 'The bond tenants have under them many who pay them rent, who do no more for the lord than lifting hay for two days.' The scale of subletting on a free holding was exposed at Cleeve when, a generation before 1299, the lord bought out a tenant who had fallen into debt, and became the direct lord of his twenty-one subtenants![10]

For other manors we do not need to look for hints and chance events to reveal subtenancy. Some lords accepted the reality, and insisted that both tenants and subtenants should be listed in surveys. The actual distribution of land could differ markedly from that depicted in conventional surveys. On the Bedfordshire manors of Caddington and Kensworth, near the town of Dunstable, a survey of 1297 that includes subtenants shows a clear majority of holdings smaller than 10 acres, and in one village three-quarters of peasants

9 There is a huge literature on this topic, for example the estate histories used in chapter 2. For an interpretation, see R. H. Hilton, 'Reasons for inequality among medieval peasants', *Journal of Peasant Studies*, 5 (1978), 271–84.
10 Dyer, *Lords and peasants*, p. 56.

Map 3   Location of villages and manors mentioned in chapters 5 and 6

held less than 5 acres, whereas in the county generally most tenants were recorded as having 7 acres or above. Subtenancy at Havering-atte-Bower (Essex) in 1352–3 presents a more complicated picture, because whereas many of the subtenants had very small parcels and so swelled the number of smallholders, the better-off tenants (40 per cent of whom held 30 acres or more) had built up even larger holdings by taking extra land as subtenants.[11]

Another complicating factor is the likelihood that a peasant might hold land in a number of manors or villages. In the case of the Bedfordshire manors just cited, a number of apparently poor subtenants were in fact townsmen from Dunstable. Free tenants mentioned in the Hundred Rolls appear sometimes to have held lands in a number of villages, though if these were widely scattered we might speculate that they were worked by smallholding subtenants. There were local differences: in the tightly-knit village communities of Durham, land-holdings did not overlap, while in Norfolk the discovery of a fragment of a Hundred Roll has led to the speculation that many of the apparently impoverished tenants of 5 acres or less were really working 7 or 10 acres accumulated in different manors and villages.[12]

Subletting and the occupation of land in more than one manor should not lead us to reject the information from surveys as being entirely fictitious. Tax-lists of the late thirteenth and early fourteenth century suggest that the hierarchy of wealth in village society (reflected in the valuations of movable goods) was similar to that indicated by the contemporary surveys, except when the local economy included a strong industrial element, as in Cornwall.[13]

Tenements appear static in surveys, whereas in reality they were constantly changing. A dynamic picture can be gained from manorial court rolls, which record transfers of holdings. Some depict a

---

11 A. Jones, 'Caddington, Kensworth and Dunstable in 1297', *Ec.H.R.*, 2nd ser., 32 (1979), 316–27; M. K. McIntosh, 'Land, tenure and population in the royal manor of Havering, Essex, 1251–1352/3', *Ec.H.R.*, 2nd ser., 33 (1980), 17–31. 17–31.

12 T. Lomas, 'South-east Durham: late fourteenth and fifteenth centuries' in Harvey (ed.), *Land market*, p. 315; B. M. S. Campbell, 'The complexity of manorial structure in medieval Norfolk: a case study', *Norfolk Archaeology*, 39 (1986), 244–5.

13 J. R. Maddicott, *The English peasantry and the demands of the Crown, 1294–1341* (P. and P. Supplement, 1, 1975), pp. 8–9; J. Hatcher, *Rural economy and society in the duchy of Cornwall, 1300–1500* (Cambridge, 1970), p. 253.

rapid movement of parcels of land. At Martham in Norfolk, a manor with 364 tenants in 1292, between twenty-one and thirty-seven land transfers are recorded each year, mostly in small parcels of a half-acre or less.[14] Other manors seem to have had less eventful histories, but this may reflect the attitude of their lords who felt the need to record only the inheritance or surrender of whole tenements, while informal leasing of parcels went on beneath the surface.

One explanation of the transfer of parcels of land lies in the 'natural' land-market of a peasant society. Although a notion of families sharing equally in the resources of a village lies behind the standard units of land-holding, each household's circumstances would produce cyclical inequalities. A widow would wish to reduce her holding; a man with a large family would need to increase his. When this idea was first applied to the thirteenth-century English peasantry, it was in order to explain the 'charters of the serfs', a collection of documents made by Peterborough Abbey, recording the acquisition of land by servile tenants. It has since been shown that these charters record prosperous villeins adding free assart land to their already large holdings, in order to create profitable subtenancies, or to endow their younger sons and daughters with smallholdings. This discovery does not invalidate the idea of a natural land-market, but it does show that a number of processes lay behind land transfers. In some cases land was purchased for money in what appears to have been a commercial transaction, recorded in the manorial court as a surrender of land by a tenant *ad opus* (for the use) of another.

The land-market, whether natural or commercial, had no consistent effect on the size of holdings. In the bad harvest years of the late thirteenth and early fourteenth century on some manors in East Anglia, the sellers of land tended to outnumber the buyers, leading to the decline of the less competent or less fortunate, and the concentration of land in the hands of a minority, known as 'kulaks' from the modern Russian term.[15] Individuals built up holdings in the long-term, like Martin Suvel of Sedgeford (Norfolk) who inherited 3 acres of land, and by adding small parcels one after another had gained over 35 acres by 1282. Such successful peasants would, if they

14 J. Williamson, 'Norfolk: thirteenth century' in Harvey (ed.), *Land market*, pp. 70–6.

15 R. M. Smith, 'Families and their land in an area of partible inheritance: Redgrave, Suffolk 1260–1320' in R. M. Smith (ed.), *Land, kinship and life-cycle* (Cambridge, 1984), pp. 135–95.

had passed on their lands intact to their successors, have caused a rapid increase in the average size of holdings. However, in villages where the custom of impartible inheritance prevailed, fathers were anxious to provide for their non-inheriting sons and daughters. Custom allowed them to give away land that they had acquired in their own lifetime. Martin Suvel was therefore able to award 6¹/₂ acres to two of his sons in 1285. Such gifts of parcels and cottages were a recurring pattern in the lives of the better-off peasants of the Worcestershire village of Halesowen.[16] So the large accumulations of land were constantly being broken up to add to the numbers of smallholdings. In those places practising partible inheritance, we might expect that holdings were reduced rapidly in size as all of the larger units were divided among sons. This did not happen, partly because in a harsh world of high infant mortality many fathers were succeeded by only one son, and partly because after sons had inherited uneconomic small parcels, one would buy up his brothers' shares, so reconstituting a holding of viable size.[17] The land market can therefore be seen to have both prevented and caused the parcellization of holdings.

In a society influenced by a free market there would have been a 'centrifugal tendency', flinging more land into the hands of fewer successful families, leaving a growing majority of poor cottagers. This did not happen fully in the period 1200–1350. The middling layers of the peasantry persisted, and very large units of over 50 acres were scarce. Family loyalties, the pressure of the village community and the lord's interest in having a numerous middling tenantry all conspired to inhibit the full impact of market forces.

Having examined changes in the size of holdings, can we generalize about long-term trends? Recorded tenements diminished in size, with a different pace depending on the region. In the west, at Taunton, the amount of land per head fell from 3.3 acres in 1248 to 2.5 acres in 1311, representing a significant but not precipitate fall. On the Westminster Abbey estate in the midlands and the home counties, 48 per cent of tenants held 10 acres or less in the early thirteenth century, compared with more than a half, sometimes three-quarters, in the early fourteenth. For a dramatic change we

---

16 Williamson, 'Norfolk', pp. 94–101; Z. Razi, *Life, marriage and death in a medieval parish. Economy, society and demography in Halesowen, 1270–1400* (Cambridge, 1980), pp. 56–62.
17 Williamson, 'Norfolk', pp. 83, 102–5; Smith, 'Redgrave, Suffolk', pp. 135–95; F. R. H. Du Boulay, *The Lordship of Canterbury* (London, 1966), pp. 147–9.

must turn again to the volatile peasant society of East Anglia, where at Martham in 1220 18 per cent of tenants had holdings below 2 acres, and the proportion had grown to 60 per cent by 1292.[18] Perhaps such figures should lead us to appreciate the economic vitality of East Anglia, where a minority made a fortune from commodity production, while the rest had opportunities for wage-earning, craft work, fishing and turf digging. Or perhaps such rapid change should be seen as evidence of an over-heated economy fuelled by desperation, in which poor people sold parcels of land to keep themselves alive for another year.

We must also consider whether the land problem was alleviated by internal colonization and the leasing of demesnes. An impressive amount of new land was won from forest and marsh in the thirteenth century. Enquiries into encroachments on royal forests reveal totals of 780 acres in Rockingham Forest (Northamptonshire) in 1255, or 485 acres at Cannock (Staffordshire) in 1286. Drainage projects added 50 square miles to nine parishes in south Lincolnshire between 1170 and 1240.[19] However, this land was distributed among thousands of peasant households, and the large-scale clearances were restricted to a limited number of localities. The peasants of Bishop's Cleeve, for example, had assarted vigorously in the twelfth century, but no land was left for further clearance in the thirteenth, unless they were to lose more of their precious pasture and wood. Sometimes assarts were added to the land-holdings of wealthier peasants, as at Wakefield (Yorkshire) where many early fourteenth-century assarters were tenants with an oxgang or more.[20] The clearance of new land encouraged the proliferation of smallholdings, as better-off peasants acquired assarts to endow their children, and the assarts were sold off and broken down into smaller units. Demesne lands are found in the thirteenth century in the hands of tenants of those old-fashioned estates, like that of Worcester Cathedral Priory, where demesnes continued to be held on short leases by whole

---

18 J. Z. Titow, 'Some evidence of the thirteenth-century population increase', *Ec.H.R.*, 2nd ser., 14 (1961), 218–23; B. Harvey, *Westminster Abbey and its estates in the middle ages* (Oxford, 1977), pp. 213, 435–7; Williamson, 'Norfolk', p. 70.

19 C. R. Young, *The royal forests of medieval England* (Leicester, 1979), p. 121; J. R. Birrell, 'Medieval agriculture' in *V.C.H. Staffordshire*, vol. 6, p. 7; H. E. Hallam, *The new lands of Elloe* (University of Leicester, Dept of English Local History Occasional Papers, 6, 1954), p. 41.

20 M. Stinson, 'Assarting and poverty in early fourteenth-century west Yorkshire', *Landscape History*, 5 (1983), 53–67.

Table 9. *Mean yield ratios on the estate of the bishopric of Winchester,*
1209–1453

Date	Wheat	Barley	Oats
1209–70	3.85	4.32	2.63
1271–99	3.79	3.36	2.21
1300–24	3.90	3.57	2.21
1325–49	3.96	3.74	2.25
1349–80	3.66	3.53	2.43
1381–1410	3.88	4.13	2.93
1411–53	3.66	3.64	3.03

Source note: D. L. Farmer, 'Grain yields on the Winchester manors in the later middle ages', *Ec.H.R.*, 2nd ser., 30 (1977), 560

village communities. A growing quantity of land was leased out to tenants in parcels by lords of all kinds when the estate managers calculated that the rent income would be higher or more stable than the profits of direct agricultural exploitation. On the estates of the bishopric of Winchester, 5,000 acres were leased between 1270 and 1350.[21] There is a widespread suspicion that the new land acquired by the peasantry from wastes and from demesnes was of poor quality.

To sum up, the Bishop's Cleeve peasants can be seen to be not untypical, except that in other parts of England, especially in the east, smallholdings were even more numerous. In the Cleeve survey of 1299, 42 per cent of holdings were of less than a half-yardland. The average from surveys and the Hundred Rolls varied between 42 and 45 per cent, and in East Anglia the figure was nearer to 80 per cent. The surveys may give a false picture because of the prevalence of subletting, and if we estimate the size of holdings actually worked rather than that officially recorded the national figure for smallholdings would probably rise above 50 per cent. If the rural population of England in 1300 is estimated at 5 millions, living in a million households, then 600,000 of those households (allowing for the high

21 R. H. Hilton, *A medieval society*, 2nd edn (Cambridge, 1983), p. 153; E. Miller and J. Hatcher, *Medieval England: rural society and economic change, 1086–1348* (London, 1978), p. 244.

proportion of the population in eastern England), depended on smallholdings. Demographic growth had contributed to this problem.

The productivity of peasant agriculture

One method of assessing the success of agriculture is to calculate cereal yields, of which the best series, from the demesnes of the bishopric of Winchester, is summarized in table 9. The first conclusion to be drawn must be to note the low level of productivity. The wheat yield stayed just below four times the seed sown, compared with a figure of ten in the eighteenth century and twenty in the twentieth. The other observation is that yields were declining in the thirteenth century. The pronounced fall of barley, which was more sensitive to the soil's loss of fertility, may be a significant indication of the damaging effects of over-cultivation. The slight recovery in the early fourteenth century followed the leasing-out of part of the demesne, perhaps the least fertile part, to peasant tenants.[22]

Various explanations can be offered for the low yields on demesnes. The land lacked manure because there was a shortage of pasture and animals. The demesnes were ill-managed: weeding was neglected, and the labour force stole corn and lacked motivation.[23] When better yields were achieved they sometimes reflect special circumstances, like the wheat yields of ten and sixteen at Little Humber in Holderness (Yorkshire) in the 1280s, harvested after the old sheep pastures, manured and rested for many years, were ploughed up in the great sheep scab epidemic. Other cases point to the superiority of different agrarian systems resulting from policy rather than mere chance. On the Battle Abbey estate in Sussex the conventional rotations were ignored, and a number of years of continuous cropping were followed by a period under grass, resembling the 'up-and-down' husbandry of later centuries. Later in the fourteenth century, thick sowings smothered the weeds and enabled wheat to yield 12 or 13 bushels per acre, significantly better than the Winchester figures which usually fell below 10 bushels. Yields per acre as high as 20 bushels were achieved in north-east Norfolk, where fallows were virtually eliminated, labour intensive methods such as repeated ploughings were employed, and much

22 J. Z. Titow, *Winchester yields* (Cambridge, 1972), pp. 1–33.
23 T. H. Aston, 'The external administration and resources of Merton College, to *c.*1348' in J. I. Catto (ed.), *The history of the University of Oxford*, vol. 1 (Oxford, 1984), pp. 322–3, 341–9.

attention was given to manuring by the folding of sheep and even carrying muck by boat from Norwich.[24]

All of the information about corn yields given so far derive from demesnes, because they are recorded abundantly in manorial accounts. Did peasant holdings produce comparable yields? There are grounds for assuming a general similarity, because demesne land and peasant holdings adjoined one another in the same fields. Information from tithes suggests that peasants grew much the same crops as the lords, though with some significant variations. In many west midland examples, including Cleeve, the peasants grew more barley, which yielded higher than other crops, so that all else being equal, peasant holdings would have produced a little more grain. However, all else was not equal. If the key factor in keeping down demesne yields was the unenthusiastic attitude of the work-force, then peasant yields might be expected to have been superior, as the peasants were cultivating their own crops for their own benefit. Also peasant households, especially those cultivating smaller holdings, would be better able than the demesne managers to cultivate intensively, by repeated weeding for example. The peasants' disadvantages lay in their smaller supplies of manure, because of the limited numbers of animals. Those that they did own were often folded on the lord's demesne, so the lord's land gained most benefit from the muck. Peasant efforts to use household refuse on the fields would benefit only a few acres each year, judging from the archaeological evidence for the concentration of such manuring in the vicinity of settlements. By the terms of a lease between two Cambridgeshire tenants in 1311, land was to be manured, 1/2 acre at a time, only once in every five years.[25] Peasant farming equipment, draught power and storage facilities were all inferior to those of the demesnes. And peasants might have been taken away from their holdings at critical times to perform labour services. Direct information about peasant yields comes from the mid- to late-fourteenth century, but is still worth quoting here. A reeve of Hampton Lucy

24 M. Mate, 'Profit and productivity on the estates of Isabella de Forz (1260–92)', *Ec.H.R.*, 2nd ser., 33 (1980), 332–3; E. Searle, *Lordship and community. Battle Abbey and its banlieu 1066–1538* (Toronto, 1974), pp. 272–86; P. F. Brandon, 'Cereal yields on the Sussex estates of Battle Abbey during the later middle ages', *Ec.H.R.*, 2nd ser., 25 (1972), 403–20; B. M. S. Campbell, 'Agricultural progress in medieval England: some evidence from eastern Norfolk', *Ec.H.R.*, 2nd ser., 36 (1983), 26–46.

25 J. G. Hurst, 'The Wharram research project: results to 1983', *Med. Arch.*, 28 (1984), 99; Cambridge U.L., EDR c8/1.

Table 10. *Number of animals per tax-payer or per tenant, 1225–91*

	Horses and oxen	Cattle	Sheep	Pigs
Wiltshire, 1225	1.8	2.8	15.6	0.3
Blackbourne Hundred, Suffolk, 1283	1.0	3.2	10.5	1.4
Liberty of Ramsey, 1291	2.35	4.5	6.2	3.8
Mickleover, Derbyshire, 1280	1.7	1.25	12.6	1.9

Source note: M. M. Postan, 'Village livestock in the thirteenth century' in M. M. Postan, *Essays on medieval agriculture and general problems of the medieval economy* (Cambridge, 1973), pp. 214–48; J. F. R. Walmsley, 'The estate of Burton Abbey from the eleventh to the fourteenth centuries' (University of Birmingham Ph.D. thesis, 1972), pp. 234–5

(Warwickshire), the tenants of Bourton-on-the-Hill who died in 1349 and a serf of Chevington (Suffolk) who fled in 1371 all left their crops to be harvested by their respective lords and consequently to be recorded. Their grain yielded rather less than the demesnes, in the first case 8 bushels per acre for wheat, and 13½ bushels for drage, in the second less than 8 bushels for all crops, and in the third 8 bushels per acre for both wheat and oats.[26]

Demesne yields may give a guide to peasant returns, and help us to understand regional variations in the peasant economy. At first sight, the peasant of north-east Norfolk with 5 acres was much poorer than a Gloucestershire half-yardlander. But if the Norfolk peasant managed his holding in the same fashion as his lord's demesne, as part of the local agrarian system, then he grew crops on the whole holding every year, and even if his yields were 20 per cent lower than those of the lord, the peasant could still harvest 10 quarters, or enough to provide next year's seed and most of his family's food needs.

Peasant farming depended on a combination of productive activities. Animals contributed food, cash, pulling power and manure. Their value depended crucially on their numbers. Table 10 gives some examples of assessments for subsidies, and of stock confiscated from some Derbyshire peasants by their landlord. The subsidies

26 R. H. Hilton, *The English peasantry in the later middle ages* (Oxford, 1975), p. 202; Westminster Abbey Muniments, 8282; Suffolk R.O. (Bury St Edmunds branch), E3/15.3/1.15.

must be treated with suspicion because of their tendency to under-count. The most reliable are likely to be the earliest, before the peasants learnt the skills of evasion. The averages relate only to those more prosperous peasants who fell within the net of taxation (by the end of the thirteenth century, less than half of households), and averaging conceals a wide variety in animal ownership. Take the very early assessments for Wiltshire, when evasion may have been least prevalent. At West Hatch in 1225 William atte Putte was assessed on a mare, six oxen, four cows, four younger cattle, a pig and fifty-two sheep. Two other tax-payers owned more, and the other eighteen in the village much less, down to Sybil the widow with only two cows. All of the 233 sheep assessed for taxation belonged to the three leading tax-payers, leaving the rest looking very poorly endowed.[27] The small quantity of stock implied by the tax records are confirmed by other sources, such as stints (restric-tions on the number of grazing animals) declared in villages anxious to prevent overburdening of pastures, which might limit a yardlan-der to forty sheep and three cattle. If the poorest tax-payer owned only a cow or two, we can infer that many of those exempt from tax owned no animals at all. This is confirmed by records of heriot payment where as many as 40 per cent of the tenants dying or surrendering their holdings in the late thirteenth and first half of the fourteenth century had no 'best beast', not even a sickly sheep or decrepit pig, that could be seized for the lord's profit. Our con-clusion must be that in much of lowland England, including areas now regarded as sheep country, such as the Wiltshire Downs, the peasant flocks and herd were insufficient to contribute fully to the fertility of the arable.

A couple of cows and a pig would make a valuable supplement, if on a small scale, to the peasant family's diet. The significant earnings from wool sales would be confined to a few leading villagers like William atte Putte. The Bishop's Cleeve yardlanders were especially fortunate because they had access to an area of hill pasture, and their Cotswold wool fetched a high price. In the lowlands of Oxfordshire, by contrast, sheep-keeping was limited by the lack of pasture, and fleeces in the 1280s, for example, fetched only 4s. or 5s. per stone compared with 6s. for the Cotswold product.[28] Peasants in much of

---

27 F. A. and A. P. Cazel (eds.), *Rolls of the fifteenth and rolls of the fortieth* (Pipe Roll Soc., new ser., 45, 1976–7), pp. 70–1.

28 T. H. Lloyd, *The movement of wool prices in medieval England* (Ec.H.R. Supplement, 6, 1973), pp. 38–44.

lowland England were limited by their agrarian system, which was designed to produce as much grain as possible. A more pastoral economy is found on the uplands of the Pennines, on the moors of the south-west, and in the fens of eastern England. In the Cambridgeshire fens, flocks of 200 and 300 sheep are recorded in the early fourteenth century and even cottagers owned ten, twenty and fifty sheep: Adam Buk of Downham, with a holding of 8 acres, in 1328 asked permission to have a fold separate from the lord's for 120 sheep.[29]

The emphasis on cereals also limited the cultivation of other crops. Even in areas of relatively large-scale apple, vegetable and flax growing in parts of Suffolk and Hampshire, the proportion of tithe revenues from such crops rarely exceeded 6 per cent of the total.[30] Similarly peasants collected from commons and wastes, wild plants such as furze, broom, heather and thorns, or sedge, rushes, reeds and osiers in the fens, mainly for use on their holdings but also sometimes for sale. These resources were limited and quarrels broke out when individuals took more than their share. We would be mistaken to assume that there was much free food in extensively cultivated and heavily-grazed lowland England where, for example, rabbits lived in a state of semi-domestication under the close protection of lords. The fens were again unusual in the large amounts of fish available for peasant communities.

Evidence of assarting and tithe revenues suggests that the thirteenth century saw a long-term shift from pastoral to arable farming, encouraged by such short-term disasters as the late thirteenth-century sheep diseases.

Non-agricultural sources of income

The numerous smallholders of thirteenth-century England depended on sources of income additional to their own agricultural production. Employment in agriculture came primarily from the largest productive units, the lords' demesnes. They had originally relied for ploughmen, carters, shepherds and dairy-maids on a category of peasants who were liable to serve continuously as a condition

29 J. Ravensdale, *Liable to floods. Village landscape on the edge of the fens A.D. 450–1850* (Cambridge, 1974), p. 75; M. C. Coleman, *Downham-in-the-Isle. A study of an ecclesiastical manor in the thirteenth and fourteenth centuries* (Woodbridge, 1984), pp. 59–61.

30 *Nonarum inquisitiones* (Record Commission, 1807), pp. 63–105, 126–7.

of their tenure. In the thirteenth and early fourteenth century these were often replaced by full-time farm servants, called *famuli*, who were hired by the year, in numbers that varied on each manor from as few as four to as many as thirty, depending on the size of the demesne.[31] In addition on demesnes which lacked labour services, workers were employed by the day for tasks such as threshing, hay-making and harvesting. Specialist work on the buildings of the manor, or the iron-work of the ploughs and carts, was often done by hired craftsmen. Rectors would provide employment, both agricultural work on the glebe, and domestic service. Within the peasant community the presence of living-in servants was regarded as so commonplace that they were stated in descriptions of labour services as being liable to accompany the rest of the household to help with the lords' harvest boons. The temporary employment of poor villagers at harvest was mentioned in village bye-laws that set out their rates of pay. Village communities acted as employers of common herdsmen, and through the church-wardens the parishioners hired labour to work on the church.

Industrial and craft work were widely spread through peasant society. Many villages had a smith or a carpenter. Textile workers were dispersed in the southern and eastern counties where consumers were plentiful and, judging from the numbers of fulling mills built by lords, in relatively thinly-populated pastoral areas like the Lake District. The frequent finds of spindle whorls in excavations on village sites show that spinning yarn with a distaff (an activity that could be combined with other jobs about the house or holding) was an almost universal practice among peasant women. Food-processing and above all brewing for sale went on everywhere, and provided more employment than any other trade. Large-scale industrial employment was often localized, like the tin-mining and smelting which occupied as many as one in ten of the population of Cornwall. Industries were often sited in uplands and woodlands, so that many peasants with holdings of poor land, or who depended on pastoral farming, were able to make up their slender profits from agriculture. The woods themselves provided an environment for a wide range of crafts, for potters, glass-makers, coopers, turners, wheelers, cartwrights, fletchers (arrow-makers), bow-makers and charcoal burners. Likewise coastal and fenland villages, or those on the banks of major rivers, could profit from fishing on a commercial scale. Many of these occupations were seasonal, so that mining

31 M. M. Postan, *The famulus* (Ec.H.R. Supplement, 2, 1954).

would take place in the early summer or fishing in the winter and spring, which would allow those involved to return to the land for the harvest or planting.[32]

Were these varied activities sufficient to provide work for the hundreds of thousands of thirteenth-century smallholders? Individual craftsmen can often be shown to have held only small acreages, like the potters of Crockerton (Wiltshire), most of whom held 4 acres each. One of the regular brewers of Redgrave (Suffolk), Reginald Warrenner, who also sold bread, was otherwise dependent on an acre of land. A high proportion of brewers were single women, including many widows.[33]

Three problems faced smallholders in their efforts to make a living. Firstly, there was fierce competition for employment. Even those with larger holdings entered the labour market as miners, craftsmen and agricultural wage-earners, and their equipment, such as carts, must always have given them advantages over the cottagers. Secondly, the quantity of employment and the demand for goods and services were severely limited. In many villages, unlike Cleeve and Ducklington, half-yardlanders formed the upper layer of peasants; of these only a minority would need hired labour. There was a limited demand for manufactured goods, and English industry was underdeveloped in relation to that of the continent; in particular English cloth-making seems to have been stagnating or even in retreat until the early fourteenth century. And thirdly, as a consequence of the large pool of labour, rates of pay were very low at the end of the thirteenth century, with unskilled workers often earning no more than 1d. per day, and full-time *famuli* commonly received annually 2s. to 5s. in cash and 4½ to 6½ quarters of cheap corn, which was barely enough to keep a family alive without income from land or a wife's employment. The rewards of trades such as potting must have been similarly meagre. The multiplicity of small-scale food and drink retailers, as in the modern third world, indicates the wide-

32 E. Carus-Wilson, 'An industrial revolution of the thirteenth century' in E. Carus-Wilson, *Medieval merchant venturers* (London, 1967), pp. 183–210; E. Miller, 'The fortunes of the English textile industry during the thirteenth century', *Ec.H.R.*, 2nd ser., 18 (1965), 64–82; A. R. Bridbury, *Medieval English clothmaking* (London, 1982), pp. 16–26; J. Hatcher, *English tin production and trade before 1550* (Oxford, 1973), pp. 43–88; J. R. Birrell, 'Peasant craftsmen in the medieval forest', *Ag.H.R.*, 17 (1969), 91–107.

33 H. E. J. Le Patourel, 'Documentary evidence and the medieval pottery industry', *Med. Arch.*, 12 (1968), 105; R. M. Smith, 'Kin and neighbours in a thirteenth-century Suffolk community', *Journal of Family History*, 4 (1979), 245.

spread poverty that drove people into an activity which yielded at least some small profit.

The size of the family

In turning from income to expenditure, the numbers of mouths to be fed was one of the main variables in a peasant's budget. Peasant households were once thought to have been large and extended, containing married brothers or three generations living together. Now it is believed that the great majority of peasant households were simple, containing a nuclear family of husband, wife and children. According to one serf census from Lincolnshire in 1268–9, the average family size was 4.68 persons. Brothers sometimes shared a household, and retired people commonly lived with their heir or an unrelated younger successor, but these tended to be short-term arrangements, part of a cycle, and therefore affecting a small minority of households at any one time. Also, family sizes varied with wealth. At Halesowen it has been argued that around 1300 the better-off peasants would have an average of five children and the poorest only two.[34] In the light of this information, in our budget calculations we should perhaps have assigned Robert le Kyng, the yardlander, another child or two, and John le Gavisare one less. Smallholders would have had few children because they married late (reflecting their low earnings), and because their children were more likely to die in infancy.

Food consumption

The food needs of a peasant family have been estimated at 11,000 calories per day, on the basis of the modern recommendation that an adult male needs 2,900, a female 2,150, and the three children about 6,000. It is thought, again on the basis of analyses of modern foods, that this would be provided by an annual 6 quarters 5 bushels of grain, made up of wheat, barley and oats as indicated in table 7, eaten as bread and pottage, which would provide about 9,000 calories per

34 H. E. Hallam, 'Some thirteenth-century censuses', *Ec.H.R.*, 2nd ser., 10 (1957), 340–61; R. M. Smith, 'Some reflections on the evidence for the origins of the European marriage pattern in England' in C. Harris (ed.), *The family* (Sociology Review Monograph, 28, 1979), pp. 74–112; Razi, *Life, marriage and death*, pp. 83–97.

day, the other 2,000 coming from two flitches of bacon each year, milk and cheese from a cow, garden produce, and ale brewed from an annual 3 quarters of barley. All of these calculations are very speculative, of course, but the types of grain consumed, and the ratio of bread/pottage to other foodstuffs is based on thirteenth-century evidence (see table 13 and fig. 4). The numbers of calories can be debated. The allowances are for 'moderately' rather than 'very' active people, on the assumption that medieval agricultural work involved great surges of effort interspersed with episodes of enforced idleness. They may have needed less calories because they were of slightly smaller stature than ourselves.[35]

Rents and taxes

A high proportion of labour services had been commuted for cash by the late thirteenth century, and surveys give a cash value for services, so we can attempt to use money as a basis for comparing tenant obligations. The Bishop's Cleeve customary tenants paid rents, estimated above at about 26s. per yardland, at a rather higher rate than most of their contemporaries, but payments were often made up of much the same elements. The fixed annual rent of assize, which often included commuted labour services, could be as low as 7s. or as high as 40s. per yardland, with the majority falling between 10s. and 20s. Contributions to dues such as common fines and tallages usually added a few shillings to the individual tenant's total. Many other payments were occasional and variable. Entry fines, paid when the tenant took up a new holding, could be set by custom at a few shillings, or more commonly depended on the demand for land and the 'will of the lord', and could rise above £2, even up to £10, £20 and more. Recognition fines were paid to acknowledge the arrival of a new lord. Heriots were often defined as the best beast, but in the north midlands lords took a number of animals and chattels when a tenant died. Every tenant was liable to amercement in the manor courts at 2d. to 6d. for each offence. Such was the all-embracing character of the jurisdiction of the courts that almost everyone was liable to pay an amercement at least once a year, and often they

35 On recommended intakes: Department of Health and Social Security, *Recommended daily amounts of food energy and nutrients for groups of people in the United Kingdom* (London, 1979), pp. 6–7; on food values, see the appendix to C. Dyer, 'Changes in diet in the late middle ages: the case of harvest workers', *Ag.H.R.*, 36 (1988), 21–37; on stature, M. W. Beresford and J. G. Hurst, *Deserted medieval villages* (London, 1971), p. 135.

mounted up to sizeable sums. Tolls were levied on the sale of ale or draught animals. Tenants paid multure for having their corn ground at the mill, and contributed extra rents for access to pastures or parcels of demesne. Serfs owed payments on marriage (*merchet*), for fornication (*leyrwite* and *childwite*) and for absence from the manor (*chevage*).

Smallholders contributed more proportionately than tenants of half-yardlands and full yardlands, often paying 1s. per acre (taking all payments together) whereas yardlanders paid from 4d. to 10d. per acre. Free tenants averaged 1d. to 2d. per acre, and had few additional dues, apart from a relatively low and fixed relief payable when they took over a new holding. In the south, assize rents accounted for a higher proportion of tenant payments than in the north, where mill tolls, tallage and court profits often bulked larger in the tenants' obligations.[36]

The level of customary rents and the proportion of unfree tenants depended on at least three variable factors. Firstly, the local traditions might protect tenants, even those on the estates of strong lords. The total of rent paid in Kent, where customs guaranteed the personal freedom of the inhabitants, was often no more than 3d. or 4d. per acre.[37] Secondly, the power of the lord, especially power applied continuously over many generations, enabled large and ancient churches to make greater demands on their tenants than did the gentry. The Crown was the least oppressive lord of all, and unfree peasants envied the low rents and extensive privileges of the peasants on the king's manors. The third influence derived from the local economy. Lords tended to have more control over close-knit arable communities than over the scattered pastoralists of woodlands and uplands. Also peasants favourably placed to benefit from the market, or from fertile land, might have to pay relatively high rents. Entry fines and variable payments might be pushed up by competition for land, and a serf's dues were often adjusted according to the lord's judgement of his capacity to pay.[38]

Did rents make serious inroads into the income of peasants? The accepted view has maintained that rents depended on the lord's power, and that therefore lords were able to demand payments according to their needs and above market levels. An alternative

36 E. A. Kosminsky, *Studies in the agrarian history of England in the thirteenth century* (Oxford, 1956), pp. 244–5; Harvey, *Westminster Abbey*, pp. 444–6.
37 Du Boulay, *Lordship of Canterbury*, pp. 179–80.
38 R. H. Hilton, *The decline of serfdom in medieval England* (London, 1969), pp. 17–26.

argument suggests that customary rents were actually below the 'market rate', so that for example in one Gloucestershire village in the late thirteenth century the customary tenants paid 8·7d. per acre, while leasehold rents negotiated according to the laws of supply and demand varied from 9d. to 3s. So the argument goes that if holders on lease were prepared to pay such high sums, then the villeins had a good bargain. The customs under which the villeins held their land were not adjustable at the lord's whim, but protected the tenant against the chill winds of market forces.[39] A number of objections can be made to this opinion. Firstly, a great deal of leasehold land was let on rents below the rate for customary land.[40] In any case, leasehold land was in such short supply on many manors (because the area in customary and free tenure took up most of the tenant land), that the rent reflected a scarcity value. We just do not know the level of 'economic rent' for land because in a society influenced by lordship, custom, patronage and other non-economic forces, the 'pure' market had limited scope for operation. Secondly, we must note the effort of lords in the thirteenth century to prove their rights over villeins. In the previous century there had been a large number of tenants owing labour service whose precise legal status was in doubt. From about 1180 lawyers applied a series of tests to establish whether peasants were servile or free. An obligation to do a regular two, three or four days' work each week, or to pay marriage fines or tallage would be used to prove servility. At the end of the process about a half of the rural population had been classified as unfree. Disputes continued to come before the courts throughout the thirteenth and early fourteenth century.[41] We must presume that the lords thought that there were material advantages in establishing their rights over their serfs, especially in the rents and dues that they could exact. Thirdly, the behaviour of the tenants indicated a similar (if opposite) appreciation of the economics of serfdom. Groups of servile tenants and individuals hired lawyers to fight cases in the royal courts against the lord's assertion of their unfree status. Individuals bargained with their lord for a concession of their holdings at a fixed leasehold rent, for which the tenant was prepared to pay a

39 J. Hatcher, 'English serfdom and villeinage: towards a reassessment', *P. and P.*, 90 (1981), 3–39.

40 Harvey, *Westminster Abbey*, pp. 234–7, 444–6.

41 R. H. Hilton, 'Freedom and villeinage in England' in R. H. Hilton (ed.), *Peasants, knights and heretics* (Cambridge, 1976), pp. 174–91. For an alternative view, P. R. Hyams, *Kings, lords and peasants in medieval England* (Oxford, 1980), pp. 221–65.

substantial premium. A common theme that runs through both the legal disputes and the more peaceable bargains is the tenants' dislike of the variable dues – heriots, entry fines, tallage, marriage fines, and recognitions – which they hoped to remove through the law or to buy off with a single lump sum.[42] Evidently they felt that regular and fixed payments of rents were more acceptable than unexpected and fluctuating payments. These dues increased as the market and the lord's needs expanded. For example, on the Ramsey Abbey estate the rate of entry fine rose from 20s. per yardland in the 1250s to 66s. 8d. in the period 1303–10.[43] As our budget calculations have suggested, the death of a tenant, because of the exactions of heriots and entry fines, could have a more damaging effect than a very bad harvest. The enviable characteristic of free tenure lay in the certainty of the obligations as well as their overall low level. If contemporaries felt that the rents and dues of customary tenants were important enough to spend good money on disputing or proving their legality, who are we to question their judgement?

Similarly, some seek to minimize our assessment of the impact on the peasantry of royal taxes. The main type of direct tax, the lay subsidy, even after it had become established as the main source of finance for war towards the end of the thirteenth century, was not levied every year. Although the tax was imposed from outside, the assessors were local people who understood their neighbours' circumstances. After 1334 the degree of local control increased when each village was assigned a quota of tax and decided among themselves how to levy the money. A combination of official exemption and bending of the rules by local assessors meant that most people were deemed too poor to contribute. Only about 40 per cent of the peasantry paid, and in any case, they contributed an affordable 2s. or so, the price of a sheep or a quarter of oats.

In fact there are a number of reasons for regarding the tax burden as a significant one for the peasantry. The incidence of taxes rose at a time when economic growth was ending, and the years of tax demands sometimes coincided with bad harvests like those of the 1290s. The taxes were also combined with levies of local troops, and of purveyance (requisitioning of goods for which in-

---

42 R. H. Hilton, 'Peasant movements in England before 1381' in R. H. Hilton, *Class conflict and the crisis of feudalism* (London, 1985), pp. 122–38; R. H. Hilton, 'Gloucester Abbey leases of the late thirteenth century' in Hilton, *English peasantry*, pp. 139–60.

43 J. A. Raftis, *The estates of Ramsey Abbey* (Toronto, 1957), pp. 237–8.

adequate payment was made). There were complaints that the taxes were assessed and levied unfairly, and that bribes had to be paid.[44] The poor were not exempt from the indirect effects of the taxes. Villages were economic communities, and the removal of a quantity of cash from the better-off peasants must have left them with less to spend on the services and goods provided by their poorer neighbours. All peasants must have been under extra pressure from their lords, who needed more rent money to pay their taxes. The competition for the peasants' money between the lords and the state lies behind the complaints by grumbling magnates that if pressed too hard by the king, the people might rebel.

Demands for taxation from 1290 onwards, reaching a peak in 1332–41, imposed an extra burden on the peasantry, especially on half-yardlanders who owned just enough animals to be included among the tax-payers, but who could ill afford an extra shilling on top of other commitments. Nor should we forget that some villages suffered directly from the wars, which provoked Scottish raids deep into northern England from the 1320s. For example, fifty-four places in the Carlisle area were reported as seriously impoverished after the Scottish raid of 1345.[45]

We have now examined the various elements that went into the budget calculations for the Bishop's Cleeve peasants. It can be seen how risky were some of the figures used in the budgets, and how much of the information is uncertain, such as the way in which subletting affected the size of holdings, or whether peasant and demesne crops produced similar yields. The budgets have been offered as a balance of probabilities rather than proven certainties. The Cleeve example is not in any sense typical of the rest of England because each area had its own farming system. Other midland villages often had less pasture than was available to the Cleeve peasants, but they did not have to pay so much rent. In north-east Norfolk the holdings were tiny compared with those in Gloucestershire, but the land was worked more intensively, there were more sources of paid employment, and rents were lower. It is difficult to tell if one region had a poorer peasantry than another, though the peasantries were certainly different. Most of the changes in the thirteenth and early fourteenth century did not favour the peasants,

44 Maddicott, *Demands of the Crown, passim.*
45 H. J. Hewitt, *The organization of war under Edward III* (Manchester, 1966), pp. 126–30.

because holdings were becoming smaller, the pastoral element more restricted, and rents and taxes higher. High grain prices benefited a minority with a saleable surplus, and even their profits were reduced if yields declined. The gloomiest prospects faced the smallhold-ers, whose earnings were low and costs high. A combination of circumstances from the 1320s brought lower grain prices, a serious decline in arable cultivation, and industrial growth, pointing the way towards a new age.[46]

1350–1520

After the famine of 1315–18, in which 10–15 per cent of the peasantry in some villages died, the population in different places either con-tinued to decline, or climbed back. The plague epidemic of 1348–9 caused a virulent and universal mortality, killing about a half of the population. Recovery was prevented by a succession of epidemics of plague and other diseases. A reduction of the birth-rate contributed also to the decline and long-term stagnation of the population, which showed signs of recovery after 1470 but did not grow again until after 1520 (see fig. 1).[47] The conventional interpretation of this period is to attribute most social and economic developments to the shortage of people.

The peasantry did not merely react to changes in their environ-ment. The falling birth-rate suggests that they behaved in unpredict-able ways in new circumstances, not immediately replacing the losses from disease, but maintaining the advantages enjoyed by the survivors of the plagues. Social relationships between lords and tenants, and between masters and servants, did not naturally adjust themselves in the light of the shortage of peasants and workers, but were changed by the assertiveness of the lower orders. Agrarian systems could be modified only through conscious decisions by peasants. We will look firstly at the variable factors, and then return to reconstruct Cleeve budgets again.

---

46 A. R. H. Baker, 'Evidence in the *Nonarum Inquisitiones* of contracting arable lands in England during the early fourteenth century', *Ec.H.R.*, 2nd ser., 19 (1966), 518–32; Miller and Hatcher, *Medieval England*, pp. 240–51.
47 L. R. Poos, 'The rural population of Essex in the later middle ages', *Ec.H.R.*, 2nd ser., 38 (1985), 515–30; J. Hatcher, *Plague, population and the English economy, 1348–1530* (London, 1977), *passim*; J. Z. Titow, *English rural society 1200–1350* (London, 1969), pp. 70–1; Dyer, *Lords and peasants*, pp. 218–35; J. Hatcher, 'Mortality in the fifteenth century: some new evidence', *Ec.H.R.*, 2nd ser., 39 (1986), 19–38.

Table 11. *Long-term changes in the size of holdings*

Holywell, Huntingdonshire (free and customary holdings only in 1252, customary and leasehold in 1451–7)

	30 acres or more	26–9 acres	18–25 acres	11–17 acres	10 acres or less	total
1252	2	0	18	0	36	56
	(4%)		(32%)		(64%)	(100%)
1451–7	7	1	12	9	20	49
	(14%)	(2%)	(25%)	(18%)	(41%)	(100%)

Stoughton, Leicestershire (free, customary and leasehold in both)

	31 acres or more	24–30 acres	12–23 acres	11 acres or less	total
1341	2	25	3	32	62
	(3%)	(40%)	(5%)	(52%)	(100%)
1477	14	3	3	4	24
	(58%)	(13%)	(13%)	(16%)	(100%)

Source notes: E. B. Dewindt, *Land and people in Holywell-cum-Needingworth* (Toronto, 1972), pp. 56, 114; Bodleian Library MS. Laud misc. 625, fols. 128–31, 191–3

The size of peasant holdings

In the two centuries after 1320 thousands of settlements were abandoned and hundreds of thousands of acres of arable land fell out of cultivation. The population diminished more than the amount of land in productive use, so the quantity per head increased. A peasant wishing to add to the size of his holding could buy land from another tenant, marry a widow, or acquire it directly from a landlord who had been left with holdings 'in his hands' after the death or departure of tenants. Judging from the declining entry fines paid to lords, which virtually disappeared on many manors, holdings could be obtained with relative ease. Lords added to the pool of available land by leasing out their demesnes. Many gentry, merchants and clergy were better provided than peasants with the capital and the managerial skills needed to run such large units, but at least 40 per cent of the new breed of demesne farmers were of peasant origin.[48] Peasants were most likely to take on leases of demesnes when lords chose to split the land into manageable parcels, and some of the demesnes apparently leased as a unit to a gentleman farmer were divided and sublet to peasants.

Who gained from the newly available land, everyone in the peasant community, or only its wealthier members? Table 11 shows long-term changes in the distribution of land in two east midland villages. Holywell typifies a pattern in which the number and proportion of both the middling and upper peasantry increased. Stoughton shows a pronounced decline among the cottagers, and the yardlanders (each with 24 acres) diminished also with a corresponding increase in holdings larger than 30 acres. Holywell looks like a peasant community modestly prospering, with many people remaining as cottagers, while Stoughton seems to be going through a transformation into a society of wealthy yeomen. The larger holdings at Holywell included only two which were in excess of 48 acres, while at Stoughton eleven held 48 acres or more. Both types of development are found all over the country, and the predominant pattern, or the reasons for the divergence, are not as yet known. The land-market, involving the rapid transfer of holdings, continued as before the Black Death. In declining villages, newcomers and cottages could easily take on large holdings though these were often assets of doubtful value. In more prosperous places, such as Halesowen, the wealthier villagers had a great advantage in acquiring new land because they had the resources to pay the lord's fine and the vendor's price, and to stock the holding. The large holdings emerged rather slowly, not in the immediate aftermath of the plagues but over two or three generations. At Forncett in Norfolk, for example, the largest holdings did not appear until the middle of the fifteenth century.[49] Land circulated from family to family, with sons acquiring smallholdings from their fathers or on their own initiative, and then building up their lands, only to shed parcels later in life. Large holdings were very fragile in the fifteenth century. Peasants put together three, four, or more tenements, only for these

48 J. N. Hare, 'The demesne lessees of fifteenth-century Wiltshire', *Ag.H.R.*, 29 (1981), 1–15 and works cited by him; Harvey, *Westminster Abbey*, pp. 148–63.

49 For example, B. M. S. Campbell, 'Population pressure, inheritance and the land market in a fourteenth-century peasant community' in Smith, *Land, kinship and life-cycle*, pp. 87–134; R. J. Faith, 'Berkshire: fourteenth and fifteenth centuries' in Harvey (ed.), *Land market*, pp. 106–77; F. G. Davenport, *The economic development of a Norfolk manor 1086–1565* (London, 1906), pp. 76–97.

accumulations to break up in the next generation. Only at the end of the fifteenth century or in the early sixteenth did large holdings pass intact from one generation to another. Part of the explanation must lie in the economics of farming.

The productivity of peasant agriculture

Arable yields on lords' demesnes changed in divergent ways according to the accounts, which become meagre after 1400 and rare after 1450. On the great estates, including that of the bishopric of Winchester, the system of cultivation continued, but the low corn prices and increased labour costs discouraged large-scale production, so the sown area diminished. There was more manure, but less weeding or fallow ploughing. The resulting yield ratios are similar to those prevailing before 1349 (see table 9), with a marked improvement after 1376, when there was a run of good weather, but a slip back after 1400 to yields lower than those of the thirteenth century. An alternative approach, followed on the estates of Durham Priory at Elvethall, and on a grange on the Bordesley Abbey estate at Bidford-on-Avon, Warwickshire, as well as on some of the manors of Tavistock Abbey in Devon, such as Hurdwick, was to concentrate labour and manure on a limited area so as to secure higher productivity.[50] The Tavistock monks spent a great deal on beat burning (spreading ash on the land after burning pared-off turf) and carrying loads of sea sand to the fields. The Bordesley managers paid for sheep flocks to be folded on their land. The introduction of more legumes (peas and beans) increased the fertility of the soil. As a result they achieved some of the highest known medieval yields, six to eight times the seed sown.

Which course did the peasants follow? They did not share the lords' problems in the same measure, because they used family labour, but tenants of larger holdings could still have incurred high wage costs. Individual peasants consolidated their holdings, enclosed their lands piecemeal, and adopted new methods.[51] One

50 R. A. Lomas, 'A northern farm at the end of the middle ages: Elvethall Manor, Durham, 1443/4–1513/14', *Northern History*, 18 (1982), 26–53; P.R.O., SC6/1038/4–5; H. P. R. Finberg, *Tavistock Abbey*, 2nd edn (Newton Abbot, 1969), pp. 86–128.

51 For example, H. S. A. Fox, 'The chronology of enclosure and economic development in medieval Devon', *Ec.H.R.*, 2nd ser., 28 (1975), 181–202; C. Dyer, *Warwickshire farming, 1349–c.1520* (Dugdale Soc. Occasional Paper, 27, 1981), pp. 22–35.

strategy was to cultivate a small area intensively and continuously for some years, by concentrating manure on it and including legumes in the rotation. Then, in the classic pattern of 'convertible husbandry', they put the land down to grass, while transferring cultivation to another area. This gave better grazing on the former arable, and grain should have yielded more abundantly after the period under grass. Reliable yield figures are, as always, elusive; John Kent of Stivichall (Warwickshire) may have produced as much as 20 bushels to the acre in 1481, but such isolated examples are too sparse to indicate a trend.

Grazing land expanded as whole fields were turned into pastures, or individual parcels were grassed over as leys within an arable field. More peasants owned animals, to the point that most widows and cottagers had a beast that lords could take as a heriot. At the other end of village society, yeomen owned large flocks and herds – 300 sheep or 20 cattle – which grazed in villages in the midlands where such quantities would have been impossible in the thirteenth century. All of this was potentially good for the peasants' diet, which could include more meat; good for their pockets because of the continued market for animal products; and good for arable production if the manure was well-used.

The route to increased pastoralism was not a smooth one. Perhaps it was easiest in the uplands or woodlands where there had always been more animals. For much of lowland England a new balance had to be struck between arable and pastoral husbandry, often in the context of common fields in which one peasant's expanding sheep flock could do real harm to his neighbours. Villages made and repeated bye-laws seeking to prevent overgrazing by fixing stints and discouraging peasants from taking in outsiders' animals. A typical series of bye-laws from Great Horwood (Buckinghamshire) of 1483–1503 reveals the tensions: tenants were forbidden to put their animals on the common pasture until 29 September, or to cut the hay in the common meadow until the agreed time. Hedges were to be kept in repair, and cattle pastured near to sown crops were to be tethered. There was even an order to keep arable under cultivation.[52]

Perhaps the rules were often broken, but their existence shows that more conservative peasant arable farming continued throughout the period. Nor should we assume that all of the advantages lay with the innovators. They were often frustrated by the limited

---

52 W. O. Ault, *Open-field farming in medieval England* (London, 1972), pp. 134–6.

quantity of common pasture, and the resistance to change of their fellow villagers. It must have been extremely difficult for those who attempted to farm holdings of 50 acres and above to recruit workers, unless they were able to move into large-scale pastoralism, for which less labour was needed. In addition, although the prices of animals and their products held up better than cereal prices, the average price of wool declined from over 4s. per stone in the late fourteenth century to below 3s. in the late fifteenth, and the weights of fleeces declined at the same time.

Non-agricultural sources of income

Every change favoured the wage-earners. They diminished in number, initially because they were especially vulnerable to disease, but also because some of the surviving smallholders were able to take on more land, until they had no need to earn wages. Employment opportunities came from the growing number of large holdings and the demesnes under their new farmers. In a period of acute labour shortage the bargaining position of the employees was greatly improved, and wage-earners won more pay and better conditions, usually preferring short-term engagements at higher pay. Workers became more mobile, and a growing number of smallholders acquired horses to enable them to find work at a distance. Wives and children contributed more to the family income because employers were willing to give them jobs previously done by men.

Industrial employment expanded at this time. Although output in many industries fell, as in the case of lead- and tin-mining, and their labour forces were much reduced, they probably kept in employment a similar proportion of the working population. The numbers of workers in the iron and cloth industries grew, of which the latter in particular employed tens of thousands of part-time rural workers, especially in the regions where the industry was concentrated, such as the south-west, the Cotswolds, west Yorkshire and East Anglia. Of those listed in the 1522 muster of Babergh Hundred, a clothing district of Suffolk, 19 per cent had occupations in the textile and clothing trades, and many more would have found part-time employment, especially women as spinners.[53]

53 J. Pound (ed.), *The military survey of 1522 for Babergh Hundred* (Suffolk Records Soc., 28, 1986), pp. 4–10.

Industrial employment was by no means confined to smallholders, and in clothing, metalworking, fishing and mining districts many households of prosperous husbandmen and yeomen lived on a 'dual economy' in which farming was combined with industry.[54]

The size of the family and its food consumption

Whether because of the high rates of mortality or the lower birthrate the peasant families of the late fourteenth and fifteenth century were considerably smaller than in the period 1250–1350. Figures from serf lists and wills suggest an average of two children, with a small growth in family size in the late fifteenth and early sixteenth century. Nor is there any reason to believe, as happened in southern Europe, that the labour crisis after the Black Death encouraged more complex households in which married sons and daughters remained under the paternal roof. Rather, the new opportunities for employment liberated individuals from family ties, allowing them to move away from home. The direct evidence for food consumption will be discussed in chapter 6. In organizing their budgets peasants were faced with the choice of expanding the quantity and quality of their diet, or of living modestly and investing their surpluses. One plausible interpretation of the period is that the feckless labourers, with no other use for their cash, squandered their earnings on ale and leisure, while a different régime operated among the sober and thrifty tenants of larger holdings.[55]

Rents and taxes

The rent burden was reduced by a fall in annual payments, and by the disappearance of services and extra dues. Statistical analysis is made difficult by changes in the form in which rent was paid, such as the commuting of labour services and the conversion of customary tenure into leasehold. Nor can we be certain that the rent owed by a tenant was really being paid, in view of the mounting totals of arrears that bothered many lords.

Most fifteenth-century tenants were apparently paying rents at

---

54 I. S. W. Blanchard, 'The miner and the agricultural community in late medieval England', *Ag.H.R.*, 20 (1972), 93–106.
55 I. S. W. Blanchard, 'Labour productivity and work psychology in the English mining industry, 1400–1600', *Ec.H.R.*, 2nd ser., 31 (1978), 1–24.

least 20 per cent lower than their predecessors before the Black Death. To what extent did this still represent a real burden? For those who believe that medieval rents were fixed by market forces, the decrease in rent reflects the falling demand for land and the lower profits of cultivation. This is supported by the observation that leasehold rents for pasture behaved differently from arable rents, sometimes even rising when other rents declined.[56] Entry fines, which were sensitive to demand, did not decline in areas enjoying a favourable market for produce, while in some decaying villages rents of individual tenements fell by 50 per cent. However, some of the dues paid to lords declined because of non-economic pressures. Serfdom and servile dues withered away, often because the remaining serfs escaped by migration. The reduction in court profits shows that the lord's political power had diminished. Payments such as recognition fines, tallage and common fines were simply refused by the tenants, who threatened to leave their holdings if payment was enforced.[57] The market situation strengthened the tenants' hands, because they could use as an ultimate sanction flight to lands and jobs available in other villages. But the struggle over rent was a battle of political wills. The lords maintained a high level of rent in the late fourteenth century; this was one of the factors behind the revolt of 1381. They did not give in to the combination of market forces and obstreperous tenants until after 1400, and rents did not reach their lowest level until the middle of the fifteenth century. Because of the inertia of custom, although some leasehold rents responded to economic growth around 1500, payments often remained at their mid-fifteenth century level, below the market rate, and much to the benefit of their tenants. Another advantage of the new arrangements from the tenants' point of view was the greater regularity and consistency of their obligations, most of the uncertain payments having disappeared.

Although developments favoured the tenant, rent must be accounted a significant burden even at its lowest point. Leasehold and customary tenants were still commonly paying 3d. to 9d. per acre, even 1s. per acre when the produce, less seed, could sell for only 4s. 6d. Lords expected payment in cash, which again gave tenants difficulties when the market was slack and coin in short supply, as in

---

56 I. S. W. Blanchard (ed.), *The duchy of Lancaster's estates in Derbyshire* (Derbyshire Archaeological Soc. Record series, 3, 1967), pp. 1–13.

57 C. Dyer, 'A redistribution of incomes in fifteenth-century England?' in Hilton (ed.), *Peasants, knights and heretics*, pp. 192–215.

the middle of the fifteenth century. Free tenants, whose land accounted for almost a half of the total, lay outside this complex combination of economic and social struggles, but in a curious way they lost out. Because their rents were unchangeable, they ironically paid reliefs when entry fines had become tokens. They were still much better-off than customary tenants of course, and joined in the general movement to avoid occasional dues by wriggling out of heriots and reliefs.

While rents failed to decline after the Black Death, the peasants in the years from 1369 to 1381 faced an unprecedented series of demands for taxation. The quotas for the subsidy often remained at the same level as fixed in 1334, which forced the reduced numbers of tax-payers to increase their individual contributions. And the experimental poll taxes of 1377–81 brought the previously exempt smallholders temporarily into the tax system. The poll tax was not repeated after the 1381 revolt, but subsidies were still being demanded (with slightly lower contributions after 1433 and 1446) at irregular intervals until the end of the Hundred Years War in 1453, and more sporadically thereafter, until new assessments and more frequent taxes were introduced by Henry VIII.

Returning to the budget calculations for Cleeve, we can choose our sample from the fifty-three tenants – a half of the 1299 total – listed in a rental of 1475.[58] Our customary yardlander, William Newman of Woodmancote, was one of only two. His land was certainly worked on a three-course rotation (the arrangement was recorded in 1468), but it is most unlikely that he planted as much as Robert le Kyng. We will assume that each year he put 5 acres down to grass as leys, and cultivated 15 acres. If his yields were 20 per cent higher than those of 1299, reflecting the input of manure and the beneficial effects of convertible husbandry, he would have harvested 28 quarters and have 22 quarters left after deducting the seed. His family of two adults and two children, smaller than Robert le Kyng's, would consume 8 quarters in food and drink, and after deducting mill tolls he had almost 14 quarters to sell. Grain prices were 25 per cent lower than in 1299, so this surplus fetched only 47s. on the market. Newman could have kept more stock than Kyng had done because cows could be tethered on his leys, and the common grazing on Cleeve Hill had been increased in the fourteenth century when the hamlet of Wontley had been abandoned and its fields turned to grass (see map

58 Hereford and Worcester R.O., ref. 009:1, BA2636/161 992113 2/6.

2). He could have kept forty-five adult sheep, producing 60 lbs of wool, of which 6 lbs went to the rector as tithe. Cotswold wool had declined in price earlier in the fifteenth century, but as it had recovered in the 1470s it seems reasonable to assign to Newman a profit of 23s., together with 7s. for dairy produce and 15s. from the sale of animals. The assize rent that he paid was (unusually) similar to that of his predecessor, but the extra dues had lapsed, apart from a few amercements. His tithes would have risen with his production of cheese and hay, so he would pay out 26s. from his cash income of £4 12s. 0d., leaving a disposable surplus of £3 6s. 0d. He would have spent much more than Kyng on labour and equipment, because of rising wages and prices of manufactured goods, and he would have used more of his corn than our budget has allowed on animal feed. In the end he would have been only slightly more wealthy in cash terms than a 1299 yardlander. His position was more secure, because there were few really bad harvests, the Crown was no longer demanding taxes to fight foreign wars, and on his death his lord would charge his heir a modest entry fine of perhaps 10s. Robert Smyth, one of the three customary half-yardlanders at Cleeve in 1475, is assumed to have harvested half as much corn as a yardlander, and after deducting seed would have had 11 quarters remaining. If he fed his family on 8 quarters and paid mill toll, the remaining 2 quarters 6 bushels would have given him a return of about 8s. 4d. on the market, with a larger number of animals also contributing a cash income of at least 20s. Rents and tithes cost him about 13s., so he would have been considerably better-off than Henry Benet, his equivalent in 1299.

The most significant change would have been at the bottom of Cleeve society, where John Gamell junior, with a cottage and curtilage, in contrast with John le Gavisare, could have earned enough to buy wheat for his family (5 quarters) in only seventy-five days of employment at 4d. per day. With his wife contributing to earnings, and the produce of their curtilage and a cow on the common pasture, Gamell could have afforded to drink ale and generally live in a way that would have been inconceivable for his forebears.

An important change in Cleeve society lay in the redistribution of land among the peasantry. Some of the former holdings, as we have seen, had been turned over to common grazing. Most had been combined to make larger units, with the result that there were only six tenant holdings of 6 acres or below, compared with twenty-eight in 1299; almost a third of the tenants, sixteen in all, had a yardland or more. Some holdings had become very large, like John Sewell's 96 acres, and Thomas Yardington's 400 acres, by virtue of his lease of the demesne. As we have seen from Newman's budget, these large holdings may not have been very profitable because of the problems of low prices and high labour costs, but their tenants would have enjoyed better living standards in the sense of a plenty of goods, even if they had a limited cash surplus.

The peasant budgets presented here are hypothetical. They involve surmise and estimation, based as much as possible on the evidence. How does the picture that they give compare with the more direct indications of peasant consumption?

6

PEASANTS AS CONSUMERS

—— • ——

This chapter considers direct evidence for peasant food, buildings, possessions, clothes and other items of expenditure. As before we must continue to take account of the stratification of the peasants, their differing regional character, and changes in their standards of living over the three centuries of our enquiry.

FOOD

A typical example of a maintenance agreement, the prime source for peasant diet, arose at Alciston (Sussex) in 1348 from the surrender of two wists of land (the wist was the local version of the yardland) by Godfrey Welshe to his son. Godfrey was retiring, and his son promised in return for the holding to provide for him annually, as long as he lived, 4 bushels of wheat and a quarter of barley.[1] Such contracts provide an uncertain guide to the food actually eaten by peasants. Most of them state simply that the recipient should have 'food and drink' without details, or promise the retired peasant a share of the family meals. Sometimes the grants of corn are described as an alternative to participation in the common diet of the household, which makes them appear as a realistic description of everyday food. However, they also resemble an annuity in kind, as if the retired peasant might use them for sale or exchange. Some of the grants seem so large as to make this explanation of them very likely and

1 East Sussex R.O., Gage 18/6a.

Table 12. *Annual corn allowances in maintenance agreements,*
1240–1458
(analysed by quantity (in bushels))

No. of bushels	Annual allowance of corn given in agreements (sometimes for more than one person)	Annual allowance of corn for individuals, calculated by dividing allowances for couples
1–8	35 (25%)	5 (29%)
9–16	40 (28%)	10 (59%)
17–24	24 (17%)	0
25 or more	42 (30%)	2 (12%)
Total	141 (100%)	17 (100%)

they no doubt were granted by new tenants who were willing to make sacrifices to obtain scarce land. Others are so small that they can have provided no more than a fraction of the peasant's 'pension'. They must have had alternative sources of support, such as small-scale production, or grants from relatives. Even allowances like those in Welshe's agreement must be incomplete, lacking as they do any reference to non-cereal food, perhaps because unwritten custom gave the old person access to a garden or a share of milk from a cow. Most grain allowances in maintenance agreements were apparently intended to provide the basic necessities of life. They varied with the size of the holding, the bargaining power of the retiring tenant, and the additional sources of income available. Some agreements imply that the diet would resemble that of the new tenant's family, or that of the old person previous to retirement, or to some commonly understood norm – 'the common custom of the vill'.

By the terms of 141 agreements (see table 12) dating from 1240 to 1458, with the majority from before 1349, various quantities of corn were promised.[2] The median figure was 1½ quarters (12 bushels), the

2 The maintenance agreements are those cited in C. Dyer, 'English diet in the later middle ages' in T. H. Aston *et al.* (eds.), *Social relations and ideas* (Cambridge, 1983), pp. 198–9, with the following additions: a collection of forty-nine transcripts of agreements by Dr. J. Z. Titow and generously made available to me, from the Pipe Rolls of the bishopric of Winchester (Hampshire R.O.) and Longleat MS. 6369, 10773; E. B. Dewindt (ed.), *The Liber Gersumarum of Ramsey Abbey* (Toronto, 1976), nos. 1,730, 2,768, 3,041, 3,351; C. Howell, *Land, family and inheritance in transition* (Cambridge, 1983), p. 159; M. C. Coleman, *Downham-in-the-Isle. A study of an ecclesiastical manor in the thirteenth and fourteenth centuries* (Woodbridge, 1984), pp. 141–4; Nottingham U.L., Parkyns, Pa D29.

Table 13. *Corn allowances in maintenance agreements, 1240–1458,
analysed by counties, in percentages*
(nos. of agreements contributing to the totals appear after the county)

	Wheat	Maslin	Rye	Barley	Drage	Oats	Bere-mancorn	Peas/beans	Total
Bedfordshire (6)	41	–	–	40	–	5	–	14	100
Cambridgeshire (11)	40	–	4	33	6	–	–	17	100
Essex (18)	73	1	–	2	–	16	–	8	100
Hampshire (35)	36	3	2	48	–	8	1	2	100
Huntingdonshire (7)	51	–	–	21	2	7	–	19	100
Norfolk (5)	–	–	21	74	–	5	–	–	100
Somerset (8)	63	8	2	4	–	10	–	13	100
Suffolk (11)	43	–	–	43	–	–	–	14	100
Surrey (6)	72	–	–	16	–	12	–	–	100
Worcestershire (13)	37	3	11	13	8	24	–	4	100

same as in Godfrey Welshe's agreement. Many of the larger allowances were for two or more people (some of the wealthier recipients
kept a servant), and to gain a better guide to the quantity for an
individual those seventeen agreements stated to be for the upkeep of
a couple have been selected. The majority can be seen to have
allowed an individual between 9 and 16 bushels, again centred on 12
bushels. Depending on the proportions of each, 12 bushels of wheat
and barley would have been sufficient to give a daily allowance of
about 1½ or 1¾ lbs of bread. A pound of cereals per head per day is
regarded in modern famine relief programmes as sufficient to sustain
life; 1¾ lbs would yield almost 2,000 calories, enough to allow a
retired person some energy for light work. A younger man involved
in heavier work would need about 2½ lbs.

The more generous agreements gave retired people a diet of bread,
pottage and ale. Emma del Rood of Cranfield (Bedfordshire) in
1437–8 was promised annually 12 bushels of wheat (2 lbs of bread per
day), 2 quarters of malt (2½ pints of strong ale per day), and a peck of
oat-meal (for pottage). The pottage element seems to have been
omitted from some of the largest allowances, such as that for a
Nottinghamshire woman in 1380, who was to receive a bushel of
wheat and two of malt every three weeks, evidently envisaging a diet
mainly of bread and ale. Better-off peasants received malt, showing
that they were expected to drink ale regularly. The less generous
allowances gave unmalted barley, and because it would lose much of
its food value if brewed, the recipients must have eaten it as bread or
boiled it in a pottage. Two maintenance agreements from the same
place, Langtoft (Lincolnshire), in successive years in 1330–1 demon-

strate the social inequalities of peasant diet. Beatrice atte Lane, who was surrendering 24 acres, was promised 1¹/₂ quarters of maslin and 1¹/₂ quarters of drage, sufficient for an ample diet of bread and ale, while a smallholder with 4¹/₂ acres, Sara Bateman, received a quarter of maslin and 4 bushels of barley, the ingredients of a menu of bread and pottage, accompanied mainly by water.

The types of grain issued under maintenance agreements reveal marked regional differences (see table 13). In Essex and Surrey peasants ate a great deal of wheat, while in Hampshire and Worcestershire the proportion of wheat was low, and none of the Norfolk maintenance agreements mention it at all. In the last two counties rye acted as a substitute for wheat, but its absence in some counties, for example Bedfordshire, suggests that barley was used as a bread corn. Oats, peas and beans formed the bases of pottages, except in Essex where oats were malted for brewing. A few maintenance agreements from the northern counties can be supplemented with evidence from mill tolls, servants' allowances and tithe corn to suggest that in the east, from Lincolnshire through eastern Yorkshire to County Durham, both wheat and rye formed an important element in the diet, whereas in north Staffordshire, Derbyshire and much of the north-west, oats bulked large in the diet of peasants and servants alike. Studies of later centuries have emphasized the rôle of rye in lower-class food, but the maintenance agreements show the widespread importance of barley as bread or pottage corn.[3]

A few maintenance agreements make reference to supplies of meat and dairy produce, like the Warwickshire yardlander, John Stappe of Blackwell, who in 1347 was to receive a pig and a quarter of an ox-carcass, enough to give him a daily allowance, on meat days, in the region of ¹/₂ lb. Other agreements allow the retired peasant to keep a pig, or a cow, or poultry, pointing to supplements of bacon, milk products and eggs in their diet. A few were able to keep sheep. The ideal peasant foods in the context of limited supplies of animal products were bacon, sausages and cheese, because they could be preserved and eaten in small quantities over a long time. The importance of bacon in peasant households is shown by occasional tax assessments which included it in the goods valued. At Cuxham (Oxfordshire) in 1304 most of the tax-payers (half-yardlanders) owned one, two or three flitches, and at the same place in 1349 the relatively wealthy reeve had four or five flitches, a 'carcass' and

---

3 W. Ashley, *The bread of our forefathers* (Oxford, 1928).

Table 14. *Animal bones from village sites, 12th–15th century, by percentage*

Site	Horse	Cattle	Sheep	Pigs	Game and poultry	Total
Gomeldon, Wiltshire (buildings 1 and 2)[a]	1	20	61	13	5	100
Grenstein, Norfolk[b]	20	23	37	13	7	100
Lyveden, Northamptonshire (1972 season)[c]	8	35	34	14	9	100
Martinsthorpe, Rutland[d]	8	17	64	6	5	100
Seacourt, Berkshire[e]	3	39	43	13	2	100
Upton, Gloucestershire[f]	5	22	69	3	1	100
Wharram Percy, Yorkshire[g] (Area 10, peasant houses)	7	25	58	8	2	100

(*N.B.*: The *dates* at which the bones were deposited is often uncertain. Most samples cover the whole period from *c.* 1100 to *c.* 1500, except Upton where occupation ceased in the fourteenth century; at Lyveden the bones came from fifteenth-century deposits. The reservation must be made that bones are un-datable, and some may have survived on the site from earlier phases of occupation.

Sheep may include goats, the bones of which are often indistinguishable. The *game and poultry* includes deer, rabbit and bird bones, except at Seacourt and Wharram Percy, where deer only are included.)

Source notes:

a. J. Musty and D. Algar, 'Excavations at the deserted medieval village of Gomeldon, near Salisbury', *Wiltshire Archaeological and Natural History Magazine*, 80 (1986), 166–9

b. P. Wade-Martins, 'Grenstein (Greynston)', *East Anglian Archaeology*, 10 (1980), 158–9

c. J. M. Steane and G. F. Bryant, 'Excavations at the deserted settlement at Lyveden', *Journal of the Northampton Museums and Art Gallery*, 12 (1975), 152–7

d. J. S. Wacher, 'Excavations at Martinsthorpe, Rutland, 1960', *Transactions of the Leicestershire Archaeological Soc.*, 39 (1963–4), 17

e. M. Biddle, 'The deserted medieval village of Seacourt, Berkshire', *Oxoniensia*, 26–7 (1961–2), 197–20

f. R. H. Hilton and P. A. Rahtz, 'Upton, Gloucestershire, 1959–64', *Transactions of the Bristol and Gloucestershire Archaeological Soc.*, 85 (1966), 139–43; P. A. Rahtz, 'Upton, Gloucestershire, 1964–8', *Transactions of the Bristol and Gloucestershire Archaeological Soc.*, 88 (1969), 124–6

g. J. G. Hurst (ed.), *Wharram* (Soc. for Med. Arch. Monograph, 8, 1979), pp. 135–6

ten cheeses.[4] Another guide to peasant meat consumption comes from the bones found on village sites (table 14), which demonstrate different local patterns of animal husbandry and consumption. They include the remains of animals that were not normally eaten, such as horses, showing that the bones derive from farm rubbish as well as kitchen waste. Pork consumption is under-represented, presumably because pigs were slaughtered young and their bones have not been preserved. Poultry, rabbits and wild birds are less likely to be preserved or discovered because of their small size and fragility. The large number of sheep bones creates an illusion of peasants as mutton eaters, but even at Upton or Martinsthorpe where sheep bones were especially plentiful the superior weight of cattle meant that beef was eaten more than mutton. A simple transposition of the Gomeldon bones into meat weights would make beef even more prominent in peasant than in aristocratic diets (compare with table 4). In reality, pork consumption would have made the predominance of beef less overwhelming. Cattle and sheep were usually killed at the end of their useful lives as providers of pulling-power, milk and wool.

The maintenance agreements give a rather false impression of peasant self-sufficiency; peasant foodstuffs were in fact often obtained from retailers. This is especially true of ale: for example, forty-eight to seventy people each year were fined for brewing offences at the large Suffolk village of Redgrave in the late thirteenth century. Brewing was most efficiently done on a large scale, producing more ale than could be consumed in a normal peasant household. So the village's needs were served in rotation, with better-off households brewing for their own needs and selling the surplus, or buying their supplies from poorer neighbours. Bakers also plied a trade in villages, especially in parts of eastern England. The sale of dairy products is known from debt cases, for example those at Ombersley (Worcestershire) in 1377, which revealed that thirteen people had bought cheese from John Deye.[5] Likewise, although peasants would kill pigs and preserve their bacon at home, they would sell other animals to a butcher, whether one living in the village or more commonly in the local market town, and buy their meat supplies in small quantities as they were needed or could be afforded. Many of

4 P. D. A. Harvey (ed.), *Manorial records of Cuxham, Oxfordshire, c. 1200–1359* (Oxfordshire Record Soc., 50, 1976), pp. 153, 712–14.
5 R. M. Smith, 'English peasant life-cycles and socio-economic networks' (University of Cambridge Ph.D. thesis, 1974), chapter 4; Hereford and Worcester R.O., ref. 705:56, BA3910/39.

the bones found on peasant sites, therefore, are likely to represent the remains of joints bought from butchers. Sea-fish were obtained inland as items of long-distance trade. Fish bones have been found at Wharram Percy and herrings were widely available, for example from a stall in the main street of Chaddesley Corbett (Worcestershire) in the early fifteenth century. In sophisticated market centres like Lakenheath (Suffolk), 'take-away' meals, eel pasties, could be bought in the early fourteenth century.[6]

There were two types of food that came from the peasants' resources rather than the market. Firstly, the peasant's garden was an important source of onions, leeks, garlic and cabbages, and apples and pears. Though small in quantity (as tithe records show, see pp. 115 and 131), vegetables and fruit made important contributions to the nutritional quality and the flavour of meals. Peasants valued them highly, judging from the number of maintenance agreements in which access to the garden was written into the contract. One Essex widow, for example, was given 'half of the garden for her own use', and a couple from Bishop's Waltham (Hampshire) in 1457 with a half-yardland received an annual pipe of cider (c. 120 gallons). Secondly, the surrounding countryside provided some foodstuffs, from hunting, fishing and gathering. In much of the country, extensive agriculture had reduced the wastes to negligible proportions (see p. 125), but peasants who lived in royal forests could go on poaching expeditions, and in forest settlements like Lyveden (see table 14) venison provided a significant part of the meat supply. Small birds could be caught without infringing any laws. Wild plants such as blackberries and the 'weed' fat hen could be collected to supplement limited garden supplies. Fishing provided food for peasant households, as well as saleable catches. At Alrewas (Staffordshire) in the Trent valley, a good number of tenants were allowed, according to customs written down in 1342, to fish on the meatless days (Wednesdays, Fridays and Saturdays) 'for their table'.[7]

Most peasants before the Black Death lived on a cereal based diet of bread and pottage. The better-off drank ale regularly, the rest as circumstances allowed. The main sources of animal protein – dairy

6 J. G. Hurst (ed.), *Wharram* (Soc. for Med. Arch. Monograph, 8, 1979), p. 136; Shakespeare's Birthplace Trust R.O., Stratford-upon-Avon, DR5/2798; Cambridge U.L., EDC 7/15/11/2/15 (transcript by J. A. Cripps in School of History, University of Birmingham).

7 J. R. Birrell, 'Who poached the king's deer? A study in thirteenth-century crime', *Midland History*, 7 (1982), 20–2; J. Greig, 'Plant foods in the past', *Journal of Plant Foods*, 5 (1983), 179–214; B.L., MS. Stowe 880, fol. 29.

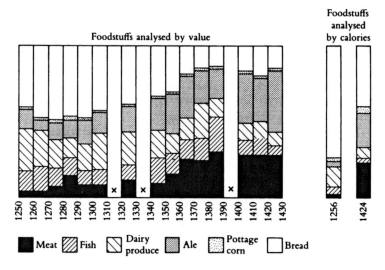

Fig. 4   Harvest workers' diet, at Sedgeford, Norfolk
(Data derive from a sample year in each decade; X = no data in this decade)
The various elements in the diet are compared by value in the main series, and by their
calorific value in two sample years.
Source: C. Dyer, 'Changes in diet in the late middle ages: the case of harvest workers',
Ag.H.R., 36 (1988), 21–37

produce, beef and bacon – were consumed in quantity only by the
upper ranks of village society. They also ate fish, but for many
peasants, observance of fast days meant that they ate cheese or
onions with their bread and pottage. Garden produce provided a
valuable dietary supplement. The types of grain and animals consumed, and the availability of game, fish and wild plant-foods
depended on the locality.

In the fourteenth and fifteenth centuries peasant diet changed in
three ways. Firstly, wheat consumption increased, even, according
to maintenance agreements from Walsham-le-Willows, in the bar-
ley-dominated agricultural landscape of north Suffolk. Farm servants were given increased wheat allowances. Peasants baked more
bread rather than boiling grain in pottages, and more houses acquired individual ovens instead of depending on common ovens.
Secondly, peasants drank more ale on a regular basis, leading to the
development in many villages of permanent ale-houses, licensed by
the lord of the manor, instead of the multiplicity of part-time brew-

ers.[8] And thirdly, they ate more meat, providing rural butchers with a growing trade.

The long-term changes in rural diet can be indicated statistically by analysing the food given to harvest workers, who were a privileged group among wage-earners because they were expected to work hard at a season of fierce competition for labour. They included peasants with smallholdings and peasants' adult children as well as servants. As fig. 4 shows, the thirteenth-century harvesters consumed a great deal of bread, modest quantities of ale and dairy produce, and very little meat (compared here in terms of both value and calories). Through the next century the importance of bread and dairy produce diminished, and expenditure on ale and especially meat increased. By the early fifteenth century, harvest workers were allowed a pound of meat for every two pounds of bread, compared with an ounce or two of meat for every two pounds of bread 150 years earlier. The harvest workers improved the quality of their diet, with wheat replacing barley or rye as the main bread corn, fresh beef and mutton increasing at the expense of bacon, fresh fish instead of salt cod and herring, and strong ale instead of small ale, cider, milk and water. Presumably peasant diet moved in similar directions, particularly in greater meat consumption, as did lower-class diets throughout western Europe.[9] We might question whether the new diet in every respect represented an improvement in nutrition, because of its higher proportion of white bread and animal fats. There is no doubt that contemporaries derived a sense of psychological well-being from its consumption. In other respects peasant diet, with its emphasis on dairy produce and vegetables, and occasional offal and herrings, must have provided a range of vitamins. Perhaps the garden was not always productive enough to supply every member of the household with the modern recommended daily intake of 30 mg of Vitamin C, but perhaps they consumed enough leeks, cabbage and apples to prevent serious deficiency diseases. The chief shortcoming of the pre-Black Death diet arose from the shortage of animal protein, and the periodic emergencies which forced a dangerous reduction in consumption, and recourse to such famine foods as acorns and roots. The main dietary improvements of the later middle ages lay in the correction of the imbalance between

8 P. Clark, *The English ale-house: a social history, 1200–1830* (London, 1983), pp. 20–38.
9 C. Dyer, 'Changes in diet in the late middle ages: the case of harvest workers', *Ag. H.R.*, 36 (1988); B. Bennassar and J. Goy, 'Contribution à l'histoire de la consommation alimentaire du XIVᵉ au XIXᵉ siècle', *Annales E.S.C.*, 30 (1975), 402–30.

animal products and cereals, and the growing infrequency of serious food shortages.

The diet of peasants was subject to constant short-term changes. Although they might seek to maintain supplies through the year by storing corn in barns and bins, by salting and smoking meat and by making cheese, many foodstuffs did not keep, and had either to be consumed in season (like eggs and vegetables), or prepared repeatedly, as in the case of ale. Peasants, unlike the aristocracy, were involved in an annual cycle of temporary indulgence and *real* deprivation, with a feasting season from autumn until Christmas, and belt-tightening in the spring and early summer induced more urgently by the realities of short supplies than by the religious obligations of Lent. Peasant eating was not entirely governed by utilitarian considerations. Meals were served with some ceremony, on a table covered with a linen or canvas cloth, the single chair being occupied by the male head of the household, the others being seated on forms or stools. In better-off households hands were washed, using a metal basin and ewer, and a linen towel (see table 15). If the English observed the same practices as the continental peasants, the women served the men.[10] Even poorer families could adorn the table with a decorative ceramic jug. The meal maintained the unity of the domestic group, just as attendance at Christmas meals in the manor house, and Whitsun ales at the parish church, reinforced the village's sense of community.[11]

HOUSING

The excavation of village sites is our main source of information about thirteenth-century peasant buildings. For the succeeding two centuries, architectural evidence (from the study of standing buildings) and documents add a great deal to the information obtained from archaeology.[12] At the beginning of our period the main building tradition, dating back to before the Conquest and even earlier, involved the use of vertical posts or horizontal beams set into the ground. This 'earthfast' technique provided a secure basis for walls and roof, but its disadvantage lay in the tendency for the base of the

---

10 M. Closson, 'Us et coutumes de la table du XIIᵉ siècle au XVᵉ siècle à travers les miniatures' in D. Menjot (ed.), *Manger et boire au moyen âge* (2 vols., Publications de la faculté des lettres et sciences humaines de Nice, 28, 1984), vol. 2, pp. 21–32.

11 C. Phythian-Adams, *Local history and folklore* (London, 1975), pp. 17–27.

12 The details of evidence on which this section is based are set out in C. Dyer, 'English peasant buildings in the later middle ages', *Med. Arch.*, 30 (1986), 19–45.

posts to rot and therefore to need constant replacement. Over a long time span, from the late twelfth to the early fourteenth century, building methods changed with the introduction of stone walls. On peasant sites in the south-west, granite was used; in the downlands of the south, flints; in the Cotswolds, oolitic limestone; and in the Yorkshire Wolds, chalk blocks. The stones were mortared together at Hangleton (Sussex); elsewhere they were normally bonded with earth or clay. Where stone was scarce, especially in the east, houses were founded on pad-stones, single blocks of stone on which timbers rested, or walls were made of earth, using such techniques as 'cob'. The new style of building might involve setting horizontal timbers on the ground surface, without any real foundation at all. Sometimes the stone walls were built high enough – 6 feet – to support the rafters directly. More often the walls were quite low, little more than a foundation of two or three courses, on which a horizontal cill beam, or vertical posts, could be set. So the function of the stonework was often to provide a dry and level foundation for a superstructure of timber and wattle and daub, or cob walls, depending on the local building tradition. Roofs were generally covered with straw or reed thatch, or turf. A few stone slates or ceramic tiles might be set around the smoke hole lest sparks set light to the thatch.

In western and northern areas at the end of our period the timber frame was founded on crucks, which were inclined timbers stretching from a low level, even from the ground, to the apex of the roof, and serving as the trusses of the roof.[13] (See fig. 5.) They seem to have been adopted at much the same time as the introduction of stone foundations. Indeed, one building at Gomeldon (Wiltshire) of the late twelfth century represents a transitional stage, with flint walls and sockets for crucks.[14] Normally no trace survives of crucks when a building is excavated because their bases were either set into a horizontal cill beam (which has rotted away), or they rested on pad-stones, which were removed when the building went out of use. Documentary references to crucks in Worcestershire and Staffordshire, and two surviving houses at Harwell and Steventon (Berkshire) which have been dated scientifically to the years 1285–95 and 1305, show that peasants were using cruck construction around 1300. This has implications for the quality of peasant buildings

13 N. W. Alcock, *Cruck construction* (C.B.A. Research Report, 42, 1981), pp. 2–4.
14 J. Musty and D. Algar, 'Excavations at the deserted medieval village of Gomeldon near Salisbury', *Wiltshire Archaeological and Natural History Magazine*, 80 (1986), 135–6.

(a)

(b)

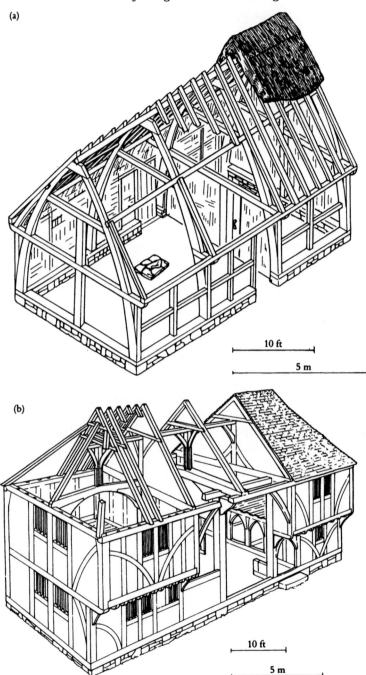

because, as the survival of the Berkshire houses eloquently illustrates, cruck structures were often sturdy, using substantial timbers
for the uprights, and the framing normally required the skilled work
of a carpenter. The timber building tradition of eastern England was
based on vertical posts rather than crucks. Again, it has been argued
that its origins lie in the thirteenth century, with the development
firstly of 'primitive framing', followed by the full timber-framing
technique. Small buildings of apparent peasant origin of the late
thirteenth and early fourteenth century still survive in Essex, representing the eastern equivalents of the Berkshire houses. Timber
superstructures everywhere were solid enough to justify fitting
secure doors and shutters, hanging on iron hinges or pivoted on
stones, and fitted with iron locks and keys.

The earthfast buildings of the early middle ages were often twice
as long as they were wide, and this is also true of their thirteenth-
century successors, which were 12 to 15 feet wide and 25 to 30 feet
long.[15] Many were longer, often in the range of 35 to 45 feet long and
up to 90 feet. Many thirteenth-century peasants lived in long-
houses, in which people and animals were accommodated under the
same roof, at separate ends of the building. Since the sixteenth
century the type has been confined to the highland fringe, but in the
thirteenth century they were more widespread, extending into
Gloucestershire and Northamptonshire. Further south and east a
separate dwelling house was more usual. The house or house-with-
byre was usually accompanied by a barn or other outbuilding, such
as a bake-house. The buildings were often arranged around a yard.

15 S. James, A. Marshall and M. Millett, 'An early medieval building tradition',
Archaeological Journal, 141 (1984), 182–215.

Fig. 5   Two peasant house traditions
(a) The cruck house shown here is a midland type. Four pairs of cruck blades stand on
a low stone foundation wall, defining a building of three bays, divided into two
rooms, the commonest type found on peasant holdings of *c.* 1350–1450. The walls
were built of timber with panels of wattle and daub, and the roof was thatched.
Source: E. Mercer, *English vernacular houses* (London, 1975), p. 17, with modifications,
for which advice was given by Dr N. W. Alcock.
(b) The fifteenth-century wealden house from Surrey is typical of many examples
scattered over south-east England. It has an open hall flanked by two storeys at each
end. The size and architectural pretension show that it was built for an upper peasant,
and indeed houses of this type were sometimes owned by those superior to the
peasantry. The building materials – stone foundations, timber and wattle and daub –
are similar to those used in the cruck house, but the timber was more plentiful, and the
roof was tiled.
Source: M. W. Barley, *Houses and history* (London, 1986), p. 154.

(a)

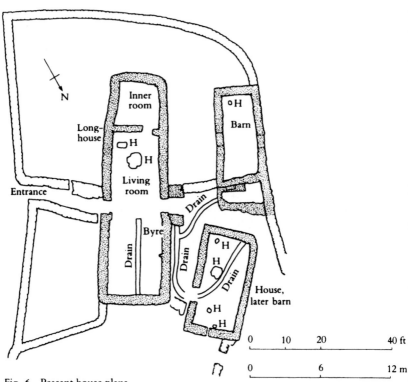

Fig. 6 Peasant house plans
(H marks the sites of hearths)
(a) The thirteenth-century buildings at Houndtor on Dartmoor (Devon) had foundations of granite blocks (building walls are shown stippled, boundary walls unstippled). The stonework probably rose to a considerable height. The largest building, a long-house, contained a byre, a hall or living room, and an inner room or chamber. Nearby stood a smaller house which was used originally as a dwelling, perhaps for an elderly relative or subtenant, but which was later turned into a barn. The other building seems to have been used as a barn throughout its life. The buildings were surrounded by walled enclosures used as gardens or animal pens.
Source: G. Beresford, 'Three medieval settlements on Dartmoor', *Med. Arch.*, 23 (1979), 98–158
(b) At Goltho (Lincolnshire) the buildings of the fourteenth century were entirely of timber and earth, but the lines of the walls are marked by lines of pad-stones. The dwelling house was divided into three rooms, all for the use of people. Cattle were kept in the cobbled crew yard (heavy stippling marks the cobbled area) on one side of which lay a barn for storing crops and farming gear. A turf bank (light stippling) enclosed the yard and buildings on two sides.
Source: G. Beresford, *The medieval clayland village: excavations at Goltho and Barton Blount* (Soc. for Med. Arch. Monograph, 6, 1975), p. 17.

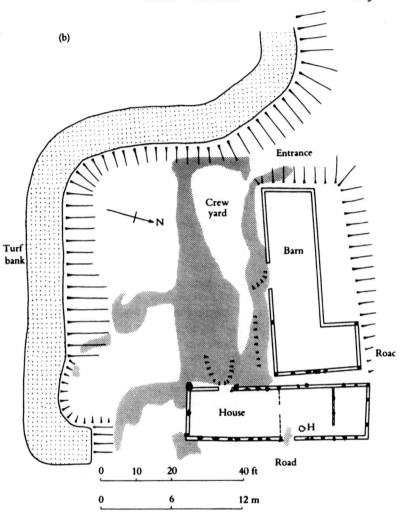

The dwelling house (or the dwelling end of a long-house) usually consisted of two rooms, one a living room with a central hearth (the hall), the other an inner chamber or sleeping room which may also have served for storage. Houses were normally provided with opposed doorways in the long walls, with a screen or internal porch for draught protection. There were few windows, for example only two in a house in Halesowen described in 1281; they were small and unglazed. Cooking may sometimes have taken place in the hall, or in a separate room or building designated as a kitchen (see fig. 6).

The changes in peasant buildings in the thirteenth century were connected with a number of economic developments of the period. The growth of the market meant that peasants could buy materials more easily, not just such fittings as hinges and locks, but also the timber itself in the case of villages lacking abundant local supplies. The cutting and fitting of the timber required the skilled labour of craftsmen, which is typical of the growth of specialized occupations in the period. The whole package of changes suggests a move away from peasant self-sufficiency and the adoption of a superior and more expensive standard of construction. The initial expense of building would be partly justified by reduced maintenance costs because timber would not need frequent renewal. The cost of a house (probably a cruck building) at Belper (Derbyshire) is revealed in a dispute over a marriage contract in 1312, in which a father had agreed to build a new house for a married couple at a cost of £2. All of this points to a rising standard of peasant building in the thirteenth century, though the reservation must be made that much of our evidence relates to midland, western and northern England where the abandoned village sites, untouched since their desertion, are available for excavation. The good quality houses, such as those still standing in Berkshire, and some of the excavated examples, belonged to relatively prosperous peasants, half-yardlanders and above. References in early fourteenth-century documents to landlords running up apparently flimsy cottages for about 10s. may indicate a poorer standard of housing among the smallholders.

In the late fourteenth and fifteenth century, thousands of peasant buildings fell into decay. Many remained for centuries as empty sites, but some were still needed by the dwindling number of tenants, who often rebuilt them in a superior style. They had at least as many domestic and farm buildings as in the previous century, and animal houses and barns tended to increase in number and size because of the expanding scale of agricultural operations. At Caldecote (Hertfordshire) in the fifteenth century a house was dwarfed by its two adjoining barns. In order to accommodate the growing flocks and herds, either the long-house was replaced by separate housing for animals, or very large long-houses were built, as at Wharram Percy (Yorkshire). In the east midlands cattle were sheltered in crew yards, that is, pens partially roofed. Building sizes did not change greatly: four-fifths of west-midland houses and barns were of two or three bays (30–45 feet long), the bay being a standard unit of building

16 G. C. Homans, *English villagers of the thirteenth century* (Cambridge, Mass., 1941), pp. 140–1.

measuring about 15 by 15 feet. A few one-bay houses are known, on smallholdings, and a minority with four and five bays.

The foundations of houses resembled those of earlier periods, but the standard of carpentry of the superstructure seems to have improved. Large numbers of buildings still survive; many of the 3,000 of the cruck type probably date from this period, and there are much larger numbers in the framing tradition of the south-east, about a thousand in Kent alone, of the late fourteenth and fifteenth century.[17] The distinctive wealden houses of Essex, Kent, Surrey and Sussex show the adoption by the upper ranks of the peasantry of a style of building which could be very imposing, with an open hall flanked by two-storey end bays, giving the inhabitants five instead of the usual two or three rooms (see fig. 5). By 1500, Kentish houses were being built in which the whole structure was of two storeys, the hall being ceiled over in the modern style. Two-storey buildings were not uncommon throughout the south-east and East Anglia, and upper rooms were being inserted into the formerly one-storey peasant houses of the west, from Devon to Warwickshire, in the fifteenth century. The open hall was heated by a hearth, with a smoke hole in the roof or a louvre arrangement to remove the smoke. More efficient fireplaces and chimneys, sometimes with smokehoods suspended over the hearth, were making their appearance in peasant houses. The use of roofs of stone slates and, more rarely, of ceramic tiles on a minority of peasant buildings in the fifteenth century were expensive improvements in themselves, and required a sturdy timber structure to support them. In some respects the advances in housing of 1350–1520 anticipated on a small scale the 'Great Rebuilding' of 1570–1640.

Peasants spent more on houses because they built to a higher specification, and materials and labour became more costly. When lords provided houses for their tenants (as they did in the early fifteenth century, despairing of the decay of the housing stock on their estates) they paid as little as £2 (using timber from a dismantled building) and as much as £7. They generally built to a rather higher standard than the peasants would have done when they were organizing the work for themselves. With timber for a building costing at least 10s. to 15s., and a carpenter's wages 2s. 6d. per week, and other payments for materials and labour, peasants would require an outlay of £2 to £3 for a three-bay building.

What was the quality of life in a late medieval peasant house? Floors were sometimes built of flags or cobbling, but more often

17 E. Mercer, *English vernacular houses* (London, 1975), p. 14.

consisted of the bare subsoil, covered with straw or rushes. Frequent sweepings gave the soft chalk floors of the peasant houses at Wharram Percy a U-shaped profile, so peasants should not be assumed to have lived in squalor. Floors must always have been damp, and indeed were subject to flooding, judging from the drains sometimes built across them. Open hearths were inefficient sources of heat, and although modern reconstructions show that holes in the roof were capable of removing most of the smoke, some must have remained in the atmosphere. The internal partitions, doors and shutters cannot have prevented winter draughts, and in the warmer weather the small windows left the inner chamber dark and stuffy. Thatch was warm, but encouraged vermin, so that it is likely that the plague spread rapidly in 1348–9 because of the close proximity of people to infected rats. Sanitary arrangements consisted of privies over cesspits in the garden, from which the contents were periodically carried to the fields. An arrangement adopted by a peasant of Methwold (Norfolk) caused complaints in 1443 from his neighbours because his privy ran into the 'common water'. Heaps of animal dung lay in close proximity to houses. A few houses would have had a supply of clean water from their own well, but more often the women of the household carried water from a common well or stream.[18] The supply may not always have been pure, though the fact that we hear of pollution from bye-laws seeking to control it shows a concern for cleanliness. An objective test of housing quality is to measure floor area per person, and on that basis conditions seem to have been relatively spacious. A single person, such as a widow, was sometimes assigned a bay, and at Enstone (Oxfordshire) in 1341 a non-inheriting brother was allowed (as long as he remained single) a room 20 by 12 feet.[19] Space for a person in excess of 200 square feet is quite generous, and the more normal individual share for an average family in a two-bay house (70–90 square feet) is superior to' that found in southern Europe in the later middle ages or in the modern third world. The introduction of upper storeys increased the floor area (to more than 1,000 square feet in total in the case of a wealden house), and promoted the separation of the house from the life of the farmyard.

Money spent on a dwelling house can be regarded as the largest consumption expenditure that a peasant made, both for the initial construction, and for regular maintenance that could have cost a

18 Norfolk R.O., Bantoft, P190B; B. Hanawalt, *The ties that bound* (Oxford, 1986), pp. 26–7.

19 Gloucestershire R.O., D678.96.

shilling or two each year. Expenditure on agricultural buildings should be regarded as investment, bringing benefits to the efficiency of the farm in terms of better storage, healthier animals and well-protected implements. Spending on buildings, at least for the better-off peasants, increased in the thirteenth century, and for all of the peasantry after the mid-fourteenth century.

POSSESSIONS

Lists of goods and chattels were made on the various occasions that a tenant's or serf's goods were seized by the lord. These could be *principalia* (the principal goods) attached to a customary tenement deemed to belong to the lord and therefore listed on the transfer of a customary holding; or *terciars*, the third part of a dead tenant's goods, taken in addition to the heriot; or the goods and chattels of felons or debtors. Also individual items would appear in court records as stolen property, or because they caused a death (the *deodand*), or as heriots, or as goods taken in distraint; and tenants might sue one another for goods borrowed but not returned. Wills and tax assessments make selective reference to possessions. Archaeological finds are especially useful for revealing items not regarded as sufficiently valuable by contemporaries to be mentioned in writing.[20]

It seems useful to classify peasant possessions into farming equip-

20 The main sources for this section are: R. K. Field, 'Worcestershire peasant buildings, household goods and farming equipment in the later middle ages', *Med. Arch.*, 9 (1965), 137–45; transcriptions of *principalia* lists from Ombersley (Worcestershire) of the late fourteenth and early fifteenth century, kindly given to me by G. Scardellato; W. F. Mumford, 'Terciars on the estates of Wenlock Priory', *Transactions of the Shropshire Archaeological Soc.*, 58 (1965), 68–76; F. W. Weaver, *Somerset medieval wills* (Somerset Record Soc., 16, 1901); A. E. Levett, *Studies in manorial history* (Oxford, 1938), pp. 208–34; Suffolk R.O. (Bury St Edmunds branch), 1C500/2/9, 11; Norfolk R.O., NCC will registers, Grey; A. T. Gaydon (ed.), *The taxation of 1297* (Bedfordshire Historical Records Soc., 39, 1959); A. C. Chibnall (ed.), *Early taxation returns* (Buckinghamshire Record Soc., 14, 1966); archaeological reports listed in the notes to table 14; D. Austin, 'Excavations in Okehampton Park, Devon, 1976–78', *Proceedings of the Devon Archaeological Soc.*, 36 (1978), 191–239; E. W. Holden, 'Excavations at the deserted medieval village of Hangleton, Part 1', *Sussex Archaeological Collections*, 101 (1963), 54–181; J. G. and D. G. Hurst, 'Excavations at the deserted medieval village of Hangleton, Part 2', *Sussex Archaeological Collections*, 102 (1964), 94–142; G. Beresford, *The medieval clayland village: excavations at Goltho and Barton Blount* (Soc. for Med. Arch. Monograph, 6, 1975); E. M. Jope and R. I. Threlfall, 'Excavations of a medieval settlement at Beere, North Tawton, Devon', *Med. Arch.*, 2 (1958), 112–40. A useful general survey of the archaeological evidence is M. W. Beresford and J. G. Hurst, *Deserted medieval villages* (London, 1971), pp. 140–4.

Table 15. *Two peasant inventories*

	Robert Oldman of Cuxham (Oxfordshire), 1349–52a		Richard Sclatter of Elmley Castle (Worcestershire), 1457b	
Farming equipment	1 (iron)-bound cart	4s.	1 spade and shovel	3d.
	Foot iron of plough	5d.		
	2 yokes	4d.		
Craft equipment	3 masons tools	9d.	1 axe	5d.
	1 trowel (?)	6d.	1 auger	3d.
			1 spinning-wheel	10d.
Household goods				
a) Food preparation	2 brass pots (not valued)		1 vat	4d.
	1 (brass) pot	2s.	1 barrel	3d.
	2 pans and a tripod	1s.	1 brass pan of 2 gallons	2s.
	Hoops for wooden vessels	1s.	1 pail with bucket	3d.
			1 tub	4d.
			8 trenchers	1d.
			1 bottle	4d.
			2 buckets	1s.
b) Furnishings	1 (metal) ewer	6d.	3 badly worn coverlets	2s.
	1 (metal) ewer (not valued)		2 worn canvasses	4d.
	1 basin and ewer	8d.	1 sheet	4d.
	1 basin and ewer	2s. 8d.	1 mattress	2d.
	Canvas cloth	9d.	4 pillows	4d.
	1 tapet*	3d.	3 boards for a bed	4d.
	1 tapet* with sheets	3s. 4d.	2 boards with 2 trestles	
			(i.e. a table)	6d.
	1 tapet*,		1 table board	3d.
	2 sheets, 4 blankets	5s. 4d.	1 chair	3d.
	(Table) cloth	1s. 6d.	1 form	2d.
	Towel	6d.	1 chest with various	
			necessaries in the same	2s. 2d.
	2 cloths	8d.	1 chest	6d.
	1 coffer	1s.	1 other chest	6d.
	2 stools	8d.	(Illegible item	1s. 3d.)
	1 form	1½d.		
	Total value	27s. 11½d.	Total value	15s. 5d.
	(Estimated value	c. 33s. 0d.)		

Other goods:	
Grain	61s. 0d.
Stock	56s. 0d.
Foodstuffs	10s. 5½d.
Clothes	33s. 11½d.

*=carpet, in this case, a bed covering

Source notes:
a. P. D. A. Harvey (ed.), *Manorial records of Cuxham, Oxfordshire c. 1200–1359* (Oxfordshire Record Soc., 50, 1976), pp. 153–9
b. Hereford and Worcester R.O., ref. 899:95 BA989/2/28

ment, tools and implements used in crafts, and household goods, the
latter being subdivided between those used in food preparation and
as furnishings. In the peasant's world, in which production and
consumption were intermeshed, the same object would have a variety of functions. For example, a brass pot would have cooking as its
primary purpose, but it might be used to warm milk to feed lambs,
or in commercial brewing. Two inventories are given by way of
illustration, from peasants of contrasting wealth (see table 15). The
relatively low values of the goods is worth emphasis. A better-off
peasant, Robert Oldman the Cuxham reeve, had animals and crops
worth almost four times as much as his goods and chattels.

Oldman was unusually affluent, but his goods were not very
different in type from those of most yardlanders or half-yardlanders.
They usually owned the major items of farming equipment, including some form of wheeled vehicle, either a horse-drawn cart or a
heavier ox-drawn wain. They could be 'bare' or iron-bound, referring to the iron tyres on the wheels, depending on whether the
cart was to be used mainly on journeys to and from the fields, or if it
was intended to run for a distance on hard roads to market. The
iron-work made a considerable difference to the value, because a
wooden cart could be worth as little as a shilling or two, while the
tyred kind could cost 10s. or even 18s. The valuation often included
the harness, cart-saddle, rope and horse-collar. The wooden parts of
ploughs were so cheap that inventories often omit them, concentrating instead on the iron share and coulter, which were usually valued
at 2s. (Oldman's list omits these, perhaps because he used the lord's
plough as reeve of the manor). Other plough fittings included such
metal items as chains, feet, ears, staples and hooks, and wooden
yokes for the oxen or horse-collars, which together could raise the
value of the whole implement to 3s. or 4s. Many peasants with
half-yardlands or above owned a harrow, its value depending on
whether or not it was fitted with iron teeth.

Smallholders with no plough, the great majority, may have borrowed or hired them from wealthier neighbours, but so many of
them (like Richard Sclatter in table 15) owned hand tools such as a
spade or mattock that we must assume that they dug their land. All
types of peasants owned smaller farming tools, the most common
being sickles, scythes and forks, and equipment for stacking, threshing, storing and sowing grain – ladders, flails, winnowing fans,
sieves, riddles, sacks and seed-lips. Contemporary illustrations and
archaeological finds add to the list with smaller items such as ox-
goads, sheep-shears, weeding-hooks, sheep-bells, horse-shoes,

wooden rakes, vessels for the dairy and whetstones.[21] Large and expensive iron pieces, such as plough shares, are rarely found on village sites because the frugal peasants, unlike a modern farmer, would not throw away worn-out equipment, but have it re-cycled by the smith. Peasants owned wood-cutting tools (axes, saws, bills, wood-hooks and wood-knives) mainly for obtaining their own fuel, and for hedge-laying and lopping branches for fodder. Tenants of larger holdings owned a bushel, that is a measure for selling grain, which is indicative, together with the iron-bound carts, of their marketing activities. Perhaps an Essex peasant who in 1376 had bushel, half-bushel and peck measures, sold grain in these small quantities to his poorer neighbours.

Rural crafts and trades rarely required expensive equipment, except for the fisherman with his boat and nets, or the smith like John Smyth of Long Marston (Warwickshire) whose inventory in 1391 includes an anvil, hammer, tongs, bellows and grindstone.[22] Perhaps the most valuable trade equipment of all was that needed for brewing, not so much the wooden vats, tubs, stands and barrels, but the lead vessel for heating the wort, which could cost as much as 10s. Many of the processes of cloth-making required equipment worth little more than a few pence, such as the combs, cards, heckles and weighted distaffs used to produce yarn. Even a spinning-wheel (worth 1s. or less) or a loom and treadle (valued at 2s. in 1432 in a Norfolk peasant's goods) were relatively modest investments.[23] Many crafts relied more on skill than equipment, like Richard Sclatter's trade of tiling roofs with stone slates (table 15), for which he needed only an auger to bore holes in roof-slates. Many households, judging from archaeological finds, owned minor items for hunting or fishing (arrowheads or hooks), and shears, scissors, needles and thimbles, which presumably were used in day-to-day food gathering and domestic activities rather than in specialized occupations. The manufactured goods themselves were the most valuable items found in the possession of rural craftsmen, like the 2,000 tiles owned by a Fingrith (Essex) peasant in 1376, the forty-six pairs of shoes taken in distraint from an Earl Soham (Suffolk) shoemaker in 1370, and the hides valued at 4s. 6d. in the tax assessment of a Bedfordshire tanner in 1297.[24]

21 Bodleian Library, *English rural life in the middle ages* (Oxford, 1965).
22 Gloucestershire R.O., D678/98C.
23 Norfolk R.O., 11262, 26A4.
24 Essex R.O., D/DK M108, no. 48; Suffolk R.O. (Ipswich branch), V5/18/1.2; Gaydon, *Taxation of 1297*, p. 24.

Kitchen equipment often included a hand-mill (an alternative to taking corn to a mechanised mill), and a stone mortar. Kneading troughs and salting tubs were among the many wooden receptacles. By far the most expensive items were the metal cooking pots, of cast bronze, with a capacity of 1 to 6 gallons, for which 3s. to 5s. were common values, and pans of riveted copper plates worth a shilling or two. Poorer households (like Sclatter's) had to make do with a pan. Gridirons and spits appear only sporadically among peasant possessions, and in upland areas, iron plates or 'bakestones' for cooking oat cakes. Ceramic pots, bowls and pans were much used in dairying and cooking, some shallow forms being employed as dripping pans and as fish dishes. Ale was carried and stored in pottery cisterns, and served and drunk in jugs and (in the fifteenth century) cups. Most ceramic vessels cost as little as $^1/_4$d. or $^1/_2$d. each, and wooden trenchers, plates, bowls and cups, the main items of tableware, were even cheaper. An increasing number of better-off peasant households owned a few pewter vessels, like the two dishes and two saucers of a wealthy Harwell (Berkshire) peasant, John Bonde, in 1403.[25] William Harrison, writing in the 1580s, thought that only wealthy peasants had more than four pewter vessels in the early sixteenth century, and that the ownership of pewter had multiplied in his own day.[26] Silverware, a rarity in peasant households, was usually confined to a set of spoons for wealthier yeomen.

Wooden furniture in the hall usually included a trestle table, forms and a chair, which could be cleared to one side between meals, in view of the limited space. Chests were kept in the kitchen to store grain, and were the main items of wooden furniture in chambers. They were used to store textiles ('for linen and woollen clothes', in the case of one belonging to Robert Pypere of Shouldham, Norfolk in 1436), and were often fitted with locks.[27] They could be decorative, being made of good quality wood (a chest of spruce is mentioned in a Norfolk will) and were sometimes provided with ornamental metal fittings. Wooden bed frames are rarely mentioned; much more common were mattresses (sometimes stuffed with feathers, more often with straw), pillows, linen sheets, coverlets, and *tapets* (carpets). In contrast with aristocratic beds, they were usually valued at a few shillings. Other household fittings included candle-holders and candlesticks, and occasional ceramic cresset

25 *Calendar of inquisitions miscellaneous*, vol. 7, 1399–1422, p. 128.
26 G. Edelen (ed.), *The description of England of William Harrison* (Ithaca, New York, 1968), pp. 200–2.
27 Norfolk R.O., Hare 2453.

lamps. Prosperous peasant households kept a riding horse, equipped with saddles and other leatherwork, bits and spurs. Free sokemen at Alrewas (Staffordshire), tenants of yardlands owing low rents, were expected in 1342 to pay a heriot of a horse, saddle, bridle, sword, lance or bow. Their actual heriots, and the equipment of those joining in rebellion or civil war, show that peasants sometimes owned cheaper swords (worth 6d.) and bows and arrows.[28] The arrowheads found on village sites are partly of the barbed, hunting form, but also include the armour-piercing type designed for military use.

Most of the information for peasants' chattels dates from the period after 1380. Is there evidence for long-term changes, as we have seen for diet and housing? The wheeled vehicles on peasant holdings of the late twelfth century were more often ox-drawn wains than carts, and they were not owned by every substantial tenant. In the thirteenth century lighter but faster carts replaced wains, and almost every tenant with a half-yardland invested in one to allow easy market contacts.[29] In the same century, the brass pot and pan seem to have come into widespread peasant use, and had been adopted even by cottagers by the 1380s.

In the fourteenth and fifteenth centuries household textiles may have become more plentiful, but there is no certain evidence for this. Pewter tableware and metal ewers replaced some wood and pottery vessels for more substantial peasants, and ceramic cisterns supplanted wooden casks. Potters began to supply cups, which had all previously been made of wood. The technical quality of ceramics improved with a higher proportion of glazed wares. There was an element of display in some peasant possessions, like the decorative horse equipment designed to flash and jingle as the animal moved. The dice, cards, chessmen, footballs, musical instruments and 'nine-men's morris' boards show that resources could be spared sometimes from drab utilitarianism. The prevailing impression, however, is of goods kept in use as long as possible, so that inventories often describe items as old, worn or broken. Peasants thought it worthwhile to mend a ceramic cooking post (cost, ¹/₂d.) with a plug of lead. If they had a little more disposable wealth in the period 1350–1520, not much of it was evidently spent on goods and chattels. William Harrison stressed the great 'improvement' in the ownership of pewter and household textiles in the sixteenth century,

28 B.L., MS. Stowe 880, fol. 29.
29 J. Langdon, 'Horse hauling: a revolution in vehicle transport in twelfth- and thirteenth-century England?', *P. and P.*, 103 (1984), 37–66.

as is confirmed by a comparison between late medieval lists of chattels and later probate inventories. Many peasants' goods before 1520 were valued at between £1 and £10; in the late sixteenth century, husbandmen's inventories in Oxfordshire mostly ranged from £10 to £80, an increase well in excess of the intervening inflation. This is supported by the finds from rural settlements occupied, like Riplingham in Yorkshire, up to the eighteenth century, where the modern metalwork is much more plentiful than that of the medieval period.[30]

CLOTHING

Maintenance agreements for old people occasionally mention an allowance of clothing as part of their upkeep. Anicia atte Hegge, for example, of Crondall (Hampshire), in 1313 inherited her brother's holding, and, presumably because of her advancing years, immediately surrendered it to her daughter and son-in-law, in exchange for an annual allowance of grain, a chemise (linen under-garment) worth 8d. and a pair of shoes worth 6d., each to be received annually, and a woollen garment worth 3s. every other year.[31] Gathering together the information for this and other late thirteenth and early fourteenth-century agreements, interpreted in the light of contemporary illustrations, we can see that peasants usually wore linen underclothes (a chemise for women, and a type of loin-cloth for men), leather shoes and loose woollen tunics containing about 2¼ to 2½ yards of cloth. Some had an outer garment of woollen cloth also, called a super-tunic, but as this was worn less often, it did not need annual or biennial replacement. It seems that hose of woollen cloth were not always worn, so many men went bare-legged, protected to some extent by their tunics which stretched down sometimes to the ankles. Illustrations also depict hats, caps and hoods, which do not appear in agreements concerned with annual provisions. There are exceptional references to expensive garments with fur lining costing 6s. 8d. or more, but our better-off retired peasants would normally receive each year clothing worth about 4s. 6d. (a tunic for 3s., shoes for 6d. and linen for 1s.), or about 3s. annually if the tunic was renewed every other year. We must presume that the

30 M. A. Havinden (ed.), *Household and farm inventories in Oxfordshire, 1550–1590* (Oxfordshire Record Soc., 44, 1965), p. 12; J. S. Wacher, 'Excavations at Riplingham, East Yorkshire, 1956–57', *Yorkshire Archaeological Journal*, 41 (1963–6), 608–69.
31 Winchester Cathedral Library, manorial rolls, box XIII/J.

arrangements for old people reflected the standards of those who had not retired.

Peasant clothes were not made from the cheapest materials available. The textiles used for tunics cost 8d. to 1s. 3d. per yard, not very different from the cloth bought by some gentry households (see p. 78–9). Peasants evidently economized on the dyeing of their clothes, because they often wore 'white', the natural colour of the fleece, or russet, a shade of grey. Women were more likely to wear dyed clothes, judging from a couple at Taunton in 1348: the man was to wear white and his wife a coloured garment, though because of the extra expense his tunic was to be renewed annually and hers every two years.[32] Wealthy peasants like Robert Oldman, the reeve of Cuxham (see table 15), with his robe of murrey (dark brown) worth 6s. 4d., his red robe worth 5s. 3d. and cheaper blue garment, must have stood out among his drably clad neighbours. Few peasants of his generation (he died in the Black Death) can have afforded such a wardrobe, valued at 34s. At the other end of village society we find a very different picture, like the landless serfs of Alrewas (Staffordshire) who by an oddity of local custom were liable to heriot, and whose most valuable goods were often tunics worth 1d. to 6d.[33]

After 1350 peasant clothing was transformed by changes in fashion. A new style of dress spread through European courtly circles in the 1340s, and gradually permeated the rest of society. The male tunic became shorter and closer fitting, and hose were invariably worn. Women's clothes became tighter. Both sexes wore loose outer garments, often consisting of cloaks with hoods. The new trend shocked contemporary moralists, partly because the clothes revealed the shape of the body, and because they were more expensive. From this innovation developed the male costume of the doublet and hose. Doublet implies a lined (doubled) garment, so although shorter than the old tunic, it used almost twice as much material. For example, John Herfrey of Framlingham (Suffolk) in 1389 retired and surrendered his holding. His promise of maintenance included a doublet of russet (on the outside) and cheaper blanket as the lining, with a hood, also lined, two pairs of hose and three pairs of shoes. His wife also received a double tunic and hood, a pair of hose and a pair of shoes.[34] Other agreements of this period specify the quantity of cloth, 4 yards, needed to make a short, lined garment. References increase to hose, cloaks, hoods and shirts for men, and

32 Hampshire R.O., Church Commissioners, 159357.
33 Staffordshire R.O., DO/3 (from a transcript by J. R. Birrell).
34 Pembroke College, Cambridge, Framlingham court rolls, B.

belts for women, all the result of the acceptance of the new style. Peasants could have resisted the change, as did those of eastern Europe, but their greater spending power enabled them to buy the more costly clothes. They could indulge in the greater comfort of the linings, and dress more colourfully, with blues and greens to some extent replacing the old whites and russets. There were touches of luxury for the wives of the peasant élite, in the form of silk kerchiefs and belts with silver buckles and ornaments. The more common-place decorative bronze buckles, brooches and rings which are found on village sites may have become more plentiful in the later middle ages, though this is difficult to prove because they are not closely datable. They certainly seem to have been more numerous at a lowland village like Seacourt (Berkshire) on the edge of a large town, than in more remote upland settlements. The complaints that the lower orders were wearing expensive cloth and luxurious orna-ments, first voiced formally in the legislation of 1363, was evidently based on real developments. Such grumbles could have been made for at least the following century-and-a-half, as the cloth industry expanded to supply the home demand as well as markets overseas.

FUEL

Peasants used the same variety of fuels as the aristocracy (p. 73) – peat in the east and north, coal where it was locally available, for example in north Worcestershire and Nottinghamshire, and everywhere wood. The customs which limited supplies from common woods and turbaries reflected the stratification of village society. An agree-ment in 1344 at Cottenham (Cambridgeshire) allowed a yardlander to dig a stack of peat twenty-one turves high and four broad, which was 36 feet long, while a cottager's stack would be only 10 feet long.[35] Such an unequal allocation was presumably based on the smaller size of the cottagers' families and houses, the concentration of their cooking and domestic heating on a single hearth, and their limited need of fuel for such operations as malting. Fuel probably became more easily available after the Black Death with the reduc-tion in the number of consumers. The Crown and landlords seem to have relaxed some of their earlier vigilance in restricting access to woodland, and the spread of individual ovens in this period may point to higher fuel consumption. There would certainly have been a

35 J. Ravensdale, *Liable to floods. Village landscape on the edge of the fens* A.D. 450–1850 (Cambridge, 1974), p. 52.

greater quantity of raw material for artificial lighting, as tallow became more plentiful as a by-product of meat consumption.

PEASANT RESOURCES IN GENERAL

There are many indications that upper-ranking peasants could own quite large amounts of cash. Inventories of goods and details of thefts recorded between 1350 and 1500 usually mention no more than a few shillings, but individuals are known to have had sums as large as 20s., 24s., 33s. 4d., £2 6s. 8d. and £3.[36] Accumulations of cash were made at an earlier period. Peasants may well have owned some of the hoards of coins containing a pound or two, which were concealed on the Anglo-Scottish border at the time of war and disorder in the reigns of Edward I and Edward II.[37] Tenants seem also to have been able to pay large sums of money in a remarkably short time. For example, on 24 March 1279 at Stratton St Margaret (Wiltshire) John le Bedel agreed to take a messuage and 10 acres of land from his lord, and three pledges guaranteed that he would pay half of the entry fine of £4 6s. 8d. on 21 July, and the other half on 18 October. These dates would give him opportunities to raise cash from the sale of wool and grain, but the sums were well in excess of the surplus of a modest holding, so much of the money must have come from savings or loans. Customary tenants wishing to convert their tenancies to leasehold in the mid-to-late thirteenth century on the Gloucester Abbey estate were prepared to pay 5, 10 and even 25 marks (£3 6s. 8d. to £16 13s. 4d.) for the privilege. Manumission from serfdom later in the period could require larger payments. In 1412–13 three of Ramsey Abbey's serfs had agreed to pay a total of £50 for their freedom; two of them had paid up fully by the end of the year (£10 and £20), while the other contributed a first instalment of £5 towards a sum of £20.[38] Those acquiring land also paid consider-

36 J. Hatcher, *Rural economy and society in the duchy of Cornwall 1300–1500* (Cambridge, 1970), p. 255; C. Dyer, *Lords and peasants in a changing society. The estates of the bishopric of Worcester, 680–1540* (Cambridge, 1980), p. 352; M. K. McIntosh, *Autonomy and community. The royal manor of Havering 1200–1500* (Cambridge, 1986), p. 231; Suffolk R.O. (Ipswich branch), v5/18/1.2.

37 J. D. A. Thompson, *Inventory of British coin hoards A.D. 600–1500* (Oxford, 1956), p. 68 (Hesleyside, Northumberland, 257 coins, mostly pennies); p. 108 (Newminster, Northumberland, 472 coins, mostly pennies). The use of hoards as a guide to peasant accumulation was suggested to me by Dr J. Laszlovszky.

38 R. B. Pugh (ed.), *Court rolls of the Wiltshire manors of Adam de Stratton* (Wiltshire Record Soc., 24, 1968), p. 167; R. H. Hilton, *The English peasantry in the later middle ages* (Oxford, 1975), p. 152; J. A. Raftis, *The estates of Ramsey Abbey* (Toronto, 1957), pp. 284–5.

able sums of cash to the vendors, the previous tenants. In 1260 Richard Mogge of Alrewas (Staffordshire) paid 22s. for a quarter-yardland, and even after the fall in land values, holdings in eastern England changed hands for large sums: 26s. 8d. for 1³/₄ acres and a cottage at Blickling (Norfolk) in 1430, or £12 for 20 acres at Fingrith (Essex) in 1378.[39] These sums were in addition to entry fines paid to the lord, though the instalments were sometimes payable over two to five years. Marriages were occasions for the payments of dowries, some of which are revealed by disputes to have consisted of cash and goods worth 13s. 4d., 35s. 11d., 57s. and 63s. 4d.[40] If the family were servile, the lord also had to be satisfied with a merchet, which could be as small as a shilling or two or, if they seemed able to afford it, as high as 5s., 6s. 8d. and 13s. 4d. On the day of the marriage the clergy received a payment, as did the church-wardens, and a feast had to be provided. At Brigstock (Northamptonshire) in 1306 a wedding feast ran to 20s., and on some manors the expense was increased by the lord's insistence that his farm servants should be invited along.[41] An upper peasant marriage could easily have cost £3 to £4, more than the expense of a new house. Finally, peasants coming before the royal courts were expected as defendants or as litigants to pay fines and amercements of 6s. 8d., 10s. and 13s. 4d. Leading villagers would club together to mount expensive law suits against their lords, like those of South Petherton (Somerset) who in 1278 raised a common fund to pay £3 6s. 8d. to a lawyer, as a first instalment of a total fee of £6 13s. 4d.[42]

Peasants could save up coins by putting their surpluses in concealed pots, but many of the large payments detailed above, or the sums needed to build a house or to buy a cart, must have been raised by means of credit. Pleas of debt in manorial courts show that a certain amount of cash could have been borrowed within the peasant community itself. However, the bulk of the recorded loans were for quite small sums – two-thirds of those in the court at Wakefield in 1331–2, and 50 per cent in the west midlands in the late fourteenth and fifteenth centuries, were for 5s. or less.[43] Larger sums might

39 W. N. Landor (ed.), *Alrewas court rolls, 1259–61* (Staffordshire Record Soc., new ser., 10, 1907), p. 271; Norfolk R.O., 11262, 26A4; Essex R.O., D/DHt M93.
40 Homans, *English villagers*, p. 140; E. Searle, 'Merchet in medieval England', *P. and P.*, 82 (1979), 20; S. S. Walker (ed.), *The court rolls of the manor of Wakefield* (Yorkshire Archaeological Soc., Wakefield court roll ser., 3, 1982), p. 85.
41 J. M. Bennett, *Women in the medieval English countryside* (New York, 1987), p. 94; Coleman, *Downham-in-the-Isle*, p. 86.
42 G. O. Sayles (ed.), *Select cases in King's Bench* (Selden Soc., 55, 1936), pp. 80–1.
43 Walker (ed.), *Court rolls of . . . Wakefield*; Hilton, *English peasantry*, pp. 46–7.

Table 16. *Values of chattels of felons from the Shropshire eyre of 1256*

Below 2s.	2s.– 4s. 11d.	5s.– 9s. 11d.	10s.– 19s. 11d.	20s.– 39s. 11d.	40s. or above	Total
21	13	18	20	21	6	99

Source note: A. Harding (ed.), *The roll of the Shropshire eyre* (Selden Soc., 96, 1981)

have been built up by negotiating a number of loans, or more likely by going outside the peasant community to the parish clergy, or to the towns, where cornmongers and woolmongers might have advanced cash in anticipation of future crops. The best security was provided by land, and a few known mortgages may in fact be stray recorded examples of a much more widespread practice. A typical case, exposed by a dispute, arose from William Jonot of Wakefield mortgaging an acre in 1348 in order to raise 24s.[44] Debt is scarcely itself evidence of prosperity, but the willingness of lenders to risk their cash suggests that they judged some peasants to have the resources to pay back the loans. In the same way, the demands of lords for large fines and payments for manumissions must have been based on some notion that the sums could be paid. Tenants may have been reduced sometimes to abject destitution by unrealistic extortions, but the best interests of the lord lay in extracting as much cash as possible while leaving the tenant with enough to live, and to pay, another day.

Deep strata of poverty existed in peasant society. Firstly, there was the almost hidden group of non-tenants, like the cottar subtenants of Bishop's Cleeve (see p. 120), or the landless serfs of Alrewas, who accounted for a third of the 192 deaths there in the 1349 epidemic, or the shadowy outsiders, who cannot 'be identified with any particular family grouping' encountered in any analysis of manorial court rolls.[45] Although some may have made a decent living as subtenants, or as servants, most must have lived precariously from

---

44 H. M. Jewell (ed.), *The court rolls of the manor of Wakefield* (Yorkshire Archaeological Soc., Wakefield court roll ser., 2, 1981), p. 45.

45 *V.C.H. Staffordshire*, vol. 6, pp. 37–8; E. Britton, *The community of the vill* (Toronto, 1977), pp. 13, 234–41.

casual labouring, gleaning, begging, prostitution and sheaf-stealing. This poverty-stricken underworld is revealed by the valuations put on the chattels of criminals who had either fled or been hanged, as reported to the royal justices on eyre. In the Shropshire eyre of 1256 a third of felons had goods worth less than 5s. (see table 16). Some chattels were valued at 3d. and 4d., presumably the clothes the accused had been wearing. There is no need to speculate about the size of the second pool of rural poverty, because it included a large section of the smallholding peasantry. These were the people, often a half of the potential tax-payers, whose goods were valued at so low a figure that they were exempted from contributing even 8d. to the lay subsidy. A similar proportion of tenants in the early fourteenth century paid a heriot of some decrepit animal, or wretched article of clothing, or small sum in cash. A minority of them were judged to be unable to pay amercements of 3d. or 4d. in their lord's court, and were let off 'because poor'.[46] Such was the state of this section of the population that they could only pay for food in years of high grain prices, especially in East Anglia, by selling parcels of land.[47] An index of their desperation was the rising tide of crime during the bad harvest years in the early fourteenth century.[48] Their needs for a few shillings account for a high proportion of small debts recorded in the manorial courts. If the better-off peasants became drawn into seasonal loans, borrowing in the lean times of early summer, and repaying in the autumn, how much more necessary was short-term credit to keep the smallholders afloat as their grain stores were exhausted well before the next harvest?[49] These groups were vulnerable in the period 1285–1348 when death-rates rose in bad harvest years.[50]

There is some direct evidence of changes and improvements in peasant living standards in the late fourteenth and fifteenth centuries.

---

46 A. N. May, 'An index of thirteenth century peasant impoverishment? Manor court fines', *Ec.H.R.*, 2nd ser., 26 (1973), 389–402.

47 B. M. S. Campbell, 'Population pressure, inheritance and the land market in a fourteenth-century peasant community' in R. M. Smith (ed.), *Land, kinship and life-cycle* (Cambridge, 1984), pp. 110–20.

48 B. Hanawalt, 'Economic influences on the pattern of crime in England, 1300–1348', *American Journal of Legal History*, 18 (1974), 281–97.

49 E. Clark, 'Debt litigation in a late medieval English vill' in J. A. Raftis (ed.), *Pathways to medieval peasants* (Toronto, 1981), p. 267.

50 M. M. Postan and J. Z. Titow, 'Heriots and prices in Winchester manors' in M. M. Postan, *Essays on medieval agriculture and general problems of the medieval economy* (Cambridge, 1973), pp. 150–85.

The expectation of life among tenants increased. According to one estimate, the average for more substantial tenants in the mid-thirteenth century was 24 years at the age of 20, and this deteriorated to 20 years at the age of 20 after 1292. Using another method of measurement, the male peasants at Halesowen in the early fourteenth century could have expected to live for 25–28 years at the age of 20, and the poor 20.8 at the age of 20. In spite of the cycle of recurrent epidemics of the later fourteenth century, Halesowen peasants are thought to have increased their expectation at 20 to 32.5 years. A similar figure, 31 years, at Ombersley (Worcestershire) has been calculated from examples observed in the period 1360–1429, rising to 36 at 20 in 1430–1500. In much the same time-span, tenants of the bishops of Worcester who took up holdings in their mid-twenties are believed to have lived for at least another 23 to 25 years.[51] The smallholders in particular, who formed a good proportion of the tenants even in the later period, were living very much longer than had their forebears in the pre-Black Death era. The implication of these calculations is that better diet and improved housing conditions had more influence on the lives of the peasantry than the ravages of epidemics.

In his analysis of modern peasantries, Wolf talks of a 'ceremonial fund' which absorbs a good deal of peasant production.[52] The medieval English equivalent of this fund can be seen in the activities of the parish, and in particular, the levying and spending of money by the church-wardens, the laymen who from the thirteenth century were responsible for the fabric of the nave of the church, and for books and vestments. The church-wardens were able to draw on considerable resources from the parishioners at all periods, judging from the widespread building and ornamentation that went on in the thirteenth century as well as later. The sums involved are not fully recorded until the church-wardens' accounts become available after 1400, when the flow of cash often seems to have been substantial. Wardens of Tintinhull (Somerset), for example, could raise an annual average of 51s. in the 1430s from 300 parishioners at most. The

51 *Ibid.*, p. 154; Z. Razi, *Life, marriage and death in a medieval parish. Economy, society and demography in Halesowen, 1270–1400* (Cambridge, 1980), pp. 43–5, 130–1; G. Scardellato, 'Medieval records of Ombersley manor (rentals and court rolls, 1300–1500)' (University of British Columbia Ph.D. thesis, 1983), chapter 4, p. 28; Dyer, *Lords and peasants*, p. 229.

52 E. R. Wolf, *Peasants* (Englewood Cliffs, N.J., 1966), pp. 7–9.

sums included gifts or legacies from individuals, and accumulations of small payments from church ales, when the wardens would brew and sell at a profit.[53] The success of such fund-raising is well attested by the numerous rebuildings and additions to parish churches of the period 1350–1520, which in East Anglia and the south-west were on a large scale. The rebuilding of the nave of a parish church in the new perpendicular style sometimes contrasts with the survival of a twelfth- or thirteenth-century chancel, which was the responsibility of the rector or a monastery that had appropriated the rectorial revenues. Regional patterns of church building show that the surplus wealth of the rural population was unequally distributed. The woodlands of north Warwickshire, for example, had more fifteenth- and early sixteenth-century church building than did the corn-grow-ing south of the county, where a greater proportion of pre-1350 structures survived unaltered.[54] The increasing size of the ceremonial fund is also indicated by the rising membership of religious fraterni-ties, which many peasants joined by paying a few shillings' entry fee. Richer peasants in East Anglia bequeathed in their wills sums of money (£5 for a year, in some cases) for a priest to pray for their souls.

Tax records reflect the changing wealth of the tax-payer in only the crudest fashion. Very little significance can be seen in the chang-ing yield of the lay subsidies in the decades around 1300, because their decline had administrative as well as economic causes. Impor-tance should, however, be attached to the many complaints of poverty and untilled fields reported in the records of the exper-imental ninth of 1341, as the gloomy reports can be corroborated from other sources. The new tax was evidently being collected in some regions at a time of profound economic depression that had forced many peasants to abandon their holdings.[55] The main impor-tance of the subsidy records lies in their testimony to regional variety in the wealth of rural communities. The tax of 1334 shows a marked superiority in the taxable wealth of the south and east, with pockets of abnormally high taxation in such areas as the Thames valley,

53 E. Hobhouse (ed.), *Church-wardens' accounts* (Somerset Record Soc., 4, 1890), pp. 175–9.
54 J. Trainor, 'Medieval churches in Warwickshire' (University of Birmingham B.A. dissertation, 1971).
55 A. R. H. Baker, 'Evidence in the *Nonarum Inquisitiones* of contracting arable lands in England during the early fourteenth century', *Ec.H.R.*, 2nd ser., 19 (1966), 518–32.

north Kent and north Norfolk. Comparison with the newly assessed taxes of the early sixteenth century shows in the intervening 180 years a shift towards the London area, the south of East Anglia and Essex, parts of the west riding of Yorkshire, and above all a remarkable rise in the south-west. This reflects both the influence of the prospering cities of London and Exeter, and the rise of rural industries. Some peasants participated in industry directly, and others benefited from the demand for agricultural products by the artisans.[56]

In general terms the models of the peasant economy presented earlier are compatible with the more direct evidence of peasant consumption and resources. Both approaches define a pronounced peasant hierarchy of wealth. Both identify the late thirteenth and early fourteenth centuries as hard times, especially for smallholders, and suggest a degree of amelioration in peasant living conditions in the late fourteenth and fifteenth centuries. However, as is commonly found in such studies, our expectations based on models are not entirely borne out by the more direct evidence.[57] The models suggest profound differences between the yardlanders and the half-yardlanders. Yet the gap between yardlanders' and half-yardlanders' houses or farming equipment does not seem to have been so wide. The reconstruction of the half-yardlander's budget in 1299 left him with a very slender margin, yet somehow half-yardlanders of that period were able to build houses that were considerably superior to the cheap shack that we might expect. They regarded it as possible on their retirement to have 3s. or so annually to spend on clothes. Smallholders really seem to have suffered in the early fourteenth century, yet Richard le Knyth of Monkton Deverill in Wiltshire in 1308 was required to produce 26s. 8d. as an entry fine on a quarter-yardland within six months, presumably in expectation that he could raise the sum.[58] The reconstruction of a smallholder's budget is

56 R. E. Glasscock, *The lay subsidy of 1334* (London, 1975), pp. xxiv-xxix; R. Schofield, 'The geographical distribution of wealth in England, 1334–1649' in R. Floud (ed.), *Essays in quantitative economic history* (Oxford, 1974), pp. 79–106; H. C. Darby *et al.*, 'The changing geographical distribution of wealth in England: 1066–1334–1525', *Journal of Historical Geography*, 5 (1979), 247–62.

57 The problems are aired in M. Aymard, 'Autoconsommation et marchés: Chayanov, Labrousse ou Le Roy Ladurie', *Annales E.S.C.*, 38 (1983), 1392–1410.

58 Longleat MS. 9658.

entirely compatible with evidence of rising death-rates in bad harvest years – but perhaps we should expect the death-rate to have been even higher?

Historians puzzling over these discrepancies have suggested hidden factors that might have raised living standards above the low levels predicted by conventional budget calculations. Perhaps the ill-documented garden was large and productive enough to supply a high proportion of food needs, and therefore compensate for the small size and limited productivity of the main arable holding? Have we underestimated the penetration of the market into the rural economy – was there really much more paid work than is normally assumed? Perhaps the contribution of gathering to the peasant's household economy has been underestimated, particularly in the case of the smallholders of East Anglia, who could make a good living in the marshes and fens by fishing, fowling, salt-making, cutting sedge, rushes and reeds, and digging peat?[59] There may be truth in all of these suggestions, but not enough to raise so many budgets above the predictions. Perhaps the fault of the models lies in their individualism, because they inevitably treat each peasant household as an island, whereas in reality peasants were embedded in a community which had important influences on the economy of each holding. Households were involved in a network within the village in which goods, labour and produce were exchanged without much use of cash. The system occasionally spilled over into the written accounts of lords who became involved in an arrangement of 'counters'. A peasant owing rent to a small monastery would pay no cash but would do harvest work for the monks and provide them with a bullock for the kitchen, so cancelling his debt. The transactions would appear in a formal account as a series of payments, but in reality no money changed hands. Inter-peasant transactions are known at Havering (Essex), where 'balances could go uncollected for years'.[60] Such arrangements within a village would make house building much more affordable for those without accumulations of cash. Similarly, the borrowing of animals and equipment compensated the smallholders for their lack of capital. Labour was exchanged, not for cash, but for meals and other payments in kind. A

---

59 For example, Britton, *Community of the vill*, pp. 157–9; B. F. Harvey, 'The population trend in England between 1300 and 1348', *T.R.H.S.*, 5th ser., 16 (1966), 23–42.
60 P.R.O., sc6/1258/11; McIntosh, *Autonomy and community*, p. 169.

cottager's children would be taken into a yardlander's household as servants, providing their master with cheap labour, and relieving the cottager of the burden of feeding them.[61] The extreme inequalities of budgets between yardlanders and cottagers might have been partially evened out, if the yardlanders had households of six or seven people, and the cottagers only two or three.

The common fields always represented a compromise between collective and individual interests. Of course the cultivation of each strip was the responsibility of a single tenant, and the resulting crops belonged to him, but there were many ways in which a little of the produce could be shared with poorer neighbours, like the well-established custom that the poor could pick green peas from the edge of the strips. The rules of gleaning after the harvest could have been interpreted generously enough to give the poor of the village more than a few ears of corn from each strip. The peasants who managed the demesne could have been especially tolerant of intensive gleaning on the lord's stubble. If the system of moneyless credit was extended sufficiently to allow poor people to pay back over a number of years, they could have survived bad harvest years. In return, the better-off peasant would have expected to receive free labour, and might also have built up a clientage that raised his status in the village. These complex relationships were revealed only when tacit agreements broke down, and a plea of debt or broken contract was brought before the manorial court. They give a glimpse of the exchanges that spread through each peasant community. They tend to show a high level of contact between middling peasants, but this may be misleading, as the cottagers and smallholders who broke their bargains were too poor for it to be worth suing them.[62] Like the other explanations of peasants' ability to live a little above the level predicted from budget calculations, this cannot be regarded as a full answer to the problem, and we should presume that it was no more than a palliative, incapable of saving many peasants in the decades around 1300

61 Hilton, *English peasantry*, pp. 37–53; K. R. G. Glavanis, 'Aspects of non-capitalist social relations in rural Egypt: the small peasant household in an Egyptian Delta village' in N. Long (ed.), *Family and work in rural societies* (London, 1984), pp. 30–60.

62 Z. Razi, 'Family, land and the village community in later medieval England', *P. and P.*, 93 (1981), 3–36; R. M. Smith, 'Kin and neighbours in a thirteenth-century Suffolk community', *Journal of Family History*, 4 (1979), 219–56.

from an early grave. As peasants became more prosperous in the late fourteenth and fifteenth centuries, this partly hidden economy certainly continued, but as a lifeline for the poor it diminished in importance.

Finally the character of the peasant family had a strong influence on living standards. Perhaps the English peasantry throughout our period practised prudential marriage, and so delayed reproduction until they had land or another steady source of income. A sizeable minority, in accordance with the 'European marriage pattern', may have remained celibate. In the economic problems of the late thirteenth century many women may have waited until their mid-twenties before marrying, and some found it impossible to marry at all. This would have reduced the numbers of births and ultimately contributed to a slowing in the growth in population. Those who did marry could have contributed to the same trend by practising some form of birth control, which would not have prevented all conceptions, but would have increased the intervals between births. Such moves would have prevented a crisis of 'overpopulation' in general, and made life easier for individual families. However, the existence of this form of peasant family has not been proved. The most detailed study of peasant demography suggests that they sometimes behaved incautiously. The habit of better-off fathers of providing younger sons and daughters with smallholdings gave couples the opportunity to marry young and have children without a stable economic base. The thirteenth-century economic expansion may have tempted many young people into abandoning the normal restraints on marriage. Perhaps in any case children were seen not as a burden but as a blessing and a potential source of income, and couples conceived often to offset the inevitably high rates of infant mortality. These rival views of the peasant family have still not been resolved. Everyone would agree that by the end of our period late marriage was practised, so that families were less likely to find themselves struggling to bring up numerous children without an adequate income.[63]

---

63 R. M. Smith, 'Human resources', in G. Astill and A. Grant (eds.), *The countryside of medieval England* (Oxford, 1988), pp. 188–212; Razi, *Life, marriage and death*, pp. 27–98.

7

URBAN STANDARDS OF LIVING

Each medieval town had such a strong sense of identity that we tend to think of them as social and economic units, and talk of a whole town prospering and declining. Our purpose here is to examine the individuals living in towns, and we cannot assume that their changing wealth and living standards coincided precisely with the growth or decay of the urban community to which they belonged. The thirteenth century was a period of urban expansion, yet many of the people who crowded into the larger centres or who formed the population of the new market towns were clearly making a precarious living as occasional wage-earners and petty traders. Likewise later in the period, and especially in the fifteenth century, many larger towns went into decline, suffering a loss of population, a shrinkage of the built-up area and a diminution in commerce and industry. Some small towns declined so far as to lose their urban character. Even in these circumstances, individuals would not necessarily have experienced long-term impoverishment. They could have migrated from declining places to towns that retained their prosperity, like London or Exeter, or to one of the small towns or industrial villages where the expanding cloth industry was often located. One of the main symptoms of urban decline was not so much the wholesale emigration of the inhabitants, but the failure of the place to continue to attract immigrants. Disastrous urban crises, of the kind that struck Coventry in 1518–25, when an economic malaise was combined with a serious food shortage, undoubtedly caused much hardship and suffering; most towns that experienced difficulties did not undergo such traumas, but decayed gently.[1]

Medieval towns generated their own distinctive environment. Historians may define an urban settlement in terms of its economy, one in which a large concentration of people pursued a variety of occupations, but contemporaries would have recognized a town by its appearance, feel, sounds and smells. Houses were more closely packed than in a village, without spaces between the buildings along the street frontage. In Winchester, a large provincial town with about 7,000–8,000 inhabitants in 1400, the population density averaged twenty-nine people per acre within the walls, and as much as eighty-one per acre in the centre, which exceeds the densities in modern British cities.[2] In the early days of urban growth, townsmen had been assigned plots of a quarter- or half-acre on which to build their houses, leaving plenty of space for out-buildings, gardens and animal pens. As the larger towns developed, the plots became built-up and subdivided, and the houses were occupied by more than one family. Town houses rose to three or four storeys, which were sometimes divided into the equivalent of modern flats. Multi-occupation in London's Cheapside meant that people lived in close proximity to one another, sometimes housed in single rooms, with living accommodation adjacent to their neighbours' privies, and in some cases, to a churchyard.[3] High densities of people, many of whom kept animals and pursued trades and crafts using organic materials, inevitably created problems of disposing of effluents and rubbish. Privies ran into open drains or cess-pits, which had a tendency to leak. Heaps of manure lay in the streets, butchers dumped entrails, blood and hair in unsuitable places, and pigs rooted among the garbage. Water supplies were endangered by industrial and domestic wastes, and the air was filled with odours and smoke. London citizens in *c.* 1300, according to one estimate, burnt each year 40,000 metric tonnes of wood and 600 tonnes of sea-coal, all in a space of about two square miles. The hundreds of hearths for cooking,

---

1 C. Phythian-Adams, 'Urban decay in late medieval England' in P. Abrams and E. A. Wrigley (eds.), *Towns in societies* (Cambridge, 1978), pp. 159–85; R. B. Dobson, 'Urban decline in late medieval England', *T.R.H.S.*, 5th ser., 27 (1977), 1–22; C. Phythian-Adams, *Desolation of a city. Coventry and the urban crisis of the late middle ages* (Cambridge, 1979).

2 D. J. Keene, *Survey of medieval Winchester* (2 vols., Oxford, 1985), vol. 1, pp. 370–1.

3 D. J. Keene, 'Social and economic study of medieval London' (Summary report for Economic and Social Research Council, 1979–84), and personal comments.

Map 4   Location of towns and rural places mentioned in chapters 7 to 10

heating and industry threatened the surrounding buildings, and the history of many towns was punctuated by major fires.[4]

The town authorities exerted themselves to keep these problems under control. Rubbish disposal was organized, whether by making each householder responsible for his own, often resulting in the digging of pits in back-yards, or by the provision of a public street-cleaning service, as happened in London from the late thirteenth century. Butchers were assigned places to dump their wastes, or required to keep a cart for transporting them out of town, and threatened with penalties for failing to comply.[5] Bye-laws and building regulations sought to control the more noisome privies and cess-pits, and most large towns insisted that thatch be replaced by less flammable roofing materials, such as shingles or ceramic tiles.[6] Initiatives in public works provided larger towns with piped water supplies, drains and public latrines. The relative success of these measures is suggested by the judgement of archaeologists that towns were less filthy in the later middle ages than they had been a few centuries earlier.[7] We should remember that, unlike their modern successors, the men of influence and power in medieval towns lived in the town centres, and they therefore had a direct and personal interest in maintaining decent standards.

Towns, though densely populated, occupied a relatively small area, and few of their inhabitants lived more than a quarter-mile from open spaces. The wealthier townsmen kept gardens even in the centres, and as the built-up zone contracted in the later middle ages, gardens, orchards and yards expanded over the sites of decayed houses. Urban decay, at least in this respect, improved the living conditions of the remaining town-dwellers.[8]

We are prevented, however, from adopting excessively optimistic views about the quality of the urban environment by the abundant evidence for serious health problems. In the fifteenth century, urban populations could not maintain their numbers, and in earlier cen-

---

4 P. Brimblecombe, 'Early urban climate and atmosphere' and D. J. Keene, 'Rubbish in medieval towns' in A. R. Hall and H. K. Kenward (eds.), *Environmental archaeology in an urban context* (C.B.A. Research Report, 43, 1982), pp. 18–22, 26–30.

5 J. Schofield, *The building of London* (London, 1984), pp. 78–9, 95–8; E. Sabine, 'Butchering in mediaeval London', *Speculum*, 8 (1933), 335–53.

6 Toulmin Smith and F. Brentano (eds.), *English guilds* (Early English Text Soc., O.S., 40, 1870), p. 386.

7 H. K. Kenward *et al.*, 'The environment of Anglo-Scandinavian York' in R. A. Hall (ed.), *Viking age York and the north* (C.B.A. Research Report, 27, 1978), p. 68.

8 Keene, *Winchester*, pp. 151–5.

turies it seems likely that urban growth was sustained by substantial levels of immigration rather than by natural increase. Counts of family sizes (mostly from after 1400), from both England and the continent, reveal that few couples had as many as two children, presumably because of the high levels of infant and child mortality. In London, between 16 and 49 per cent of the orphans left by merchants in the period 1318–1497 died before they reached the age of twenty-one; the children of the poor presumably had even lower chances of survival.[9] Epidemic diseases tended to strike towns more often than rural communities, and to cause higher rates of mortality; at the end of our period bubonic plague had become an 'urban disease'. Archaeological research has revealed something of the dangers of town life. Analysis of the contents of cess-pits shows that people were carrying large numbers of intestinal parasites, such as whip-worms. The cemetery of the York church of St Helen-on-the-Walls was in use between the tenth and sixteenth century, and we may suppose that many of the burials belong to our period. Children accounted for 27 per cent of those buried, which understates their rate of mortality because their fragile bones have been more likely to be disturbed or decayed, and so escape the notice of modern archaeologists. Of the women and men who survived into adulthood, 56 and 36 per cent respectively died before they reached the age of thirty-five, and only 9 per cent of the burials were of people who had died aged sixty or over.[10] London merchants lived longer than the inhabitants of St Helen's parish, their median age of death being about fifty, but that is not surprising in view of the contrast between the wealth of the capital's élite and the relative poverty of the people of an undesirable part of York.[11] There is little evidence of major dietary deficiencies among those buried at St Helen's, apart from one case of rickets; there are enough examples of 'Harrison's lines' on bones and horizontal ridging of tooth enamel to suggest that some of the inhabitants went hungry or suffered major illnesses at some stage of their lives. Infectious diseases were the most likely cause of the relatively early deaths of so many people. The poor were more vulnerable because of their closely-packed living conditions, while

---

9 Phythian-Adams, *Desolation of a city*, pp. 221–37; S. Thrupp, *The merchant class of medieval London* (Chicago, 1948), pp. 202–3.
10 A. W. Pike and M. Biddle, 'Parasite eggs in medieval Winchester', *Antiquity*, 40 (1966), 293–6; J. D. Dawes and J. R. Magilton, *The cemetery of St Helen-on-the-Walls, Aldwark* (The archaeology of York, fascicle 12/1, York, 1980).
11 Thrupp, *Merchant class*, p. 194.

the rich could move out of the towns in times of epidemics. Just as those attending parliaments shied away from visiting a town suffering high mortality, so would-be immigrants were discouraged from taking up residence in such a dangerous environment.

URBAN INCOMES

Contemporaries tended to assess a townsman's wealth in terms of the value of his goods and chattels, while we need to learn their annual income in order to make comparisons with aristocrats and peasants. It is helpful to be told by those drafting the 1363 sumptuary law that 'merchants, citizens and burgesses' with goods worth £500 were equivalent to an esquire with a landed income of £100 per annum.[12] This must have been the roughest rule of thumb, not capable of being extended with too much precision, but it is still worth noting that of a sample of London merchants who died between 1350 and 1497, 14 per cent had an estate worth £1,000 or above, suggesting that they were the equivalents of rich knights and barons with incomes of £200 or more. This would certainly be in accordance with less tangible evidence of the close social links and shared culture which existed between the top rank of London citizens and the landed aristocracy. Some townsmen themselves enjoyed landed resources; in 1436 eighty Londoners, mostly merchants, were in possession of land worth £20 per annum or above, according to the (underassessed) income tax of that year.[13] However, this gives no real guide to merchants' total revenues, because rents tended to form a relatively small part of their resources, and to learn about their income from trade we need to know something about their margins of profit and the volume of goods in which they were dealing.[14] The fifteenth-century London grocers, it is thought, made a profit on their transactions of about 10 per cent, as did Colchester clothiers in the late fourteenth century. Estimates on the profits of the overseas wool trade vary, but from a range of 17–43 per cent in the late fifteenth century, the average is thought to have been near to 20 per cent. Many wool staplers shipped annually forty sacks or more, and on such a volume of trade they are unlikely to have made

12 *Statutes of the realm* (11 vols., Record Commission, 1810–28), vol. 1, p. 380.
13 Thrupp, *Merchant class*, pp. 110–26.
14 R. H. Hilton, 'Some problems of urban real property in the middle ages' in R. H. Hilton, *Class conflict and the crisis of feudalism* (London, 1985), pp. 165–74.

less than £50 in profit, depending on the quality of the wool. And in view of the unspecialized nature of medieval trade, wool would have been only one of a range of commodities in which they dealt.[15]

The well-documented Cely brothers, when they operated as Merchants of the Staple in the 1470s and 1480s, were each making profits in excess of £100 per annum. A merchant with a primary interest in the import trade, a Winchester vintner called Mark le Fayre, in the early fifteenth century is thought to have combined an income from rents of £26 per annum with trading profits in a normal year of £100 or more. In London, a merchant of the second rank with a finger in many pies but with a strong interest in the iron trade, Gilbert Maghfeld, handled goods worth £1,150 in 1390 which, on the assumption of 10 per cent profits, cannot have brought in less than £100. Richard Whittington, the outstanding merchant who became a legend, sold luxury textiles to the royal household worth £3,475 over a two-year period in 1392–4, again yielding a large sum if his profit margins were about 10 per cent, and this was by no means his whole trade. The £5,000 in cash, jewels and plate that he left on his death in 1423 is hardly surprising in view of his capacity to accumulate large profits.[16] At the other end of the scale were many traders called merchants, who, if we see significance in the valuation of their goods at £50 or below, could have expected an annual income of no more than £10 per annum.

The long-term trends in merchant incomes must be judged from the indirect evidence of the changes in patterns of trade. Although the volume of trade was very high in the thirteenth and early fourteenth century, many of the lucrative overseas transactions were in the hands of non-English merchants. The fifteenth century, when the overall quantity of commerce tended to decline, saw a paradoxically high level of English merchant activity, because merchants controlled a considerable proportion of the export trade, as Merchants of the Staple in the case of wool, and Merchant Adventurers

15 S. Thrupp, 'The grocers of London: a study of distributive trade' in E. Power and M. M. Postan (eds.), *Studies in English trade in the fifteenth century* (London, 1933), pp. 252–3; R. H. Britnell, *Growth and decline in Colchester, 1300–1525* (Cambridge, 1986), p. 62; A. Hanham, *The Celys and their world. An English merchant family of the fifteenth century* (Cambridge, 1985), p. 128; H. L. Gray, 'English foreign trade, 1446–1482' in Power and Postan (eds.), *English trade*, pp. 12–16.

16 Hanham, *The Celys*, pp. 420–1; Keene, *Winchester*, pp. 232, 272; M. K. James, *Studies in the medieval wine trade* (Oxford, 1971), p. 212; C. M. Barron, 'Richard Whittington: the man behind the myth' in A. E. J. Hollaender and W. Kellaway (eds.), *Studies in London history* (London, 1967), pp. 199–229.

for cloth. From the mid-fourteenth century they were also able to participate on a large scale in loans to the government, in which the Italians had been prominent in the reigns of the first two Edwards. A high proportion of the wealthy merchants lived in London, and they concentrated a growing share of the country's internal trade in their hands. There were still opportunities in the provinces for mercantile profit, especially for entrepreneurs involved in the manufacture of woollen cloth; this product supplied both the home market and an increasing share of European needs as well. The peak of merchant prosperity came in the years around 1400, when there was a boom in trade. Merchant wealth declined in the middle of the fifteenth century, as a pronounced overseas trading depression coincided with a decline in urban rents.[17]

Wealth in towns was distributed with extreme inequality, as any analysis of urban tax assessments soon reveals. A sizeable proportion of a town's assessment in 1524–5 might be borne by a single very wealthy individual, like Thomas Spryng's widow at Lavenham in Suffolk, who paid £50 towards the clothing town's total of £180.[18] The craftsmen who made up the middling ranks of larger towns and could form the upper crust of smaller places, overlapped in economic terms with the lower end of the mercantile class, like the butchers who were allowed, according to one local custom, a profit margin of 8½ per cent, but who in practice took 12 per cent or more. The turnover for those with interests in meat wholesaling must often have exceeeded £100 per annum.[19] Most craftsmen were in receipt of much lower sums. At the wealthy end of the group, a founder, hosier and tailor among York craftsmen owned goods according to inventories worth about £30. Poorer craftsmen are more rarely documented, but a characteristic example would be a York stringer (with a primary occupation of making bow strings), who died in 1436 leaving goods totalling £6. Many trades involved very small investments in equipment; a glover could be set up for work on an outlay of only £2 to £3, compared with a minimum for some merchants (London mercers) of £40.[20] Perhaps the best guide to a

17 E. M. Carus-Wilson and O. Coleman, *England's export trade, 1275–1547* (Oxford, 1963), pp. 122–3, 138–9; on rents, see, for example, A. F. Butcher, 'Rent, population and economic change in late-medieval Newcastle', *Northern History*, 14 (1978), 67–77.
18 S. H. A. Hervey, *Suffolk in 1524* (Woodbridge, 1910), pp. 24–9.
19 Keene, *Winchester*, p. 258.
20 H. Swanson, 'Craftsmen and industry in late medieval York' (University of York D.Phil. thesis, 1980), pp. 405–21.

craftsman's annual income is provided by the pay of building workers, such as masons and carpenters, who could earn £3 to £5 in the late thirteenth century, and £5 to £7 in the late fifteenth (see below, pp. 226–7). Because these craftsmen would have had to bear some expenses out of these earnings, it seems reasonable to estimate their profit in the fifteenth century at £3 to £5. Master craftsmen, like Bristol hoopers and Coventry cappers, who were paying their servants and journeymen £2 annually with food, or 1s. per week, must have made substantially more than this for themselves.[21] Some lesser craftsmen, such as the semi-skilled workers in the building trade, would have received much the same incomes as these servants.

Below the merchants and craftsmen, who together formed a minority in most large towns, came less wealthy groups, including the servants and journeymen already mentioned, the casually employed labourers, petty traders like chapmen, and hucksters selling bread and dairy products from baskets. Towns had a disproportionate number of single person households, often those of widows, who made a living by casual earnings and profits from the sale of foodstuffs or ale. And below them came vagrants and beggars who had been attracted by the town's wealth and the concentration of potential alms-givers. At Coventry in the early 1520s the estimate of those living in 'wretched poverty' has been put at a fifth of the population. This was in a time of profound crisis for that city, and a generation or two earlier a smaller pool of severe poverty can be assumed to have existed.[22]

URBAN CONSUMPTION

Townsmen made some contribution to their food supplies from their own land, whether from strips in open fields, which surrounded places as large as Cambridge or Leicester, or from the rural manors held by some merchants. Many craftsmen might have garden plots at the backs of their houses and would keep pigs. Still, the bulk of food consumed in towns came from the market, and food traders made up a high proportion of the occupational groupings found in any town. For example, the court of the modest town of Ely (population, *c.* 3,000–4,000) in 1422 dealt with offences against

---

21 W. Bickley (ed.), *Little Red Book of Bristol* (Bristol, 1900), pp. 159–67; M. D. Harris (ed.), *The Coventry leet book* (4 parts, Early English Text Soc., 134, 1907, 135, 1908, 138, 1909, 146, 1913), part 2, pp. 572–4.

22 Phythian-Adams, *Desolation of a city*, p. 134.

price controls and other regulations, in reality payments for licences to trade in many cases. One session of the court dealt with three bakers, thirty-seven brewers, seventy-three ale retailers, two vintners, twelve butchers, eleven dealers in fish and two cooks.[23] Some food traders sold ingredients for processing at home, and others sold food ready prepared, not just the bakers and brewers, but also the cooks, who in large towns are known to have sold pies, puddings, sauces and ready-roasted poultry.

Townsmen viewed *en masse* seem to have enjoyed a better diet than their country counterparts. Wheat bread was eaten in towns at all times, even in the thirteenth century. Rye was sometimes used, but not the quantities of barley bread found among the peasantry. Some bread was baked from wheat even in a town like Norwich in a barley-growing county. The large numbers of brewers suggest high levels of ale consumption: at Colchester there was a brewer for every thirty people in 1311. However, the brewing and selling of ale was an occasional and transient trade, so most brewers were selling for only a short time. Although wine-drinking was evidently confined to a minority, it was a very widespread practice judging from the appearance of vintners in quite small towns, such as Market Harborough in Leicestershire in 1422.[24] The numerous sellers of meat and fish demonstrate a high demand for these relatively expensive items. A high proportion of the meat came from young animals, as is shown by the analysis of bones from excavations on urban sites. This implies that the choicest beasts were sent for sale in towns, while the rural producers ate the meat of the more mature animals. Analysis of the contents of cess-pits and latrines reveals the importance in the urban diet of fruits, because the pips and stones show that people were eating apples, plums, cherries, grapes, gooseberries and other cultivated species in profusion, as well as wild fruit such as blackberries and sloes. One botanist has referred to the abundance of species as a 'medieval fruit salad'.[25] The greatest concentrations of gardens in medieval England were located in towns or their suburbs,

23 Cambridge U.L., EDR c6/1.
24 W. H. Hudson (ed.), *Leet jurisdiction in the city of Norwich* (Selden Soc., 5, 1891), p. 74; Britnell, *Colchester*, p. 21; James, *Wine trade*, p. 192.
25 B. Noddle, 'A comparison of the animal bones from 8 medieval sites in southern Britain' in A. T. Clason (ed.), *Archaeozoological studies* (Amsterdam, 1975), pp. 248–60; G. G. Astill, 'Economic change in later medieval England: an archaeological review' in T. H. Aston *et al.* (eds.), *Social relations and ideas* (Cambridge, 1983), pp. 242–5; J. Greig, 'The investigation of a medieval barrel-latrine from Worcester', *Journal of Archaeological Science*, 8 (1981), 265–82.

and gardeners and female hucksters sold fruit and vegetables in the streets.

Food supplies were problematic for the towns, as is evident from the numerous regulations of all aspects of the victualling trades.[26] Some of these rules were concerned with maintaining food quality and with protecting public health, such as those allowing for the inspection of fish, or forbidding the sale of measled pork and reheated pies. But their main purpose was to provide the urban population with as plentiful a supply of foodstuffs as possible, at the cheapest price. Urban authorities pursued an ideal of producers selling directly to the consumer, cutting out all middlemen, whose profit margins would raise the price. In reality, urban life was too complicated for such a perfect market to work, and consequently the town governments became involved in constant tussles with an army of traders, bakers, brewers, cooks and hucksters. The regulations forbade the interception of supplies as they came to town by cart or boat by forestallers who would resell the grain or fish at a higher price. Once the food had reached the market, consumers had priority to make their purchases before the processors, such as bakers and brewers, could buy. Brewers again were expected to sell first to consumers, rather than let the retailers, called tapsters and gannockers, take all the ale for resale. Ale and other foodstuffs had to be sold publicly, not at the back door to people in the know. Food traders were forbidden to form conspiracies to restrict supplies or to fix artificially high prices. Retailers were prohibited from combining two food trades; for example butchers were not allowed to act as cooks. Indeed, the prices were set by law, in the case of bread and ale by the sliding scale of the assizes, depending on the price of grain, and in the case of other foods (the cooks' products, for example) by local regulations. In the case of foodstuffs like meats, where no fixed price system could be used, the retailers' profit margins were limited by law. The constant reiteration and refinement of these measures show that the food traders often broke them, or found new ways of profiting at the public's expense. Sometimes a confrontation developed, as when the bakers of Coventry went on strike in 1484 by withdrawing to the nearby village of Baginton. A mixture of motives lay behind the food policies of the urban governments. Those who made the rule were themselves consumers, and on quite a large

---

26 This is based on Bickley (ed.), *Little Red Book*; Harris (ed.), *Coventry leet book; L'approvisionnement des villes de l'Europe occidentale au moyen âge et aux temps modernes* (Centre culturel de l'Abbaye de Flaran, Auch, 1985).

scale in the case of the wealthier merchants. In the fifteenth century, a London merchant's household could cost as much to feed as that of an esquire or knight, £30 to £60, or even £100 per annum.[27] More important, however, was a concern for the social and political equilibrium of the urban community. Every government feared disorder, and if the people of the town felt that they were the victims of unfettered profiteers they would have had ample grounds for grumbling and rebellion. Governments sought to avoid such problems by aligning themselves on the side of the consumers. Finally, the town lived on its trade, and the products of the towns' workshops had to be reasonably priced in order to compete on the market. If foodstuffs were sold at the lowest possible price, this would make a contribution to containing wage costs. Some of the regulations demonstrate a concern to make cheap food available at the bottom of the market: brewers were ordered to sell their 'remnants', and butchers their offal, to the poorer inhabitants. For all of their efforts, the cost of living in towns was higher than in the countryside (see p. 210 below), but perhaps the disparity would have been even greater without the local regulations and their enforcement.

Towns felt themselves to be vulnerable to famine, because of their dependence on outside supplies. They made some long-term precautions, such as the building of granaries, and in bad years took measures to conserve stocks and increase supplies, by forbidding the export of grain, and sometimes by buying ship-loads for sale to the inhabitants. Wealthier townsmen were forbidden to waste grain on inessentials, and on at least one occasion there were enquiries into the private stocks of individuals.[28]

Improvements in urban diet in the long term are suggested by a number of changes in the food trade. The quality of wheat loaves varied with the fineness and whiteness of the flour used, the rich being able to afford the whitest 'wastel', and the poor eating coarse brown varieties such as 'treat'. In London in the early fourteenth century, the bakers of brown bread outnumbered those making white bread by thirty-two to twenty-one, but later the increased domination of the trade by white bakers suggests a move towards the more refined product. At Winchester, the prominence of fishmongers as compared to butchers in the early fourteenth century has suggested demand for the cheaper sources of protein, while the reversal of the trend after 1350 implies that as people became more

27 Hanham, *The Celys*, pp. 324–8; Thrupp, *Merchant class*, p. 143.
28 Harris (ed.), *Coventry leet book*, part 3, pp. 674–8.

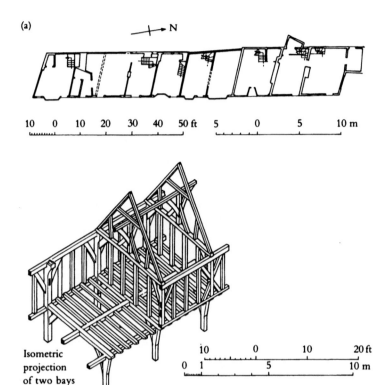

(a)

N

10   0   10   20   30   40   50 ft   5   0   5   10 m

Isometric
projection
of two bays

10   0   10   20 ft

0   1   5   10 m

Fig. 7 Urban houses
(The black lines on the ground plans indicate walls of the fourteenth century, the
shaded walls were built between 1400 and 1550, and the unshaded walls are modern)
(a) The early fourteenth-century Lady Row in Goodramgate in York was built
originally as a terrace of eleven one-bay, two-storey houses, with a living room (hall)
on the ground floor and sleeping quarters (chamber) above. Although built for poor
people's accommodation, the landlords used high-quality carpentry as a long-term
investment.
Source: Royal Commission on Historical Monuments, *City of York* (London, 1981),
vol. 5, p. 144
(b) Hampton Court, King's Lynn, developed as a superior merchant's house from the
late fourteenth to the early sixteenth century. It was built around a courtyard, with
ample domestic accommodation in one wing for the merchant's family and servants,
shops on the street frontage, and a warehouse facing the river.
Sources: W. A. Pantin, 'The merchants' houses and warehouses of King's Lynn', *Med.
Arch.*, 6–7 (1962–3), 180; W. A. Pantin, 'Medieval English town-house plans', *Med.
Arch.*, 6–7 (1962–3), 234

(b)

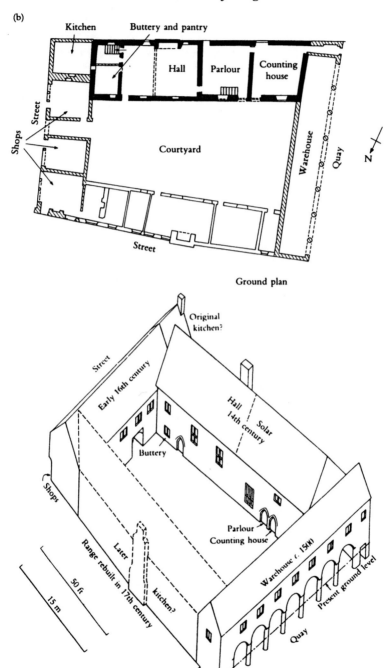

Kitchen

Buttery and pantry

Hall

Parlour

Counting house

Street

Shops

Courtyard

Warehouse

Quay

N

Street

Ground plan

Original kitchen?

Street

Early 16th century

Hall 14th century

Solar

Buttery

Shops

Parlour Counting house

Warehouse (. 15M)

Later

Range rebuilt in 17th century

kitchen?

Present ground level

Quay

50 ft

15 m

wealthy they ate more meat. As in the country, consumption of pigs declined as bacon was rejected in favour of fresh beef and mutton. This shift towards meat-eating, and a decline in the consumption of cereal foods, was a feature of the diets given to employees as part of their pay. By the early fifteenth century, non-cereal foods accounted for 37 per cent of the cost of urban building workers' diet.[29] That this was a new situation is suggested by the attempt in 1363 to restrict urban employees to only one meal per day containing meat or fish, evidently the normal practice before 1349, but now abandoned in the face of the workers' superior bargaining power.

The familiar changes in house construction, by which vertical posts set in the ground were replaced by timber framing and stone foundations, occurred in the towns at about the same as in the countryside, in the thirteenth and early fourteenth century.[30] The exceptions were the houses of the wealthiest inhabitants in larger towns such as Canterbury, Southampton and Lincoln, which had been built entirely of stone since the twelfth century. Regional building traditions were very influential; in Norwich, the relatively impermanent but cheap method of construction with clay walls continued in some cases throughout the fifteenth century, as it did in the surrounding villages. In King's Lynn in the same county, wattle and daub were the main wall materials. The distinctive character-istics of the medieval townscape came from the large number of houses of two or more storeys. Some buildings were only partly storeyed, being of the 'wealden' type with an open hall flanked by bays with upper chambers. The impetus to build upwards was strongest in the centres of large towns, where space was scarce and property values at their highest, and houses rose to three or four storeys. The space on the upper levels was increased by jettying, by which the floors projected as an overhang. The necessary accompa-

---

29 S. Thrupp, *A short history of the worshipful company of bakers of London* (London, 1933), pp. 119–22; Keene, *Winchester*, pp. 259–60; Astill, 'Economic change', p. 244; R. H. Hilton, 'Pain et cervoise dans les villes anglaises au moyen âge' in *L'approvisionnement des villes*, p. 222.

30 This section uses W. A. Pantin, 'Medieval English town-house plans', *Med. Arch.*, 6–7 (1962–3), 202–39; M. Biddle, 'Excavations at Winchester', *Antiquaries Journal*, 47 (1967), 264–5; 48 (1968), 265–6; P. Short, 'The medieval rows of York', *Archaeological Journal*, 137 (1980), 86–137; P. A. Faulkner, 'Medieval undercrofts and town houses', *Archaeological Journal*, 123 (1966), 120–35; J. Munby, 'Medieval domestic buildings' in J. Schofield and R. Leech (eds.), *Urban archaeology in Britain* (C.B.A. Research Report, 61, 1987), pp. 156–66; W. A. Pantin, 'The merchants' houses and warehouses of King's Lynn', *Med. Arch.*, 6–7 (1962–3), 173–81; and studies of individual towns cited in notes 2, 5, 9, 15, 32 and 34.

niments of multi-storey living were internal staircases, or at least ladders for the less well-off, and chimneys, which seem to have proliferated in some towns in the fourteenth century, though they were still coming into places like York and Worcester in the following century. Those living on upper floors were provided with internal latrines which ran into stone-lined cess-pits at ground level. Buildings in towns tended to adopt the use of superior materials such as roofing tiles and bricks rather more quickly than in the villages; in the case of tiles this was partly because of their enforced use as a fire precaution.

The urban poor lived in single-room dwellings, either a sublet room in a larger house, or as part of a terrace. In a row of the early fourteenth century excavated at Brook Street in Winchester each house measured 15 by 15 feet; the internal space was subdivided with partitions into areas of different functions, and if these really housed whole families we must assume that they made very cramped homes. In York in the early fourteenth century, builders ran up terraces of housing to be let to poorer townsmen, and by a unique combination of circumstances, not only do the houses still survive, but their inhabitants in 1381 can sometimes be identified from the poll tax records (see fig. 7). A labourer apparently occupied a two-storey house in such a row, measuring 17 by 11½ feet at ground level, while a craftsman, a tailor, is known to have lived in a three-storey building of similar floor area. Labourers worked on other people's premises but craftsmen needed an extra room as a workshop, where goods could be made and sold to customers. The shop occupied the ground floor, a living room (hall) would be on the first floor, and the sleeping accommodation (chamber) on the second floor. The two-storey houses occupied by most craftsmen could be set at a right angle to the street frontage, with a shop in the ground floor of the end-bay nearest the street, and a hall behind, with chambers above. When space was less restricted the whole building might lie parallel with the street. A superior craftsman's house was described when a Coventry weaver, Thomas Brone, in 1425 made a building agreement with his landlord to erect a three-bay house, 45 feet long, of which one bay would be used for an open hall (so this was a house of 'wealden' type), another bay for an entrance with two small chambers (for apprentices, perhaps?) and a solar above, and the third bay for a ground floor chamber and a solar upstairs, making a total of six rooms in all. Two chimneys were to be provided, for hearths in the hall and one of the chambers.[31]

Larger houses suitable for merchants might be built as a double range parallel to the street, with a shop or shops at the front (some of them being sublet) and the hall and living accommodation behind. The house could be extended upwards, with shops occupying the ground floor, the hall and kitchen the first floor, and the chambers on the second floor. Extra storage space, or a shop, could be created by providing a stone undercroft. These basements were also used as taverns. The ultimate luxury in merchant housing would consist of four ranges built around a courtyard, in the same style as an inn or an aristocratic town house. Shops would occupy the street frontage, again most of them rented out, and access would be gained through an impressive gateway. The other sides of the rectangle would provide ample living space; in the case of one of the best preserved surviving examples, Hampton Court at King's Lynn, the rear backed onto the quay and was used as a warehouse (see fig. 7).

Urban decline in the fourteenth and fifteenth centuries caused the abandonment of many former house sites. At Southampton merchants ceased to build new houses in stone as they had done before 1300.[32] However, the houses that were built or rebuilt in English towns in the fifteenth century – and they were many – indicate that individual living standards were rising. For the upper class, the reduced size of the hall and the proliferation of private chambers run parallel to the trends in aristocratic accommodation. For the less wealthy, although existing rows continued to be inhabited, there was a trend at York, for example, towards more individual houses, of the type occupied by Thomas Brone the Coventry weaver. Chimneys were built in greater numbers, as were tiled roofs. Glazed windows were by no means common, but examples can be found in houses below the merchant level. The quality of the construction of urban houses, especially of their carpentry, is attested by the numbers still surviving, both in towns that were declining and those that were thriving. Eighty houses built before 1500 have been identified in the town of Salisbury alone, and the total over the whole country, especially in many small towns, must run into thousands. If buildings alone provided evidence for the changing fortunes of the inhabitants of fifteenth-century towns, we would have to conclude that they were passing through a period of unparalleled prosperity.

The high quality of surviving urban building reflects the fact that much of it was put up by landlords for letting, for which some invested in highly competent craftsmen and used good quality ma-

---

32 C. Platt, *Medieval Southampton* (London, 1973), p. 145.

terials. Building costs could be as low as £2 for a one-bay two-storey cottage, but the individual dwellings of the well-built York rows in the early fourteenth century required as much as £5 each. A two-storey craftsman's house of two or three bays with a tiled roof could be erected for £10 to £15, and the cost of a merchant's house would amount to between £33 and £66, with a large building of the court-yard type needing expenditure of £90 or above.[33]

Wealthy townsmen behaved like aristocratic consumers in that, after spending a good proportion of their income on food for their households, their other main areas of expenditure were building and textiles. Inventories of their possessions (see table 17) show them as owners of large quantities of clothing, bedding and household tex-tiles, including in the later part of the period tapestries and hangings. They also displayed and stored their wealth by buying silver plate and jewels. Just as a high proportion of a knight's goods consisted of the stock and equipment of agricultural production, so merchandise bulks large in a wealthy townsman's inventory of possessions (see p. 76). As we have seen, the minimum capital for a mercer starting up in business was set at £40, and at any one time a leading merchant could have had goods worth a thousand pounds lying in his ware-house. The merchandise belonging to Simon de Leverington of King's Lynn accounted for 38 per cent of his goods assessed for subsidy payment in the late 1280s (table 17). Urban craftsmen could have obtained the tools of their trade quite cheaply, often for a few shillings, and the most valuable of their possessions consisted of raw materials and finished products awaiting sale (see p. 172). We must presume that expenditure on food took up a very high proportion of a craftsman's budget, and that textiles, judging from their invento-ries, accounted for much of their other spending. Prosperous crafts-men could afford to buy a few pieces of plate, often a mazer (a cup of high-quality turned wood, with silver fittings) or silver spoons. Metal domestic utensils, especially cooking equipment, seem to have been owned in quantity by middle-ranking townsmen. Richard le Barbur of King's Lynn (see table 17) owned a lead and a tripod for brewing worth a sixth of his whole inventory. The quantity in a single kitchen is strikingly illustrated by a find at Norwich, among the debris of a fire of 1507, of cooking pots, a frying pan, spits, basting spoons and a pothook. The small finds

---

33 R. Machin, 'The mechanism of the pre-industrial building cycle', *Vernacular Architecture*, 8 (1977), 15–19; Thrupp, *Merchant class*, pp. 132–3; L. F. Salzman, *Building in England, down to 1540*, 2nd edn (Oxford, 1967), pp. 517–19.

Table 17. *Urban goods and chattels. A King's Lynn tax assessment of c. 1285–90, comparing the goods of a merchant with those of a craftsman (a barber, whose wife span)*

	Simon de Leverington		Richard le Barbur	
Money	Cash	6s. 2d.	Cash	10s. 0d.
	Debts	£23 17s. 0d.		
Jewels and plate	Jewels	£1 15s. 0d.		
	Silver spoons & plate	£2 1s. 8d.		
	4 mazers	£1 10s. 0d.		
Textiles and bedding	Silk quilt	10s. 0d.		
	Bedspreads (16) Sheets (20) }	£3 1s. 0d.	Bedspreads (2)	2s. 0d.
	Featherbeds (8) Cloths (6) and towels (8)	14s. 0d.	Cloth (1) and towels (3) }	2s. 0d.
Clothing	2 robes* for men and 3 for women, a cloak }	£3 7s. 4d.	Supertunic and tabard	3s. 0d.
Kitchen equipment	Lead†	£2 12s. 9d.	Lead†	7s. 3d.
	100lb brass (pots)	£1 0s. 0d.	Wooden vessels, etc. }	10s. 0d.
	Tripod etc.	3s. 4d.	Tripod etc.	1s. 3d.
	7lb tin in vessels	10½d.		
Furniture	4 chests	6s. 0d.	1 chest	2s. 0d.
			Boards and chequer	1s. 0d.
Foodstuffs	1 last herring	£3 0s. 0d.	1 qr maslin	4s. 0d.
			Larder	3s. 6d.
Stock	1 cow	6s. 0d.	Piglets	3d.
Fuel, lighting etc.	Turfs, tallow etc.	£1 15s. 6d.	Turfs, wood	3s. 6d.
Misc.	Armour	5s. 0d.		
Merchandise etc.	Charcoal, boards, etc.	£17 6s. 0d.	Wool and linen yarn	3s. 0d.
	Merchandise in ship	£12 0s. 5½d.		
	Total	£75 18s. 1d.		£2 12s. 9d.

* robe = suit of clothes   † lead = lead vessel used in brewing
(*N.B.*: Some personal possessions and tools of trade were excluded. In any tax, goods would be omitted and under-valued.)
Source note: D. M. Owen (ed.), *The making of King's Lynn* (Oxford, 1984), pp. 235–6, 246–7

from urban excavation sites in general are difficult to relate to any specific social group, but they suggest quite a rich material culture, exceeding the objects from rural sites both in their quantity and variety.[34] Among the most common metal finds are modest articles of dress such as belt and scabbard fittings. The iron-work of houses included locks, keys and hinges from doors, and there is much commonplace domestic equipment – knives, spoons, needles and thimbles. Enough townsmen owned horses to make the accoutrements of riding – spurs, bits, horseshoes, stirrups, and decorative harness fittings – common finds. Carved bone was used to make pins, knife handles and toggles, and mortars and whetstones were the most used stone objects. Urban deposits in waterlogged conditions, as at King's Lynn, reveal the great variety of wooden and leather utensils which have normally decayed, and which, especially in the case of treen table ware, spoons and pot covers, are rarely mentioned in the documents because of their cheapness.

The increase in the spending power of the urban wage-earners and artisans after 1349 attracted a good deal of contemporary comment, and indeed they were the groups at which the sumptuary law of 1363 was principally directed. Expenditure on clothing was stressed in that law, and increased purchase of household textiles is indicated by the references to hangings, even if only painted cloths, in modest houses. Use of pewter ware became more widely dispersed through urban society. There is also some indication that the quality of wooden furniture was increasing; it scarcely merited valuation in the thirteenth century, but later inventories mention such articles as 'jointed cupboards', evidently of superior workmanship.[35] Inventories of cottagers which total no more than a few shillings, and the market for second-hand clothes, even those of hanged felons, are reminders of pockets of continued urban poverty.

CONCLUSION

The urban economy was characterized by an intensity and variety of activity, leading to great rewards and high costs. Trade, especially

---

34 M. Atkin, A. Carter and D. H. Evans, *Excavations in Norwich, 1971–1978* (East Anglian Archaeology, 26, 1985), pp. 77–85; H. Clarke and A. Carter, *Excavations in King's Lynn* (Soc. for Med. Arch. Monograph Series, 7, 1977), especially pp. 286–377; J. H. Williams, *St Peter's Street, Northampton* (Northampton, 1979), pp. 248–302.
35 Keene, *Winchester*, pp. 176–7.

on a large scale and at long distance in valuable commodities, gave good returns, and for the urban masses there was a multiplicity of small jobs and chances for retail trade, none of which would have been especially rewarding in themselves, but which in combination gave families the ability to make a living. The attractions of town life for migrants lay in the range of opportunities unavailable in the countryside.[36]

Houses, as we have seen, were more complex than those of villages, and two or three times as expensive. Most townsmen did not pay for the construction, which was often borne by landlords confident of a profitable investment. The rents reflect the costs of building and the competition for accommodation; they varied with the size of the town and the state of its economy, but an annual rent of 5s. for a cottage, 20s. for a craftsman's house, and £2 or £3 for a more pretentious merchant's house were not unusual. Rents and tithes were closely linked, because in some places tithes were paid at a rate of a penny per week for every 20s. of annual rent, which would give many cottagers a tithe burden of 1s. 1d. per annum (a week's cash wages for many journeymen).[37] Every ascent through the social hierarchy of the town had to be paid for. To gain the freedom of the town, for those not fortunate enough to have inherited it, or for those who had not earned it by the hard road of apprenticeship, a payment of between 3s. 4d. and 20s. was required. Membership of a fraternity or company, essential for the pursuit of many trades and crafts, could cost another 6s. 8d. to £3, depending on the rewards and exclusiveness of the occupation. Membership of fraternities and participation in civic life led the more successful townsmen into the expenses of office, such as the feast that guild masters or town officials were expected to fund for the other members of the élite.[38] Towns, as centres of money-making, were expected to contribute a large share of taxation. The lay subsidies were levied on many larger towns at the rate of a tenth, instead of the rural rate of a fifteenth. Townsmen were also required to produce extra taxes, like the tallages of the thirteenth century and the loans and benevolences of the fifteenth. Many of the larger towns paid a substantial fee-farm of £30 to £100 per annum to the Crown. The Crown's indirect taxes on wool and other traded goods were paid initially by merchants, even

36 R. H. Hilton, 'Lords, burgesses and hucksters', *P. and P.*, 97 (1982), 3–15.
37 Keene, *Winchester*, p. 123.
38 J. I. Kermode, 'Urban decline? The flight from office in late medieval York', *Ec.H.R.*, 35 (1982), 179–98.

if they were able to pass the tax on to their customers and suppliers. The towns which enjoyed a good deal of financial autonomy were able to levy indirect taxes to pay for wall building and street paving, which drew the poor, who were largely exempt from the property taxes, into contributing to civic expenditure. They were subject to the jurisdiction of the borough courts, which gained a good proportion of their revenues from amercements for trading offences, especially breaches of the assize of ale by relatively poor retailers. The Justices of the Peace joined in this activity in the late fourteenth century by fining those who broke the rules on trading practices (for example, by forestalling and regrating, again usually affecting food traders). Financial autonomy gave the oligarchies the chance to shift financial burdens onto the lower classes, and periodic complaints reveal the grievances of those who felt themselves unfairly treated.

Townsmen contributed a large proportion of their resources to the 'ceremonial fund' of their communities, because many larger towns had a high density of parish churches, religious fraternities, friaries and hospitals, all of which pressed the surrounding laity into making donations. The towns themselves organized processions and ceremonies, which became increasingly expensive with the elaboration of civic drama (plays performed by the crafts on pageant wagons), the costs of which could fall heavily on relatively small craft fraternities.[39]

The cost of living was high for townsmen because of their lack of opportunities for self-sufficiency. All goods consumed, not just food, had to be brought in from outside. Some towns were fortunate enough to have rights over commons, from which fuel and building materials could be obtained. The usual source of supply was the market, with the inevitable expense of transport as well as the middleman's profit margins. Everything had to be paid for, even water, which would be carried to the householder's door. Cess-pits were emptied at an understandably high cost (6s. 8d. was a not unusual charge), reflecting not just the unpleasantness of the task, but also the sheer quantity of work. A London latrine, in 1425–6, contained almost a thousand gallons of ordure. Rubbish of all kinds was carried away at a price, like the sum paid by the fellows of King's College Cambridge to have a dead dog removed from outside their

39 C. Phythian-Adams, 'Ceremony and the citizen: the communal year at Coventry, 1450–1550' in P. Clark and P. Slack (eds.), *Crisis and order in English towns* (London, 1972), pp. 57–85.

gates.[40] Above all, food cost more in large towns. When the bishop of Bath and Wells moved from Somerset to London in late January or early February 1338, his household account reveals a leap in prices of between 33 and 100 per cent. Candles went up from 1¹/₂d. per pound in the country to 2d. to 2¹/₂d. in the city. In Somerset, pigs were bought for 2s. and wethers for 9d. or 10d. In London they were 3s. and 1s. 5d. respectively. Oats rose from 1s. to 2s. 2d. per quarter, and best ale from ³/₄d. to 1¹/₄d.[41] Some imported luxuries cost less in the capital if bought in bulk from the wholesaler, giving the aristocratic consumer some advantages. But the foodstuffs and goods recorded here as day-to-day small-scale purchases reflect the cost of living of ordinary citizens who, unlike the bishop, could not withdraw into the cheapness of a rural retreat.

In the intensity of a thriving urban economy, high costs could be afforded out of high incomes. Problems multiplied after 1400, both the short-term slumps and, more seriously, the long-term depression of the mid-fifteenth century. Two structural changes in the economy damaged the trade of a number of larger towns: firstly, the growth of rural cloth manufacture, and secondly the changes in the trade in luxury goods, which became concentrated in the hands of London merchants, and which simultaneously diminished in volume with a decline in aristocratic demand. As the towns experienced these troubles, expenses became harder to bear, and complaints proliferated about the size of the fee-farm, the weight of taxation and the costs of civic office. One suspects that those who complained were comparing their plight in the fifteenth century with the recent years of urban boom around 1400, and even then that their consciousness of civic poverty was at variance with their experience as individuals. The evidence for incomes, diet, housing, possessions and the environment suggests a degree of material improvement for many sections of urban society.

40 D. Keene, 'The medieval environment in documentary records', *Archives*, 16 (1983), 137–44; King's College, Cambridge, Mundum Book, vol. 4, no. 2, fol. 111.
41 J. A. Robinson (ed.), 'The household roll of bishop Ralph of Shrewsbury, 1337–8', in *Collectanea* vol. 1 (Somerset Record Soc., 39, 1924), pp. 134–51.

8

THE WAGE-EARNERS

Medieval wage-earners ought to be easier to investigate than peasants, merchants or craftsmen. Surely their incomes can be established with certainty, and their continued existence into modern times makes their style of life more readily understandable? In fact they pose as many problems as any other group, and we must establish firstly who earned wages. Two broad categories can be identified: servants, who were employed full-time by the year, and tended to live in their masters' homes, and labourers or journeymen, who took on short-term jobs, often by the day, and lived in their own houses. Both types have a long ancestry, as far back as Domesday, and by the thirteenth century both had become very numerous, through urbanization and the proliferation of smallholdings. Increased production for the market stimulated producers in country and town to employ labour.

In a small village like Cuxham (Oxfordshire) in 1300, about thirty households contained 150 or more people. The lord employed nine full-time *famuli*, and there were peasant employers with servants, notably John ate Grene, a free-holding kulak, Alice Beneyt, a widow, and the more prosperous half-yardlanders. The fourteen cottagers obtained some employment from the lord (£3 per annum was spent on agricultural wages), and were occasionally hired by their wealthier neighbours. At least twenty-eight wage-earners, full and part-time, amounted to more than half of the adult male population.[1] This was in a mainly agricultural village with a high proportion of self-sufficient half-yardlanders, in which the lord used a great deal of labour services. The wage-earning sector would have been larger in East Anglian villages, which contained more smallholders and more kulaks. Much wage-earning is hidden from us because there is little record of the work of women and children. The latter have been recognized as 'life-cycle servants' in the early modern period, and there is also much medieval evidence for their existence. These were young workers, mostly aged from twelve to twenty-five, who lived with their employers and who received much of their pay in the form of their keep. They were given a training through apprenticeship or 'work experience' of crafts, domestic tasks, agriculture or retail trade. They were regarded as part of the family, and indeed often were related to their employer. In some poll tax records, the phrases 'son and servant' and 'daughter and servant' were used to describe children living with their parents. The links between families and servants who were not relations were close enough for servants to marry the son or daughter of the house, or to receive bequests of goods, cash or land on their employer's death. Life-cycle service ended with the acquisition of land, house or independent employment, which was often accompanied by marriage.[2] Not all servants were young, however. The Cuxham *famuli* included adult cottagers who had worked on the lord's demesne for decades.

Our first widespread indication of the scale of wage-earning comes in the detailed returns of the poll taxes of the years 1377–81, especially those of 1380–1. There was much avoidance of this tax, and many of the evaders would have been wage-earners. For all their faults, the poll tax returns come nearer than any other medieval document to giving an occupational census. Take the Essex village of Pentlow, where twelve male free tenants paid the tax, nine of them with their wives. Two labourers and their wives were also listed, and a weaver. The rest were called 'servants (*famuli*) and labourers', seven of them married couples, and eleven single, of whom three were women. The tenants mostly paid 1s. to 1s. 3d.

1 P. D. A. Harvey, *A medieval Oxfordshire village. Cuxham 1240 to 1400* (Oxford, 1965), pp. 75–86, 113–35.
2 A. S. Kussmaul, *Servants in husbandry in early modern England* (Cambridge, 1981); P. J. P. Goldberg, 'Female labour, service and marriage in the late medieval urban north', *Northern History*, 22 (1986), 18–38; J. M. Bennett, 'Medieval peasant marriage: an examination of marriage licence fines in *Liber Gersumarum*' in J. A. Raftis (ed.), *Pathways to medieval peasants* (Toronto, 1981), pp. 193–246.

each, while the servants and labourers contributed 4d., 6d., 9d. or
11d. Of the total of fifty-one persons, twenty-nine were servants,
labourers or their wives, accounting for 57 per cent of the tax-
payers.[3] Over whole hundreds and counties the percentage of servants and labourers could be as low as 18 in south Staffordshire, 30 in
Leicestershire, in excess of 40 in Gloucestershire, and between 50 and
63 in Essex and Suffolk.[4] All of these figures tend to undercount the
wage-earners, because of the evasion already noted, the official
omission of those under the age of fifteen, the appearance of married
women simply as wives and the uncertain status of craftsmen and
peasants, many of whom were at least in part-time employment.
The proportion of people who obtained most of their living from
wage work must have exceeded a third over the whole country,
rising to two-thirds in parts of the east. There were concentrations of
wage-earners in large towns; in York, for example, 32 per cent of the
contributors to the poll tax were called servants.[5]

We cannot be sure how the wage-earning sector changed in the
fourteenth and fifteenth centuries. In the countryside, the landless
and smallholding population dwindled as land became more easily
available. There may have been a reduction in employment because
of urban decline. On the other hand, the demand for employees
continued as agricultural holdings increased in size, and the cloth
industry, especially in the country, expanded. There could have
been a movement into full-time service because of the special needs
of pastoral farming.[6] However, the numerous disputes over the
wages paid for short-term employment found in manorial court
rolls, and the mass of complaints that after 1349 workers refused
annual contracts and preferred to be hired by the day, suggest that
the part-timers were becoming more important sources of labour
than the servants.[7]

---

3 C. Oman, *The great revolt of 1381* (Oxford, 1906), pp. 178–9.
4 W. K. Boyd (ed.), *Poll-tax of 2–4 Richard II 1379–81 for the hundreds of Offlow and
   Cuttlestone* (Staffordshire Record Soc., 17, 1896), pp. 157–205; L. M. Midgley,
   'Some Staffordshire poll-tax returns, 1377', *Staffordshire Record Soc.*, 4th ser., 6
   (1970), 1–25; R. H. Hilton, 'Some social and economic evidence in late medieval
   English tax returns' in R. H. Hilton, *Class conflict and the crisis of feudalism* (London,
   1985), pp. 253–67; R. H. Hilton, *Bondmen made free* (London, 1973), pp. 170–2.
5 Goldberg, 'Female labour', p. 21.
6 Implied in Kussmaul, *Servants in husbandry*, pp. 97–119.
7 Z. Razi, 'Family, land and the village community in later medieval England', *P. and
   P.*, 93 (1981), 31–3; N. Ritchie, 'Labour conditions in Essex in the reign of Richard
   II' in E. M. Carus-Wilson (ed.), *Essays in economic history* (3 vols., London, 1954–
   66), vol. 2, pp. 91–111.

Another opportunity to estimate the importance of the wage-earners is provided by the records of the 1522 muster and 1524–5 lay subsidy, which in some counties state the occupation of the tax-payers, and distinguish between those who were assessed on land, goods or wages. It seems reasonable to count as wage-earners, in addition to those who paid tax on their earnings, those who were assessed below the low figure of 40s. on goods (most of whom would have been labourers) and to include an informed estimate for those exempted because of their poverty. Using these methods of calculation in a sample of six counties the average percentage of wage-earners was thirty-six, with a variation from thirty-two in Gloucestershire to forty-one in Rutland. The highest concentration is found in centres of rural industry, such as the Forest of Dean in Gloucestershire and the cloth-making area of west Suffolk. Small towns overall show no higher proportion than in rural areas, but a large city like Coventry, even in a state of chronic decline, had a proportion of well over a half.[8] Again the tax must have omitted many people who earned wages, such as women, and those who paid on goods assessed above 40s. who might nonetheless have occasionally accepted employment. The taxes of 1380–1 and 1524–5 were based on different principles of assessment and cannot tell us if wage-earning had increased or diminished in the century-and-a-half that separated them. They both confirm, however, that wage earn-ing was widely diffused in English society. A high proportion of the population worked for others at some stage of their lives, and employers were numerous, including not just the wealthy gentry, clergy and yeomen, but also a wide range of craftsmen and peasants, and even the occasional labourer. As the unit of production was the peasant holding or the craftsman's workshop, few employees worked in a group larger than two or three. In towns, a workshop in one of the metal industries sometimes employed more than ten but this was exceptional. There was no medieval proletariat, in the sense of large numbers of people depending entirely on wage labour for the whole of their lives, nor was there a single employing class.[9]

---

8 J. Yang, 'Wage-earners in early sixteenth-century England' (University of Bir-mingham Ph.D. thesis, 1986); C. Phythian-Adams, *Desolation of a city. Coventry and the urban crisis of the late middle ages* (Cambridge, 1979), pp. 130–4.

9 R. H. Hilton, 'Capitalism – what's in a name?' in Hilton, *Class conflict*, pp. 268–77; H. Swanson, 'Craftsmen and industry in late medieval York' (University of York D.Phil. thesis, 1980), p. 186.

Table 18. *Daily wage rates of building workers, 1260–1520*
(in pence (d.))

	Thatcher	Thatcher's mate
1261–70	2	–
1271–80	2^1/$_2$	1
1281–90	2^1/$_4$	1
1291–1300	2^1/$_2$	1
1301–10	2^1/$_2$	1
1311–20	3	1^1/$_4$
1321–30	3	1
1331–40	3	1^1/$_4$
1341–50	3	1^1/$_4$
1351–60	3^1/$_2$	2
1361–70	3^1/$_2$	2
1371–80	4^1/$_4$	2^1/$_2$
1381–90	4	2^1/$_4$
1391–1400	4^1/$_4$	2^3/$_4$
1401–10	4^1/$_2$	3
1411–20	4^3/$_4$	3
1421–30	4^1/$_2$	3
1431–40	4^1/$_2$	3^1/$_4$
1441–50	5^1/$_4$	4
1451–60	5^1/$_2$	3^1/$_4$
1461–70	4^3/$_4$	3^3/$_4$
1471–80	5^1/$_4$	3^3/$_4$
1481–90	6	3^3/$_4$
1491–1500	5^1/$_2$	3^1/$_2$
1501–10	5^3/$_4$	4
1511–20	5^1/$_4$	4

N.B.: These are *decennial* averages, calculated from many different manors in different parts of the country, and do not therefore form a single coherent series. Thorold Rogers gave his averages to the nearest eighth of a penny. These have been corrected to the nearest farthing (^{1}/$_4$d.)
Source note: J. E. Thorold Rogers, *A history of agriculture and prices in England* (7 vols., Oxford 1866–1902), vol. 1, p. 321; vol. 4, p. 524

Plenty of information survives about the payment of wages:

And to Robert of Whitfield, mason, for eight days, 32d.

says the building account for Dover Castle for Easter, 1221, among hundreds of similar entries.[10] Having established Robert's daily

10 H. M. Colvin, *Building accounts of King Henry III* (Oxford, 1971), p. 41.

wage as 4d., we can gather together figures for other types of worker and other years, work out annual and decennial averages, arrange them in series, and define trends in wage-rates. If we add information about prices, real wages can be calculated. For example, Robert's 4d. could have bought him four loaves of bread, a gallon of ale and a large piece of meat; and a mason's wage in 1421 would have bought much more. A succession of researchers beginning with Thorold Rogers have been able to show that cash wages increased gradually in the thirteenth century, and more rapidly in the fourteenth, especially after the Black Death, and reached a peak in the fifteenth (see table 18). When expressed in terms of the goods that people bought, wages are seen to have been declining in the thirteenth century. Farmer has calculated that agricultural workers on the Winchester estate needed to do 24–6 units of work in the early thirteenth century to buy a 'shopping basket' of goods, rising to 27–36 units in the years 1270–1330, which then improved slightly to 22–3 units in the twenty years before the Black Death.[11] The study of building workers in southern England by Phelps Brown and Hopkins is based on another 'shopping basket', the price of which was charted from year to year, along with the movement in wage-rates.[12] The purchasing power of the wage was then expressed as an index number (see fig. 8). The series begins in 1264, and the index, after staying around 50 in the late thirteenth and early fourteenth century, rises to about 60 in the 1360s, 80 in the period 1378–1400, and hovers around 100 throughout the fifteenth century, at double its pre-Black Death level. Unskilled workers' wages rose more rapidly than those of the skilled after 1349, a sure indication of a labour shortage, and confirming Thorold Rogers's aphorism that the period was the 'golden age of the labourer'.[13] The series continues until the twentieth century, and puts medieval wages into a long-term perspective. The index fell in the sixteenth century to 29 in 1597 (when Shakespeare wrote patronizingly about rude mechanicals in *A midsummer night's dream*), and did not return to its medieval peak until 1880.

---

11 D. L. Farmer, 'Prices and wages' in H. Hallam (ed.), *Agrarian history of England and Wales*, vol. 2 (Cambridge, 1988), p. 778.

12 E. H. Phelps Brown and S. V. Hopkins, 'Seven centuries of the price of consumables, compared with builders' wage rates' in Carus-Wilson (ed.), *Essays in economic history*, vol. 2, pp. 179–96; reprinted in E. H. Phelps Brown and S. V. Hopkins, *A perspective on wages and prices* (London, 1981), pp. 13–59.

13 W. Beveridge, 'Wages in the Winchester manors', *Ec.H.R.*, 7 (1936), 22–43.

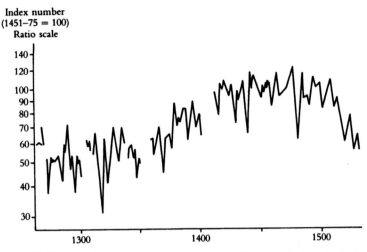

Index number
(1451–75 = 100)
Ratio scale

Fig. 8   Building workers' wages, 1264–1532, expressed in terms of a shopping basket of consumables
(The wage-rates used are those of craftsmen employed in southern England)
Source: E. H. Phelps Brown and S. V. Hopkins, 'Seven centuries of the price of consumables compared with builders' wage rates' in E. M. Carus-Wilson (ed.), *Essays in economic history* (3 vols., London, 1954–66), vol. 2, p. 186, reprinted in E. H. Phelps Brown and S. V. Hopkins, *A perspective on wages and prices* (London, 1981), pp. 13–59

Before we can conclude that wage-earners experienced a low and declining standard of living in the thirteenth century and relative plenty in the fifteenth, there are many doubts and qualifications to be raised. These concern the nature of medieval wages; the extent to which the trends are clear and continuous; the choice of the items in the 'shopping basket of consumables' used to calculate real wages; the typicality of the sample of workers; and the translation of wage-rates into earnings.

MEDIEVAL WAGES

We must doubt if all of the payments made to workers on demesnes can be regarded as wages in the normal sense. On thirteenth-century manors, 'wages' may in some cases have been customary payments given to tenants who had previously done the work by servile labour services.[14] This would explain their failure to change for many years

14 Farmer, 'Prices and wages', p. 732.

together. We must also question the freedom of wage bargaining when demesne *famuli* were often recruited from the lord's serfs, and work by the day came from cottagers holding by servile tenure.

EXCEPTIONS TO THE LONG-TERM TRENDS

Both the money supply and social controls complicate the analysis of wage-rates and sometimes they appear to have slowed down or reversed long-term movements. The decline or stagnation in real wages in the period 1200–1320 accords with our expectations of a period of rising population. Labour became more plentiful, and food more scarce. The events of 1320–48 are problematic, with some series showing a slight rise in cash wages, others a slight decline and others stability, though a definite drop in grain prices ensured that real wages increased.[15] The evidence is contradictory, but one possible underlying depressive influence on money wages was a shortage of coin, acting in opposition to a decline in population and a growth in industrial employment.[16] Another difficult period is the thirty years after 1349. If the labour supply alone determined wages, a rapid and decisive increase should have followed the Black Death. In fact the rise in wages was at first modest, and the striking improvement often came in the last quarter of the fourteenth century. One possible explanation is that a small army of previously unemployed and under-employed people came forward to replace those who died in the epidemics, and the labour-force was not eroded seriously until the successive epidemics of the 1360s and 1370s had had their full effect. This is unlikely because the existence of the shadow work-force ought to have depressed wages to rock-bottom before 1348, and all the direct evidence for mortality shows that the later plagues were much less virulent than the epidemic of 1348–9. The monetary factor cannot be invoked because of the high level of prices. Other influences may have been social and institutional restraints. The Ordinance of Labourers of 1349 and the Statute of Labourers of 1351, which sought to peg wage levels and enforce contracts between masters and servants, are usually thought

15 Farmer, 'Prices and wages', pp. 814–17; Beveridge, 'Wages in Winchester manors', pp. 38–43; information from N. Belford and C. Lloyd-Jones, kindly communicated to me in advance of the completion of their Economic and Social Research Council project on medieval wages.

16 M. Prestwich, 'Currency and the economy of early fourteenth century England' in N. J. Mayhew (ed.), *Edwardian monetary affairs (1279–1344)* (British Archaeological Reports, 36, 1977), pp. 45–58.

to have been ineffective. It is however possible that the Justices of Labourers in the 1350s and the Justices of the Peace thereafter, even if they could not chase every offender, had some inhibiting effect on wage increases. More widespread effects could have come from the local pressure on servile employees by lords wishing to pay 'reasonable' (i.e. low) rates. The gentry who were most involved in enforcing the law may sometimes have received cooperation from wealthier peasants and craftsmen, small-scale employers themselves, who acted as jurors and local officials.[17] In towns and villages, local regulations had set wage-rates even before the epidemics, and attempts at restriction continued after 1349. In towns these pressures were countered by the leagues and plots among workers uncovered by courts enforcing the labour laws, and by illicit religious fraternities, like that of the journeymen spurriers of London, which was banned in 1381.[18] We should not underestimate the time that people took to adjust to new social circumstances. The employers clearly felt a deep sense of shock at the 'unnatural' demands of their servants, and the employees also may have needed time to overcome deferential attitudes towards their social superiors.

So the new deal for wage-earners emerged slowly from a combination of complex supply and demand factors which we still do not fully understand, complicated by social struggles. Even after this period of adjustment, detailed studies of wage-rates show short periods of decline within the overall growth, and the fifteenth-century 'bullion famine' has been cited in explanation.[19]

THE 'SHOPPING BASKET OF CONSUMABLES'

Phelps Brown and Hopkins calculated building workers' real wages in terms of a shopping basket derived from the account-book of

17 B. H. Putnam, *The enforcement of the Statute of Labourers* (New York, 1908); L. R. Poos, 'The social context of Statute of Labourers enforcement', *Law and History Review*, 1 (1983), 27–52; N. Goose, 'Wage labour on a Kentish manor: Meopham 1307–75', *Archaeologia Cantiana*, 92 (1976), 203–23; M. Mate, 'Labour and labour services on the estates of Canterbury Cathedral Priory in the fourteenth century', *Southern History*, 7 (1985), 55–67; C. Dyer, 'Social and economic background to the rural revolt of 1381' in R. H. Hilton and T. H. Aston (eds.), *The English rising of 1381* (Cambridge, 1984), pp. 25–6.

18 R. H. Hilton, 'Popular movements in England at the end of the fourteenth century' in L. S. Olshki, *Il tumulto dei ciompi* (Florence, 1981), pp. 162–3.

19 J. H. Munro, 'The behaviour of wages during deflation in late-medieval England and the low countries', paper at the International Economic History Congress at Bern, 1986; J. Day, 'The great bullion famine of the fifteenth century', *P. and P.*, 79 (1978), 3–54.

Munden's chantry. Now this was a justifiable decision because the source has detailed information on the spending habits of chantry priests at the base of the clerical hierarchy. Building workers who were repairing chantry properties often ate at their table. However, the two priests with an income approaching £20 were a good deal wealthier than any craftsman. They paid no rent, and their household contained a single servant, not a wife and a brood of hungry children. If we assess their diet in terms of the ratio between cereal products (bread, pottage and ale) and other foods (*companagium*, that which goes with bread) we arrive at a figure of 55:45, whereas building craftsmen in the fifteenth century received from their employers diets with a ratio of 60:40, and earlier the figures were probably nearer to 70:30 (see p. 202). In this case the real wages index for the period 1264–1330 is too high, because corn was then relatively expensive. In other words, the Phelps Brown and Hopkins indices tend to understate the improvement in real wages, which in terms of cereal prices were even more depressed in the decades around 1300 than the already gloomy index suggests.

THE TYPICALITY OF BUILDING WORKERS

Historians must inevitably study building workers because they are the only group to be paid by the day for whom enough usable evidence survives. Though we must continue to cite them in the absence of any better example, we ought to be aware of their special characteristics. Firstly, they were few in number, accounting for perhaps one in twenty of the working population of towns and an even smaller proportion in the countryside. Their wages might include the cost of materials and tools, and were also used to pay assistants and to keep apprentices. Sometimes an apparent daily wage conceals a 'price for a job', in which the carpenter or mason was really acting in an organizational rôle like a modern building contractor. Many building workers who lived in rural areas (near to their supplies of raw materials) held land, so their wage does not represent their main source of income. There were also considerable local differences in the rates of pay; Thorold Rogers, Phelps Brown and Hopkins and others tend to use rates from the south-east, where building workers were strongly in demand. While a fifteenth-century carpenter in London or Oxford received 6d. per day, his counterpart in Stratford-upon-Avon was paid only 5d. Our knowledge of building wages depends on the records of the large institutions, who could seek out the best craftsmen and pay wages in cash rather than in kind, and at more consistent rates than the smaller employers.[20]

By contrast, in other fields of work many employees received a high proportion of their pay in the form of shelter, food and clothing. In the country they might be given a piece of land to cultivate, a share of pasture on which they could keep animals, or a part of the grain harvest. In towns, craftsmen's servants were assigned some of the goods that they had helped to produce, so cordwainers would pay their employees partly in shoes. The full amount of cash wages is difficult to assess, because servants in particular were given tips and rewards in unknown quantity. Demesne *famuli* are the servants about whom we know most. Before the Black Death their annual cash wage was very small, often 2s. to 5s., depending on the region, up to an unusually high 9s. on a Kentish manor in the early fourteenth century.[21] The grain allowance of $4^1/2$ to $6^1/2$ quarters per annum was worth much more than the cash wage. After 1349 the cash payments rose to 10s., 20s., or even 30s. per annum, and the grain allowance improved in quantity and quality, with a greater wheat content. As a proportion of the total package of rewards the grain livery dwindled in significance. Living-in servants in the late fourteenth century, we gather from contemporary comments, demanded good ale instead of water and dishes of fresh fish and meat, rather than cabbages and bacon. Direct comparison between the pay of *famuli* and day labourers is not easy because of the variety of payments, but the general impression is that in the late fourteenth century servants' wages advanced more than daily wages, presumably to counteract the unpopularity of annual contracts and the resulting drift into casual employment. Peasants employed living-in servants, of whom many were young. Their pay, known when disputes reveal the details of the contract, involved a smaller sum in cash than that paid to the demesne *famuli*, often in the region of 6s. 8d. or at most 13s. 4d. in the late fourteenth century, but they had the benefit of more home comforts. In towns during the period 1350–1520 servants who accepted annual contracts received about 40s.

20 D. Knoop and G. P. Jones, *The medieval mason*, 3rd edn (Manchester, 1967); T. H. Lloyd, *Some aspects of the building industry in medieval Stratford-upon-Avon* (Dugdale Soc. Occasional Paper, 14, 1961); H. Swanson, *Building craftsmen in late medieval York* (Borthwick Paper, 63, 1983); D. Woodward, 'Wage-rates and living standards in pre-industrial England', *P. and P.*, 91 (1981), 28–46.
21 Mate, 'Labour and labour services', p. 58.

annually, with meals and other benefits, or 1s. to 1s. 6d. per week, if their employers observed the regulations. In reality they were probably paid rather more.[22]

Workers' individual pay could be concealed behind contracts made with a team, often for piece-work. Work-gangs would be taken on in the harvest and paid at a rate per acre, or groups of Welsh dikers would be employed in the midlands to dig moats, ponds and ditches for a price agreed 'in gross' (for the whole job). Piece-work was the usual form of payment in many urban crafts. Spinners were paid for the pound of yarn, weavers by the ell of cloth, and shoemakers by the dozen pairs. We should remember that building workers' pay and conditions in many ways differed from those of other employees, but we should still be grateful that at least one section of the medieval work-force is so fully documented.

WAGE-RATES AND EARNINGS

In order to translate information about rates of pay into annual earnings of individual workers, we need to know for how many days they would have been employed.

As a result of a century or two of collective experience of industrial discipline, modern western societies are accustomed to a regular pattern of daily work, to the point that its absence because of unemployment or retirement can cause psychological disturbance. We should not expect the rhythm of medieval work to accord with such modern notions of routine. Firstly, the working year was punctuated by numerous and irregular holidays, mostly saints' days sanctioned by the church, and others of more popular origin. Local cults had grown up in the early middle ages, and reforming bishops in the early thirteenth century sought to codify and regularize the observance of holidays, dividing them into three categories, those on which no work was to be done, those when all work stopped except for ploughing, and those applying only to women's domestic work. The former type of universal compulsory holiday affected forty to fifty days in the year, in addition to Sundays, which meant that ninety to a hundred were officially designated as non-working days. The rules could be flouted, but offenders were liable to the discipline of the church courts if they worked on prohibited days.

---

22 E. Clark, 'Medieval labor law and English local courts', *American Journal of Legal History*, 27 (1983), 330–53; W. Bickley (ed.), *Little Red Book of Bristol* (Bristol, 1900), pp. 41–4, 159–67; Phythian-Adams, *Desolation of a city*, pp. 132–3.

Records of the performance of labour services on demesnes, and of work on building sites, shows that at least in these activities holidays were observed.[23]

Secondly, medieval work was episodic and seasonal. In agriculture the periods of intense effort at sowing, lambing, hay-making and harvest were separated by relatively slack times. Mining tended to be a summer-time activity because of flooding in the workings at other seasons. Woodcutting was related to demand and was therefore concentrated in the winter. Shoe-makers were at their busiest in the autumn, and fishermen in the spring. Workers could often combine complementary seasonal activities, or practise a trade with periods of intense work together with pastoral farming, which required constant but undemanding attention.

Thirdly, the main problem facing workers before 1349 was the lack of sufficient work to keep everyone occupied. Many activities were on a small scale, such as building a peasant house or ploughing a half-yardland, both of which could have been accomplished in a few weeks. Industries like cloth-making and mining were subject to periodic booms and slumps. While a modern post-industrial society combines employment for most people with substantial unemployment, the well-populated, pre-industrial England of the thirteenth century suffered from the underemployment of the majority.

After 1349, work-patterns became even more fragmented, as employees broke away from the long-term commitments of annual contracts, preferring to work by the day. Most of the people caught in the net of the late fourteenth-century labour laws had been involved in periods of employment lasting from two to twenty days. In both agricultural and industrial employment, workers moved from job to job, leading to accusations of vagabondage. A Suffolk labourer worked in a typically discontinuous way between 1 November 1363 and 2 February 1364. Out of a total of ninety-four days we know that he spent forty days with one employer.[24] He may have worked for others, but with his earnings of 5s. in that time, together with savings from lucrative harvest earnings earlier in the year, it is possible that he rested for a high proportion of the other fifty days.

23 E. C. Rodgers, *Discussion of holidays in the later middle ages* (New York, 1940); B. F. Harvey, 'Work and *Festa Ferianda* in medieval England', *Journal of Ecclesiastical History*, 23 (1972), 289–308.
24 This and other cases cited here from the proceedings under the labour laws derive from S. A. C. Penn, 'Wage-earners and wage earning in late fourteenth century England' (Report on Economic and Social Research Council project, School of History, University of Birmingham, 1986), p. 35.

Sundays, Christmas, Plough Monday and other festivals would in any case have occupied more than twenty days of the period. The positive virtue of leisure in the minds of medieval people should not be underestimated. Such tasks as threshing with flails or weaving were arduous, repetitive and tedious. Hours were very long, with town governments imposing on the crafts working days of twelve to fourteen hours defined by the new-fangled clock. Before the adoption of such precise measurement of time, work began at dawn and ended at night-fall. In the building trade, meal breaks were limited to no more than an hour and a quarter to two hours per day.[25] Lengthy working hours must have detracted from the productivity of labour, and indeed when comparison can be made between medieval and modern workers they do seem to have proceeded very slowly.[26] The problem lay not in medieval laziness, but in an understandable antipathy to drudgery. A work ethic was advocated by the clergy (for others), but it met with considerable resistance. In the late fourteenth and fifteenth century the reiteration of regulations about the working day, the disapproval of journeymen 'disporting themselves in the streets', the attempt to enforce annual contracts, the move to reduce the number of religious holidays and the growing disapproval of time-consuming sports and games serve to reinforce the impression of the anxiety of employers to combat workers' strong preference for leisure.

A plausible reconstruction of workers' attitudes in the period 1349–1520 is that they set themselves goals in cash or consumption needs, and worked until they had achieved their aims. Then they ceased to work. A peasant might wish to earn his rent money, or a labourer enough to buy a desirable diet of wheat bread, ale and meat. Harvest work helped this purpose very well, because a few weeks' labour brought in enough to keep a family for weeks. Then the labourers could behave like John Hogyn, who shocked a Hampshire bench of justices in 1371 by refusing to serve when asked, sleeping all day, and spending his nights in taverns playing 'peny prick'. Such behaviour shows that we should not assume that a rise in wages resulted in a comparable expansion in earnings. A worker on 4d. per day in the late fourteenth century could in theory have earned more

25 J. Le Goff, 'Labor time in the "crisis" of the fourteenth century: from medieval time to modern time', in *Time, work and culture*, pp. 43–52; Knoop and Jones, *Medieval mason*, p. 105.
26 W. Endrei, 'The productivity of weaving in late medieval Flanders' in N. B. Harte and K. G. Ponting (eds.), *Cloth and clothing in medieval Europe* (London, 1983), pp. 108–19.

than £4. In practice he might have judged that £3 would cover his needs, and accept sufficient employment to attain that sum. When his wage-rate rose to 6d. per day, he could well have increased his earnings to, say, £3 10s., and taken another six weeks of holiday.[27]

The long-term changes in wages and earnings can best be investigated by looking at the patterns of work on large building sites. Vale Royal Abbey in Cheshire is the first example. This Cistercian monastery was founded by Edward I; work began in 1277 and proceeded at a cost to the crown of about £500 per annum.[28] The building accounts cover payments to many types of workers because this pioneering project involved site clearance, tree-felling and the erection of masons' lodges as well as the more skilled carving of stone by masons. The wage-rates, typical of the thirteenth century, were characterized by marked differentials. Summer rates exceeded winter rates, reflecting the longer working hours. In 1278, the summer pay of the labourers was 8d., 9d., and 10d. per week; tree-fellers, daubers and colliers were given 12d., quarrymen 18d., carpenters, sawyers and smiths from 20d. to 24d., and masons up to 36d. Among the masons, small gradations of experience and skill were recognized by six rates of pay, 30d., 29d., 28d. and so on. On other sites at this period the numbers of rates among masons was even greater, thirteen at Caernarvon Castle in 1316, for example.[29] The poorly paid unskilled workers outnumbered the skilled. Of the 187 men working at the site's peak of activity on 1 June 1278, 96 were earning 12d. or less, and only 37 earned more than 24d. The skilled minority enjoyed the double advantage of higher pay and more continuous employment. Masons and carpenters tended to keep working steadily through summer and part of the winter (activities were drastically scaled down in the worst weather), while labourers were often taken on for a shorter time in the summer. Carpenters worked on the site from 30 January to 24 December, while no diggers were hired until 6 March; their numbers were built up to fifty-nine in May, and then dwindled again towards the end of the year.

27 I. S. W. Blanchard, 'Labour productivity and work psychology in the English mining industry 1400–1600', *Ec.H.R.*, 2nd ser., 31 (1978), 1–24; G. Persson, 'Consumption, labour and leisure in the late middle ages' in D. Menjot (ed.), *Manger et boire au moyen âge* (2 vols., Publications de la faculté des lettres et sciences humaines de Nice, 28, 1984), vol. 1, pp. 211–23; Penn, 'Wage-earners', p. 25.

28 J. Brownbill (ed.), *The ledger-book of Vale Royal Abbey* (Record Soc. of Lancashire and Cheshire, 68, 1914), pp. 192–230.

29 Knoop and Jones, *Medieval mason*, p. 98.

To make comparisons between earnings we can select a range of workers. A middle-ranking mason could have worked for 286 days, earning £5 1s. 4d., and a carpenter with a maximum of 262 days could have received £4 1s. 0d. A quarryman's earnings could have been £2 1s. 4d., and a labourer with a possible 243 days would have gained £1 11s. 8d. These were the maximum possible earnings, and most individuals would not have done as much work on this site. Among the carpenters, for example, only the inappropriately named Richard le Jobbere appears continuously in the accounts throughout the year. Many of the workers were migratory, the skilled coming from as far afield as Gloucestershire, and the labourers from other parts of Cheshire. The general pattern of earnings is confirmed by the accounts for work on Exeter Cathedral in 1299–1300, which was conducted on a smaller scale with local labour. A mason called Richard de la Streme was employed for a total of forty-six weeks at a rate of 1s. 6³/₄d. to 2s. 3d. per week, depending on the number of days worked. His total earnings were £4 17s. 2¹/₄d. Adam de Chudleigh, a carpenter, whose services were needed only for twenty-six weeks received £2 13s. 10d., and a labourer (their names are not given) might have been able to work for forty-eight weeks and earn £1 19s. 4d., though it is unlikely that any one employee worked for so long.[30]

In the late thirteenth century, therefore, the maximum earnings of a building craftsman could have been in the region of £4 to £5, and of a labourer in the range of £1 10s. to £2. In 1278, when a quarter of barley cost 3s. 9d., a labourer could have fed his family on 6 quarters 5 bushels for 24s. 10d. and have a little cash left for other purposes. When the price of barley rose to 5s., a diet of bread and water would have absorbed all of his earnings. He would have depended on some other source of income, such as a smallholding of land, to raise his standard of living to a point where he could regularly have drunk ale or bought clothing. His chief problem would have been the discontinuous nature of the available employment, and the gaps spent searching for work. This would not have been such a problem for the craftsmen, who with £4 could have afforded some wheat bread in years of average prices, together with ale, meat, clothing and rent. In 1278, for example, 6 quarters 5 bushels of wheat would have cost 30s., 3 quarters of barley for brewing 11s. 3d., a pig 3s. and clothing for two adults 6s. to 8s. As already mentioned, craftsmen's wages

30 A. M. Erskine (ed.), *The accounts of the fabric of Exeter Cathedral, 1279–1353* (Devon and Cornwall Record Soc., 24, 1981, and 26, 1983).

were expected to cover expenses, such as the cost of tools, some
materials and assistants.

Two centuries after work began on Vale Royal, William Lord
Hastings was building a new castle at Kirby Muxloe in Leicestershire. A manor house had stood on the site previously, but the
project was in effect to build an entirely new castle in the latest style,
appropriate to a magnate who had relatively recently been promoted
to great power.[31] Construction cost £200 to £400 per annum, but
after three years, in 1483, work was interrupted by Hastings' sudden
arrest and execution. In 1481–2 more than eighty-seven workers
were employed on the site, including a similar variety as at Vale
Royal, but with the addition of brick-layers specially brought in
from East Anglia, some of whom were of Flemish origin. In line
with the general tendency of the period, differentials between workers had lessened in importance. There were both fewer grades of pay
(8d. per day for the overseers of masonry and carpentry, 6d. for most
craftsmen, and 3d. to 4d. for labourers and dikers), and the gulf
between the top and bottom of the hierarchy had lessened, with the
highest-paid mason receiving between two and three times the
labourer's wage, compared with four times or more at Vale Royal.
Earnings benefited both from the higher rates of pay, and the improved conditions which gave the workers paid holidays. Except for
dikers and brick-layers who worked in teams, the earnings of each
man can be calculated exactly. Robert Steynforth, a leading mason,
was paid in the accounting year 1481–2, for 290 days, £7 5s. 0d.
Another mason, Robert Bardolf, received £7 2s. 0d. Among the
labourers Simon Phelyp worked 218 days for £3 0s. 5³/₄d., and Roger
Hudson after 236 days obtained £3 5s. 0³/₄d. The wainmen who
carried materials to the site were paid quarterly with cash and food
allowances totalling £3 4s. 2d. per annum. The labourers could not
have afforded to eat wheat bread in the exceptionally bad year of
1481–2 when 6 quarters 5 bushels of wheat cost £2 17s. 0d. In a
normal year of the late fifteenth century, when wheat would have
cost 30s., it would have absorbed only a half of a labourer's earnings.
Steynforth and Bardolf could have lived very well, even allowing for
the expenses of their trades. Many vicars managed on less.

In order to obtain some idea of possible annual earnings, workers
have been selected who stayed in the same job for a long time, which
gives a misleading impression of the normal working patterns.

31 A. Hamilton Thompson, 'Building accounts of Kirby Muxloe Castle, 1480–
1484', *Transactions of the Leicestershire Archaeological Soc.*, 11 (1913–20), 193–345.

Steynforth and Phelyp belonged to an untypical minority: at Kirby
Muxloe in 1481–2, of the eighty-seven named workers, sixty-two
were employed for less than 50 days, and only a dozen stayed on the
Hastings pay-roll for more than 100 days. This does not necessarily
mean that a labourer like Richard Hancok who worked on the site
for only ten days earned much less than Phelyp. He may have
worked for a dozen employers during the year and so built up a
sizeable income. However, the likelihood is that his working time
was reduced by the need to pick up news about jobs, travel to them
and negotiate with new employers. On the other hand, Hancok
would have justified his working pattern on the grounds that he
found the jobs with the best pay, so he earned as much as Phelyp in
less time. He also doubtless gained satisfaction from his freedom,
and from his lack of dependence on a single employer. The difference between a thirteenth- and fifteenth-century labourer's existence, in addition to the rates of pay, was that the former worked
discontinuously not through any choice but because the jobs were
not available. Major sites like Vale Royal were insufficient in
number to employ more than a small fraction of the working
population.

The problem of inadequate levels of pay in the late thirteenth and
early fourteenth century was not confined to England. The most
detailed investigation of real wages and earnings in medieval Europe
has exposed conditions of considerable poverty even in the sophisticated and thriving city of Florence.[32] A single adult in *c.*1290, in
order to maintain his 'physiological and socio-psychological health',
that is to buy wheat bread, beans, meat, olive-oil and wine, and to
pay for rent and clothing, needed 43s. 3d. per month (the Florentine
coinage was worth much less than English money). At that time a
labourer was paid about 52s. 6d. per month, so a single man could
live on the wage, but not a family. Even a skilled worker on 96s. per
month would not have been able to afford all of the elements in the
ideal family budget. And periodic bad harvests and bouts of unemployment eroded the workers' living standards still further. In
hard times they bought less *companatico (companagium* in the English
documents), and even descended to 'grey' bread made from grains
other than wheat. In the severe shortages of 1329 and the 1340s,
families could not have obtained even enough barley bread to have
sustained normal life. In the late fourteenth century, Florentine

---

32 C. de la Roncière, *Prix et salaires à Florence au XIV* siècle* (Rome, 1982), pp.
381–461.

wages and prices both rose, so that a labourer in 1370 earned 199s. 6d. per month, and each person 'needed' 132s. to live, so families were still hard-pressed. In Florence, as in England, some households may have received two incomes, but women's earnings, for example as spinsters in the cloth industry, were so low that a labourer's family with both parents at work would still not have been able to afford a full diet and the other costs. If the inhabitants of one of Europe's centres of culture and industry lived so precariously, it is hardly surprising to find labourers of Cheshire in difficult straits.

After such a lengthy critical examination of the conventional view of medieval wage-earners we must still conclude that there is no need to *overturn* such useful aids as the Phelps Brown and Hopkins index of real wages. We need to make more allowance for the south-eastern bias of the wage-rates, and the use of a clerical 'shopping basket', and we should give more consideration to earnings rather than rates of pay, but the main conclusions drawn from the indices are still valid.

In a whole variety of ways, not just rates of pay, the conditions of wage-earners improved in the fourteenth and fifteenth centuries. They gained more freedom of choice, of occupation, of employer and even whether they should work at all. In spite of the many areas of contraction in the economy, the demand for labour continued. Employers were accused of poaching each other's servants, like John Saunderson, a baker of Boston in Lincolnshire, who in 1396 'procured' the services of Henry Bramlee who was contracted to work for another baker for a 'reasonable' salary.[33] Despite urban regulations forbidding the offer of inducements to persuade a worker to transfer employment, their repetition suggests that this was a not uncommon practice.

In addition to the increased pay of individuals, the incomes of families expanded. Women could contribute to the household economy by extensions of their traditional domestic duties, by brewing for sale or spinning yarn. Rural women joined in agricultural work at peaks of activity. Coroners' records show that they left children unsupervised, with tragic results. In towns, women helped in their husband's trade or craft, either in making goods or selling them. Women were much involved in small-scale trade as hucksters, dealing in bread, dairy products and other foodstuffs from baskets in the streets. Children and young people were mainly employed in do-

---

33 E. G. Kimball (ed.), *Some sessions of the peace in Lincolnshire, 1381–96* (Lincolnshire Record Soc., 49, 1955), p. 71.

mestic service and as assistants to adults. There were various tasks commonly performed by boys, for example as shepherds' helpers at lambing time. Before 1349 the opportunities for women and children were limited by the abundance of male labour, and their rates of pay were markedly below those of men.

After 1349 women continued to perform their traditional tasks, in harvesting, the food and drink trades, and in textiles. Their occupations were extended into heavy work previously monopolized by men, such as ploughing or iron-making.[34] Employment of children apparently also increased. For example, the court at Writtle in Essex in 1381 heard complaints that tenants who owed labour services, instead of sending a man as custom specified, were substituting 'a boy aged fourteen years' and a boy 'who harvested badly'. Legislators in 1388 assumed that twelve-year-olds were performing valuable agricultural work, and sought to prevent them moving to towns.[35] Differentials in pay narrowed to the benefit of both female and child labour. The increasing value of women's earnings often benefited family incomes, but it also gave females more independence, enabling them to make a living, either as the bread-winner of a single parent family, or as a single woman both before marriage and as a widow. Widows were in a better position to resist pressure to remarry.

Men and women alike were able to maximize their earning capacity by their flexibility in changing occupations and their geographical mobility. The enforcement of the labour laws in the late fourteenth century revealed some remarkable cases of workers refusing to accept employment in one job in order to take up some entirely different activity. Ploughmen gave up their annual contracts to become carpenters, weavers and mariners, and a shepherd became a tiler. Workers had always been prepared to travel. In the late thirteenth century, a large town like York was capable of attracting

---

34 R. H. Hilton, *The English peasantry in the later middle ages* (Oxford, 1975), pp. 95–110; B. A. Hanawalt, 'Childrearing among the lower classes of late medieval England', *Journal of Interdisciplinary History*, 8 (1977), 1–22; S. A. C. Penn, 'Female wage-earners in late fourteenth-century England', *Ag.H.R.*, 35 (1987), 1–14; M. Kowaleski, 'Women's work in a market town: Exeter in the late fourteenth century' in B. A. Hanawalt (ed.), *Women and work in pre-industrial Europe* (Bloomington, Indiana, 1986), pp. 145–64; R. H. Hilton, 'Women traders in medieval England' in Hilton, *Class conflict*, pp. 205–15; G. T. Lapsley, 'The account roll of a fifteenth-century iron master', *E.H.R.*, 14 (1899), 509–29.

35 Essex R. O., D/DP M189; *Statutes of the realm* (11 vols., Record Commission, 1810–28), vol. 2, pp. 56–9.

42 per cent of its migrants from a radius in excess of 20 miles, and long-distance migration into towns continued in later centuries, so that Oxford in the early sixteenth century recruited many of its apprentices from Staffordshire. Workers are found moving distances of 10 to 24 miles to obtain a few days' or a few weeks' work in the harvest season, and building workers would commonly find employment 8 miles distant from their homes.[36] Contemporary upper-class observers were worried about the increase in wandering workers in the late fourteenth century, which they associated with vagabondage and crime.

There were, however, some drawbacks to the life of the wage-earners in the 170 years after 1349. Once they took a job, they seem to have worked harder. Perhaps in the glut of labour of the late thirteenth century some servants found that their time was not fully occupied. Employers did not need to be too vigilant in keeping workers at their tasks because labour was so cheap. 'Walter of Henley' in his treatise on husbandry, despaired of controlling the 'malice of the ploughmen' which would lead them to work slowly. After 1349, labour time was expensive and had to be well-used. Ploughmen were expected to cover more ground in a year, and shepherds were given larger flocks to keep. The increased output of iron forges may have been due to more intensive work-régimes as well as to the greater use of water power. For workers in some occupations, higher wages may therefore reflect increases in productivity.[37] A problem which helped to perpetuate the labour shortage lay in the reluctance of people to become wage-earners. In all of the power relationships that governed medieval society, they were invariably at the receiving end of discipline and coercion. At home, young people were pressurized to stay and become the 'son and servant' or 'daughter and servant' of their parents. In the country, bye-laws ordered those capable of work at harvest time to accept employment, and not to glean or leave the village. Lords linked the recruitment of wage labour with their power over serfs, in some cases requiring tenants to nominate *famuli* from among the serfs and also expecting serfs to be available for short-term hiring in the

36 Penn, 'Wage-earners', pp. 43–7; P. McClure, 'Patterns of migration in the late middle ages: the evidence of English place-name surnames', *Ec.H.R.*, 2nd ser., 32 (1979), 181; C. I. Hammer, 'The mobility of skilled labour in late medieval England: some Oxford evidence', *Vierteljahrschrift für Sozial und Wirtsschaftsgeschichte*, 63 (1976), 194–210; Lloyd, *Building industry*, p. 11.

37 D. Oschinsky (ed.), *Walter of Henley* (Oxford, 1971), pp. 316–19; H. R. Schubert, *History of the British iron and steel industry* (London, 1957), pp. 139–41.

harvest. Town authorities, through their influence on the regulations of the 'craft guilds', attempted to control the recruitment, terms of service, hours of work and rates of pay of servants and journeymen. The state stepped in between 1349 and 1445 to aid the employers with eight pieces of legislation which, if implemented, would have fixed pay, enforced contracts of employment, made work compulsory if offered and required migratory workers to carry a form of internal passport.[38] These laws were very unevenly enforced. In the early days after the Black Death attempts seem to have been made to deal with every offender in some villages. For example, in 1352 at South Shoebury in Essex, no less than sixty-eight people were fined under the Statute of Labourers.[39] Later enforcement became haphazard and occasional. Every worker lived continuously in breach of one or more of the regulations, and therefore in constant danger of punishment, if by some chance or malice an accusation was made.

Economic reality may have strengthened the bargaining position of the employee, but in law and custom the employer still enjoyed considerable advantages. We should resist the tendency to idealize the apparently close relationship between masters and servants. In a study of the wage-earners of Paris in the later middle ages, the cloak of apparent paternalism has been shown to conceal a harsh and exploitative attitude on the part of employers in the various crafts.[40] The cosy modern image of life-cycle servants in the English countryside is tarnished by records of disputes between employers and young servants' parents over unpaid wages, and clothing that was not provided.[41] Not all servants may have had influential parents able to defend them through legal action. The occasional marriages between a female servant and her employer's son give us a favourable impression of the servant's rôle and treatment, but there was also a dark side of sexual exploitation of female servants, which was sometimes revealed before the church courts. The position of the urban apprentices demonstrates another aspect of the vulnerability of the employee, or rather trainee. The whole system, with the long terms of seven years and more, greatly in excess of the time actually taken to learn some trades and crafts, was clearly designed to provide the masters with a pool of cheap labour. The master entered into an

---

38 Clark, 'Medieval labor law'.
39 Poos, 'Statute of Labourers enforcement', p. 48
40 B. Geremek, *Le salariat dans l'artisanat parisien aux XIIIe–XVe siècles* (Paris, 1968).
41 Hilton, *The English peasantry*, pp. 51–2.

agreement to treat the apprentice well, in exchange for a promise of good behaviour from the youth. In the case of London, for example, occasional disputes arose from accusations that masters took on apprentices informally, without registering them with the authorities, left the city in the middle of the apprentice's term, failed to teach the trade, failed to provide adequate food and chastised them 'horribly'.[42]

In addition to the wage-earners' legal and social disadvantages, their economic position was always precarious. While fifteenth-century earnings may have been high, they ceased immediately if the worker was injured, ill, or old. The only sure protection against loss of earning capacity came from the acquisition of land or property, and many wage-earners, as we have seen, were able to gain enough to keep themselves and give up working for others.

For both practical and ideological reasons, wage-earning was a low status activity. Among the various types of wage-earners, servants occupied the lowest position of all. Some of them may have enjoyed the closeness of their relationship with their employers, and the sense of belonging to a household. However, their lack of separate identity is suggested by the many records which deny them a surname, describing them simply as John or Agnes, 'servant of John Taylor', or in English as 'John Taylor's servant' or 'Agnes parson's servant'. Life in an employer's household smacked of dependence or even servility, and long before seventeenth-century complaints that service was 'pottage for freeborn Englishmen', servants left as soon as circumstances allowed.[43] Those who received rising wages in the late fourteenth and fifteenth century gained not a rewarding and satisfying life of comfort, but some compensation for demeaning labour for others. They looked forward to temporary release into leisure, or for some, permanent escape into a more secure life based on land, or independent work as a craftsman.

---

42 P. E. Jones (ed.), *Calendar of plea and memoranda rolls of the City of London, 1437–57* (Cambridge, 1954), *passim*.

43 C. Hill, 'Pottage for freeborn Englishmen: attitudes to wage labour in the sixteenth and seventeenth centuries' in C. H. Feinstein (ed.), *Socialism, capitalism and economic growth. Essays presented to Maurice Dobb* (Cambridge, 1967), pp. 338–50.

9

POVERTY AND CHARITY

——— • ———

Poverty was experienced at many social levels in the later middle ages, frequently for smallholders and wage-earners, and occasionally among the urban artisans and middle-ranking peasants. Most people were vulnerable to deprivation in old age and as parents of young children. They also felt the effects of long-term economic cycles and short-term slumps. Everyone was prone to fall victim to the ill-fortune which visited medieval people more often than ourselves, and from which recovery was more difficult – illness, accidents, premature death of breadwinners, fire, robbery, pillage in war, natural disasters and bad weather.

Poverty, defined as life-threatening deprivation, seems to have been a permanent condition for some and a periodic problem for many, and yet not all of its victims went to an early grave, or otherwise the population could not have grown in the thirteenth century, or maintained its numbers in the fifteenth. A possible answer to the question of 'How did the poor survive?' could lie in the abundance of charity, so initially we must devote some attention to alms-giving and poor relief, both as advocated by moralists and as it was practised.

Much is known of the theory of charity, because throughout Europe it provided a constant theme for writers of all kinds, theologians, canon lawyers, authors of sermons and devotional works, poets and chroniclers.[1] A modern observer cannot but notice the irony of members of the clerical hierarchy, writing either for an audience of fellow clergymen or to influence the lay aristocracy, advocating that the rich should give to the poor, when both the authors and their readers lived comfortably on the proceeds of rents, tithes and taxes that flowed from the lower to the upper ranks of society.

The common medieval view, drawing on the biblical notion that 'the poor you have with you always', was that the eternal and incurable nature of poverty meant that alms-giving would be a constant process. No-one expected a remedy for poverty, just some amelioration. The poor were defined not in economic but in political and legal terms: they lacked power. They might include 'poor knights' and 'poor priests', who had lower incomes than their fellows, and had difficulty in maintaining their status, but who rose well above indigence. The poor were seen as a natural part of the social scene. They received sympathy, but did not create much anguish. They were valued by the rich, because alms-giving, an act of justice and mercy, wiped away sin, and the poor, for all of their low status on earth, kept the gates of heaven.

There were many strands of thinking about poverty, and in the thirteenth century the different traditions diverged to the point of fierce controversy. One approach had been to stress the sin and guilt associated with the possession of riches. Christ had used the analogy of a camel passing through the eye of a needle to convey the difficulty of a rich man gaining salvation. A much retold biblical parable was that of Dives and Lazarus, in which the rich man feasted while his dogs licked the sores of the beggar at his gates. In eternity the positions were reversed, and while the pauper lay in the bosom of Abraham the wealthy man suffered the torments of hell. This story

---

1 B. Tierney, 'The Decretists and the "deserving poor"', *Comparative Studies in Society and History*, 1 (1958–9), 360–73; B. Tierney, *Medieval poor law* (Berkeley, Cal., 1959); F. Graus, 'The late medieval poor in town and countryside' in S. Thrupp (ed.), *Change in medieval society* (New York, 1964), pp. 314–24; M. Mollat (ed.), *Études sur l'histoire de la pauvreté* (Paris, 1974); M. Mollat, *The poor in the middle ages* (New Haven, Conn., 1986); L. K. Little, *Religious poverty and the profit economy in medieval Europe* (London, 1978); C. Lis and H. Soly, *Poverty and capitalism in pre-industrial Europe* (London, 1979); M. A. Moisa, 'Fourteenth-century preachers' views of the poor: class or status group?' in R. Samuel and G. Stedman Jones (eds.), *Culture, ideology and politics* (London, 1982), pp. 160–75; D. Aers, '*Piers Plowman* and problems in the perception of poverty: a culture in transition', *Leeds Studies in English*, new ser., 14 (1983), 5–25; M. Rubin, *Charity and community in medieval Cambridge* (Cambridge, 1987).

was intended to illustrate the dangers of the sins of avarice and gluttony, and to encourage the rich to embrace the poor. In the view of the clergy, the rich and poor could be bound together in a complementary relationship, in which the rich exhibited mercy and pity by their gifts, and the poor reciprocated with gratitude and prayers. A social contract was thus advocated; the rich were morally improved, and the poor, by accepting their lot with patience and resignation, would also gain salvation. The emphasis on the spiritual value of alms-giving encouraged the idea that the donors should avoid discrimination – who were mortal men to reject one beggar for another, because they cannot know who enjoys the favour of god? Nor should the rich become self-satisfied with their generosity, as this might add pride to their existing burden of sin.

The church had inherited a long tradition of poverty. The apostles had shown little concern for material goods, and the desert fathers had established an austere tradition of asceticism. Monasteries denied private property to their members, and new orders like the Cistercians revived the idea that conventual life should be sparse and bare. Religious houses fitted the secular poor into their organization by providing guest-houses for travellers and pilgrims, and almonries to distribute food at the gates. None of this could hide the immense wealth enjoyed by the church, and there was a growing criticism of possessions. In the thirteenth century, the friars enjoyed much success and popular good will by refusing to accept endowments and instead living as beggars. Their advocacy of voluntary poverty, particularly when voiced with millenarian enthusiasm by the spiritual wing of the Franciscan Order, led to criticism of the main body of the church. Dangerously radical suggestions were made about the rights as well as the duties of the poor, and on the morality of the poor taking property to satisfy their needs. A socially conservative thinker of the thirteenth century, Thomas Aquinas, contemplated the proposition that the poor were entitled to steal in times of famine, and he had to accept that in real emergencies such actions might be justified. The new ideas reflected changing social realities, especially those consequent on urbanization.

Another group of ideas regarded wealth as a moral problem, but not one demanding urgent remedies. The reception into Christian thinking of views ultimately deriving from ancient Greek philosophers allowed property and power a legitimate rôle in the world. Without property, how could the virtue of alms-giving be practised? There was some criticism of the poor. Poverty could be an ugly sight, bringing shame to the pauper, and might have resulted from his own sinful actions. Lepers, for example, although worthy of receiving alms, were segregated from the rest of society not just because of the supposedly contagious nature of their disease, but also because they were thought to be morally tainted. It was believed that they possessed unquenchable sexual appetites, and were given to malice towards the uninfected world. Some beggars deserved sympathy more than others. Pope Gregory the Great had distinguished between public beggars and modest paupers, giving more to the latter, and thirteenth-century writers preferred to give to the 'shame-faced poor'.[2] Such phrases anticipate the distinction between the deserving and undeserving poor, and the notion of discriminatory charity. Donors were advised that they should give alms while taking into account their own resources, the qualities and needs of the recipients, and the effect of the gift on the pauper. Too much charity might encourage begging – as a Victorian would put it, pauperize those receiving relief – or be squandered on luxuries.

A practical guide to charitable discrimination was provided in the model account-book of the Cistercian monastery of Beaulieu in Hampshire, compiled in 1269–70.[3] The rules decreed that the porter (gate-keeper) give thirty pairs of new shoes and the monks' old clothes to 'lepers and other paupers', and to distribute left-over bread on three days of each week. At harvest time, when there was plenty of work for the poor, alms should not be given except to pilgrims, old people, children and those incapable of work. Women who were suspected of being prostitutes should be given alms only in times of grave famine. The number of paupers to be maintained by the porter and guest-house, thirteen, is that commonly chosen in the administration of medieval charity, and derives from the number present at the Last Supper. Strict limits were set at Beaulieu on the quantity and the quality of charity; in the lay infirmary the poor sick were to be aided to recovery by being fed the meat of animals that had died of disease. In the guest-house, once the quota of poor had been accommodated, preference was to be given to aristocratic visitors. The attention to economy, the discrimination and the distrust of the poor would not have been out of place among the zealous administrators of the new Poor Law in the nineteenth century.

2 Rubin, *Charity and community*, pp. 72–3.
3 S. F. Hockey (ed.), *The account-book of Beaulieu Abbey* (Camden Soc., 4th ser., 16, 1975), pp. 172–82, 269–81.

These varied perceptions of poverty came into direct conflict in the controversy aroused by the friars. The struggle between the friars and the secular clergy, and the internal argument within the Franciscan Order, forced the church to defend itself on the grounds that its property was not held by individuals but in common, and ultimately for the benefit of the poor. The voluntary poverty advocated by the spiritual wing of the Franciscans was seen as arrogant, hypocritical and ultimately subversive. In 1323, Pope John XXII condemned their doctrines, though the controversy continued for many more decades.

In the early fourteenth century, the admirers of poverty were losing the argument within the church. Perhaps the changing climate of opinion reflected both the momentum of debate and the higher clergy's own economic problems. The growing hostility to the poor came at a time when the price scissors were beginning to pinch (see pp. 101–3). Fitzralph, an Englishman holding an Irish bishopric, revived the controversy against the friars in 1349, and wrote a great deal about poverty in the 1350s. He believed that property could be found in Paradise, and that poverty, not wealth, was a product of sin. He saw labour as an alternative to poverty, and he was beginning to develop a 'work ethic': 'He who will not work neither shall he eat'.[4] The same idea was advocated by the poet William Langland, writing in the 1370s and 1380s. He idealized the working peasant, and criticized the greed and idleness of the mendicant orders and secular beggars, whom he believed should be disciplined into work by Hunger. With typical intellectual complexity, he also showed some sympathy for the old virtue of voluntary poverty.[5] These harsher attitudes towards beggars have been ascribed to purely intellectual developments, but there can be little doubt that they were also strongly influenced by the late fourteenth-century labour shortage. The employers, burdened with rising costs, turned against those who begged when work was available. The roads seemed full of sinister vagabonds and criminals, who mingled with wage-earners tramping between jobs. The bonds of society seemed to be breaking, and respectable people felt threatened. The poor provoked a 'moral panic', not unlike the hysterical

---

4 Moisa, 'Fourteenth-century preachers' views'; J. D. Dawson, 'Richard Fitz Ralph and the fourteenth-century poverty controversies', *Journal of Ecclesiastical History*, 34 (1983), 315–44.
5 Aers, '*Piers Plowman*'; G. Shepherd, 'Poverty in *Piers Plowman*' in T. H. Aston *et al.* (eds.), *Social relations and ideas* (Cambridge, 1983), pp. 169–89.

reactions to Jews, lepers and heretics in earlier times, and the surge of witchcraft accusations of the sixteenth and seventeenth centuries. In its most extreme form, in France for example, beggars were accused of the same crimes as were imagined in anti-Semitic fantasies.[6] They were said to poison wells, and to kidnap and mutilate children (a child without a foot, for example, would attract the sympathy of alms-givers). More frequently, the critics of the beggars stressed the social inversion that had occurred: the hierarchy had been turned upside-down, and now the beggars had become proud. The haughty beggar (*pauper superbus*) had replaced the cringing and grateful receiver of alms of the good old days, and prostitutes wore furs like fine ladies. In fact, beggars and other marginals were not especially subversive, because they depended too much on the productive capacity of orthodox society as a source of alms. The moral and social order *was* threatened at this time, not however by the extreme poor, but by rebel bands of peasants and artisans, whose revolts were fuelled by rising expectations.

Social attitudes shifted among the clergy and literate laity, so the pride of the rich was mentioned less often, and the sin of envy received fresh emphasis from such writers as Froissart, who wrote to please an aristocratic public. The poor, in the eyes of the wealthy, were now sharply divided between the idlers and criminals who deserved no charity, and the real poor, those incapable of work and who had fallen on hard times after a period of respectability. Because of the confident identification of the deserving poor, alms could be concentrated on them in the hope of relieving their plight. New religious attitudes, connected with the doctrine of purgatory and the advocacy of good works, kept up the pressure on the rich to practise charity both in their lifetime and through bequests after their death. Many of the ideas commonly supposed to have been introduced in the sixteenth century, such as discriminatory charity, the work ethic and the search for solutions to poverty, all developed before 1500. It is not even likely, as was once believed, that the quantity of charitable gifts increased after the Reformation.[7]

These, then, were some of the shifting opinions of the clergy and

---

6 B. Geremek, *The margins of society in late medieval Paris* (Cambridge, 1987), pp. 199–210.

7 W. G. Bittle and R. Todd Lane, 'Inflation and philanthropy in England: a reassessment of W. K. Jordan's data', *Ec.H.R.*, 2nd ser., 29 (1976), 203–10; and the ensuing controversy in *Ec.H.R.*, 2nd ser., 31 (1978), 105–28.

upper classes towards the poor. The church's insistence on the duty of charitable giving provides a common theme throughout the middle ages. Now it is time to see how alms were organized and to judge their effectiveness as remedies for poverty.

MONASTIC ALMS

Monastic almonries were among the oldest of medieval charitable institutions. Worcester Cathedral Priory's almonry provides a characteristic example, being run by a monk obedientiary on a cash budget of £64 in 1345–6, and £89 in 1521–2.[8] The bulk of the income was absorbed in administration, wages and expenditure within the monastery. The gifts to the poor were made up of numerous customary elements, the accretions of the centuries, including a daily dole of bread, special doles on St Wulfstan's day (the day of the cathedral's own saint), Maundy Thursday and days marking the anniversaries of the deaths of former monks. At least three paupers lived in almshouses maintained in the city by the almoner. The total value of the almoner's charity in 1521–2, £23, amounted to 2 per cent of the monastery's income. The *Valor ecclesiasticus* shows that this was typical of the early sixteenth century, and individual monastic accounts confirm that a similar percentage prevailed throughout our period. Some monasteries organized practical charity that would provide a regular clientele with basic food and clothing. Regulations at Gloucester Abbey in 1327 insisted that 249 quarters of wheat, peas and beans (mostly the latter), should be distributed each year, enough to feed perhaps 150 people, and 30 paupers were each to receive enough woollen cloth to make a garment. Some monasteries concentrated their charity on the inmates of a hospital, as Peterborough Abbey did in the case of St Leonard's. Otherwise much monastic charity served liturgical purposes, one aim being to assemble a large crowd on a saint's day, or to provide a focus for the Maundy ceremonies. The needs of the poor came rather a long way down the list of monastic priorities, and is shown by Bolton Priory's cut in charity during the famine of 1315–18, from £10 in cash before

8 S. G. Hamilton (ed.), *Compotus rolls of the priory of Worcester of the XIVth and XVth centuries* (Worcestershire Historical Soc., 1910), pp. 49–54; J. M. Wilson (ed.), *Accounts of the priory of Worcester for the year 13–14 Henry VIII, 1521–2* (Worcestershire Historical Soc., 1907), pp. 9–13; J. H. Bloom (ed.), *Liber elemosinarii: the almoner's book of the priory of Worcester* (Worcestershire Historical Soc., 1911).

1314 (about 2 per cent of money income) down to £1 3s. od. in 1317–18.[9]

Bishops had a special responsibility to set an example to other churchmen. In the bad harvests of the mid-thirteenth century, the bishops of Winchester and Worcester gave to poor tenants on their estates cash at a rate of $^1/_4$d. per day each through the difficult summer months (early April to early July), and such necessities as shoes. The most lavish scheme for episcopal charity was that proposed by an early fourteenth-century bishop of Bath and Wells, to give 240 paupers on his manors $^1/_4$d. per day, with clothes at Michaelmas, at a total cost of £130 per annum, or about 5 per cent of the estate's income.[10] Episcopal charity seems to have declined in the late fourteenth and fifteenth centuries, being concentrated on small numbers of named tenants. Bishops continued to encourage charity in others, by emphasizing the responsibilities of parishes in the case of Bishop Carpenter of Worcester, or by granting indulgences to those who gave alms to especially deserving cases, such as those who had suffered from fires or other misfortunes. A bleak picture of the bishop of Lincoln's charity emerges from a record in his household account of 1506 of the gift to the poor of fish that had become 'corrupt and defective'.[11]

9 A. Savine, *English monasteries on the eve of the dissolution* (Oxford, 1909), pp. 234–40; R. H. Snape, *English monastic finances in the later middle ages* (Cambridge, 1926), pp. 112–18; R. M. Haines (ed.). *A calendar of the register of Wolstan de Bransford* (Worcestershire Historical Soc., new ser., 4, 1966), pp. 512–14; J. Greatrex (ed.), *Account rolls of the obedientiaries of Peterborough* (Northamptonshire Record Soc., 33, 1984), p. 197; I. Kershaw, *Bolton priory. The economy of a northern monastery, 1286–1325* (Oxford, 1973), pp. 141–2.

10 J. Z. Titow, *English rural society 1200–1350* (London, 1969), p. 96; N. S. B. Gras and E. C. Gras, *The economic and social history of an English village* (Cambridge, Mass., 1930), pp. 225–6; C. Dyer, *Lords and peasants in a changing society. The estates of the bishopric of Worcester, 680–1540* (Cambridge, 1980), p. 111; E. Hobhouse (ed.), *Church-wardens' accounts* (Somerset Record Soc., 4, 1890), p. 250.

11 Suffolk R.O. (Ipswich branch), HA12/C2/65; R. M. Haines, 'Bishop Carpenter's injunctions to the diocese of Worcester in 1451', *Bulletin of the Institute of Historical Research*, 40 (1967), 203–7; Rubin, *Charity and community*, pp. 264–9; Lincolnshire Archive Office, B.P.Min.Acct. 10.

HOSPITALS AND ALMSHOUSES

More than a thousand hospitals and almshouses are known to have existed in England at some time in the later middle ages, the majority of them in or near towns.[12] Larger towns commonly had six or more. They varied as institutions from well-endowed groups of priests and brethren living under the Augustinian rule, with charity as one of the functions of a religious community, to a few 'bedesmen' with a master, observing some purpose-made regulations. The buildings of the former type would include a cloister and chapel, and for the latter no more than a row of cottages.[13] In the first wave of foundations of the eleventh to thirteenth century, bishops and monasteries played a major rôle. Later on townsmen, whether individually or collectively, became the main founders, and the nobility sometimes included almshouses in their collegiate churches. Their income came from endowments of property, occasionally rural manors, but more commonly urban rents. Annual revenues usually ranged from £5 to £60, and the well-provided St Leonard's at York (£308 in 1535) and the Savoy in London (£567) were quite exceptional. Because of their modest endowment they were more dependent than most church institutions on casual income from entry fees and gifts. Often they sheltered a (symbolic) thirteen paupers; at St Leonard's in 1370, 224 inmates and 23 orphans were accommodated.

Hospitals were supervised by a variety of external authorities, such as bishops, monasteries or town governments. Within a hospital, a disciplinary system depended on the master or warden. The rules usually stressed that the hospital should have a communal life, and a large hall often served as the living accommodation. The inmates ate together, and wore a badge or livery. They were expected to take part in religious observances, and to behave in a seemly fashion, avoiding ale-houses, gambling and the company of the opposite sex. Rules of conduct were especially strict in the leper houses, to the point that the prior of the hospital of Sherburn (Co. Durham) was provided under the early fourteenth-century rules with a stick for beating the disobedient, 'and to encourage the faithless and negligent'.[14]

12 D. Knowles and R. N. Hadcock, *Medieval religious houses: England and Wales*, 2nd edn (London, 1971), pp. 310–410, 494–5; R. M. Clay, *Medieval hospitals in England* (London, 1909).

13 W. H. Godfrey, *The English almshouse* (London, 1955), pp. 15–47.

14 P. Richards, *The medieval leper and his northern heirs* (Cambridge, 1977), pp. 125–8.

Hospitals were primarily religious institutions, and often lacked any medical function.[15] Even leper hospitals had constitutions, like those of Sherburn, which began with arrangements for priests, altars and masses, though they also stressed the importance of a healthy environment, such as a fresh water supply. Some hospitals specialized in the care of those with particular health problems, such as pregnant women or the insane, but often the intended inmates were defined in religious and social terms. In early hospitals pilgrims, converted Jews and retired clergy were named as groups to be helped. Indeed, some hospitals specifically excluded those with serious illnesses: St John's Cambridge would not admit lepers, the insane, pregnant women or people suffering from wounds, and St John's Oxford regarded as ineligible those with paralysis, dropsy, epilepsy and ulcers.[16]

Most hospitals and almshouses gave some relief to the poor and the old. Some issued doles to outsiders, like the hundred meals per day at St Mark's, Bristol, in the early thirteenth century.[17] The great majority provided long-term residential places for people selected on the grounds of their poverty (those who were incapable of work, for example), or those who were 'lame, crooked, blind and bed-ridden', to quote the ordinances of the Saffron Walden almshouses in 1400.[18] Almshouses attached to colleges or fraternities with an educational rôle might house scholars who were 'poor' only in a relative sense. Hospitals also cared for people who were well above any poverty line that we might draw, as is shown by the entry fees, of £5 at Dover for example, or the boarding charges, like the annual 26s. 8d. that the families of the insane paid to the London hospital of St Mary of Bethlehem (Bedlam). Many hospitals accepted corrodians, who gave a substantial endowment of land or cash in exchange for their keep for the rest of their lives. A few hospitals served as soft havens for masters and brethren, and luxurious rest-homes for decayed aristocrats. God's House at Ospringe in Kent is a good example, founded by the Crown in the early thirteenth century partly as a convenient stopping-place for the royal household on the

15 C. Rawcliffe, 'The hospitals of later medieval London', *Medical History*, 28 (1984), 1–21.

16 Rubin, *Charity and community*, pp. 157–8.

17 C. D. Ross (ed.), *Cartulary of St. Mark's hospital, Bristol* (Bristol Record Soc., 21, 1959), p. xii.

18 F. W. Steer, 'The statutes of the Saffron Walden almshouses', *Transactions of the Essex Archaeological Soc.*, 25 (1958), 172–83.

road from London to Dover, and as a retirement home for royal servants. By 1293–4 it enjoyed a cash income of £137 per annum, from which the master was provided with robes costing more than £2. Purchases for the kitchen included peacocks, sugar and wine. In addition to the normal hospital diet, which was like that of any small monastery with much bread, ale and meat, the sick at Ospringe were given special delicacies of almonds, pullets, milk and fresh goat's meat. The community was housed in high quality buildings, decorated with Caen stone, Purbeck marble, painted plaster, painted glass and ornate floor tiles.[19]

Hospitals and almshouses grew in numbers up to a peak of almost 700 in 1300, and after a decline to about 500 in the late fourteenth century, they increased again to nearly 600 on the eve of the Reformation. These overall figures conceal the tendency for hospitals to decay, either because of their inadequate endowments, or as a result of the decline in pilgrimage and leprosy which deprived them of their original functions. Almshouses increased in number, and as they provided more places at less cost than did the hospitals, the population of inmates may not have been greatly reduced in the fourteenth and fifteenth centuries. In view of the general demographic decline, the proportion in residential places may actually have risen. At any time, however, the numbers were tiny, probably less than 10,000, or below a half of one per cent of the English population.

The character of the post-1349 almshouse foundations reflected new attitudes towards poverty. There was more emphasis on the selection of the genuinely indigent. The poor were treated as individuals, often living in separate rooms arranged in a row or around a quadrangle. And the inmates were subject to a strict and improving discipline. At Saffron Walden in Essex once a year the twenty-four 'most worshipful' townsmen, who formed the fraternity governing the almshouse, read the ordinances to the poor and sick, who were no doubt expected to listen to the fourteen pages of exhortation with gratitude and respect. Four times each year the house was visited, to ensure 'that they have of good rule and clean living [and that there are] no ribalds, quarrellers, drunkards or latemakers'. After two warnings any dissidents were to be expelled. The concern

19 St John's College, Cambridge, MS. 2/1/2; 2/1/3; S. E. Rigold, 'Two Kentish hospitals re-examined', *Archaeologia Cantiana*, 79 (1964), 31–69; G. H. Smith, 'The excavation of the hospital of St Mary of Ospringe', *Archaeologia Cantiana*, 95 (1979), 81–184.

for the morality of the poor, and the insistence on discipline and godliness, have rightly been compared with the puritanical attitudes of later centuries, and show that the emergence of such values pre-dates the Reformation.[20]

The well-documented almshouse at Sherborne in Dorset can stand as an example of late medieval institutional charity.[21] At the centre of this small town, next to the church, stood in the early fifteenth century an almshouse for a dozen paupers, who received so little from the endowment that they must have relied on the variable day-to-day charity of the townspeople. In 1437–8 a scheme was initiated to increase the income of the almshouse to £30 per annum or more, enough to give each of twelve men and four women food worth 7½d. per week, clothing costing 6s. 8d. annually and a bed. This expressed both the civic pride and the charitable impulses of the leading townsmen, twenty of whom formed a fraternity acting as governors, who expected the building and its inmates to be a credit to Sherborne. The new foundation seems to have won a generous response from the townspeople, 146 of whom subscribed an initial £80.

The Sherborne almshouse was set up as a respectable institution for those deserving charity. The 'poor, feeble and impotent' were eligible for entry, preference being given to 'continual householders' of the town, or at least local residents. This reflected civic consciousness, the desire to exclude vagrants, and the need to guarantee that admission was restricted to people of good character. The choice was made by the twenty governors, who would have known the applicants and their circumstances. In every respect the institution reinforced the social hierarchy of the town. The selection process strengthened the authority of the élite, who could reject undesirables. Even among the twenty, some had higher status than others, because a tied vote was to be decided by the 'most worthy men'. The new recruits to the almshouse swore to obey the rules, and would be ejected for misbehaviour. They were explicitly forbidden to beg, and any unruliness would have been noticed in a small town, especially as they were required to wear a badge. Some entrants were not desperately poor, judging by the gift of 66s. 8d. made by one

---

20 Steer, 'Saffron Walden almshouses', pp. 175, 183; M. K. McIntosh, *Autonomy and community. The royal manor of Havering 1200–1500* (Cambridge, 1986), pp. 235–63; B. Pullan, *Rich and poor in renaissance Venice* (Oxford, 1971), pp. 197–215.
21 Dorset R.O., D 204/A1–A35; C. H. Mayo, *Historic Guide to the almshouse of St John, Sherborne* (Oxford, 1933), pp. 20–40.

'pauper' to the almshouse funds in 1451–2, and from the fact that some of the inmates' surnames were the same as those of wealthy townsmen. If one of the twenty hit on hard times, he was entitled to receive 20d. per week, well above the allowances for the paupers. No poverty needed relief so much as that of a member of the oligarchy who was down on his luck.

One can detect in the arrangements for this almshouse the influences not just of piety, charity and local loyalty but also of social solidarity among the rich that left many poor people out in the cold. The labourer with many children, who may sometimes have drunk too much and who engaged in petty crime, would never gain access to this narrowly defined charity, while the widow of a leading trader might well have been eligible. We can see in the administration of the almshouse that the institution depended on social inequalities for its existence – on the widows and artisans who were persuaded to contribute 6d. or 12d. to the original fund; on the labourers employed on the building work at 4d. per day during the period of very high food prices in 1439–40; and on the tenants charged with high rents, such as 4s. for a cottage, out of which the charity was endowed. In 1484–5 one such tenant, John Nodebyll, had fallen behind in his rent payments. Many landlords turned a blind eye to such lapses at this period, but the twenty worthies of Sherborne moved against him, seizing goods worth 3s. 2d. in distraint and selling them. As his goods (including such tools as an axe and two knives) were carried off for the benefit of the 'paupers' in the almshouse, John could well have mused on the different treatment meted out to the various categories of poor.

FRATERNITIES

In England there were no large fraternities devoted primarily to charitable works comparable with those of the great Italian cities. The fraternities which played such an important rôle in the government of some towns, like the Holy Cross Guild of Stratford-upon-Avon, founded and maintained almshouses. Most of the smaller fraternities in the countryside, or the urban 'craft guilds', confined themselves to making modest cash grants to poor members, and paying for funerals. Many guilds, judging from the formal statements of their rules submitted to a royal enquiry in 1389, had no formal charitable rôle at all, and as they tended to attract members from the wealthier section of society, their assistance was perhaps not often needed. They were not sufficiently well-endowed to hand out large sums: one Cambridgeshire guild could give a single claimant 7d. per week, but if there were two, the relief would fall to 4d. each! An enigmatic Norwich fraternity, called the Poor Men's Guild, was presumably open to those who could not afford membership of grander organizations. It offered a meagre 3d. per week to indigent members.[22] Perhaps the main charitable function of the fraternities, rather than providing formal grants, was to reinforce the neighbourliness and sense of community of their members, and thus encourage informal giving.

THE PARISH

Lacking the continental 'poor tables', the English parish was not provided with a permanent institution for channelling alms to a selected list of paupers. Under canon law, the parish clergy were obliged to devote a quarter or a third of their revenues to the poor. If this had been observed, most parishes would have had access to a regular annual fund of £2 or £3. Though it has been argued that if the rules had not been obeyed, we would hear more complaints in the records of bishops' visitations, there is little evidence that the clergy gave more than a few shillings. Parishes were either served by a rector or by a vicar if the rectory had been appropriated by a monastery or college. Contemporaries complained that appropriation led to a decline in charity, but rectors were not especially generous. At Bishop's Cleeve at the end of the fourteenth century, a rector with an income of £100 per annum gave to the poor an annual quarter of wheat worth 4s. or 5s., on one occasion to be divided among six named individuals. In appropriated parishes, alms of 5s. 5d. were given at Barford (Norfolk) in 1335, and at the valuable living of Writtle in Essex around 1400 the gifts varied from 1½ bushels of wheat (worth 8d.) to 1 quarter 1 bushel, the bulk of this last amount going to a 'beggar of this parish' called Andrew Haukyns. The same appropriator, New College Oxford, paid 12d. for the rent of a house for a local pauper at Steeple Morden (Cambridgeshire) in 1400, apparently its only act of charity in that parish. Sometimes we hear of a large amount of charity, only to find that it was a folk memory rather than a well-attested payment, like the 2

---

22 Rubin, *Charity and community*, pp. 250–9; Toulmin Smith and F. Brentano (eds.), *English guilds* (Early English Text Soc., O.S., 40, 1870), pp. 40–1.

bushels of wheat and 4 bushels of malt once distributed each week at Bibury (Gloucestershire) according to a local jury in 1482, but which had been discontinued for some years.[23] In 1391 and 1403 parliamentary statutes, which reflected a growing concern about poverty, reminded appropriators of their charitable duties, and required bishops vetting new appropriations to order that 'a convenient sum of money' be set aside from the parochial revenues for alms. The second enactment was obeyed, and in the resulting agreements the sum suited the convenience of the clergy rather than the poor, varying from 3s. 4d. to 15s., usually at the lower end of that range, for vicarages worth £6 13s. 4d. to £10.[24]

The laity may have been more effective organizers of charity than the clergy. They participated in customs like the 'holy loaf' by which the congregation brought bread to church for eventual distribution, and some form of discreet charity may have been practised at the church ales whereby the poor were given drink and food normally offered for sale. By the mid-fifteenth century, church-wardens were keeping a parish box for donations, from which alms were distributed at their discretion.[25] Unfortunately the scale of their activities is not recorded.

LAY ARISTOCRATIC CHARITY

The royal household set a charitable example in the thirteenth century: Henry III fed 500 paupers daily, and Edward I spent £650 per annum (1 per cent of his revenues). After this the scale of royal alms-giving seems to have declined. A similar pattern is found among the aristocrats who in the late thirteenth and early fourteenth century kept groups of paupers as part of their entourage. There were as many as thirteen living sparsely on a diet of maslin bread and herrings in the household of Katherine de Norwich, the widow of a

23 Tierney, 'Medieval poor law', pp. 89–109; Corpus Christi College, Oxford, B/14/2/3/1–B/14/2/3/7; H. W. Saunders, *An introduction to the obedientiary and manor rolls of Norwich Cathedral Priory* (Norwich, 1930), p. 64; New College, Oxford, MSS. 7312, 7317–7319, 6824; H. E. Salter (ed.), *Cartulary of Oseney Abbey* (6 vols., Oxfordshire Record Soc., 98, 1935), vol. 5, pp. 12–13.

24 *Statutes of the realm* (11 vols., Record Commission, 1810–28), vol. 2, pp. 80, 136–7; W. E. L. Smith (ed.), *Register of Richard Clifford, bishop of Worcester, 1401–1407* (Toronto, 1976), pp. 128–37; R. N. Swanson (ed.), *A calendar of the register of Richard Scrope, archbishop of York, 1398–1405* (York, 1981), p. 8; R. A. R. Hartridge, *A history of vicarages in the middle ages* (Cambridge, 1930), pp. 159–60.

25 Haines, 'Bishop Carpenter's injunctions', p. 206.

rich knight, in 1336–7. Later the aristocracy are revealed by their accounts as great donors, but not necessarily to the poor. Lady Katherine Beauchamp, for example, in 1421–2 had a section of her accounts headed 'The lady's gifts'. Of a hundred items totalling £9 2s. od. only 5s. 2d. went in alms. Perhaps the main aristocratic contribution came through the largely undocumented distribution of left-overs from meals, and the equally mysterious gifts from the privy purse. The aristocrats of the late fourteenth and fifteenth century reflected the new approaches to charity by careful selection of the recipients of alms, who belonged in some way to their clientage, whether as tenants, or servants to be provided with spare cottages for their retirement.[26]

BEQUESTS

Medieval will-makers were expected to dispose of a third of their goods 'for the good of their soul' in religious and charitable works. They did not distinguish clearly between gifts to churches and poor relief, and charity was so broadly defined that it included bridge repairs and road-works as well as alms to the poor.

Most of the medieval wills that survive date from after 1370; the testators tend to come from the wealthier sections of society and especially the urban rich. The attitudes expressed in wills were not necessarily the personal opinions of the testator, but were influenced by the conventional formulae in which the will was written and the suggestions of the clergyman who drew up the document.[27] An example is that of a Bristol merchant, John Shipward the elder, who made his will on 14 December 1473.[28] He wished a good deal of his money to be spent on doles to the poor: bread and ale worth £3 6s. 8d. at his funeral and at his 'month's mind', and 1d. each to a

---

26 H. Johnstone, 'Poor relief in the royal households of thirteenth-century England', *Speculum*, 4 (1929), 149–67; C. Given-Wilson, *The royal household and the king's affinity* (Yale, 1986), pp. 69–70; B.L. Add. Roll 63207; Hereford and Worcester R.O., ref. 705:99 BA.5540/2; Lord Grey of Ruthin gave a cottage 'to John Cartere in alms', I. Jack (ed.), *The Grey of Ruthin valor* (Bedfordshire Record Soc., 46, 1965), p. 76.

27 M. M. Sheehan, *The will in medieval England* (Toronto, 1963); M. Zell, 'Fifteenth-and sixteenth-century wills as historical sources', *Archives*, 14 (1979), 67–74. This discussion is based on the will collections cited in n. 20 of chapter 6, and J. Raine (ed.), *Testamenta Eboracensia* (Surtees Soc., 4, 1836; 30, 1885; 45, 1865).

28 T. P. Wadley (ed.), *The great orphan book of Bristol* (Bristol, 1886), pp. 158–61.

hundred attending a memorial service on the anniversary of his death. Twenty-four poor men who attended the funeral ceremony were to be given black and white clothes which they could keep. These suggest a primary interest in attracting large crowds and in making a public show, yet Shipward expressed some concern for the effects of his hand-outs by specifying that most of them should be in kind, thus preventing the poor from misusing any cash. A discriminatory bequest was for £10 to be spent on bedding for poor householders in St Stephen's parish, according to the discretion of the executors, with the advice of the vicar. Here every precaution was being taken to ensure that idle beggars did not thus obtain money for buying ale. By specifying a respectable class of poor people, by insisting that the gifts be in kind, and by ensuring that the recipients would be chosen by someone with local knowledge, the merchant closed every loop-hole. He also left money to the local almshouses, again confident that the inmates would have been selected, and the distribution supervised by responsible wardens. His other choice of institution, Newgate prison, was directed to helping debtors, among whom would be found sober citizens who had suffered misfortune. Finally he asked that if his heirs died, the proceeds from the sale of his property should go to 'poor bedridden people' and for the 'marriage of poor maidens', again selecting the 'real' poor, and hoping to rescue young women from poverty and worse.

Few wills contain as many charitable bequests as Shipward's. He was by no means unusual in combining doles with more discriminating charity. Fashions changed, so that the proportion of London wills leaving money to hospitals declined from 23 per cent in the early fifteenth century to 18 per cent during the period 1479–86, and at Norwich 36 per cent of wills in the years 1370–1439 mention St Paul's Hospital (the largest in the town) but by the early sixteenth century the percentage had fallen to 22.[29] This does not mean that selective or discriminatory charity was waning in the period, because wills commonly refer to deserving groups, such as widows, orphans, the bedridden sick, blind and lame. The definitions are sometimes elaborately precise: 'poor and decrepit and bedridden with two or three children', 'poor weavers and fullers holding houses and having wives and families', or 'poor women and children except those with husbands and fathers with goods worth more than

29 J. A. F. Thomson, 'Piety and charity in late medieval London', *Journal of Ecclesiastical History*, 16 (1965), 178–95; N. P. Tanner, *The church in late medieval Norwich* (Toronto, 1984), pp. 132–7, 222–3.

£10'. Evidently those who worked and who bore heavy family responsibilities could occasionally be admitted into the ranks of those deserving charity. Some testators also showed a concern to provide long-term relief, like the Hull merchant who left enough to give the poor of the town 20d. per week for ten years.[30] Testators could exclude the unworthy, in such categories as the litigious, the dishonest or the 'common beggars'. The quantity of bequests and the objects of charity varied between different social groups, with the gentry, for example, showing less interest in almshouses and hospitals than did the townsmen. Aristocrats might leave money for their tenants, sometimes in recompense for wrongs done to them, and peasant will-makers invariably left any alms for the poor of their own village. The greatest concentration of charitable bequests would be in towns, but even there, a relatively small amount of charity was being spread unevenly and often thinly over a large number of potential recipients. Many wills made no mention of alms, and among those that did, the sum often amounted to no more than a few shillings. An estimate for the sixteenth century, that the poor of a town of 4,000 to 5,000 inhabitants (Worcester) might in a year be left £5 to £20 by the better-off citizens, would not be very different from the scale of medieval urban bequests.[31] This amount of money could have supported no more than a dozen paupers in an average year. We should also remember that wills convey intentions which may not have been implemented. The dying may have over-estimated their resources, and they depended on executors, who were notorious for their unreliability.

GOVERNMENT

Medieval governments had no social policy in our understanding of the term, and their measures reflect the interests and attitudes of the upper classes. The taxes collected before 1334 exempted about a half of the potential payers on grounds of poverty, and the shift of opinion after the Black Death is reflected in the attempt between 1371 and 1381 to find a basis for taxation that would force more of the newly enriched wage-earners to make a direct contribution. The poll taxes of 1377–81 sought to distinguish between the 'real' poor (those living on alms, including indigent householders) who did not

---

30 J. I. Kermode, 'The merchants of three northern towns' in C. H. Clough (ed.), *Profession, vocation and culture in later medieval England* (Liverpool, 1982), p. 30.
31 A. D. Dyer, *The city of Worcester in the sixteenth century* (Leicester, 1973), p. 170.

have to pay, and the labourers and servants who did.[32] The violent reaction to the third poll tax in 1381 frightened governments from future experiments, and taxes were mostly collected, as they had been since 1334, from communities who decided their own assessments. Town authorities continued to tax the less well-off, like the labourers on 4d. per day who were expected to contribute a penny or two to the cost of Coventry's walls in 1451 along with the 'thrifty men'.[33]

The labour laws after 1349 included some 'poor law' provisions. In the atmosphere of 'moral panic' the 'valiant' or 'sturdy' beggars attracted fear and loathing. They were forbidden to beg, or even to wander without licence, and the 1388 laws included the principle of local responsibility for the poor that was to be repeated in the 1495 poor law and become the hall-mark of subsequent measures. We have also seen that the laws of 1391 and 1403 attempted to strengthen the alms-giving functions of the vill or parish.[34] The assumption on the part of the legislators that the poor should be relieved or controlled by their local communities was presumably not an innovation imposed from above, but a comment on existing social practice.

CONCLUSION

Alms-giving fell short of the expectations of clerical exhortations. Plenty of organizations dispensed charity, but much of their income went into non-charitable activities. Gifts were deployed inconsistently and unevenly, and the recipients were either not selected by need at all, or were chosen by rules that excluded many categories of poverty. The overall quantity of charity was low, whether measured as a proportion of the donors' wealth, or in relation to the needs of the poor. It might be thought that each institution, though modest in its spending, might contribute to an impressive cumulative total. If we take as an example a community well-supplied with charitable institutions, the city of Worcester in the fifteenth century, we find that the two hospitals (of St Oswald and St Wulfstan) contained

---

32 C. C. Fenwick, 'The English poll taxes of 1377, 1379 and 1381' (University of London Ph.D. thesis, 1983), pp. 113–14, 176–8.

33 M. D. Harris (ed.), *The Coventry leet book* (4 parts, Early English Text Soc., 134, 1907, 135, 1908, 138, 1909, 146, 1913), part 2, p. 258.

34 *Statutes of the realm*, vol. 2, p. 58; for later measures, P. L. Hughes and J. Larkin (eds.), *Tudor royal proclamations* (New Haven, 1964), pp. 17, 21, 23, 32–4, 85–93, 127.

about thirty inmates, and the main fraternity, the Trinity Guild, had twenty-four almshouses capable of holding forty-eight people. The cathedral almonry fed about twenty paupers each day. The clergy of the eleven parish churches and the bequests in wills can be guessed to have maintained another twenty people at most, assuming that a pauper needed a penny a day on which to live. It seems reasonable, therefore, to estimate that the formal charities of the city could provide for 120 people, or 3 per cent of the population of 4,000. This figure must represent a fraction of the poor. In contemporary Tuscany, 9.5 per cent of the population were aged sixty-five or over, and Worcester's elderly should not have been any less numerous.[35] In addition were the disabled, sick, orphans and widows. The numbers were swelled by immigrant paupers from the surrounding villages, whose departure is recorded in manorial court records. There can have been no shortage of paupers who, being unable to obtain permanent charitable relief, were forced to seek temporary aid on the occasions when it was made available, at funeral doles, or the irregular special distributions made by the Priory almoner. Worcester's poor were not adequately served by charitable institutions, even when all of the gifts are added together.

The documentation of charity can tell us something about what it was like to be poor. For example, two sums of money recur as suitable donations: ¼d. per day seems to have been an absolute minimum, given to prisoners and destitute tenants. It was the price of a loaf of bread weighing about two pounds. Guild members down on their luck, or the inmates of almshouses were given 1d. per day, which gave an individual a decent but sparse living with meat and ale to go with the bread.

The medieval upper class had a perception of poverty which seems to differ from that which we derive from our sources. Judging from foundation documents of hospitals, wills and legislation, the poor were concentrated in towns, suffered from disabilities preventing work, and multiplied after 1349. We would expect the poor to include, as well as the old and crippled, smallholders and sections of the lower-paid working population with families, in both town and country; their numbers ought to have diminished after 1349. The most plausible explanation of this discrepancy lies in the 'moral panic' which created so much comment and action on poverty in the late fourteenth century. This was not necessarily provoked by a real increase in work-shy beggars, but by a growth in the flexibility of

35 D. Herlihy and C. Klapisch-Zuber, *Les toscans et leurs familles* (Paris, 1978), p. 371.

employment, and above all by the resentment of employers at having to pay high wages to a shifting and truculent work-force. In view of their outlook and prejudices, it is scarcely surprising that their charity was ineffective.

If formal charity helped so few paupers, can we identify any solution to the problem? The answer lay partly in self-help, in which property and market forces could be used to prevent poverty, and partly in community efforts. The relative importance of these two areas of poor-relief are uncertain and controversial.

A wide range of customary as well as free tenants could obtain some measure of social security from their holdings. The free could trade their land for corrodies and free and customary tenants alike could negotiate a retirement arrangement with a promise of maintenance.[36] Urban property owners made the same kind of agreements, surrendering part of their tenement in exchange for a promise of food and drink.[37] A more informal solution to the problems of the elderly or infirm was to sublet land and to live on the resulting rents. Parcels of land could if necessary be sold off to raise cash. The market could also be a source of care for the elderly, through the hire of servants. Care for orphans could be obtained by paying wet-nurses, or by making boarding arrangements.

Inheritance customs also provided forms of social security (see pp. 120–4). Partible inheritance seems to have been the fairest system, though it excluded females if there were male heirs, and would not give much useful support if holdings became excessively fragmented. In practice, sons who acquired a small parcel as their share would often sell it to a brother. They would gain some cash to buy land or a craftsman's tools, thereby receiving a useful share of family resources. A father might help his daughters by instructing in his will that sons provide them with a cash sum. The two types of impartible inheritance, primogeniture and ultimogeniture (borough English) gave families a variety of options. A father could look after non-inheriting sons and daughters with grants of land acquired in his lifetime, or he could leave them cash and goods in his will. Some peasants bequeathed much more than they actually owned, not because of unrealistic optimism, but to build up an obligation on the

36 F. M. Page, 'The customary poor-law of three Cambridgeshire manors', *Cambridge Historical Journal*, 3 (1930), 125–33; E. Clark, 'Some aspects of social security in medieval England', *Journal of Family History*, 7 (1982), 307–20; see also pp. 151–7 above.

37 M. Bateson (ed.), *Records of the borough of Leicester* (3 vols., Cambridge, 1899–1905), vol. 1, p. 389.

part of the heir to look after a younger brother or sister. Under ultimogeniture, the youngest son who inherited was more likely to be a child at the time of his father's death, so his eldest brother would in practice have the use of the holding for a few years, long enough to make arrangements for an independent life when the heir came of age. Alternatively, the younger son might make over the inheritance to his elder brother in exchange for a promise of maintenance.[38] Widows were protected from poverty by their entitlement to dower, or free-bench, or joint tenancy; these gave them the right to keep at least a third of their husband's land, and often the whole tenement, for life. The widow could continue with farming or a trade, or she could dispose of the property in order to obtain an income.

All of these arrangements for maintenance, inheritance or subletting depended on the initial possession of property. However we would be quite mistaken to think of medieval society as being governed entirely by property rights. Family loyalties clearly played an important part in the transmission of land. Maintenance agreements were not negotiated strictly on the basis of the laws of supply and demand. The allowances depended on the 'common custom of the vill', and the community supervised the arrangements, by approving them in the manorial court, and by informing the court if agreements, even unwritten and informal ones, were being broken. We may suspect that social pressure was brought to bear on sons who neglected their duties to their elderly parents. One could say that self-interest lay at the roots of this community concern. No-one gained if a village or town was overrun by destitute beggars, who could threaten public order; everyone might one day need to obtain maintenance in their own old age. Motives are often mixed, and people's calculations of short-term and long-term advantage must have been mingled with a humane concern for their neighbours.

What happened to those without property or with smallholdings? They could make the maximum use of the labour market, by sending their children out to work at the earliest opportunity, and by working as late in life as possible, like the poor old labourers mentioned in the 1522 muster for Rutland.[39] But this was no solution to

---

38 R. Faith, 'Peasant families and inheritance customs in medieval England', *Ag.H.R.*, 14 (1966), 77–95; M. Spufford, 'Peasant inheritance customs and land distribution in Cambridgeshire from the sixteenth to the eighteenth centuries' in J. Goody *et al.* (eds.), *Family and inheritance* (Cambridge, 1976), pp. 156–76.

39 J. Cornwall (ed.), *The county community under Henry VIII* (Rutland Record Soc., 1, 1980), pp. 24, 27, 49, 72, 79, 86.

the problem of ill-health, or the burden of numerous young children; such sufferers turned to their neighbours. Village communities and urban governments could treat harshly those whom they regarded as undesirable, ordering lepers to leave, and searching out and expelling vagabonds, 'unknown women' and suspected criminals. On the other hand, villages were capable of sympathy toward beggars, like the leading men of Writtle (Essex) who, as participants in a court session in 1382, amerced a peasant 9d. for striking a beggar, and found that the victim had 'justly' raised the hue and cry.[40] Village communities distinguished between strangers and their own people, and allowed the latter rights on the common, and facilities for gleaning and pea-picking. As affeerers (assessors) in the manorial court, leading villagers could save the poor from financial penalties. The better-off villagers also practised localized charity, well-documented in their wills which contain bequests of grain, sheep, clothing and cash for the poor of their own village, often for named individuals. East Anglian peasant wills reveal the existence in the fifteenth century of a 'common box' to which donations could be made, which sometimes seems to have been connected with the tax-collecting machinery, because bequests were made to help the poor with their contributions to the subsidy. Money in the box could have been invested in some way, perhaps in land, judging from a Suffolk man's bequest in 1444 of 40s. to the township of Rougham, the profits of which were to be spent on the poor and indigent.[41] The vill could hold land as a charitable endowment and could even build almshouses. One was erected near the churchyard at Elsworth (Cambridgeshire) in 1451 'at the expense of the community of the vill'.[42] Presumably the box of the vill was the same as the one kept by the church-wardens (see p. 248). It was adopted as the basis of the state-directed poor law in 1536, the innovation lying not in the local organization, but in the state's interest in it.

By the seventeenth century, village society had become sharply differentiated between the respectable elders, who effectively governed the village, and their inferiors, who were controlled through such institutions as the poor law. The germs of that relationship can certainly be seen in the late medieval village, but it would not be idealizing the medieval community excessively to

40 Essex R.O., D/DP m189.
41 Suffolk R.O. (Bury St Edmunds Branch), 1c 500/2/9 Baldwyne, fol. 44v.
42 E. B. Dewindt (ed.), *The Liber Gersumarum of Ramsey Abbey* (Toronto, 1976), p. 349.

recognize a spirit of neighbourliness that blurred social distinctions and alleviated some poverty. In the sixteenth century there were complaints of a 'decline of hospitality' that must have had some basis in social reality, and a plausible explanation of the witchcraft accusations in the same century is that old and poor people were denied traditional informal charity, and subsequent misfortunes, such as the death of an animal, were blamed on the mutterings of the disappointed applicants.[43]

Towns were relatively impersonal communities, though the urban parish could still act as a focus for charity and maintain a common box. There was less chance to use property as a protection against poverty, but more opportunities for the old and disabled to take on light work or small-scale retailing. The concentration of institutional charity in towns must reflect the greater needs of the urban poor, in the absence of the informal charity of the countryside. In caring for orphans, governments of large towns took on the rôle that in the countryside would have been performed by kin and friends, sometimes under the supervision of the manorial court.

The survival of the medieval poor still remains something of a mystery. Given the inadequacy of charitable institutions, the networks of relatives and neighbours must be assumed to have worked with some effect. Real economics rather than social cohesion provided the main relief for poverty when employment and earnings increased in the late fourteenth and fifteenth century.

43 F. Heal, 'The idea of hospitality in early modern England', *P. and P.*, 102 (1984), 66–93; A. Macfarlane, *Witchcraft in Tudor and Stuart England* (London, 1970), pp. 168–77.

10

THE WEATHER AND
STANDARDS OF LIVING

———— • ————

The climate helped to determine living standards in any pre-industrial society. When contemporaries talked of good years and bad,
they were usually referring to the quality of the harvest and its effect
on grain prices. The unpredictability of the weather left medieval
people in a constant state of insecurity, and climatic freaks like the
great wind of 15 January 1362 were regarded as portents of the Day
of Judgement.

We can take a long-term view of the climate, and attempt to
estimate the consequences for living standards of shifts in annual
average rainfall or temperature. And we need to assess the year-to-
year fluctuations that exercised contemporaries, by comparing the
frequency of bad years from one period to another.

No subject has caused such divisions of opinion as the rôle of
climate in history. For a long time the whole field of study was
discredited by glib determinists who needed only to find simul-
taneous climatic and historical events to assume a causal connection.
A more thoughtful approach began with the plausible and well-
reasoned arguments of Scandinavian scholars, who linked the desertion of settlements and the abandonment of arable land in northern
Europe with a climatic deterioration that began in about 1300.[1]

---

1 A. Steensberg, 'Archaeological dating of the climatic change in north Europe about
A.D. 1300', *Nature*, 168 (1951), 672–4; G. Utterström, 'Climatic fluctuations and
population problems in early modern history', *Scandinavian Ec.H.R.*, 3 (1955),
3–47.

However, many of the apparent symptoms of worsening weather that they cited are capable of other explanations. The English vineyards, for example, seem to have declined because of competition from Gascon imports rather than as a result of colder weather. Scientific research based on measuring the expansion and retreat of Alpine glaciers, which are sensitive indicators of trends in average temperatures, suggested that the thirteenth century had seen a cold spell, during which the glaciers advanced. After a bout of unstable weather beginning around 1300, a relatively warm period in the late fourteenth and fifteenth century was succeeded by the 'Little Ice Age' of 1550–1850. The later middle ages underwent a less extreme movement in temperature than the sixteenth and seventeenth century; the annual average changed by only 1 °C or 2 °C. If we accept this line of reasoning, then the climate had no significant effect on the medieval economy at all.[2]

This sceptical view has now been modified. New scientific evidence based on measurement of the fluctuations in the oxygen isotope ¹⁸O, and the study of tree rings, together with systematic analysis of chronicle reports of weather, points to the thirteenth century as having been a mild period in north-western Europe, with an absence of very cold winters. There was also a high level of winter rainfall, which could explain why archaeologists encounter so much evidence of ditch-digging and ditch-cleaning on sites of that period. After the instability of the early fourteenth century, on which everyone agrees, the next century and a half is seen as a period of cool and wet summers, becoming warmer and dryer around 1500 before the onset of the Little Ice Age.[3] This chronology would support the idea of some link between the weather and the retreat of settlement and cultivation in the later middle ages. The shorter growing period for cereal crops, the wetness of the planting and harvest seasons and the proliferation of pests like 'leather jackets' would have reduced cereal yields and increased the chances of bad harvests.[4] From the point of view of assessing living standards, all of this would be

2 E. Le Roy Ladurie, *Times of feast, times of famine* (London, 1972), pp. 244–87.
3 H. H. Lamb, *Climate, present, past and future* (2 vols., London, 1977), vol. 2, pp. 426–61; M. L. Parry, *Climatic change, agriculture and settlement* (Folkestone, 1978), pp. 65–6; P. Alexandre, 'Les variations climatiques au moyen âge', *Annales E.S.C.*, 32 (1977), 183–97; M. W. Beresford and J. G. Hurst, *Deserted medieval villages* (London, 1971), pp. 121–2.
4 G. Beresford, 'Climatic change and its effect upon the settlement and desertion of medieval villages in Britain' in C. Delano Smith and M. L. Parry (eds.), *Consequences of climatic change* (Nottingham, 1981), pp. 30–9.

significant if the period had seen grain scarcity and high prices. Instead the generally low prices of the years 1375–1519 point to a great plenty of corn.

The conclusion must be reached that long-term climatic changes had a limited effect on the standards of living of the inhabitants of lowland England. In areas with thin soils at high altitudes, notably Dartmoor, the Pennines, and the hills of the north-west, the inhabitants would have encountered difficulties in cereal cultivation. Those growing corn at 1,000 feet above sea-level (for example at Tideswell in Derbyshire) would be in a similar position to their counterparts in the Lammermuir Hills in southern Scotland, whose chances of harvest failure increased seven-fold (from one harvest in twenty to one harvest in three), if the mean maximum temperature fell by 1°C, as may have happened between the thirteenth and early fifteenth century.[5] Increased rainfall tended to have a more damaging effect on cereal crops than a fall in temperature, and this probably occurred at the same time. Settlements and arable land were given up in these uplands through a combination of circumstances, to which colder and wetter weather contributed. In other difficult environments, notably the reclaimed fenlands and marshlands, some arable land was lost to cultivation through flooding.[6] From the point of view of living standards, these developments should not be regarded with unrelieved gloom. The country may have lost thousands of acres of potentially productive land, but such land was no longer needed. All of the grain to feed the population, and some more besides, could be grown more reliably on the remaining millions of acres which were neither perched on bleak hill slopes nor subject to floods. The people who moved from their Dartmoor homes in the early fourteenth century would have had a hard time because of the dense settlements in the lowlands, but after 1350 migrants from the hills would have been able to find more productive land with relative ease. We might sympathize with the disruption that they suffered in moving, or regret the extinction of an upland peasant culture, but in strictly material terms they were better-off for their move.

In general, the notion that colder and wetter weather automatically caused worsening living conditions does not convince. The

5 Parry, *Climatic change*, pp. 73–94; M. L. Parry, 'Evaluating the impact of climatic change' in Delano Smith and Parry (eds.), *Consequences of climatic change*, pp. 3–16.
6 P. F. Brandon, 'Late medieval weather in Sussex and its agricultural significance', *Transactions of the Institute of British Geographers*, 54 (1971), 1–17.

Little Ice Age of 1550–1850 saw much economic growth and it is even possible that climatic deterioration stimulated productive activity. In our period, upland peasants were encouraged to concentrate on animal husbandry, for which their land was well-suited, and which gave them higher returns. To sum up, long-term climatic shifts had considerable importance for a minority of people living in specialized environments, and everywhere exercised an influence on economic change, but did not determine living standards.[7]

By contrast, short-term fluctuations in weather had a profound effect on standards of living. When we average grain yields in 25-year periods (see table 9) we are doing violence to the experiences of those who lived through years of sudden movements in production. A quarter-century with five years of very poor harvests would have been a miserable period for contemporaries, who would have derived little consolation from a high average of all years taken together. The most direct means of identifying good or bad harvests is to calculate the yield ratios for each year and to see how far they depart from the norm. In many cases the manorial accounts confirm that unusual yields can be linked with bad weather because the reeve would offer to the auditors excuses that the autumn had been wet or the summer dry, lest he be blamed for a poor performance. The Winchester series has been analysed by Titow for such information, and table 19 records those harvests which were 15 per cent below the average.[8] Such deficient harvests were often linked with excessively wet weather, according to the reeves' explanations. Using this method of identifying bad harvests we can observe their infrequent occurrence in the thirteenth century. Nor were very good harvests common then, as yields rose 15 per cent above average in only six years. In the first three quarters of the fourteenth century the yields show a very uneven pattern, with thirteen bad harvests between 1309 and 1374, and thirteen good harvests. The years 1374–94 saw an unusual run of good harvests, and bad harvests reappeared, though less frequently than in 1309–74, in the first third of the fifteenth century.

---

7 J. L. Anderson, 'Climatic change in European economic history', *Research in Economic History*, 6 (1981), 1–34; see also his essay and the introduction to T. M. L. Wigley *et al.* (eds.), *Climate and history* (Cambridge, 1981).
8 J. Z. Titow, 'Evidence of weather in the account rolls of the bishopric of Winchester, 1209–1350', *Ec.H.R.*, 2nd ser., 12 (1960), 360–407; J. Z. Titow, 'Le climat à travers les rôles de compatabilité de l'évêché de Winchester (1350–1450)', *Annales E.S.C.*, 25 (1970), 312–50.

Table 19. *Bad harvests, 1208–1520*

1. 1208–1450 All grains	2. 1225–1300 Wheat	3. 1225–1300 Barley	4. 1274–1520 Wheat	5. 1274–1520 Barley
1224–5				
1226–7				
	1246–7	1246–7		
	1247–8	1247–8		
	1256–7	1256–7		
	1257–8	1257–8		
			1274–5	1276–7
1283–4				
1290–1				
	1293–4	1293–4	1293–4	1293–4
	1294–5	1294–5	1294–5	1294–5
	1295–6	1295–6		
1310–11				
1315–16			1315–16	1315–16
1316–17			1316–17	1316–17
			1321–2	1321–2
			1322–3	1322–3
			1331–2	1331–2
1339–40				
1343–4				
1346–7				1346–7
1349–50				
1350–1			1350–1	1350–1
1351–2			1351–2	1351–2
				1352–3
1362–3				
			1363–4	
1367–8			1367–8	
1369–70			1369–70	1369–70
			1370–1	
1374–5			1374–5	
1381–2				
			1390–1	1390–1
1396–7				

Table 19. *Bad harvests, 1208–1520*

1. 1208–1450 All grains			4. 1274–1520 Wheat	5. 1274–1520 Barley
1401–2			1400–1	1400–1
1406–7			1401–2	
			1408–9	
			1409–10	1409–10
			1416–17	
1418–19			1418–19	
1420–1				
			1428–9	1428–9
			1429–30	
1432–3				
			1437–8	
			1438–9	1438–9
			1439–40	1439–40
1447–8				
			1460–1	1460–1
			1461–2	1461–2
	2. 1465–1520 Wheat	3. 1465–1520 Barley		
		1481–2	1481–2	1481–2
	1482–3	1482–3	1482–3	1482–3
		1483–4	1483–4	1483–4
	1502–3			
		1504–5		

1 Calculated from Winchester yields, 15% or more below counting as 'bad'. Incomplete data, so that late 1430s not documented, for example
2 & 3 Calculated from Farmer's (1225–1300) and Bowden's (1465–1520) price series, 26% or more above average counting as 'bad'
4 & 5 Calculated from Thorold Rogers's averages, 26% or more above average counting as 'bad'

The years given are the accounting year (29 September–28 September) in which the yields or prices were recorded

Grain prices reflect a number of influences, including the supply of money, but the quality of the harvest provided the main cause of sudden surges in price. A number of series have been compiled, and here three overlapping ones have been employed, Farmer's for the early part of the period, Bowden's for the end of the fifteenth and early sixteenth century, and Thorold Rogers's series for the whole period (see table 19). Thorold Rogers's series is flawed by his calculation of averages from different parts of the country from an inconsistent regional sample, but his figures have the virtue of covering a wide span of time. It will be seen that when Thorold Rogers's averages are compared with more scientific series, the results are not dissimilar, suggesting that for our enquiry his figures serve a useful purpose. A crude method of identifying bad years would be to fix an horizon, such as 7s. per quarter for wheat, and to list the years when that price was exceeded. This would suggest a concentration of problems in the period 1293–1332, when there were fourteen years of high prices, and again in 1350–76, when there were twelve (according to Thorold Rogers's averages). This method takes no account of long-term movements in prices, which were inflationary at the beginning of our period and deflationary at its end. Hoskins developed a technique for identifying harvest qualities in the early modern period by comparing the price for each year with a 31-year moving average. Each year is therefore compared with its own generation of harvests and prices. For Hoskins, a bad harvest was one after which the price of grain rose more than 25 per cent above the average, so in a period when barley averaged 4s. per quarter, a year with a price of 5s. 1d. would register as 'bad'. This method has been applied to the whole of our period for the two main bread corns, wheat and barley.[9]

The series does not begin to record bad years until the mid-thirteenth century because of the incomplete information for the earliest years. If there was a longer series, there is little doubt that 1201–4 would qualify for inclusion. A group of difficult years in the 1240s and 1250s was succeeded by a period of relatively moderate weather until the 1290s. Bad years recurred in almost every decade until the 1370s. Then came the plentiful decades, coinciding approx-

9 D. L. Farmer, 'Some grain price movements in thirteenth-century England', *Ec.H.R.*, 2nd ser., 10 (1957), 112; J. E. Thorold Rogers, *A history of agriculture and prices in England* (7 vols., Oxford, 1866–1902), vol. 1, pp. 226–34; vol. 4, pp. 282–8; W. G. Hoskins, 'Harvest fluctuations and English economic history', *Ag.H.R.*, 12 (1964), 28–46; C. J. Harrison, 'Grain price analysis and harvest qualities', *Ag.H.R.*, 19 (1971), 135–55.

imately with the reign of Richard II. There was a succession of bad years until 1440, eleven in terms of wheat prices, and then a marked improvement that continued into the early sixteenth century, apart from the early 1460s and the more troubled early 1480s.

The general conclusion that can be drawn from these figures must be that after a thirteenth century with long gaps between hard years, the first three quarters of the fourteenth century had an unusual concentration of deficient harvests. Prices in the early fourteenth century were generally high, presumably reflecting the large numbers of consumers as well as the climatic problems. After 1348–9 there may have been a short-term disruption in production caused by the epidemic, but the continued high prices after the sharp fall in the numbers of consumers had depressed demand must be attributed primarily to the influence of the weather. The tendency for the worst years to fall into groups must have contributed to the discomfort of consumers. Within these hard times short respites, for much of the 1330s for example, can be identified. The early fifteenth century was not punctuated as regularly by bad years, but there was a renewal of climatic instability. By contrast two 'golden ages' stand out. Those born in 1375 or 1440 would have lived into their mid-teens without knowing a bad harvest. A fortunate individual of 1375 would have reached the age of sixty-two before experiencing a famine, and someone born in 1440 might have been troubled by the high prices of the eighties, but could have expired at a ripe old age without feeling the effects of famine.

Adverse weather had effects on harvests which are customarily classified on a scale of severity as deficient, bad and dearth. In the later middle ages, two episodes stand out because of their concentration of bad years, including dearths: 1315–18 and 1437–40. There is no universally agreed scientific definition of a famine. One view is that the word describes any period of widespread or extreme food shortage, the other insists that the low level of supplies must lead to a disruption of social and economic life, and cause starvation and an increase in mortality.[10] Both bouts of bad weather caused famines, whichever definition is employed.

The episode of 1315–18 is rightly infamous because it seems to have been the worst famine in England and indeed in northern Europe in the last millennium. It was the result of a succession of bad

---

10 A. Sen, *Poverty and famines* (Oxford, 1981), pp. 39–40; *Famine in History Newsletter*, no. 4 (1982), p. 2.

years, with exceptionally wet weather in both 1315 and 1316.[11] Grain supplies did not return to normal until after the very good harvest of 1318. Some exceptionally low yield ratios are recorded, 40 and 47 per cent below the average for wheat on the Winchester manors in 1315–16 and 1316–17, and 20 and 32 per cent below the average for barley. In the north the figures were much worse, with rye, the main bread corn, on a Bolton Priory manor in Yorkshire yielding 72 and 88.5 per cent below average in the same two years. Prices rose to 15s. or 16s. per quarter for wheat according to Thorold Rogers's averages, deriving mainly from southern England. Individual transactions show that wheat was commonly pushed to a price in excess of 20s. Consumers turned to cheaper grains, and used them economically by ceasing to brew ale. Landlords who found themselves in temporary difficulties laid-off their servants as an economy measure. The peasantry were, of course, severely affected. Court rolls are filled with land transfers as poorer people rushed to sell, lease out, or mortgage their land in order to raise money to buy corn. Those with resources were able to take advantage of their neighbours' temporary embarrassment. At Tardebigge (Worcestershire) in 1316–17, the vicar, John de Bradewas, was able to acquire four peasant holdings, by straightforward purchase or because he was foreclosing on mortgages.[12] Normally the buyers came from the wealthier peasants, who were thus able to benefit from their neighbours' problems and increase the inequalities of village society. On the manor of Wakefield great numbers of assarts were recorded, whether because peasants went out to clear land in desperation, or because the lord's officials searched out old clearances in order to boost manorial income at a difficult time. At Wakefield and other manors a flurry of pleas of debt reflected both the need of the poor to borrow to buy food, and the calling in of old debts as creditors began to feel the pinch. The social dislocation is demonstrated by a sudden crime wave, which sent offences reported to royal courts soaring to five times their normal level. The courts sometimes took an understanding view, as in the case of Peter de Synekere of King's Lynn who was accused in 1316 of burglary, in which he took a half-bushel of wheat valued at 14d. (equivalent to a very high 18s. 8d. per

---

11 H. S. Lucas, 'The great European famine of 1315, 1316 and 1317' in E. M. Carus-Wilson (ed.), *Essays in economic history* (3 vols., London, 1954–66), vol. 2, pp. 49–72; I. Kershaw, 'The great famine and agrarian crisis in England, 1315–1322' in R. H. Hilton (ed.), *Peasants, knights and heretics* (Cambridge, 1976), pp. 85–132.

12 Hereford and Worcester R.O., ref. b705:128, BA1188/12.

quarter), and clothing worth 18d. The jury said that he had committed the offence 'because of hunger and destitution'. Four other Lynn thieves convicted at the same court session were not so lucky: all of them being hanged, including a woman said to own no chattels of her own, who had stolen goods worth 3s. 4d.[13] It is sometimes alleged that the East Anglian population, because of their dependence on barley, did not suffer so much from the famine as their counterparts in other regions, but this is not supported by the evidence of the judicial records, nor by the frantic selling of land by the poor tenants of Coltishall in Norfolk in 1316. Also, the region was especially badly affected by bad harvests at other times in the early fourteenth century, notably in the early 1320s.[14]

Many people died in the great famine, as many as 10 per cent of the tenants on Winchester bishopric manors, and among the males of Halesowen and on some Essex manors the proportion rose as high as 15 per cent.[15] As often happens in times of famine, deaths were caused not so much by the direct effects of starvation as by the accompanying diseases such as typhus. These spread from the hungry to the more affluent, and better-off peasants and even clergy and gentry died in unusual numbers.

Recovery from the famine was delayed by a severe cattle plague in the early 1320s. The losses of people were eventually replaced on manors such as Halesowen by a rash of marriages, and a consequent baby boom. Elsewhere the long-term shock to the economy can be seen in an increase in vacant land and abandoned houses, for example on the north midlands manors of the earldom of Lancaster.[16]

The famine of 1437–40 is not so well-known as that of the previous century, but it had some similar characteristics. It also was felt over much of northern Europe.[17] Like the earlier famine it was caused by exceptionally wet weather in successive years, pushing

13 B. Hanawalt, 'Economic influence on the pattern of crime in England, 1300–1348', *American Journal of Legal History*, 18 (1974), 281–97; B. Hanawalt (ed.), *Crime in East Anglia in the fourteenth century* (Norfolk Record Soc., 44, 1976), pp. 117–18.

14 H. E. Hallam, 'The climate of eastern England, 1250–1350', *Ag.H.R.*, 32 (1984), 124–32; B. M. S. Campbell, 'Population pressure, inheritance and land market in a fourteenth-century peasant community' in R. M. Smith (ed.), *Land, kinship and life-cycle* (Cambridge, 1984), pp. 107–20.

15 Z. Razi, *Life, marriage and death in a medieval parish. Economy, society and demography in Halesowen, 1270–1400* (Cambridge, 1980), pp. 39–40; L. R. Poos, 'The rural population of Essex in the later middle ages', *Ec.H.R.*, 2nd ser., 38 (1985), 521.

16 *V.C.H. Staffordshire*, vol. 6, pp. 36–7.

17 W. Abel, *Agricultural fluctuations in Europe* (London, 1980), pp. 59–62.

wheat prices as high as 20s. per quarter. Thorold Rogers's average
for 1438–9, at almost 15s. per quarter is the highest after 1316–17,
and was not to be exceeded again until inflation as well as shortages
raised prices in the sixteenth century. The chroniclers report that
people in the south were reduced to eating cheaper grains such as
peas, beans and barley, in itself a comment on the extent of wheat-
eating after the late medieval revolution in diet. In the north the
effects were felt so severely that according to the chroniclers, people
were eating fern roots.[18] In Staffordshire in 1438, farm servants were
being given barley bread; rye, their normal bread-corn, cost 10s. per
quarter.[19] The proceedings of midland manor courts exhibit symptoms of hardship, such as an increase in the number of land transactions, a rash of pleas of debt, and a decline in brewing fines, but not
on the same scale as in 1315–18. The community of Elmley Castle
(Worcestershire) re-issued their harvest bye-laws, which forbade
anyone to glean who could earn a living, and took precautionary
measures against the stealing of sheafs. The crop failures in Gloucestershire led tenants in Norton and Hucclecote to excuse their failure
to roof their new buildings on the grounds that thatching straw was
unobtainable.[20] However, although a high mortality is recorded in
East Anglia at this time, this is normally blamed on an epidemic, and
on many midland manors there was no great increase in tenant
deaths in 1437–40.[21] According to a chronicler, suffering in London
was averted by the actions of the mayor in making cheap corn
available. The similarity between 1315–18 and the 1430s in weather
and prices, but the less severe social disruption in the second episode,
demonstrates that profound economic and social changes had taken
place during the century and a quarter that separates the two great
late medieval famines, which left the population much less vulnerable to the effects of shortages.

18 C. L. Kingsford, *Chronicles of London* (Oxford, 1905), pp. 145–6; J. S. Davies, *An English chronicle* (Camden Soc., 64, 1856), p. 55; R. Flenley, *Six town chronicles of England* (Oxford, 1911), p. 114; F. W. D. Brie (ed.), *The Brut* (2 parts, Early English Text Soc., O.S. 131, 1906, 136, 1908), part 2, pp. 472–3.
19 P.R.O., SC6/988/12.
20 W. O. Ault, *Open-field farming in medieval England* (London, 1972), pp. 126–7; Gloucestershire R.O., D621 M1.
21 R. S. Gottfried, *Epidemic disease in fifteenth-century England* (Leicester, 1978), pp. 96–7.

IMPLICATIONS AND CONCLUSIONS

It is sometimes stated that bad harvests had mixed effects on society. They were ill-winds indeed, but they blew some good to some people; peasants with large holdings who sold grain might make a windfall from rocketing prices. Shakespeare could write (in *Macbeth*, soon after the terrible years of the 1590s) of 'a farmer that hanged himself on the expectation of plenty'. The choice of words is important here, because farmers, with leaseholds which often ran to hundreds of acres, in the later middle ages as in the late sixteenth century, could indeed sell a large enough surplus to profit from high prices. Most peasants, including yardlanders, would not be compensated for their low yields by higher prices because most of their crops were used for seed and in the household.[22] It is true that a minority were able to increase their holdings at the expense of their neighbours, but this reflects at least as much on the desperation of the sellers as on the wealth of the buyers. There is much to recommend the view of historians of more recent pre-industrial economies that after a bad harvest everyone was a loser.[23] Most peasants produced less, and their profits were cut. The high price of grain would depress the rest of the economy, because the urban consumers and rural wage-earners spent so much on bread that they did not have enough for other goods, and the demand for manufactures would fall. Peasants and artisans would lay-off the servants that they could no longer afford to keep, and avoid employing casual labour. Unemployment and underemployment would spread, and wages would be reduced, further depressing demand. The occasional oddities of famine economies benefited no-one in the long run. For example, meat sometimes became cheap, because peasants sold their animals to raise cash, and there was a smaller demand from consumers who needed bread. However, eventually supplies of meat would have been disrupted while the producers built up their breeding stock again. Not enough work has been done on the bad harvest years of medieval England to show whether all of these phenomena were present, but some events certainly fit the pattern. Lords laid-off their servants and reduced wages in the 1315–18 famine; cheese and pig prices dipped in some of the bad years of the late thirteenth and early fourteenth

22 Cf. Abel, *Agricultural fluctuations*, p. 64–79.
23 H. Van der Wee, 'Typologie des crises et changements de structure aux pays-bas (XVᵉ–XVIᵉ siècles)', *Annales E.S.C.*, 18 (1963), 209–25; W. Kula, *An economic theory of the feudal system* (London, 1976), pp. 107–11.

century; the sales of ale dropped, which must have left the ale-wives in difficulty.[24]

We rightly concentrate our attention on the effects of weather on arable crops, because grain was the staple food of the medieval population, but the effects of adverse conditions on animal husbandry should not be forgotten. Periodic outbreaks of disease among flocks and herds could in some cases have been associated with adverse weather, and it has been argued that the long-term decline in fleece weights reflected the coldness of fifteenth-century winters.[25] Rising animal and cheese prices in or soon after years which saw a poor grain harvest suggest that supplies of cattle fodder, and especially hay, had been damaged by excessive rainfall or spring droughts.

A way of assessing the severity of the bad harvests and the vulnerability of the population is to measure rises in mortality which coincide with high grain prices. The death-rates of the 1315–18 famine are well-established, and a classic study of the Winchester estate showed that high grain prices (wheat rising above 7s. per quarter seems to have been the trigger) were significantly linked to an increase in payments of heriots, the tenants' death duties. Doubts have been cast on the statistical basis for this coincidence, but subsequent studies in other parts of the country have confirmed the Winchester discovery. At Halesowen there was a comparable sharp increase in mortality in 1293–5 and 1310–12, corresponding with years of deficient harvests. After the famine there was some correlation, for example in the early 1320s, between prices and death-rates. At Chesterton near Cambridge there were three episodes in the early fourteenth century of high death totals, in 1304–5, 1310–11 and 1321–2, as well as during the great famine.[26] There are obvious problems in distinguishing between years of epidemic diseases and

24 On the movements in prices of animal products, see D. L. Farmer, 'Prices and wages' in H. Hallam (ed.), *Agrarian history of England and Wales*, vol. 2 (Cambridge, 1988), pp. 799–810.

25 M. Stephenson, 'The productivity of medieval sheep' (University of Cambridge Ph.D. thesis, 1986), chapter 9.

26 M. M. Postan and J. Z. Titow, 'Heriots and prices in Winchester manors' in M. M. Postan, *Essays on medieval agriculture and general problems of the medieval economy* (Cambridge, 1973), pp. 150–85; G. Ohlin, 'No safety in numbers: some pitfalls of historical analysis' in R. Floud (ed.), *Essays in quantitative economic history* (Oxford, 1974), pp. 73–7; Razi, *Life, marriage and death*, pp. 36–41; C. A. Clarke, 'Peasant society and land transactions in Chesterton, Cambridgeshire, 1277-1325' (University of Oxford, D.Phil. thesis, 1985), chapter 4.

years of hunger, and even greater difficulties in unravelling the cause of death when food shortages coincided with epidemics that were killing people independently. Epidemics caused unusual numbers of deaths among parish clergy in such years as 1304 and 1309–11. These may have been diseases linked to the food deficiencies of the poorer sections of the population, which spread to the more affluent. Or there may have been epidemics of diseases unconnected with hunger.[27] The weather, notably in hot, dry summers, might assist in the spread of epidemics.

The fifteenth century presents a clear contrast. The period was punctuated by a series of peaks of mortality, among all sections of society – clergy, monks, lay aristocrats and peasants – which indicate that in most regions an epidemic struck once in almost every decade. As well as bubonic plague, people died of dysentery and influenza. The extent to which these diseases controlled the general level of population has been much debated, but no-one has seriously argued that they were linked with crises of food supply. The notable exception is the increased mortality of the late 1430s. The high death-rate seems to have been localized but the food shortages are found everywhere, suggesting that an epidemic occurred coincidentally in some regions. At other times, high prices and epidemics do not seem to have occurred in the same years. For example, the 1470s, a decade of plenty, saw the most severe epidemics of the century. The late medieval period appears to have been a watershed in English history, when the cycle of bad harvests and resulting misery was broken. Before the mid-fourteenth century, in recurring bad years, many people starved and died. Afterwards, mortality peaks were not related to food shortages, neither in the fifteenth century, nor apparently in the subsequent three centuries save in exceptional episodes and in ill-favoured regions. This seems to have marked a divergence between England and continental Europe, because food crises and resulting high death-rates troubled Castile, France and the Low Countries in the fifteenth century.[28] The relative poverty of the

---

27 R. J. Rowberry, 'Late medieval demography: a study of mortality among the beneficed clergy in western England' (University of Birmingham B.A. dissertation, 1974), pp. 9–15.

28 D. M. Palliser, 'Tawney's century: brave new world or Malthusian trap?', *Ec.H.R.*, 2nd ser., 35 (1982), 339–53, especially 345; H. Neveux, *Vie et déclin d'une structure économique* (Paris, 1980), pp. 101–9; Van der Wee, 'Typologie des crises', pp. 211–14; A. Mackay, 'Popular movements and pogroms in fifteenth-century Castile,' *P. and P.*, 55 (1972), 33–67.

French population was noted by Sir John Fortescue, writing in the 1470s, the first of many such comments over the next few hundred years:

They drink water, they eat apples, with bread right brown made of rye; they eat no flesh but if it be right seldom a little lard, or of the entrails and heads of beasts slain for the nobles and merchants . . . They wear no woollen . . . Their wives and children go bare foot . . .[29]

Finally, in making comparisons across time and space, the apparent absence of food-riots in medieval England is worthy of notice. On the continent bad harvests were linked with popular disturbances, in fifteenth-century Castile for example, and protests against high prices are found in early modern England. Many rebellions occurred in England before 1520, but not at times of hunger. The later English food-riots were directed against commercial practices which the crowd believed to have caused shortages, such as hoarding of grain.[30] In the different economy of the later middle ages the authorities, especially urban governments, claimed to be acting in the interests of consumers against such anti-social elements as the forestallers and regraters. The grievances that provoked revolts were connected with servile dues and the corruption of urban oligarchies, in which those in authority were seen to be acting against the interests of the underprivileged.

The food shortages of the late thirteenth and fourteenth century, followed by a decline in the frequency of bad harvests, could be capable of a simple climatic explanation. By accident, the weather deteriorated, and then improved, and the misery and then the relative well-being of the population can be attributed to such impersonal forces as the variations in the tracks taken by the Atlantic cyclones. This is a most unlikely proposition. It does not accord with evidence for long-term climatic change, and it ignores the changes in the structure of the economy. More grain was grown *per capita* after 1350 because of the change in the ratio of people and land. Holdings increased in size, corn-growing was concentrated on the most suitable soil and productivity probably improved. The prevalent low prices after 1375 suggest not just plenty but a degree of overproduction, and this is supported by the not uncommon practice of leaving demesne stocks for more than a year, as the managers held back sales

29 C. Plummer (ed.), *The governance of England by Sir John Fortescue* (Oxford, 1885), p. 114.
30 E. P. Thompson, 'The moral economy of the English crowd in the eighteenth century', *P. and P.*, 50 (1971), 76–136.

in the hope of a better price. The existence of such stores helped to maintain more even prices from year to year.

In the thirteenth and early fourteenth century many poorer people ate barley and oats, and had no cheaper food on which to fall back in hard times. The widespread switch to wheat-eating in the fifteenth century meant that the cheaper corn could be used as a fail-safe. This hurt people's pride, but maintained their physical well-being.

In assessing the effects of climatic change, we must consider the interaction of both the weather and society. The wet seasons of the early fourteenth century had a severe effect on mankind because of the combination of an unusual climate, and a vulnerable population. Later in the period, a less poverty-stricken society could shrug off the effects of inclement weather, in the same way that modern industrialized countries suffer less from natural disasters than those of the third world.

CONCLUSION

'Standards of living', either today or in the past, cannot be measured exactly.[1] In dealing with such a variable concept, we are not able to make precise or dogmatic judgements about the late medieval period. For example, any statistical series that can be compiled, as in the case of wage-rates, need to be assessed in the light of social circumstances, such as working practices, which are only partly understood. A further problem is raised by our need to calculate in terms of money, yet we know that much medieval exchange was conducted without direct payment in cash. Above all, in making comparisons between social groups, or in defining minimum requirements for life, we cannot be sure of our bench-marks for judging material well-being. We have seen that contemporaries believed that life could be sustained on ¼d. per day, which was the cost of a loaf of bread. Yet to maintain 'physiological and socio-psychological health' a variety of foods was required, and contributions toward the cost of clothing and housing, which would probably come near to the 1d. per head per day specified in some fifteenth-century schemes for poor relief. These sums mean very little when applied to the aristocracy, who often spent 2d. or 3d. per day on feeding each of their servants. Such figures imply that we should not expect to define a single scale of comparison, like a ladder on which different social groups occupied lower or higher rungs. There were standards of living in the plural, and different classes had

1 A. Sen *et al.*, *The standard of living* (Cambridge, 1987).

their own expectations. The contrasts are apparent even in medieval fantasies: whereas the lower orders dreamt of the coarse materialism of the Land of Cokayne, in which houses were built of food and the geese flew around ready roasted, the aristocracy enjoyed more re-fined visions of ideal courts which feasted, but also indulged in chivalric entertainments.

Assessments of living standards are bound to involve a good deal of subjective judgement, and are inseparable from considerations of the quality of life. This book has deliberately concentrated on ma-terial things, and adopted a utilitarian approach, believing that higher wages, for example, would bring greater happiness to the greater number. But we must recognize anomalies and discrepancies between non-material conditions and economic well-being. To take some examples from the thirteenth century, a servile peasant with a full yardland consumed an ample diet and could have afforded some small luxuries, but would have found his legal status irksome, because it limited his income, and lowered his standing not just in the eyes of his lord and the king's courts, but also in comparison with his free peasant neighbours. In the towns some Jews gained high profits from their financial dealings, and yet were deprived of civil rights, and suffered both heavy tax demands from the Crown and periodic hostility from christians. On the other hand, a Franciscan friar who had volunteered to beg for his living, and was consequently worse-off than many of his fellow clergy, derived spiritual satisfaction from his relative poverty. Measuring happiness is not the purpose of this book, but we can bring these subjective matters into our sum-ming-up of the whole period by considering the lives of different sections of society in terms of the choices and options that were available to them.

In the thirteenth century the higher aristocracy could choose between increased consumption and expanding their resources by buying land, or (less often) investing in production. Such was their level of prosperity that they could sometimes afford both. Better-off townsmen and the upper peasantry were enabled by the growth in the market to gain from the sale of the goods that they traded, manufactured or grew. Peasants could choose to buy more land and accumulate a large holding to pass to the next generation, or to use their acquisitions to provide for their non-inheriting children. Most opted for the welfare of all of their children, and so contributed to the growing numbers of underendowed smallholders. Most people had a limited range of options. They needed to avoid risks, for example those involved in technical innovation, because any change might have been for the worse. The ventures of the poor into small-scale commerce and crafts reflect the need of poor people to take up activities yielding some profit because a low income was preferable to no income at all. Periodic misfortunes such as bad harvests, disease among animals, and the heavy demands of lords and kings closed off avenues of choice, and jeopardized the supplies even of the basic cereals on which many of the poor subsisted.

The changes of the fourteenth and fifteenth centuries offered the underprivileged sections of society a range of uses for new wealth. Wage-earners could either raise their level of consumption of food, clothing and housing, or they could escape from the drudgery of continuous labour by taking more frequent holidays. Peasants and artisans could innovate and invest; one indication that they spent more on equipment is the increase in the domestic production of iron, and the higher volume of iron imports.[2] Not just iron-workers but also large numbers of artisans in the cloth industry, and those in the food trades such as ale-house keepers and butchers, benefited from the general level of prosperity. The new economic climate helped those who had previously been socially subordinate to develop in confidence, and so to resist the rent demands of their lords, and to insist on better conditions of work. The aristocracy were therefore threatened both with loss of income and a higher cost of living, but their continued control of vast resources, and their adapt-. ability in finding new sources of income and in cutting costs allowed them to continue their position of social primacy.

In the late fourteenth and fifteenth centuries ordinary people exercised some choice over the place in which they lived, with consequent loss of population for towns and villages that could no longer offer economic advantages. Not all decisions were made in order to benefit the individual, as can be appreciated from the use of a considerable proportion of wealth to fund such community assets as parish churches and almshouses.

All of these changes shook the structure of society, but did not turn it upside-down, as upper-class contemporaries believed. The extreme inequalities of wealth revealed by the record of the musters and tax assessments of 1522–5 show that a sharply differentiated social hierarchy had survived the upheavals of the later middle ages.[3]

---

2 W. R. Childs, 'England's iron trade in the fifteenth century', *Ec.H.R.*, 2nd ser., 34 (1981), 25–47.
3 J. C. K. Cornwall, *Wealth and society in early sixteenth-century England* (London, 1988).

There were still many social casualties, notably the new generations of widows and orphans left by the successive epidemics, and the need for poor relief continued to exercise contemporaries both in their private and their public lives. The economy was subject to recurrent instabilities, varying from the mid-fifteenth-century commercial depression to the short-term crisis in cloth-making in 1462–5. And life can scarcely have been comfortable for those living in villages on the verge of desertion or towns in the throes of decline. The late medieval economy continued to suffer from weaknesses, some of which can be attributed to the low and stagnating population. For example, it expanded to fill new demands for clothing and iron, but England did not develop into a 'consumer society' of the kind that produced new demands for a wide range of goods including furnishings, pewter ware and horticultural produce, in the sixteenth century.[4] And yet there were structural changes in society. It is true that wage-earners and smallholders were only temporarily relieved from the spectre of famine, because the virtual absence of mortality associated with bad harvests between 1375 and 1520 was to be succeeded by a return to episodes of hunger in the sixteenth century. But still, especially in comparison with continental Europe, the later middle ages does mark a stage in the disappearance of famine from England: the horrors of 1315–18 would never be repeated. Not only did the peasants no longer starve, but they also freed themselves from serfdom. Never again would they be subject to the direct legal control of their lords. And among the peasants a new stratum of prosperous yeomen and farmers emerged by 1500 who were there to stay.

4 J. Thirsk, *Economic policy and projects* (Oxford, 1978).

MEDIEVAL LIVING STANDARDS
POSTSCRIPT

This additional chapter intends to review new research and thinking about standards of living in the period 1200–1520. The chapter follows the organization of the book, beginning with the aristocracy and the peasants, and going on to consider changes in towns, wage earning, charity and the climate. It cannot provide a complete account of new discoveries and ideas since 1987 so certain themes have been chosen. The section on aristocratic incomes is concerned with the smaller landowners, and the main aspects of aristocratic expenditure to be discussed are patterns of consumption. The section on peasants focusses on their experiences in the crisis period around 1300, and the part devoted to towns includes shifts in demand and interactions between town and country.

Wage workers are discussed in relation to earnings and issues of leisure and work ethics, and the section on the poor is devoted to assessments of the effectiveness of charity.

ARISTOCRATIC INCOMES

The formative period for the gentry can be located around 1200, when a great upheaval redrew the social boundaries. In the reign of King John (1199–1216) the title of knighthood was not especially exclusive, and as many as 5,000 men at any one time could be described as *milites* or *chevaliers* - knights. The numbers of knights collapsed in the next twenty or thirty years, to a point when only about a thousand remained in the middle of the thirteenth century[1] The explanation for the retreat by so many families from this honourable title must lie in the rise in the status of knighthood, and with that increased prestige went more official reponsibilities, both in local government at home and service in war abroad, and greater financial obligations. A typical example of the burdens that were associated with knighthood was the expensive dubbing ceremony by which the title was conferred. This redefinition of titles was an aspect of the crystallization of a large social group, because as well as marking the emergence of a new elite of knights, the families that had once been knights, and those who rose to prominence after knighthood became so exclusive, formed a wealthy, influential and numerous lesser aristocracy[2] Both they and the new knights based their position on land, but in addition their roles as advisers and administrators to the magnates, functionaries of the state, and soldiers, provided many of them with a substantial part of their income. Some of them were rewarded by living in magnate households, or gained fees in cash, or had rents assigned to them, or profited as officials in expanding government. Another avenue for careers and profits was opening for the gentry as 'serjeants of the Bench', that is lawyers who pleaded before the royal courts, were being regarded as a specialized professional group by about 1240.[3] 'Bastard feudalism', by which lesser aristocrats were given liveries, fees and annuities in exchange for administrative, military or political services, was once regarded as a novelty of the late thirteenth century, which expanded in the following two hundred years. Now we appreciate that the whole network of clientage, with cash rewards for service, developed rapidly at the beginning of the thirteenth century, especially for the new generation of stewards, auditors, and financial specialists who were engaged to

1 K. Faulkner, 'The transformation of knighthood in early thirteenth century England', *E.H.R.*, 111 (1996), 1–23; P. R. Coss, *The knight in medieval England 1000–1400* (Stroud, 1993), pp. 30–71.

2 P. R. Coss, 'The formation of the English gentry', *P. and P.*, 147 (1995), 38–64.

3 P. Brand, 'The origins of the English legal profession', in P. Brand, *The making of the common law* (London, 1992), pp. 6–7. The profits of the law a little later have been documented in P. J. Jefferies, 'Profitable fourteenth century legal practice and landed investment: the case of Judge Stonor, c. 1281 to 1354', *Southern History*, 15 (1993), 18–35. His annual income of £247 as a justice from 1322, with other rewards, allowed him to buy eleven manors, with other properties besides, worth at least £200 p.a. by 1354.

run the magnate estates after they were taken back from leaseholders and managed directly by the lords.[4]

The variety of sources of income available to the thirteenth-century gentry should not lead us to underestimate the significance of their landed wealth. New small manors were being carved out of the larger estates, and the land market was growing. Detailed local study of gentry activities shows them buying land, often with a view to consolidating their holdings in a particular locality, or clearing previously uncultivated land, and organizing their acquisitions into manors which would allow them to maximize their incomes from the sale of produce and from collecting tenant rents. An example was the new manor of Caludon in Warwickshire, where the Segrave family from the 1220s assembled a grain-growing demesne, and a park, with a few tenants, which by 1254-5 was yielding at least £20 in a year from the sale of produce. This seems to resemble the better-known creation of compact and specialized granges by Cistercian monks, which was still proceeding at this time. Other gentry lords were pursuing a very different process of assembling manors with small demesnes or none at all, where peasant tenants paying cash rents provided most of the income. Gentry estates often included some urban property, both as sources of rents and as outlets for the sale of agricultural produce and the purchase of goods in the town market. The Segraves for example acquired in about 1250 a house in nearby Coventry, with shops and rents from fifteen tenants.[5]

Consumption played a crucial role in the lives of the gentry. Wise or cautious men held back from the extravagant life style associated with acquiring and maintaining knightly status. Others, knights or not, lost the battle of keeping expenditure in line with income, and fell into debt and bankruptcy. Parks, moated houses and private chapels are examples of the more costly projects that displayed a family's standing. We can put a precise figure on the cost – and the rise in cost – of some of the trappings of aristocracy. In c. 1200 horses suitable for mounted soldiers were bought for about £3–£4, and a hauberk (shirt of chain mail) and helmet, the main items of armour, for 25s. Horses later in the thirteenth century could cost as much as £50, but these were exceptional

4 D. Crouch, D. A. Carpenter and P. R. Coss, 'Debate. Bastard feudalism revised', *P. and P.*, 131 (1991), 165–203
5 P. R. Coss, *Lordship, knighthood and locality. A study in English society c.1180–c.1280* (Cambridge, 1991), pp. 93–130.

destriers, and more representative examples were valued at an average of £8 10s 0d. in Edward I's campaign in Wales in 1282. In the early fourteenth century body armour cost £6 13s 4d., a helmet 10s. and plates to protect the legs 15s.[6] A full set of armour and weapons could be worth about £10 at this time, the increase since 1200 reflecting the greater elaboration of equipment more than general price inflation. Many gentry families lived on an annual income below £20, so the purchase of a warhorse and armour could have absorbed a year's income.

In the thirteenth century the knights formed a diminishing proportion of the gentry who as a whole were increasing in numbers. To what extent did the size of the aristocracy shrink as the whole population declined in the late fourteenth and fifteenth centuries? The temptation has been to believe that the manors and other landed assets of the aristocracy were concentrated in fewer hands, as marriages brought together the assets of two or more lines. The declining value of individual manors would not therefore have reduced the income of families who could have drawn on more sources of income than their thirteenth-century predecessors. In fact this does not seem to have been the predominant trend. Although many lords died without sons, and their daughters married into other landed families, so uniting inheritances, a contrary tendency fragmented estates because they were sometimes divided to give younger sons a share. Some manors ended up on the market because families failed to produce any direct heirs, and could be bought by those who had made money in trade, war, service, or the law, and aspired to gentry status. The same upwardly mobile groups married heiresses and so gained access to gentry land. So, far from closing ranks and sharing the limited assets among the existing families, the class was constantly gaining new recruits from below.[7] Comparison over the long term, say between 1300 and 1500, is not really possible, because the gentry changed character, and the documents are dissimilar, but we can say with confidence that the numbers of gentry were increasing in the fifteenth century. In Warwickshire, for example, the total rose from 112 in 1410 to 155 in 1500. The high mortality among the established families, or at least their

6 M. Prestwich, *Armies and warfare in the middle ages. The English experiences* (New Haven and London, 1996), pp. 24–35.

7 S. J. Payling, 'Social mobility, demographic change, and landed society in late medieval England', *Ec.H.R.*, 45 (1992), 51–73.

failure to maintain a continuous male line, gave opportunities for 109 new families to enter county society during the century, at a recruitment rate of about one new family each year, though with a faster pace in the middle years of the century.[8] Far from demonstrating the weakness of the gentry, this tendency shows their social strength, in that they were able to absorb new blood without too much snobbish agonizing over the credentials of the new rich, and they added to their economic strength, because the recruits were bringing with them their assets, and the enterprise that had enabled them to prosper as lawyers, merchants and acquisitive peasants.

The gentry in the period 1349-1520 showed a remarkable capacity to maintain their incomes in an age of falling or stagnating land values. They were helped greatly by the income from their non-landed resources, such as the profits of legal practice, and service rendered to magnates or the crown. They added to the total of landed assets in aristocratic hands when hundreds of families previously described as 'franklins', yeomen, farmers, or just free tenants qualified for promotion to the rank of 'gentlemen' in the fifteenth century, transferring as they did so thousands of acres from the peasantry to the gentry. Also established families as well as newcomers bought up land previously held by peasants, and even put aside any qualms about acquiring customary holdings, which had once been held in villeinage. At about the same time some gentry took over on leasehold the demesnes of the larger estates; although lands held on lease did not become part of the gentry family's long-term inheritance, they could be profitable. For example, two manors (Deighton and South Cowton) in north Yorkshire, together with other holdings on the great estates of the Neville family, were leased in 1462 to Richard Pigot, a lawyer, for £24 per annum – no doubt he calculated that he could make, say £34 annually from the land, and so take £10 each year for himself.[9] Some gentry gained a great deal from agricultural management, especially if they had money from a successful legal career to invest, and if they could specialize in the most profitable branch of agriculture, stock raising. Perhaps the most spectacular success story of this period is provided by the Townshend family of Norfolk, who began as prosperous yeomen, though even in

8 C. Carpenter, *Locality and polity. A study of Warwickshire landed society, 1401–1499* (Cambridge, 1992), pp. 35–95.

9 A. J. Pollard, *North-eastern England during the Wars of the Roses. Lay society, war, and politics, 1450–1500* (Oxford, 1990), p. 63.

relative obscurity John Townshend, who died in 1466, enjoyed a landed income of £40. Sir Roger Townshend I used his money from the law to buy manors, and was worth £240 in 1493, and his successor increased the annual value of the estate to £350 by 1515. The land was used to grow grain, especially barley for malting, but the pastures were the estate's great asset, with a total of 12,000 sheep by 1490, exceeding in number many of the huge monastic flocks in their thirteenth-century heyday. On a smaller scale hundreds of gentry estates were managing agriculture directly, and presumably making a profit, as is shown by regional studies of landlords in the fifteenth century in north Warwickshire and in north Yorkshire.[10]

These were testing times for any landlord as rents declined and agricultural profits were hard to maintain. Many of the parish clergy expected to live in the same style as gentry from the tithes that their parishioners paid, and the profits of the glebe land with which rectories and vicarages were endowed, but tithes declined in volume and value as cultivation shrank and grain prices dipped, and glebes, like manors, suffered from diminishing profits. The decline in the value of benefices may have been a factor in the drop in the number of recruits into the clergy in the first half of the fifteenth century. Among the smaller monasteries, which were especially afflicted by debt and errors of management, some were actually so reduced to poverty that they could not maintain an adequate number of religious, and were in effect closed down. Twenty houses of the Augustinian order ceased to exist as independent institutions, mainly in the late fifteenth century, as they were either dissolved or demoted to become cells of other houses.[11]

ARISTOCRATIC CONSUMPTION

Household accounts provide the main evidence for aristocratic spending, and together with cookery books and works on

---

10 C. E. Moreton, *The Townshends and their world: gentry, law, and land in Norfolk, c.1450–1551* (Oxford, 1992), pp. 7, 115–90; A. Watkins, 'Landowners and their estates in the Forest of Arden in the fifteenth century', *Ag.H.R.*, 45 (1997), 18–33; Pollard, *North-eastern England*, p. 64.

11 R. N. Swanson, 'Standards of living: parochial revenues in pre-Reformation England', in C. Harper-Bill (ed.), *Religious belief and ecclesiastical careers in late medieval England* (Woodbridge, 1991), pp. 151–83; C. Platt, *King Death. The Black Death and its aftermath in late-medieval England* (London, 1996), pp. 79–83.

household management throw light on aristocratic social mentality and behaviour, as does archaeological evidence.[12] Aristocrats show no great variation in their diet from one part of the country to another, and indeed their tastes were under strong continental influence. Occasionally a regional speciality is revealed, like the wildfowl consumed by some households sited near the Wash in Lincolnshire, or the 'puffins' (in fact shearwaters) from the Isles of Scilly eaten in Cornwall.[13] Aristocratic consumption had to take into account practicalities and economics, but cultural influences or personal preferences led them to ignore local sources of food (the le Stranges of Hunstanton on the north Norfolk coast, for example, did not consume much wildfowl) and to make choices based on considerations of status and medical theories which required them to maintain a balance of humours.[14]

Although we might interpret indulgence in large quantities of expensive food as selfish extravagance, the wealthy elite was anxious to practise generosity and charity, and the especially detailed records of Westminster Abbey allow us to observe 'largesse' and Christian almsgiving in operation. The monks were assigned a diet capable of giving each of them 7,000 calories per day, but much of the food – probably 45 per cent of the total – was distributed among the servants and handed over to the poor.[15]

The aristocratic meal was a cultural event which sent signals at different levels both to those involved, and to those outside. It celebrated the unity of the group sharing the food, while making the hierarchy of the household, and its standing in society, very clear. The size and splendour of the occasion was established by the architectural setting in the hall, with dais, canopy, painting,

12 C. M. Woolgar (ed.), *Household accounts from medieval England*, 2 parts (Records of Social and Economic History, new ser., 17 and 18, Oxford, 1992, 1993); D. Dymond (ed.) *The register of Thetford Priory*, 2 parts (Records of Social and Economic History, new ser., 24 and 25, Oxford, 1995, 1996); T. Scully (ed.), *The Viandier of Taillevent* (Ottawa, 1988); J. Beauroy, 'Sur la culture seigneuriale en Angleterre: un poème anglo-normand dans le cartulaire des barons de Mohun', in C. Duhamel-Amado and G. Lobrichon (eds.), *Georges Duby. L'écriture de l'histoire* (Brussels, 1996), pp. 341–64; U. Albarella and S. J. M. Davis, 'Mammals and birds from Launceston Castle, Cornwall: decline in status and the rise of agriculture', *Circaea. The Journal of the Association of Environmental Archaeology*, 12 (1996 for 1994), 93–7.

13 C. M. Woolgar, 'Diet and consumption in gentry and noble households: a case study from around the Wash', in R. Archer and S. Walker (eds.), *Rulers and ruled in late medieval England* (London, 1995), pp. 17–31; Albarella and Davis, 'Launceston Castle', p. 27.

14 T. Scully, *The art of cooking in the middle ages* (Woodbridge, 1995), pp. 70–1.

15 B. Harvey, *Living and dying in England 1100–1540. The monastic experience* (Oxford, 1993), pp. 34–71.

carving and ornate windows designed to draw attention to the top table where the lord sat with his family and most important guests.[16]

The modern 'consumer revolution' centred on the eighteenth century has been represented as a complete break with a medieval society bound by rigid social distinctions. The tendencies which encouraged modern consumerism included emulation of higher ranks by inferiors, and social competition, leading to 'differentiation' whereby the elite reacted to social climbers by adopting new patterns of consumption in order to maintain their superiority. Such impulses encouraged the lesser ranks to buy 'consumer' goods such as cotton textiles, fine ceramics, mirrors and clocks, and drove the engine of 'fashion'.[17]

Consumer spending was no doubt conducted on a larger scale in the modern period, but the elements of social competition and imitation are familiar from any investigation of the late medieval aristocracy. It is true that we can find medieval consumers holding back from expenditure, as when some religious orders were restrained by their ascetic tradition from renewing or decorating their buildings, and we have already noted that the heads of some landed families refused to be dubbed knights although they were eligible. But in the period of economic expansion in the thirteenth century members of the gentry, and people who aspired to be counted as gentry, dug moats around their houses, built impressive halls, and in general adopted a material style of life imitative of the top ranks of their class. Competitive forces among the wealthy sections of society encouraged families to buy luxuries, which must have been a factor behind the surge in international trade in the thirteenth century. The goods which were imported included wine and high quality textiles which only the aristocracy or the richest merchants could afford: the cumulative value of both imports and exports was assessed at between £55,000 and £75,000 in 1204, and exactly a century later the annual total of £500,000 represents, after adjustment for inflation, a tripling in trade.[18] Similar pressures in the fourteenth century no doubt encouraged

16 For architectural features emphasizing the ceremonial and prestigious aspects of the hall, see A. Emery, *Greater medieval houses of England and Wales*, vol. 1 (Cambridge, 1996), pp. 321–3, 350–1; on the culture of the household, see E. Rassart-Eeckhout, J.-P. Sosson, C. Thiry and T. van Hemelryck (eds.), *La vie matérielle au moyen âge. L'apport des sources littéraires, normatives et de la pratique* (Louvain-la-Neuve, 1997).

17 E.g. J. Brewer and R. Porter (eds.), *Consumption and the world of goods* (London, 1993).

18 E. Miller and J. Hatcher, *Medieval England. Towns, commerce and crafts* (London, 1995), pp. 196–214

gentry to live in an appropriate fashion when they wished to qualify for the rank of esquire. The superiors who were the subject of this emulation observed the process, and deprecated it, most effectively in the writings of Geoffrey Chaucer. The process continued in the fifteenth century with the appearance of the gentleman at the base of the aristocracy. The magnates sought to differentiate themselves from those struggling to reach them by building more luxurious houses, like the Duke of Buckingham's new castle of the early sixteenth century at Thornbury in Gloucestershire with its emphasis on privacy in its chambers. The very wealthy also bought silks, rare furs such as marten, and quantities of sweet wines, or were buried in splendid tombs in collegiate churches built in honour of the family.

Changes in fashion were not confined to the aristocracy, but they often led the way in the new styles. The best-known innovation was the short and closely-fitting mode of dress adopted in the middle of the fourteenth century. But new styles were being introduced at intervals in every type of clothing, including shoes. Surviving examples from excavations in London show how footwear went through a series of changes, not just because of new techniques of manufacture or materials, but presumably because fickle consumers demanded fresh designs. So the predominantly rounded or oval shapes characteristic of the thirteenth and much of the fourteenth century were replaced by a more pointed style in the late fourteenth, including the notoriously long 'poulaine' type, with points extending beyond the toe by 4 inches (10 cm) or more, which had to be stuffed with moss to keep their shape. During the fifteenth century the more rounded shape returned, to be followed by a broad-toed shoe, sometimes almost square, soon after 1500.[19] Cultural historians claim that a 'youth culture' did not develop until modern times, and childhood in the middle ages was not accorded any special status. Again the surviving shoes show that those made for children (especially for young children) often had their own designs, though in some periods, such as that of the pointed style, footwear for all ages followed the same fashion. Games and toys suggests that childhood was regarded as a sufficiently distinct and important phase to warrant some expenditure, and that the young were being encouraged to involve

---

19 F. Grew and M. de Neergard, *Shoes and pattens* (Medieval finds from excavations in London: 11, London, 1988), pp. 15–43.

themselves in imaginative play. Adolescents had their own games, styles of dress and unruly behaviour, and while distinctive expressions of 'youth culture' developed after 1500, they were not without their precedents.[20]

We can conclude with the generalization that the medieval aristocracy were probably not living in a 'consumer society' as intense as that found in the eighteenth century, but that they did participate in forms of consumerism. There may have been no 'consumer revolution' in our period, but there were distinct phases and shifts in consumer behaviour.

PEASANT LIVING STANDARDS, *c.* 1300

The key period when peasant living standards are most fiercely debated lies in the period c. 1290-1320, which seems to contain the turning point when more than a century of growth in population, production and exchange was turned into two centuries of low and falling population, and a global reduction in output. The old explanation for the reversal of fortunes was directly related to living standards – the growth in the rural population exceeded the capacity of the land to support the extra numbers, given the existing level of technology. Holdings were reduced to dangerously small sizes, so that a substantial minority were unable to feed their families from the land that they cultivated. The fertility of the soil deteriorated, and the newly cleared 'marginal' land failed to maintain its productivity. Food shortages and high grain prices caused undernourishment and starvation. In the terminology of modern ecology, thirteenth-century agricultural growth was not sustainable, and this weakness precipitated the eventual drop in population.

Although these views have been subjected to sustained criticism, they still receive support and are bolstered by new evidence. There is now general acceptance that the society and economy received a severe shock in the early fourteenth century, and historians once wary of the term refer to a 'crisis of the fourteenth century' which was located in the period before the Black Death of 1348-9. By the 1320s the population was beginning

---

20 N. Orme, 'The culture of children in medieval England', *P. and P.*, 148 (1995), 48–88; B. A. Hanawalt, *Growing up in medieval London. The experience of childhood in history* (New York and Oxford, 1993), pp. 114–28.

to decline, and occasional clearances of new land were overshadowed by fields that were taken out of cultivation, reclaimed land that was being flooded once more, and houses that fell into decay as their tenants became impoverished, died or moved away.[21]

Symptoms of overpopulation can be found in thirteenth-century peasant communities. Peasants were normally cautious about allowing marriage and the formation of a new household until a couple had access to land or some secure basis for a family. As more land became available through clearance or the land market, parents saw the opportunity to provide the children who had no claim to the main inheritance – daughters and younger sons – with a plot on which they could set up a cottage and marry. On the intensively studied and well-documented manor of Halesowen (Worcestershire) cottages for family members were built on to the edge of the messuage (house, buildings and farmyard), to the point that a holding was overburdened with occupants – for example the Alwerd family's yardland, which at 30 acres should have assured its cultivator a modest prosperity, in 1295-1305 had six households grouped round its messuage.[22] Parents were moved by a strong sense of obligation to their offspring, but also by the belief that the newly developed market could give a living to smallholders through retail trade, craft work or employment. The market did have that capacity in good years, but the demand for manufactures and traded goods was inevitably limited by the poverty of the potential consumers, whose earnings were kept down by endemic problems of low productivity and a lack of specialization.[23] It was precisely the cottagers whose numbers had grown so rapidly in the thirteenth century who felt the worst effects of high prices and restricted incomes in the bad harvests which began in earnest in the 1290s. The market provided an initial safety net to the smallholders when grain prices increased, as their parcels of land could be sold or leased to raise cash to pay for food. But of course if the high prices continued or recurred, the impoverished peasants had lost the means to grow food as well as their source of emergency cash. The signs of social stress, notably pleas of debt before the manor court, and enforced

21 Many aspects of the crisis are examined in B. M. S. Campbell (ed.), *Before the Black Death. Studies in the 'crisis' of the fourteenth century* (Manchester, 1991).
22 Z. Razi, 'The myth of the immutable English family', *P. and P.*, 140 (1993), 8–9.
23 Miller and Hatcher, *Medieval England. Towns, commerce and crafts*, pp. 52–5.

sales and leases of land to repay creditors appear in the bad years of the 1290s as well as in the catastrophic conditions of famine in 1315-18.[24]

Further evidence of a submerged labour force has come from the manors of Glastonbury Abbey in Somerset and Wiltshire in 1262-1348, where by local custom *garciones* paid a small sum of money (between 2d. and 12d.) to the lord, and consequently their names were written into the rolls of the manorial court. The term *garciones*, which can be translated as 'boys', implies young unmarried men, who formed an underclass of workers living either in the household of their employers or occasionally in separate cottages on the edge of the village. There were many of them, equal in number to the tenants at a manor such as Pilton, where the standard holding of 20 acres could not have been cultivated by a single peasant, especially if he had no mature son to help.[25] This group of workers is known on the Glastonbury estate by an accident of documentation, and they must have existed in varying numbers everywhere, like the East Anglian *anilepimen*, and shadowy subtenants occasionally mentioned in manorial surveys. The *garciones* led a precarious existence, perhaps earning well in the harvest season, but often receiving low wages, and they were liable to be laid off in the slack times or when the crops yielded badly. Cheap labour allowed intensive agricultural methods, best known in Norfolk, where weeding, fallow ploughing and careful manuring gave good yields. But we should not forget the poverty that accompanied such technical achievements. Many peasant communities lacked adequate numbers of draught animals, and to some extent they were using human labour as a substitute for animal power.[26]

New scientific work has lent some support to the idea that agricultural land was suffering reduced fertility at this time. Statistical analysis of the grain yields at Cuxham in Oxfordshire shows that they were falling gradually between the 1290s and the 1340s. Phosphorus, which normally accumulates from the breakdown of rock particles in the soil, was carried away from the

24 P .R. Schofield, 'Dearth, debt and the local land market in a late thirteenth-century village community', *Ag.H.R.*, 45 (1997), 1–17.

25 H. S. A. Fox, 'Exploitation of the landless by lords and tenants', in Z. Razi and R. Smith (eds.), *Medieval society and the manor court* (Oxford, 1996), pp. 518–68.

26 B. M. S. Campbell and M. Overton, 'A new perspective on medieval and early modern agriculture: six centuries of Norfolk farming c.1250–c.1850', *P. and P.*, 141 (1993). 38–105, especially 83–5.

land when the grain was sold or taken to Oxford to be consumed in the household of the lord of the manor, Merton College. The manure, ashes and other material spread on the fields did not return enough of the mineral to the soil to compensate for the loss, and so the health of the cereal plants suffered.[27]

We can see that a number of studies show that the land was being required to feed a larger number of smallholders and landless, while at the same time having its fertility inhibited by chemical imbalances. The increasing number of people depended on cheaper foodstuffs. While the better-off peasants on the manor of Taunton in Somerset, like most of those in southern England, could eat wheat bread, the mills of the manor, which were grinding the corn for the mass of the population, were processing a high proportion of rye and oat meal.[28] The seriously deficient harvests of the great famine of 1315-18 found many people without a secure and sufficient income who were unable to afford the high prices, and as they already consumed inferior grains could not (like the wheat eaters) turn to cheaper substitutes.

Perhaps the death rates estimated for the Great Famine – between 10 and 15 per cent – are exaggerated. Some regions suffered more than others. The figures for the bishopric of Winchester's manors of mortality based on heriots probably includes some payments made when land was surrendered as well as those consequent on the deaths of tenants. Those who did die succumbed to disease rather than hunger, and the death toll therefore includes people who picked up an infection at a time of general social dislocation. Having made all of these qualifications, it must be said that some of the statistics, such as those deriving from tithing penny payments, an annual poll tax collected by lords of manors, provide secure evidence for a pronounced drop in numbers during the famine years.[29] Taking conservative estimates of the death rate would still leave a mortality in 1315-18 in the region of a half a million, a shocking figure, marking the decisive

27 E. I. Newman and P. D. A. Harvey, 'Did soil fertility decline in medieval English farms? Evidence from Cuxham, Oxfordshire, 1320-1340', *Ag.H.R.*, 49 (1997), 119-36.

28 C. Dyer, 'Did the peasants really starve in medieval England?', in M. Carlin and J. Rosenthal (eds.), *Food and eating in medieval Europe* (London, 1998), pp. 53-70.

29 W. C. Jordan, *The Great Famine. Northern Europe in the early fourteenth century* (Princeton, 1996), pp. 118-20; B. F. Harvey, 'Introduction: the "crisis" of the early fourteenth century', in Campbell (ed.), *Before the Black Death*, pp. 8-9; R. M. Smith, 'Human resources', in G. G. Astill and A. Grant (eds.), *The countryside of medieval England* (Oxford, 1988), pp. 192-3.

end of population growth, and a likely turning point in the history of the whole period 900-1540.

In spite of this new evidence in support of a thesis of overpopulation, falling productivity, impoverishment and crisis mortality, there are still great problems in making a direct connection between the economic and social troubles of the peasantry and the demographic decline. The famine could have been an 'exogenous' shock – an accident of nature, which had disastrous consequences because the rain rotted the crops, not because of deep-rooted social and ecological problems.[30] For example, the notion that the crisis was precipitated by the lack of fertility in the newly colonized marginal lands, where woods had been cleared and upland grasslands ploughed, can no longer be accepted. In the districts where the marginal lands could have been cultivated and then failed, such as the sandy Breckland of East Anglia, or the woodlands of the west midlands, or the hills of the Lake District and the south-west, the local people were not so foolish as to plough up large swathes of poor land. They had lived in these landscapes for generations, and had learnt how to use the resources in appropriate ways, and when the crisis came these marginal (or rather strongly pastoral) regions did not suffer so badly. In contrast, in Bedfordshire, Buckinghamshire and the Cotswolds, which were regions with a long history of dense settlement and which cannot be described as 'marginal', peasants were migrating and land was falling out of of cultivation by 1341.[31]

The notion that this was a period lacking in technical development cannot be sustained in the light of the abundant evidence for the many adjustments and innovations made by demesne managers and peasants in the methods of cultivation. Rotations were changed, legumes planted in quantity to feed animals and add nitrogen to the soil, seed was sown in different densities, new crop combinations were introduced, different balances between arable and pasture were established, and various weed control measures were taken, such as repeated fallow ploughing and removal of weeds by hand. Drainage of wetlands made more land available for intensive agriculture, and water

---

30 M. Mate, 'The agrarian economy of south-eastern England before the Black Death: depressed or buoyant?', in Campbell (ed.), *Before the Black Death*, pp. 79–109.

31 M. Bailey, *A marginal economy? East Anglian Breckland in the later middle ages* (Cambridge, 1989); C. Dyer, 'The retreat from marginal land': the growth and decline of medieval rural settlements', in M. Aston, D. Austin and C. Dyer (eds.), *The rural settlements of medieval England* (Oxford, 1989), pp. 45–57.

control could also be used to make ponds for fish culture. Building techniques with stone foundations and durable timber frames contributed to improved crop storage, and provided accommodation for livestock. Peasants acquired horses and carts, which enabled them to carry goods more conveniently to market. Lords built many windmills during the thirteenth century mainly as a source of profit, but they had the effect of releasing labour for productive purposes which had previously been spent on hand milling or travelling to a distant watermill.[32] Much of our evidence for techniques and yields comes from the well-documented demesnes of lords, and we lack information about the performance of crops on peasant holdings. The records of Wisbech in Cambridgeshire in the mid fourteenth century show that work done by peasant labour services was less productive than the labour of hired workers.[33] This could mean that the yields recorded for demesnes which made heavy use of labour services are giving too pessimistic a picture of medieval agriculture. When peasants worked on the demesne they did not put in their maximum effort, but on their own land their commitment could have given better results. However, there were many other differences between peasant and demesne agriculture, such as the numbers of animals and the quality of buildings and equipment, so that it is still not possible to be sure that there was a significant difference between demesne and peasant yields. Even if we use the statistics for grain yields from the demesnes, in the absence of any better, they must be examined critically. For example, the long-term and general deterioration in productivity on the bishopric of Winchester's estates may be a statistical illusion, caused by a period of temporarily high yields in the mid-thirteenth century when pastures were being ploughed and cropped for the first time, which gives the period around 1300 the appearance of decline.[34]

All of this new work makes it difficult to accept that the problems of food supply around 1300 inevitably followed from the misuse of land, the over-extension of cultivation, and technological stagnation.

---

32 G. Astill and J. Langdon (eds.), *Medieval farming and technology. The impact of agricultural change in northwestern Europe* (Leiden, 1997); R. Holt, *The mills of medieval England* (Oxford, 1988), pp. 17–35; J. Langdon, 'Watermills and windmills in the West Midlands, 1086–1500', *Ec.H.R.*, 44 (1991), 424–44.

33 D. Stone, 'The productivity of hired and customary labour: evidence from Wisbech Barton in the fourteenth century', *Ec.H.R.*, 50 (1997), 640–56.

34 C. Thornton, 'The determinants of land productivity on the bishop of Winchester's demesne of Rimpton, 1208–1403', in B. M. S. Campbell and M. Overton (eds.), *Land,*

In making a judgement about the state of the peasantry and the rural economy it is worth stepping back to survey the whole of society, and particularly those who were not agricultural producers. A feature of the thirteenth century was the ever increasing proportion of the population who did not live on the land, or who grew food only on a small scale. Any estimate of the size of towns presents major difficulties, but a plausible estimate would be that the urban population grew from about a quarter of a million to a million between *c*.1180 and 1300, and that as a proportion of the whole population town dwellers grew from nearly 10 per cent to a little below 20 per cent.[35] The figures can be disputed, but the urban population certainly expanded more rapidly than the rural population. This could be interpreted in a negative way – urbanization provided a safety valve for the surplus of impoverished peasants who migrated into towns, and once there they experienced a miserable and uncertain existence.[36] However, towns attracted many newcomers, so must have offered some benefits, and were able to maintain and increase their numbers, which means that the inhabitants cannot have been in a permanent state of starvation. Agricultural production could apparently cope with the needs of a fifth of people who were not direct producers which according to some estimates is near to the maximum proportion that could be sustained in a pre-industrial economy. Calculations, which began with estimates of the amount of grain needed to feed 80,000 Londoners in *c*.1300 and were then extended tentatively to the whole country, concluded that there would not have been enough grain for a population as high as five or six million, and consequently a scaling down of the population estimate should be contemplated, perhaps to as small a figure as four million.[37] Such a revision is not possible, because a projection back from the poll tax of 1377 could not arrive at a figure much lower than five million. The presumption must be that England's agriculture in *c*.1300 produced enough in normal years to feed the

labour and livestock: historical studies in European agricultural productivity (Manchester, 1991), pp. 183–210.

35 C. Dyer, 'How urbanized was medieval England?', in J.-M. Duvosquel and E. Thoen (eds.), *Peasants and townsmen in medieval Europe. Studia in Honorem Adriaan Verhulst* (Ghent, 1995), pp. 169–83.

36 E.g. R. H. Hilton, *English and French towns in feudal society. A comparative study* (Cambridge, 1992), pp. 17, 61–3.

37 B. M. S. Campbell, J. A. Galloway, D. Keene and M. Murphy, *A medieval capital and its grain supply: agrarian production and distribution in the London region c.1300* (Historical Geography Research Series, 30, 1993), pp. 43–5.

peasants, the Londoners and the other townspeople, though perhaps with less grain for ale and horse food than Londoners expected, and with a good deal of consumption of cheap grain and pulses boiled in pottages.

In addition to the towndwellers who lived on the agricultural surplus, there were numerous rural smallholders whose land provided only part of their subsistence, and who relied for their living on wage labour, work in crafts, or retail trade. Should their high and rising numbers, and their low and uncertain income, be seen as important contributors to the fourteenth-century crisis? Two qualifications must be made before too gloomy a view is taken. Firstly, the sources may exaggerate the number of smallholders, as one of our most comprehensive sources for peasant conditions, the Hundred Rolls of 1279, has been shown to include among the freeholders (who account for the bulk of the smallholding population) minor aristocrats, clergy, institutions, rich peasants and townspeople who may have held an acre or two in one village, but also had many more acres in other places.[38] This discovery does not entirely resolve the problem of the large number of smallholders, because our sources rarely reveal the full complexity of unofficial or informal subletting, which would probably account for as many new smallholders as can be discounted by eliminating the pseudo-smallholders in the Hundred Rolls and the manorial surveys. Secondly, we ought not to presume that people with smallholdings were necessarily living in a state of permanent destitution. Their successors in the eighteenth and nineteenth centuries have been shown to have practised a 'cottage economy', by which they consumed frugally, and maximized their earnings from their garden and from the commons, where they could graze animals and obtain fuel, fodder, litter and raw materials for their own use and sale. Gleaning in the cornfields, which we know was an important activity in medieval villages, subject to much regulation, could be a major source of income in the early nineteenth century: an energetic collector of ears of corn left by the harvesters could find herself with between three and eight bushels at the end of the season, the larger amount being perhaps a sixth of a family's needs for a year.[39] They picked

38 M. A. Barg, 'The social structure of manorial freeholders: an analysis of the Hundred Rolls of 1279', *Ag.H.R.*, 39 (1991), 108–15.

39 D. Levine, *Reproducing families. The political economy of English population history* (Cambridge, 1987), pp. 19–21; P. King, 'Customary rights and women's earnings: the

up income where they could from a wide range of occupations, in which the earnings of women and children were vital. For example, in the middle ages women are known to have travelled to markets and towns with baskets of foodstuffs, such as fruit and vegetables, eggs, butter, honey and other minor but still profitable products. When cottage women brewed for sale, according to one estimate they would in the early fourteenth century have made 5d. profit from 22½ gallons of ale, and many of these brewsters sold hundreds of gallons in a year.[40] The growth of the market may not have given these people the opportunity to accumulate much wealth, but it did give them a chance of a living.

While the crucial matters of life and death in the worst years lead us to focus on the smallholders, we should still consider the living standards of the middling and upper peasants. Their ability to benefit from the expanding market can be debated. They were prevented from making the best advantage of the sale of their crops by their commitments to pay rent, which forced them to sell a good proportion in September for the money due to the lord at Michaelmas (29 September), and the middling peasants were forced to sell grain that they would have preferred to consume. Rent took away cash which they could have spent on improving their holding by buying animals or constructing buildings. On the other hand the market was undoubtedly large. The urban population received most of their grain, meat and dairy produce from peasants rather than demesnes, and they were especially important sources of poultry, eggs, fruit and vegetables, which were not sold on a large scale by most lords. The peasants gained enough money to pay rents and taxes, and they had cash to spare to buy goods for their own use. The small towns that multiplied in the thirteenth century – there were more than 600 by 1300 – did not attract much patronage from the aristocracy, and were populated by small-scale artisans and traders of cheap everyday goods. Most market towns served perhaps 2,000 households living within a six-mile radius, and they sold foodstuffs and manufactured goods such as ale, bread, joints of meat, fish, cloth, shoes, nails, knives and horseshoes suitable for peasant purchasers. They could also provide country people with the services of such specialists as

importance of gleaning to the rural labouring poor, 1750–1850', *Ec.H.R.*, 44 (1991), 461–76.

40 J. Bennett, *Ale, beer, and brewsters in England. Women's work in a changing world, 1300–1600* (New York and Oxford, 1996), p. 23.

tailors and clerks. As the peasants became more involved in the market during the thirteenth century, the number of small towns and village markets increased rapidly. After about 1310 the rate of foundation slowed, and the later creations often failed, which signalled a levelling in consumer demand.[41]

What brought about the crisis of the fourteenth century? The weight of rents and services demanded by lords cannot have helped people struggling with bad harvests and other economic problems, but they had reached a high level well before the 1290s, and they varied considerably from one estate or manor to another, yet the crisis seems to have been felt everywhere. Peasants were not just the hapless victims of their social superiors, but helped to set limits on the demands made on them by taking legal action against their lord, and by minor revolts and agitations. Taxes, which began to become seriously oppressive in the 1290s, and the economic uncertainties created by the wars of Edward I and Edward III, may have tipped the balance at critical moments.[42] The 'exogenous' factor of bad weather cannot be discounted, especially as the unstable climate had long-term effects beginning in the 1290s and continuing up to 1375. But natural disasters, even one as severe as that of 1315-18, would not have had such far-reaching consequences in a healthy society.

LIVING STANDARDS IN TOWNS, AND CHANGES IN DEMAND

Towndwellers depended on the countryside for formidable quantities of food and raw materials. The feeding of each Londoner in *c.*1300 required each day 1 lb–1.25 lb of bread, baked

---

41 C. Dyer, 'Market towns and the countryside in late medieval England', Canadian Journal of History, 31 (1996), 17–35; R. M. Smith, 'A periodic market and its influence on a manorial community', in Razi and Smith (eds.), Manor court, pp. 450–81; R. H. Britnell, *The commercialisation of English society 1000–1500* (Cambridge, 1993), pp. 81–5, 119–23, 155–61.

42 On lord–peasant relations, C. Dyer, 'Memories of freedom: attitudes towards serfdom in England, 1200–1350', in M. Bush (ed.), *Serfdom and slavery: studies in legal bondage* (London, 1996), pp. 277–95; R. Evans, 'Merton College's control of its tenants at Thorncroft, 1270–1349', in Razi and Smith (eds.), *Manor court*, pp. 199–259; on taxes and war, B. M. S. Campbell, 'Ecology versus economics in late thirteenth- and early fourteenth-century English agriculture', in D. Sweeney (ed.), *Agriculture in the middle ages. Technology, practice and representation* (Philadelphia, 1995), pp. 76–108.

from wheat for the better-off, or maslin or rye for the poor, and a pint of ale brewed from oats and barley. These quantities presume that 80 per cent of their calories came from cereals rather than from meat, fish, dairy products and other foodstuffs. This grain, together with oats to feed the horses that carried the food, fuel and other loads, amounted to 1.65 qrs per head each year. As London's population apparently lay somewhere between 80,000 and 100,000 at this time, it needed to draw on a rural hinterland extending from Essex and Kent in the east to Oxfordshire and Berkshire in the south, and as far north as Northamptonshire. An elaborate system of supply involved middlemen, market towns in the provinces which acted as collecting points, and transport systems by water and road to bring the grain to the capital.[43]

The other English towns depended on smaller areas of supply, but their cumulative demand was very great – the 50 towns with populations of between 2,000 and 30,000, and the 600 market towns each with 300-2,000 inhabitants, if they ate as well as the Londoners, needed more than a million quarters of grain each year, which as we have seen must have been near to the maximum capacity of the agricultural system. The urban population must have been threatened by considerable hardship when prices rose in bad years. Supply and demand had to be matched also in providing London with wood fuel, based on the assumption that each inhabitant needed annually 1.76 tons of wood for domestic heating and food preparation. This demand was difficult to satisfy because the areas of production were limited : they had to be accessible for carts or boats and to lie within reasonable distance, like the woods on the Chiltern Hills, and rising prices at the end of the thirteenth century suggest that the capital was outstripping the resources of its hinterland. At that time some coal was being brought from Northumberland, and in the sixteenth century when London's population rose above 100,000, it switched from wood to coal as its principal fuel.[44]

The changes in London's food supplies in the late fourteenth and fifteenth centuries reflect trends in the whole country. As its population had fallen to about 50,000 in 1400, the problems of obtaining supplies of grain and fuel had eased. The proportion of wheat among the bread corns rose as the poor switched from rye

43 Campbell *et al.*, *A medieval capital*.
44 J. A. Galloway, D. Keene and M. Murphy, 'Fuelling the city: production and distribution of firewood and fuel in London's region, 1290–1400', *Ec.H.R.*, 49 (1996), 447–72.

bread. Barley replaced oats as the principal brewing grain, and a large increase in consumption of ale pushed up the quantities of barley and malt brought into the city. In the fifteenth century beer began to supplant ale, with a larger scale of production and a loss of business for numerous ale wives.[45] More consumption of meat led to an increase in the number and wealth of butchers, like those in Exeter in the late fourteenth century who accounted for a high proportion of the city's trade, and were renting much pasture land in the vicinity. The rise in the demand for meat, especially beef, had widespread repercussions in the countryside. Welsh drovers had supplied the butchers of the midland towns and London before the Black Death; this continued on a larger scale, and in the fifteenth century parts of north Devon and north Warwickshire became specialist pastures where cattle were bred and fattened for urban markets in general, but especially for London.[46]

In the fourteenth and fifteenth centuries townspeople were better fed, and their lives became more comfortable. The trend towards greater privacy in housing, with the proliferation of rooms, reached its ultimate development in about 1500 when houses were built in provincial towns such as Stamford (Lincolnshire) without open halls, and ceiled throughout the building, which used a parlour or chamber rather than a hall as the principal room. New methods of roof construction gave extra space for attics where servants and apprentices could be accommodated away from the family. Many towns were less congested, so that more houses had gardens, and indeed in more pretentious dwellings a parlour or gallery was built giving access to the garden. The convenience and comfort of the upper-class urban house was being improved with more glass windows, sometimes large in size, wainscotting in more important rooms, carpets on floors as well as on tables, and a greater use of chairs and cupboards rather than chests.[47] Urban governments showed concern for

45 J. A. Galloway, 'London's grain supply: changes in production, distribution and consumption during the fourteenth century', *Franco-British Studies*, 20 (1995), 23–34; B. M. S. Campbell, 'Land, labour, livestock and productivity trends in English seignorial agriculture, 1208–1450', in Campbell and Overton (eds.), *Land, labour and livestock*, pp. 166–9; Bennett, *Ale, beer and brewsters*, pp. 77–97.

46 M. Kowaleski, *Local markets and regional trade in medieval Exeter* (Cambridge, 1995), pp. 137–8; E. Miller (ed.), *The agrarian history of England and Wales 1348–1500*, vol. III (Cambridge, 1991), pp. 158, 319–20, 239–42; A. Watkins, 'Cattle grazing in the Forest of Arden in the later middle ages', *Ag.H.R.*, 37 (1989), 12–25.

47 J. Schofield, 'Urban housing in England, 1400–1600', in D. Gaimster and P. Stamper

cleanliness. This was not just a case of legislation which was ignored, because archaeologists find deep deposits of the thirteenth century or earlier, but the occupation of the last two medieval centuries leaves much less stratification, because refuse was carried out to collective middens rather than accumulating around the dwellings.[48]

Higher levels of expenditure by individual town dwellers are reflected in the increased use of pewter. Vessels made from this alloy, much used at table as a substitute for silver, were manufactured in London and provincial towns in the thirteenth and fourteenth centuries, but after 1400 the London pewterers increased in number, from sixty in 1410 to a hundred in 1457. Their collective output at the beginning of the century has been estimated at 200,000 pieces, many of which were exported, but inventories show that much found its way into the homes of merchants, artisans and more prosperous peasants.[49] The consumption of pottery in London and other towns shows in the fifteenth century the triumph of continental wares, such as stoneware from the Rhineland, Italian maiolica and Iberian lustreware. These imports consisted of glazed, colourful and decorative table wares, contrasting with the rather drab and functional products of the English potters. The English industry retaliated with its own range of cups, jugs, bowls and chafing dishes (the latter kept food warm on the table), the most successful products being the green-glazed wares manufactured in kilns in Surrey and Hampshire, and the thin-walled 'Cistercian ware' made in the midlands with a metallic dark brown glaze. By 1500 urban households contained a wide range of well-made and attractive pottery that could be used in the kitchen and at table.[50]

How were urban living standards in general affected by the changes of 1350–1520? Much has been made of urban decline, which undoubtedly led to a serious loss of trade and population by

(eds.), *The age of transition. The archaeology of English culture, 1400–1600* (Oxford, 1997), pp. 127–44; J. Schofield, *Medieval London houses* (New Haven, 1994), pp. 61–133.

48 P. Courtney, 'The tyranny of constructs: some thoughts on periodisation and culture change', in Gaimster and Stamper (eds.), *Age of transition*, p. 13.

49 R. F. Homer, 'Tin, lead and pewter', in J. Blair and N. Ramsay (eds.), *English medieval industries* (London, 1991), pp. 57–80; Pollard, *North-eastern England*, p. 70.

50 D. Gaimster and B. Nenk, 'English households in transition c. 1450–1550: the ceramic evidence', in Gaimster and Stamper (eds.), *Age of transition*, pp. 173–9; M. R. McCarthy and C. M. Brooks, *Medieval pottery in Britain AD 900–1600* (Leicester, 1988), pp. 424–9, 448–50.

a number of types of town – the eastern ports, such as Boston, suffered from the recession in the wool trade, and some larger provincial centres, like Lincoln and Winchester, diminished seriously in size. Many towns lost about a half of their population, but so did the whole country, so their relative position was not changed. Some towns, however, could move against the trend and grow in size. These included places which found a role in the manufacture of specific types of woollen cloth which attracted customers through their quality and price, both on the continent and in the home market. These were not always very expensive, and appealed to better-off artisans and peasants, like the russets costing about 2s. per yard in *c.*1400 made in Colchester, which enabled the town to flourish in the late fourteenth and early fifteenth centuries. A century later smaller towns, such as Tiverton in Devon, and Kendal in Westmorland, found a niche at the cheaper end of the cloth trade which enabled them to grow to a larger size than before the plagues.[51] Many larger towns lost their cloth industry to rivals in the country or in the market towns, in the West Riding of Yorkshire, East Anglia, Kent and the west country. But these changes do not seem to have been either the cause or the consequence of any long-term decline in the living standards of individuals.

The cloth industry as a whole was doing well partly because the English clothiers captured markets on the continent, but also because many consumers, including peasants and wage-earners, could buy more clothing. With the exception of some smaller places, which had probably never been very securely established, towns were not abandoned. The inhabitants could still make a livelihood, though they no doubt endured some hard times, like the depression in overseas trade in the middle of the fifteenth century. But there was a recovery, and a healthy proportion of the population, about a fifth, were town dwellers when the subsidy was assessed in 1524-5. By then some new towns had been established, like Stroud in Gloucestershire and Stourbridge in Worcestershire, both in districts of rural industry, and one of the largest urban centres in England had grown at Southwark, the southern suburb of the capital. Overseas trade expanded at the end of the fifteenth century, not just because of a growth in exports of cloth, but also through an expansion in imports of consumer

---

51 A. Dyer, *Decline and growth in English towns 1400–1640* (New Studies in Economic and Social History, Cambridge, 1995).

goods. For example, one of the prospering clothing districts, Devon, was receiving through its ports cargoes of miscellaneous goods such as hats, lace, paper and candlesticks.[52]

The growth in industries making goods which satisfied the needs of a wide range of consumers, notably woollen and linen cloth, leather goods, pewter and iron, suggests that expenditure per head rose after the fourteenth-century crisis, but were incomes generally so buoyant? Wage-earners clearly prospered, as their rates of pay doubled in the second half of the fourteenth century. But any theoretical projection of peasant fortunes sounds warnings about the difficulties facing a group who produced grain and wool for the market, the prices of which fell in the long term. They needed to employ labour, especially if they were increasing the size of their holdings as land became relatively cheap and plentiful, but the higher wages would have eaten into their profits. The theory seems contradicted by the experiences and behaviour of the peasants in their localities. Richard Heggenworth, who was active in the land market in three villages in east Sussex, by 1468 accumulated a holding of 123 acres and an unknown acreage in seven other places. Holdings in excess of 40 acres, rare before 1348-9, were now commonplace over much of the country. Families of substantial peasants, like the north Warwickshire Deys of Drakenage between the 1440s and 1470s, or the Baillys of Middleton in 1362-1450, made profitable use of their many acres by specializing in beef cattle, a sure route to profit in a carnivorous age. In Devon in villages like Stokenham in the South Hams the peasants with larger holdings (in 1390 the mean size of holding was 45 acres) attempted to solve their labour problem by acquiring the cottages in their village, and using them to house their labourers. An exception to the rule that larger holdings developed after 1348-9 comes from central Essex, where a high proportion of smallholdings is found both before and after the Black Death. The explanation must lie in the industrialized character of the region, where in 1381 a quarter of the population were recorded by the poll-tax assessors as artisans or traders, so the smallholders must have been devoting their energies to industrial work.[53]

52 C. Dyer, 'The hidden trade of the middle ages: evidence from the west midlands of England', *Journal of Historical Geography*, 18 (1992), 141–57; M. Carlin, *Medieval Southwark* (London, 1996), pp. 143–4; W. R. Childs, 'Devon's overseas trade in the late middle ages', in M. Duffy (ed.), *The new maritime history of Devon*, vol. 1 (Exeter, 1992), pp. 80–1.
53 M. E. Mate, 'The east Sussex land market and agrarian class structure in the late middle ages', *P. and P.*, 139 (1993), 55; Watkins, 'Cattle grazing', 18–19; H. S. A. Fox, 'Servants,

Further evidence that peasants enjoyed some prosperity, and were able to use their wealth to raise their living standards, comes from their still surviving houses. These structures can now be dated precisely by dendrochronology, that is by taking a sample of timber, analysing the growth rings, and matching the pattern of rings to a 'master chronology' based on timber of known date. The majority of samples derive from the original timbers of a house, not from repairs, or from old timber reused, so the dates are mostly those of new buildings. In Kent hundreds of houses still stand, which originally consisted of an open hall with two storey accommodation at one or both ends. The earliest examples belong to the 1370s, but the peak of construction came in the period 1440-1519 (see fig. 9). In the midlands peasant houses using cruck construction have a surprisingly similar range of dates. A small group in Berkshire and south Oxfordshire belongs to the late thirteenth and early fourteenth centuries, but the main series of dated houses in Leicestershire, Warwickshire and Shropshire begins in the 1380s and 1390s, and almost a half of the peasant houses begun between 1380 and 1520 belong to the period between 1440 and 1480.[54]

These dates indicate remarkably that peasants were building new houses at a time when our records are full of complaints that buildings were in ruin, or indeed had fallen down. The two types of evidence are not as contradictory as at first appears, because tenants with a number of holdings allowed the redundant houses to decay, but rebuilt, to a higher standard, on the holding on which they lived. The middle years of the fifteenth century are often depicted as a bleak economic episode, and rents were especially low and difficult to collect at that time, but the period may have presented the landlords who received the rents with more problems than the tenants who paid them. Towards the end of the fifteenth century and in the early sixteenth entirely new buildings were being constructed on new sites, some of them cottages on

cottagers and tied cottages during the later middle ages: towards a regional dimension', *Rural History*, 6 (1995), 125–54; L. R. Poos, *A rural society after the Black Death. Essex 1350–1520* (Cambridge, 1991), pp. 11–31.

54 S. Pearson, *The medieval houses of Kent* (Royal Commission on Historical Monuments, England. 1994), pp. 67–70; N. W. Alcock, 'Index of tree-ring dates for British buildings: 1976–1987', *Vernacular Architecture*, 18 (1987), 56–8; N. W. Alcock, 'Index of tree-ring dates for British buildings: 1988–1992', *Vernacular Architecture*, 24 (1993), 61–5; and subsequent issues of this journal. I am grateful to Dr Alcock for providing me with details of the dated cruck buildings.

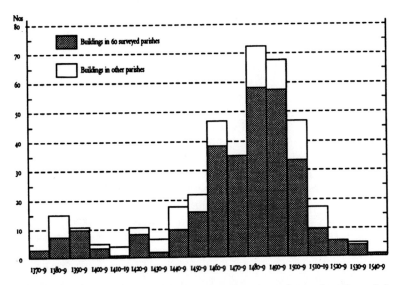

Fig. 9 The numbers of open-hall houses in Kent. This shows the number of recorded houses, or phases of houses, built in each decade. (*Source note*: Pearson, *Medieval houses of Kent*, p. 68.)

commons and wastes, associated with changing patterns of employment in agriculture and industry, and others were houses and barns for farmers who had taken over the leases of demesnes and were now managing them from new centres. Farmers who continued to occupy the old manorial sites might rebuild, or persuade the lords to replace the house and agricultural buildings. The fifteenth century was also a period of public building in the countryside, as more money was put into construction of church houses (the medieval equivalent of village halls), guildhalls for village fraternities, and churches themselves, which, if they were not rebuilt in the perpendicular style, received towers, porches or clerestories, or at least were given new fittings and furnishings. All of these strengthen the assumption that many peasant communities had surplus cash.[55]

55 For a gloomy view of the mid-fifteenth century, see J. Hatcher, 'The great slump of the mid-fifteenth century', R. Britnell and J. Hatcher (eds.), *Progress and problems in medieval England. Essays in honour of Edward Miller* (Cambridge, 1996), pp. 237–72; for new buildings, C. Dyer, 'Peasants and farmers: rural settlements in an age of transition', in Gaimster and Stamper (eds.), *Age of transition*, pp. 61–76.

The new buildings brought employment to carpenters and those who supplied building materials, and for us they also help to create a picture of consumption on some scale by peasants. This must strengthen the case for believing that peasant demand helped to keep the towns active, and encouraged some of the industrial expansion.

The generalization that the economy shrank in the later middle ages, but that many individuals enjoyed higher living standards leaves us with a demographic paradox. If a low level of population was left by the great famine, the Black Death of 1348-9, and the successive plague epidemics in 1361-2, 1369 and 1375, why was there no sustained recovery after 1375? With half as many people living on the same amount of land, peasants gained a holding early in life and could marry young. Wage-earners were receiving good money in their teens and early twenties, while in towns vacancies in trades and crafts opened up new opportunities. As food was relatively cheap and plentiful, couples should have been fertile, and their offspring would have had a good chance of a healthy childhood, yet the population remained at the low level of the 1370s, or even a little lower, until the 1530s. Two lines of explanation for this paradox have been offered.

The first argues that the two centuries after 1348 saw epidemics of plague, dysentery and influenza, and endemic disease also contributed to high levels of mortality. The monks of Westminster were a well-documented group who suffered from 'crisis' mortality (a death rate in excess of one hundred per thousand) in nine years between 1390 and 1529, and thirteen years of unusually high mortality. Their expectation of life at the age of twenty declined from twenty-nine to thirty in the early fifteenth century to below twenty at the end of the century. There are obvious difficulties in regarding monks as typical of the whole population, though their living conditions should have meant that they suffered less from disease than ordinary laypeople. The town of Westminster at this time was suffering a very high rate of mortality of fifty to sixty per thousand in 'normal' years between 1490 and 1510, so it appears that the monks were sharing in the general experience of a 'dangerously unhealthy' town. The best calculation that we have for peasants, from Essex, suggests that villages were healthier than Westminster, because expectation of life for males at the age of twelve was forty-two years in the late fourteenth century, and thirty-six in the late fifteenth. The drop in life expectation towards the end of the period suggest the effects of new diseases such as influenza, which were also killing the inhabitants of Westminster. Those historians who favour a 'mortality-driven' approach do not discount the effects of the birth rate, which they believe could have been quite high, but not enough to compensate for the rising mortality.[56]

The second explanation emphasizes the careful regulation of marriage, and the custom that no couple should marry until they were sure of land or a regular income. The couple played a major part in the decision to marry, but they were heavily influenced by families who would negotiate a contract involving property and the payment of a dowry. Marriage was preceded by employment as a servant for both young men and women, often in a household away from their parental home, in which they acquired skills, experience and savings. After 1349 the length of the episode of service might have been prolonged, so that couples married in their mid or late twenties, and a significant minority did not marry at all. Late marriage, and a good deal of celibacy, helped to reduce the number of births, and contributed to the low levels of population. But why did they delay when economic conditions favoured early marriage? In York in the late fourteenth and early fifteenth century, the labour shortage, combined with the city's relative prosperity at that time, gave women many opportunities for work. Young women enjoyed these rewards and married late.[57] The argument is closely related to the special case of York, but undoubtedly throughout the country the Black Death liberated women by opening up job prospects, so they could earn their living independently, or make a significant contribution to household income after marriage. We must doubt whether women's jobs, located mainly in the food, drink, textile and clothing trades, which tended to be tedious, unskilled and less well rewarded than men's work, were sufficient to encourage women to delay marriage, as the married state offered its traditional attractions, and did not prevent women from continuing to work.

Other factors may have been the shock of the Black Death, and a determination by the survivors to keep the better way of life that

56 Harvey, *Living and dying*, pp. 112–45; G. Rosser, *Medieval Westminster 1200–1540* (Oxford, 1989), pp. 177–80; Poos, *Rural society*, pp. 115–20; M. Bailey, 'Demographic decline in late medieval England: some thoughts on recent research', *Ec.H.R.*, 49 (1996), 1–19.

57 Smith, 'Human resources'; P. J. P. Goldberg, *Women, work and life cycle in a medieval economy. Women in York and Yorkshire c.1300-1520* (Oxford, 1992); Poos, *Rural society*, pp. 89–206.

would be threatened by a new surge in numbers. Also in the longer term the bonds of the family were weakened, so that children either did not survive long enough to inherit, or they moved away, and were less likely to help their parents in their old age. They no longer needed to inherit the family holding, as land could be easily obtained.[58] Parents could not choose whether or not to have children, but unlike earlier generations they may not have thought it vitally important to produce heirs.

Neither side of this argument has yet found sufficient evidence to prove their case conclusively. Those who emphasize changes in fertility connect the new marriage patterns to improved working conditions and changes in familial attitudes, both aspects of rising living standards. The protagonists of high mortality believe that diseases were biological accidents, and not caused by deteriorating social conditions, as this is agreed to be a period of better diet and housing, and in towns the general standard of hygiene in water supplies and the disposal of rubbish had probably improved since the thirteenth century.

WAGE-EARNERS

The Phelps Brown and Hopkins index charts the movements in real wages for building craftsmen and labourers, and shows them at a low level in the thirteenth and early fourteenth centuries, and rising from the late fourteenth until the 1440s. The trends are correctly identified, but the index provides a very imperfect guide to the standards of living of wage-earners. A new index has now been compiled by Farmer, using as a 'shopping basket' against which to measure the purchasing power of wages a realistic group of commodities, including some beef, mutton, pork and cheese, but with a high proportion of barley and peas (see table 20). The Phelps Brown and Hopkins 'shopping basket', as it was based on a clerical household's consumption, included more meat and fish than the average wage earner's family would have eaten. Farmer's index shows that a building worker in the mid-thirteenth century needed 27 units of work to buy a 'shopping basket', 35-42 in the early fourteenth century as food prices rose rapidly but wages did not, 20 in the early fifteenth, and falling to 12-14 in the period

<hr />

58 Razi, 'Immutable English family'.

Table 20. *Index of real wages, 1208–1500, based on the number of units of work needed to buy a 'shopping basket' of goods*[†]

Date[*]	Unit of agricultural work	Unit of building work
1208–20	24	–
1220–30	26	–
1230–40	24	–
1240–50	26	27
1250–60	26	27
1260–70	26	29
1270–80	36	36
1280–90	28	32
1290–1300	32	39
1300–10	27	35
1310–20	32	42
1320–30	27	40
1330–40	23	32
1340–7	22	30
1350–60	24	33
1360–70	25	32
1370–80	19	27
1380–90	15	21
1390–1400	17	23
1400–10	17	22
1410–20	16	21
1420–30	15	18
1430–40	17	20
1440–50	12	14
1450–60	11	12
1460–70	12	14
1470–80	–	13
1480–90	–	16
1490–1500	–	13

[†] Therefore the lower the figure, the higher the real wage.
[*] Years begin 29 September and end 28 September.
Source note: D.L. Farmer, 'Prices and wages', in H.E. Hallam (ed.), *The agrarian history of England and Wales 1042-1350*, vol. 11 (Cambridge, 1988), p. 778; D.L. Farmer, 'Prices and wages', in Miller, *Agrarian history*, vol. 111, p. 491.

1440-1500. The Phelps Brown and Hopkins index suggested that real wages for craftsmen doubled between the 1300 and 1450; according to Farmer's index they increased threefold. Agricultural workers did not fare quite so well, but still improved their rewards by two-and-a-half times.[59]

Historians working on the early modern period have taken the criticisms a stage further by pointing out the reliance of wage indices on the records of unrepresentative institutional employers for the wage rates, and to use as evidence for prices bulk purchases of unprocessed food such as grain, malt and animal carcasses, rather than the loaves of bread, pints of ale, small joints of meat or even take-away pies which the real wage-earners bought.[60] Future researchers should be able to compile more sophisticated indices taking note of these points, but we can already anticipate some of the conclusions. The first of these relates to the strange behaviour of wage rates in the twenty or thirty years after the Black Death, which do not appear to rise as rapidly as we would expect, or indeed as is suggested by contemporary scandalized and moralistic comments (see table 20). Various explanations have been offered, but one is that the manorial accounts are misleading because, wary of the Statute of Labourers, illegally high payments were concealed under lump sums for whole jobs rather than being itemized. Also employers would pay modest cash increases and add payments in kind to attract workers. When prosecutions of workers under the Statute mentioned specific rates of pay they varied from the sums recorded in accounts, most remarkably in the case of ploughmen and other farm servants who received 10s. per annum or less according to the accounts, but 20s. or even more according to the presentments of the juries before the Justices of the Peace enforcing the labour laws. The indices should therefore, if it was possible to correct for our misleading sources, show wage rates climbing more steeply after 1349.[61] If we were to allow for the cost of processed food, this would probably not be to the advantage of

---

59 D. L. Farmer, 'Prices and wages', in H. E. Hallam (ed.), *The agrarian history of England and Wales 1042-1350*, vol. II (Cambridge, 1988), pp. 760–79; D. L. Farmer, 'Prices and wages', in Miller (ed.), *Agrarian history*, vol. III, 467–94.

60 S. Rappaport, *Worlds within worlds. Structures of life in sixteenth-century London* (Cambridge, 1989), pp. 127–8.

61 J. Hatcher, 'England in the aftermath of the Black Death', *P. and P.*, 144 (1994), 3–35; S. A. C. Penn and C. Dyer, 'Wages and earnings in late medieval England: evidence from the enforcement of the labour laws', *Ec.H.R.*, 2nd ser., 43 (1990), 356–76.

the workers after 1349, as the labour component in baking, brewing and butchery, though supposedly controlled by law, must have pushed up the cost of bread, ale and other purchases.[62] The bias of our sources means that we draw too much of our evidence from southern and eastern England, and the records of the enforcement of the labour laws, as well as the employers' accounts, show that workers were less well rewarded in the west and north. The differences could be very substantial. For example institutional urban employers in the north of England in the period 1450–1540 were paying craftsmen 5d.–6d. per day, and labourers 4d., while on London Bridge in the same period the craftsmen were receiving 6d.–8d. and the labourers 4d.–5d.[63]

The assessment of living standards of wage workers depends more on the amount of work done and the conditions of employment than on the rate of pay. The most likely change in employment after the Black Death would have been for workers to move away from annual contracts, whereby servants worked for a whole year for limited rewards, often paid partly in kind, towards more flexible and irregular working patterns by which both skilled artisans and labourers were engaged for short terms and paid by the day or by the task. The justices enforcing the labour laws in the late fourteenth century dealt with many workers who refused to enter into annual contracts because they preferred freedom and higher pay as labourers. After 1400 both types of worker were being used by farmers, who as they took over the management of the lord's demesnes, became the largest employers in the countryside. The patterns of employment both by farmers and by the peasants with larger holdings depended on the type of agriculture that they practised. In Devon villages specializing in pastoralism living-in servants were the main labour force. In mixed farming areas labourers apparently did much of the work, though as their cottages were 'tied', being sublet to the labourer by the peasant employer, the workers may have enjoyed limited freedom.[64] Much depended also on the age of the worker, with many young people employed as servants, and adults as labourers.

62 Poos, *Rural society*, p. 210.
63 D. Woodward, *Men at work. Labourers and building craftsmen in the towns of northern England, 1450–1750* (Cambridge, 1995), p. 169; V. Harding and L. Wright (eds.), *London bridge: selected accounts and rentals, 1381–1538* (London Record Society, 31, 1994), pp. 141–5, 188–93.
64 Fox, 'Servants, cottagers and tied cottages'.

Did medieval people work hard, and was their labour, which often extended over long hours, very productive? There may have been a relationship between rates of pay and productivity, so that after the fourteenth-century rise in wages employers made sure that they received a good day's work for a high wage. On the other hand, the employees could have taken advantage of their strong bargaining position to work slowly and carelessly. In any case, whatever the rate of pay, employees would have been limited in their productivity by the technology that they were using, and general expectations of the pace of work would have differed from ours, accustomed as we are to the accurate measurement of time. The best figures available to us seem to confirm the view that productivity was low, because a tiler working on a roof in Hull in the late fifteenth century laid about 300 tiles in a day, while his modern equivalent would have laid 1,000. The comparability of the two cases is not at all certain, of course, and the medieval worker may have had to do more preparatory work.[65]

The amount earned by wage-workers in the thirteenth and early fourteenth centuries was limited by both the low rates of pay and the availability of work. The survival of labourers' families depended on the contributions of women and children either from employment, or through their involvement in the 'cottage economy'. With the rise in wages in the mid-fourteenth century households exercised some choice about whether to maximize earnings or to opt for more leisure. Were medieval attitudes towards leisure completely different from those of modern times? It is said that the distinction between work and leisure was not drawn clearly, and games and festivals were accorded great importance in the lives of communities, and took priority over productive tasks. If this view is accepted, medieval workers spent much time in idleness, and a work ethic was foreign to their thinking. Labourers would have found it easy to slip into a life of intermittent work, and after they had gained the means to buy the necessities of life, they would have rested. There is some evidence to support this view, because moralists and legislators in town and country were loud in their condemnation of those who refused work, or wasted their time in illicit sports, and kept from their beds at night in order to gamble and drink. Such reactions as always tells us more about the legislators than the objects of their indignation,

65 Woodward, *Men at work*, pp. 129–30.

and show that a work ethic did indeed prevail, at least among the better-off peasants, artisans, gentry and merchants who framed the legislation, or who might have read and approved the work of moralistic writers like William Langland.[66]

We cannot be sure that a different set of values influenced the behaviour of all wage earners. They apparently wished to better themselves, judging from the numerous cottagers or landless workers in the countryside who acquired holdings and were thereby promoted into the ranks of the middling peasantry. In towns the workers pursued a number of occupations, like the York mason who bought and sold grain. Their wives contributed to the household income by taking up such occupations as brewing and spinning, suggests a desire to maximize income and not to take the leisure option. The belief that wage-earners were content with a low level of consumption and plentiful leisure does not accord with the hostile comments on their indulgence in ale and gambling (both rather expensive pursuits), and the more objective evidence that cottages were being rebuilt in this period alongside the houses of the better-off peasants and artisans, and that labourers expected to eat quantities of meat and fish.[67] The high levels of cloth production, especially of the cheaper types, also points to the wage-earners as a significant group of consumers, who had incentives to work hard to buy these rather expensive manufactured goods.

CHARITY

The mysterious ability of the poor to survive must be our main concern. The thinking behind charitable giving seems more realistic, and its delivery more effective, than was once supposed. The monks of Westminster Abbey, for example, were contributing

---

66 The modernists' view is in P. Burke, 'The invention of leisure in early modern Europe', *P. and P.*, 146 (1995), 136–50; contrary opinions are in J.-L. Marfany, 'Debate. The invention of leisure in early modern Europe', *P. and P.*, 156 (1997), 176–91; C. Dyer, 'Leisure among the peasantry in the later middle ages', in S. Cavaciocchi (ed.), *Il tempo libero economia e societa secc. XIII–XVIII* (Istituto Internazionale di Storia Economica 'F. Datini', Prato, 1995), pp. 291–306.

67 H. Swanson, *Medieval artisans. An urban class in late medieval England* (Oxford, 1989), pp. 6–7, 136; N. W. Alcock, *People at home. Living in a Warwickshire village 1500–1800* (Chichester, 1993), pp. 40–5, referring to a new cottage of the late fifteenth century.

about a tenth of their revenues in various charitable schemes in c.1500. Much of it went to those thought to be most in need, such as the inmates of almshouses, and even the doles were directed towards poor householders and identified paupers in Westminster itself, and were not scattered indiscriminately to a crowd of anonymous beggars. A proportion of the charity consisted of surplus food, which was of practical value and less likely than money to be misused. Almshouses, as distinct from hospitals, were apparently increasing in number after the mid-fourteenth century, often being founded by townspeople, and must therefore have been able to provide residential care for a larger proportion of the population than had been the case in earlier times. Hospitals, like St Paul's and St Giles in Norwich by the late fifteenth century were giving very little relief to the poor. These institutions tended to develop an ethos of providing for a small and privileged group of inmates, who may not have been impoverished in the first place. Some did useful work in issuing outdoor relief, like the feeding of a hundred men in a hall set aside for the purpose at St Cross in Winchester.[68]

The charitable role of the religious guilds and fraternities that proliferated in the late fourteenth century has not been fully appreciated. Many fraternities built and maintained almshouses. Others gave the poor a role in their annual feast, by inviting a fixed number (thirteen at Gedney in Lincolnshire, thirty at Ely) to share in the food, or even as many poor people as there were diners (Grantham, Lincolnshire). Sometimes the poor were kept outside the hall during the meal, and either food and drink was sent outside to them, or (at Wisbech) they were invited in after the diners had departed to eat the leftovers. Fraternities would offer to help brothers and sisters who fell on hard times, though few can be shown to have done this on any large scale. The King's Lynn gild in the period 1373-1484 gave an average of more than £15 per annum to poor laity, at an average of 8s. per person. A Cambridge fraternity in the early sixteenth century limited its aid to 2d. per week, issued mainly to widows.[69]

In considering the contribution that the religious institutions made to the relief of poverty, while a greater quantity has been

68 Harvey, *Living and dying*, 7–33; N. Orme and M. Webster, *The English hospital, 1070–1570* (New Haven and London, 1995), p. 63; C. Rawcliffe, *The hospitals of medieval Norwich* (Norwich, 1995).
69 B. R. McRee, 'Charity and guild solidarity in late medieval England', *Journal of British*

revealed than was previously realised, we must still note that it was related to the priorities of the donors rather than the recipients – the numbers given alms were of religious significance (13, 30, 100) rather than reflecting the actual numbers needing help, and the timing of handouts of food and money, on saints' days and other religious occasions, did not necessarily coincide with the seasons of greatest deprivation. The poor, it has been said, were treated as 'liturgical appendages' of funerals, and much of the giving seems to have the character of a symbolic gesture. Promising to aid the poor was part of the rhetoric of the fraternities, but of course the main recipients were fraternity members, who had usually paid a substantial entrance fee, and certainly were not drawn from the lifelong poor. Above all, the charitable organizations seem to have grown in number, resources and effectiveness not during but after the period of greatest poverty. Monasteries and hospitals could not counteract disasters like the great famine, for example, or even the lesser subsistence crises of the decades around 1300.

The charity most likely to work came from families and communities who knew the poor and had the most practical means of helping them. The agreements by which elderly peasants could retire and receive food and shelter for life were obviously a very efficient form of social security. Normally the arrangement would be made within the family, and without any formal record, which explains why so many of the written contracts involve sons-in-law, remote relatives or even non-relatives. The old people trusted their sons to look after them, but preferred the security of a formal agreement in the manorial court if strangers were involved. In the period after 1348-9 the numbers of recorded agreements diminish, and the new tenants were less likely to be relatives (64 per cent were related to the retired peasant before the Black Death, 30 per cent afterwards). Some provision for old age continued, but was agreed informally, or was recorded in wills rather than in the manor court records. But with the reduction in the number of holdings changing hands through inheritance, and especially inheritance by sons, the elderly were less likely to receive the care from the younger generation that seems to have been

Studies, 32 (1993), 195–225; G. Rosser, 'Going to the fraternity feast: commensality and social relations in late medieval England', *Journal of British Studies*, 33 (1994), 436–7; V. R. Bainbridge, *Gilds in the medieval countryside. Social and religious change in Cambridgeshire c.1350–1558* (Woodbridge, 1996), pp. 99–122; A. D. Brown, *Popular piety in late medieval England. The diocese of Salisbury 1250–1550* (Oxford, 1995), pp. 181–201.

normal before the fall in population. The numbers of kin living in the same neighbourhood were also reduced, so diminishing again the chances of support for old people. The community had a role in the manor court (and more informally outside) as witnesses and enforcers of the obligations of the parties to retirement contracts, but from the late fourteenth century the community had a more important and expanding charitable role.[70]

Villages and towns were developing a more formal financial organization. From 1334 the vill was responsible for assessing and levying taxes, both to the disadvantage and advantage of the poor. The leading villagers and townsmen who ran the tax system expected the poor to make a small contribution, which amounted to a token 1d. or 2d. They were often let off, however, because wealthy individuals would donate money to pay these taxes, and the money collected for taxation seems to have formed part of a 'common box' which became the fund from which charity was dispensed. This community role was strengthened by pressure from the state which in 1388 made the vill responsible for the care of beggars who had been found wandering, and by initiatives from within the towns and villages for founding almshouses and endowing them with land. Many of the elements of the Old Poor Law, which were set up by legislation in the sixteenth century, such as community responsibility, and contributions to the 'common box', were in place in many villages in the later middle ages. More informal collective acts of charity could also play their part, like the 'helpales' in Wakefield (Yorkshire) in the fifteenth century, by which a group who wished to help someone down on their luck would brew some ale and sell it to the assembled neighbours, giving the proceeds to the unfortunate. We cannot know much about the personal acts, such as giving of alms, or inviting poor neighbours to meals, but we can appreciate from wills and sermons that acts of charity stipulated on the deathbed could have been continuations of regular practices.[71]

---

70 R. Smith, 'The manorial court and the elderly tenant in late medieval England', in M. Pelling and R. M. Smith (eds.), *Life, death and the elderly* (London, 1991), pp. 39–61; Razi, 'Immutable English family'.

71 C. Dyer, 'Taxation and communities in late medieval England', in Britnell and Hatcher (eds.), *Progress and problems*, pp. 168–90; E. Clark, 'Social welfare and mutual aid in the medieval countryside', *Journal of British Studies*, 33 (1994), 381–406; E. Clark, 'Charitable bequests, deathbed land sales, and the manor court in later medieval England', in Razi and Smith (eds.), *Manor court*, pp. 143–61; M. K. McIntosh, 'Local responses to the poor

WEATHER

The unstable climate of the fourteenth century has already been discussed. The great famine had a particularly damaging effect on crop yields in the north, and while severe food shortages came to an end in southern and midland England in 1375, the north still suffered badly in the famine of 1437-40. The poor were hard hit because in the uplands they lived on oats for which there were no cheaper substitutes, and for northern landlords the period marks a watershed in their fortunes from which they suffered for many years. By contrast, a London merchant paid in 1439 for the city to be provided with a grain store, the Leadenhall, to be used as a countermeasure against famine, but his fears proved to be unfounded, and the grand building was used as a market and wool warehouse. The north–south divide continued until the seventeenth century, when the north escaped from the threat of subsistence crises.[72]

CONCLUSION

Scientific work is adding constantly to our knowledge of features of the past for which there are no written documents. Insights into modern living standards have come from records of height, which shows differences in region, class and gender, and reductions in stature during the industrial revolution. Table 21 compares the heights of adults recorded in documents of the late eighteenth and early nineteenth centuries with heights calculated from samples of skeletons from late medieval cemeteries. The modern sample is

in late medieval and Tudor England', *Continuity and Change,* 3 (1988), 209–45; J. M. Bennett, 'Conviviality and charity in medieval and early modern England', *P. and P.,* 134 (1992), 19–41; M. Moisa and J. M. Bennett, 'Debate. Conviviality and charity in medieval and early modern England', *P. and P.,* 154 (1997), 223–42. On the apparent effectiveness of early modern local poor relief, P. M. Solar, 'Poor relief and English economic development before the industrial revolution', *Ec.H.R.,* 48 (1995), 1–22.

72 A. J. Pollard, 'The north-eastern economy and the agrarian crisis of 1438–40', *Northern History,* 25 (1989), 88–105; M. Samuel, 'The fifteenth-century garner at Leadenhall, London', *Antiquaries Jnl,* 69 (1989), 119–53; J. Walter and R. Schofield, 'Famine, disease and crisis mortality in early modern society', in J. Walter and R. Schofield (eds.), *Famine, disease and the social order in early modern society* (Cambridge, 1989), pp. 1–73.

biased towards the lower classes, but the same is true of the people buried in the cemetery of St Helen in one of the poorer districts of York.

In another approach to measuring size, table 22 shows shoe sizes from late medieval London, and those of the nineteenth and twentieth centuries, which implies that medieval people's feet, and presumably the rest of their bodies, were comparable with those of the nineteenth century.

Whatever qualifications need to be made about the methods by which this evidence has been obtained, and about its statistical interpretation, the comparison questions the common assumption of appalling medieval living conditions, from which humanity has been saved by modern progress.

Table 21. *Mean height of medieval and modern populations*

Sample	Date	Male height	Female height (in metres)·
St. Helen-on-the-Walls, York	Tenth–sixteenth centuries	1.69m	1.57m
46–54 Fishergate, York	1195–sixteenth century	1.71m	1.59m
Rothwell charnel house, Northamptonshire	Thirteenth– sixteenth centuries	1.72m	1.58m
Military recruits (aged 24–9)	1812–57	1.69m	–
Criminals	1812–57	1.66m	1.55m
Convicts transported to Australia	1770–1815	1.67m	1.55m

·some equivalents in imperial measures are
1.55 m = 61.1 ins (5 ft 1 ins)
1.66 m = 65.4 ins (5 ft 5 ins)
1.71 m = 67.3 ins (5 ft 7 ins)
Source note: J.M. Lilley, G. Stroud, D.R. Brothwell and M.H. Williamson, *The Jewish burial ground at Jewbury* (York Archaeological Trust, The Archaeology of York, 12, fasc. 3, 1994), pp. 435–7; P. Johnson and S. Nicholas, 'Male and female living standards in England and Wales, 1812–1857: evidence from criminal height records', *Ec.H.R.*, 48 (1995), 470–81.

Table 22. *Shoe sizes: medieval and modern*

	Adult male	Adult female
Medieval	4–6	1–3
1900	2–7	1–4
1990s	6–11	4–8

Note: these are modern British shoe sizes, in which the lengths are:
1 : 221mm/8⅔ ins long; 4 : 246mm/9⅔ ins; 7 : 271mm/10⅔ ins
Source note: Grew and de Neergaard, *Shoes and pattens*, pp. 102–5.

BIBLIOGRAPHY

This is intended to indicate the main published works relevant to the theme of this book. Only works in English have been included, and space allows mention of no more than a few of the numerous articles and essays on the subject. Many more will be found cited in footnotes, together with primary sources and works on related topics for the modern period.

GENERAL WORKS

Two books survey the whole of late medieval social and economic history: the most comprehensive is J.L. Bolton, *The medieval English economy 1150–1500* (London, 1980); M.M. Postan, *The medieval economy and society* (London, 1972) is more controversial. A useful survey of the rural scene in the early part of the period which gives a good deal of support to Postan's interpretation is E. Miller and J. Hatcher, *Medieval England – rural society and economic change 1086–1348* (London, 1978). Also sympathetic to Postan, and covering a similar period with illustrative documents, is J.Z. Titow, *English rural society 1200–1350* (London, 1969). England is set into the European scene in G. Duby, *Rural economy and country life in the medieval west* (London, 1968) and C.M. Cipolla (ed.), *The Fontana economic history of Europe*, vol. I (London, 1972). There are essays about England and parallel studies of Europe in the first three volumes of the *Cambridge economic history of Europe*: vol. I, *The agrarian life of the middle ages*, 2nd edn (Cambridge, 1966); vol. II, *Trade and industry in the middle ages* 2nd edn (Cambridge, 1987); vol. III, *Economic organization and policies in the middle ages* (Cambridge, 1965). Alternative views to Postan are presented in A.R. Bridbury, *Economic growth. England in the later middle ages* (London, 1962) and, more soberly, in R.H. Britnell, *The commercialisation of English society 1000–1500* (Cambridge,

1993). For a variety of interpretations of the period, turn to T. Aston and C.H.E. Philpin (eds.), *The Brenner debate. Agrarian class structure and economic development in pre-industrial Europe* (Cambridge, 1985). Essay collections with work relevant to living standards include E.M. Carus-Wilson (ed.), *Essays in economic history*, vol. II (London, 1962); R.H. Hilton (ed.), *Peasants, knights and heretics* (Cambridge, 1976); T. Aston (ed.), *Landlords, peasants and politics in medieval England* (Cambridge, 1987). Collected essays of individual scholars include M.M. Postan, *Essays on medieval agriculture and general problems of the medieval economy* (Cambridge, 1973) and *Medieval trade and finance* (Cambridge, 1973); R.H. Hilton, *Class conflict and the crisis of feudalism* (London, 1985); and C. Dyer, *Everyday life in medieval England* (London, 1994). There are also relevant essays in T.H. Aston *et al.* (eds.), *Social relations and ideas* (Cambridge, 1983), and R. Britnell and J. Hatcher (eds.), *Progress and problems in medieval England* (Cambridge, 1996).

The social history of the period is surveyed in two contrasting works: M. Keen, *English society in the later middle ages* (Harmondsworth, 1990) which is urbane and cultural, and the grittily theoretical S. Rigby, *English society in the later middle ages. Class, status, and gender* (Basingstoke, 1995). A regional approach to social and economic history was pioneered by R.H. Hilton, *A medieval society. The west midlands at the end of the thirteenth century*, 2nd edn (Cambridge, 1983); it has been continued in two works with a focus on the aristocracy: M.J. Bennett, *Community, class and careerism* (Cambridge, 1983), and A.J. Pollard, *North-eastern England during the Wars of the Roses. Lay society, war, and politics, 1450–1500* (Oxford, 1990). Two districts in eastern England have been studied intensively: M. Bailey, *A marginal economy? East Anglian Breckland in the later middle ages* (Cambridge, 1989), and L. Poos, *A rural society after the Black Death. Essex 1350–1520* (Cambridge, 1991). There are two surveys of historical geography, the first emphasizing maps: H.C. Darby (ed.), *A new historical geography of England before 1600* (Cambridge, 1973); the other containing more interpretation: R.A. Dodgshon and R.A. Butlin (eds.), *An historical geography of England and Wales*, 2nd edn (London, 1990). General surveys of archaeological evidence include C. Platt, *Medieval England. A social history and archaeology from the conquest to 1600 AD*, (London, 1978); D.A. Hinton, *Archaeology, economy and society. England from the fifth to the fifteenth century* (London, 1990); J.M. Steane, *The archaeology of medieval England and Wales* (London, 1985); D. Gaimster and P. Stamper (eds.), *The age of transition. The archaeology of English culture, 1400–1600* (Oxford, 1997). The latter work deals with a specific part of the period in a wide-ranging way, and the same is true of three historical works dealing with different aspects of the fourteenth-century crisis: B.M.S. Campbell (ed.), *Before the Black Death. Studies in the 'crisis' of the fourteenth century* (Manchester, 1991); C. Platt, *King Death. The Black Death and its aftermath in late medieval England* (London, 1996); M. Ormrod and P. Lindley (eds.), *The Black Death in England* (Stamford, 1996). And for the fifteenth century, J.I. Kermode (ed.), *Enterprise and individuals in fifteenth-century England* (Stroud, 1991).

LANDLORDS AND ARISTOCRACIES

The most influential study of the secular aristocracy is K.B. McFarlane, *The nobility of later medieval England* (Oxford, 1973). The same author's collected essays, *England in the fifteenth century* (London, 1981), contains pieces of social as well as political interest. For an earlier period, S. Painter, *Studies in the history of the English feudal barony* (Baltimore, 1943) is still useful. Estate economics and social relationships are discussed in G.A. Holmes, *Estates of the higher nobility in fourteenth-century England* (Cambridge, 1957), and the distinctive lordships of the' Welsh border are illuminated in R.R. Davies, *Lordship and society in the march of Wales* (Oxford, 1978), C. Given-Wilson, *The English nobility in the late middle ages* (London, 1987), concentrates on social and political aspects of the fourteenth-century aristocracy. The effects of the Black Death are discussed in S.J. Payling, 'Social mobility, demographic change, and landed society in late medieval England', *Ec.H.R.*, 45 (1992), 51–73. A survey of the lesser aristocracy concentrating on the early part of the period is P.R. Coss, *The knight in medieval England 1000–1400* (Stroud, 1993) and has progressed through studies of counties and localities, notably P.R. Coss, *Lordship, knighthood and locality. A study in English society c.1180–c.1280* (Cambridge, 1991); N. Saul, *Knights and esquires: the Gloucestershire gentry in the fourteenth century* (Oxford, 1981); S.M. Wright, *The Derbyshire gentry in the fifteenth century* (Derbyshire Record Soc., 8, 1983); C. Carpenter, *Locality and polity. A study of Warwickshire landed society, 1401–1499* (Cambridge, 1992), and E. Acheson, *A gentry community. Leicestershire in the fifteenth century, c.1422–c.1485* (Cambridge, 1992). M. Jones (ed.), *Gentry and lesser nobility in late medieval Europe* (Gloucester, 1986) contains some important essays.

Studies of monastic landlords include D.M. Knowles, *The religious orders in England* (3 vols., Cambridge, 1948–59) and E. Power, *Medieval English nunneries* (Cambridge, 1922). On the secular clergy as well as the monasteries, a comprehensive study is R.N. Swanson, *Church and society in late medieval England* (Oxford, 1989).

The traditional English approach to medieval landlords is to study their estates, and a good deal of general economic and social history is contained in these estate histories. For secular magnates there are the following: M. Altschul, *A baronial family in medieval England. The Clares, 1217–1314* (Baltimore, 1965); J.M.W. Bean, *The estates of the Percy family, 1416–1537* (Oxford, 1958); J. Hatcher, *Rural economy and society in the duchy of Cornwall 1300–1500* (Cambridge, 1970); C. Rawcliffe, *The Staffords, earls of Stafford and dukes of Buckingham 1394–1521* (Cambridge, 1978). Political biographies, for example, J.R. Maddicott, *Thomas of Lancaster, 1307–22* (Oxford, 1970), and A.J. Pollard, *John Talbot and the war in France, 1427–1453* (London, 1983), often include information about estates and incomes.

The larger number of studies of church estates reflects the better preservation of their records. They include F.R.H. Du Boulay, *The lordship of Canterbury* (London, 1966); C. Dyer, *Lords and peasants in a changing society. The estates of the bishopric of Worcester, 680–1540* (Cambridge, 1980); H.P.R. Finberg, *Tavistock Abbey. A study in the social and economic history of Devon*, 2nd edn (Newton Abbot, 1969); B. Harvey, *Westminster Abbey and its estates in the middle ages* (Oxford, 1977); R.H.

Hilton, *The economic development of some Leicestershire estates in the fourteenth and fifteenth centuries* (Oxford, 1947); S.F. Hockey, *Quarr Abbey and its lands, 1132–1632* (Leicester, 1970); I. Kershaw, *Bolton Priory. The economy of a northern monastery, 1286–1325* (Oxford, 1973); E. King, *Peterborough Abbey 1086–1310* (Cambridge, 1973); E. Miller, *The abbey and bishopric of Ely* (Cambridge, 1951); M. Morgan, *The English lands of the abbey of Bec* (Oxford, 1946); F.M. Page, *The estates of Crowland Abbey* (Cambridge, 1934); J.A. Raftis, *The estates of Ramsey Abbey* (Toronto, 1957); E. Searle, *Lordship and community. Battle Abbey and its banlieu 1066–1538* (Toronto, 1974); R.A.L. Smith, *Canterbury Cathedral Priory* (Cambridge, 1943). On the last estate, a number of studies by M. Mate have supplemented and modified Smith's work, notably 'The estates of Canterbury Cathedral Priory before the Black Death', *Studies in Medieval and Renaissance History*, 8 (1987), 3–31, and 'Agrarian economy after the Black Death: the manors of Canterbury Cathedral Priory, 1348–91', *Ec.H.R.*, 2nd ser., 37 (1984), 341–54.

Individual gentry or gentry families are discussed with some consideration of life-style and expenditure in C. Richmond, *John Hopton* (Cambridge, 1981); N. Saul, *Scenes from provincial life. Knightly families in Sussex, 1280–1400* (Oxford, 1986); and C.E. Moreton, *The Townshends and their world: gentry, law, and land in Norfolk, c.1450–1551* (Oxford, 1992).

Household accounts have been edited by C.M. Woolgar in *Household accounts from medieval England*, 2 parts (Records of Social and Economic History, new ser., 17 and 18, Oxford, 1992, 1993) with a useful introduction. They have been used to write C.D. Ross, 'The household accounts of Elizabeth Berkeley, countess of Warwick, 1420–1', *Transactions of the Bristol and Gloucestershire Archaeological Soc.*, 70 (1951), 81–105, and a popular work, M.W. Labarge, *A baronial household in the thirteenth century* (London, 1965). On aristocratic food there is B.A. Henisch, *Fast and feast* (Pittsburgh, 1976) and T. Scully, *The art of cooking in the middle ages* (Woodbridge, 1995); and on dress S.M. Newton, *Fashion in the age of the Black Prince* (Woodbridge, 1980). For their buildings and residences see F.A. Aberg (ed.), *Medieval moated sites* (C.B.A. Research Report, 17, 1978); M.W. Barley, *Houses and history* (London, 1986); L.F. Salzman, *Building in England, down to 1540*, 2nd edn (Oxford, 1967); M.E. Wood, *The English medieval house* (London, 1965); M.W. Thompson, *The decline of the castle* (Cambridge, 1988) and the same author's *The medieval hall* (Aldershot, 1995). The most thorough study of a household is B. Harvey, *Living and dying in England 1100–1540. The monastic experience* (Oxford, 1993) which is based on Westminster Abbey, but has general significance. On the ideas and institutions that influenced aristocratic spending see M. Keen, *Chivalry* (New Haven, Conn., 1984) and V.J. Scattergood and J.W. Sherborne (eds.), *English court culture in the later middle ages* (London, 1983).

PEASANTS

H.S. Bennett, *Life on the English manor* (Cambridge, 1937) still provides a readable if old-fashioned introduction. More austerely scientific is E.A. Kosminsky, *Studies in the agrarian history of England in the thirteenth century* (Oxford, 1956). R.H. Hilton has defined the peasantry as a social class and explored their relations both with their lords, and among themselves, in *The decline of serfdom in medieval England* (London, 1969); *Bondmen made free* (London, 1973); and *The English peasantry in the later middle ages* (Oxford, 1975). The latter includes both a lengthy study of the peasantry in the post–1350 period, and reprints of articles on earlier centuries. A legal view of serfdom is in P.R. Hyams, *Kings, lords and peasants in medieval England* (Oxford, 1980). Works which emphasize peasant communities and families are G.C. Homans, *English villagers of the thirteenth century* (Cambridge, Mass., 1941); W.O. Ault, *Open-field farming in medieval England* (London, 1972); B.A. Hanawalt, *The ties that bound* (New York, 1986); J.A. Raftis, *Tenure and mobility* (Toronto, 1964). The latter author has also edited a volume of essays: *Pathways to medieval peasants* (Toronto, 1981). For examples of peasant prosperity after 1349, see A. Watkins, 'Cattle grazing in the Forest of Arden in the later middle ages', *Ag.H.R.*, 37 (1989), 12–25.

Two essay collections concentrate on the transfer of land among peasants: P.D.A. Harvey (ed.), *The peasant land market in medieval England* (Oxford, 1984) and R.M. Smith (ed.), *Land, kinship and lifecycle* (Cambridge, 1984). Another is focussed on the court records of the manor: Z. Razi and R. Smith (eds.), *Medieval society and the manor court* (Oxford, 1996).

The estate histories listed above almost all devote space to the peasantry, but a greater concentration on peasants is found in village or manorial histories, such as F.G. Davenport, *The economic development of a Norfolk manor 1086–1565* (London, 1906); P.D.A. Harvey, *A medieval Oxfordshire village. Cuxham 1240 to 1400* (Oxford, 1965); M.K. McIntosh, *Autonomy and community. The royal manor of Havering, 1200–1500* (Cambridge, 1986); J.R. Ravensdale, *Liable to floods. Village landscape on the edge of the fens A.D. 450–1850* (Cambridge, 1974); Z. Razi, *Life, marriage and death in a medieval parish. Economy, society and demography in Halesowen, 1270–1400* (Cambridge, 1980). The Toronto school of historians have published a number of histories of villages or manors, for example, E. Britton, *The community of the vill* (Toronto, 1977).

The material culture of the peasantry is surveyed in M.W. Beresford and J.G. Hurst (eds.), *Deserted medieval villages* (London, 1971); G.G. Astill and A. Grant (eds.), *The countryside of medieval England* (Oxford, 1988); M. Aston et al. (eds.), *The rural settlements of medieval England* (Oxford, 1989). Of the many excavation reports, examples are G. Beresford, *The medieval clay land village: excavations at Goltho and Barton Blount* (Soc. for Med. Arch. Monograph, 6, 1975); J.G. Hurst (ed.), *Wharram* (Soc. for Med. Arch. Monograph, 8, 1979); D.C. Mynard and R.J. Zeepvat, *Great Linford* (Bucks. Arch. Soc. Monograph, 3, 1992). On houses, N.W. Alcock, *Cruck construction* (C.B.A. Research Report, 42, 1981); E. Mercer, *English vernacular houses* (London, 1975); S. Pearson, *The medieval houses of Kent* (Royal Commission on Historical Monuments, England, 1994).

TOWNS

General surveys are C. Platt, *The English medieval town* (London, 1976), which combines archaeology and history, and the more historical S. Reynolds, *An introduction to the history of English medieval towns* (Oxford, 1977). The controversy over 'urban decline' is summed up by A. Dyer, *Decline and growth in English towns 1400–1640* (Cambridge, 1995). The earlier urban growth is described in E. Miller and J. Hatcher, *Medieval England. Towns, commerce and crafts* (London, 1995), and its underlying causes in R.H. Britnell and B.M.S. Campbell (eds.), *A commercialising economy. England 1086–c.1300* (Manchester, 1995).

Valuable studies of individual towns include R.H. Britnell, *Growth and decline in Colchester, 1300–1525* (Cambridge, 1986); M. Carlin, *Medieval Southwark* (London, 1996); D.J. Keene, *Survey of medieval Winchester* (Oxford, 1985); M. Kowaleski, *Local markets and regional trade in medieval Exeter* (Cambridge, 1995); C. Phythian–Adams, *Desolation of a city. Coventry and the urban crisis of the late middle ages* (Cambridge, 1979); C. Platt, *Medieval Southampton* (London, 1973); G. Rosser, *Medieval Westminster 1200–1540* (Oxford, 1989); D.G. Shaw, *The creation of a community. The city of Wells in the middle ages* (Oxford, 1993); S. Thrupp, *The merchant class of medieval London* (Chicago, 1948); G. Unwin, *The gilds and companies of London*, 4th edn (London, 1963). The essays in R. Holt and G. Rosser (eds.), *The medieval town. A reader in English urban history* (London, 1990) include some on small towns. The relevance of small towns to consumption patterns is discussed in C. Dyer, 'Market towns and the countryside in late medieval England', *Canadian Journal of History*, 31 (1996), 17–35. An important section of urban society is analysed in H. Swanson, *Medieval artisans. An urban class in late medieval England* (Oxford, 1989). On urban food supplies, B.M.S. Campbell, J.A. Galloway, D. Keene and M. Murphy, *A medieval capital and its grain supply: agrarian production and distribution in the London region c.1300* (Hist. Geography Research ser. 30, 1993). There are useful essays on London (and Paris) as centres of consumption in a special issue of the journal *Franco-British Studies*, 20 (1995).

A.R. Hall and H.K. Kenward (eds.), *Environmental archaeology in an urban context* (C.B.A. Research Report, 43, 1982) and J. Schofield and A. Vince, *Medieval towns* (Leicester, 1994) survey recent archaeological research in towns. Individual excavation reports are too numerous to list here, but examples are C. Platt and R. Coleman-Smith, *Excavations in medieval Southampton, 1953–1969* (Leicester, 1975) and H. Clarke and A. Carter, *Excavations in King's Lynn 1963–1970* (Soc. for Med. Arch. Monograph, no. 7, 1977). The York Archaeological Trust publishes its reports in fascicles, under the general title *The archaeology of York*. The Museum of London has published a series on 'Medieval finds from excavations in London', by various authors, on knives, shoes, dress accessories and horse equipment. On houses see J. Schofield, *Medieval London houses* (New Haven, 1994) and J. Grenville, *Medieval housing* (Leicester, 1997).

OTHER GROUPS

Among wage-earners the best studied groups are the building workers: D. Knoop and G.P. Jones, *The medieval mason*, 3rd edn (Manchester, 1967); T.H. Lloyd, *Some aspects of the building industry in medieval Stratford-upon-Avon* (Dugdale Soc. Occasional Paper, 14, 1961); H. Swanson, *Building craftsmen in late medieval York* (Borthwick Paper, 63, 1983). A book mainly on modern building work has important points to make relevant to our period: D. Woodward, *Men at work. Labourers and building craftsmen in the towns of northern England 1450–1750* (Cambridge, 1995). On agricultural labour, H.S.A. Fox, 'Servants, cottagers and tied cottages during the later middle ages', *Rural History*, 6 (1995), 125–54.

Professionals are neglected, though C.H. Clough (ed.), *Profession, vocation, and culture in later medieval England* (Liverpool, 1982) makes a start. A thorough study has been made of the lawyers: E.W. Ives, *The common lawyers of pre-reformation England* (Cambridge, 1983).

Women are examined in J.M. Bennett, *Women in the medieval English countryside. Gender and household in Brigstock before the plague* (New York, 1987); B.A. Hanawalt (ed.), *Women and work in pre-industrial Europe* (Bloomington, Indiana, 1986); C. Barron, 'The golden age of women in medieval London', *Reading Medieval Studies*, 15 (1989), 35–58; P.J.P. Goldberg, *Women, work and life cycle in a medieval economy: York and Yorkshire c.1300–1520* (Oxford, 1992); P.J.P. Goldberg (ed.), *Woman is a worthy wight* (Stroud, 1992); J.C. Ward, *English noblewomen in the later middle ages* (London, 1992); C. Barron and A. Sutton (eds.), *Medieval London widows 1300–1500* (London, 1994); R.M. Karras, *Common women: prostitution and sexuality in medieval England* (New York and Oxford, 1996); J. Bennett, *Ale, beer and brewsters in England. Women's work in a changing world, 1300–1600* (New York and Oxford, 1996).

INDUSTRY AND TRADE

Most works concentrate on production rather than on consumption. General surveys are D.W. Crossley (ed.), *Medieval industry* (C.B.A. Research Report, 40, 1981); and J. Blair and N. Ramsay (eds.), *English medieval industries* (London, 1991). On specific industries J. Hatcher, *English tin production and trade before 1550* (Oxford, 1973); J. Hatcher and T.C. Barker, *A history of British pewter* (London, 1974); H.R. Schubert, *History of the British iron and steel industry* (London, 1957); J. Hatcher, *History of the British coal industry, vol. I: Before 1700* (Oxford, 1993); and M.R. McCarthy and C.M. Brooks, *Medieval pottery in Britain AD 900–1600* (Leicester, 1988). We still have no full study of the cloth industry. E.M. Carus-Wilson, *Medieval merchant venturers* (London, 1967), and her contributions to the *Cambridge economic history*, (see above) were the pioneering works; A.R. Bridbury, *Medieval English clothmaking* (London, 1982) mulls over the old evidence. M. Zell, *Industry in the countryside* (Cambridge, 1994) is mainly about the sixteenth-century cloth industry in Kent, but has relevance for our period.

On trade we know more about exports: for example, E.M. Carus-Wilson and O. Coleman, *England's export trade, 1275–1547* (Oxford, 1963); E. Power, *The wool trade in English medieval history* (Oxford, 1941); and much of E. Power and M.M. Postan (eds.), *Studies in English trade in the fifteenth century* (London, 1933). Studies of imports necessarily lead to more interest in consumption, for example W.R. Childs, 'England's iron trade in the fifteenth century', *Ec.H.R.*, 2nd ser., 34 (1981), 25–47; M.K. James, *Studies in the medieval wine trade* (Oxford, 1971); E. Veale, *The English fur trade in the later middle ages* (Oxford, 1966); W.R. Childs,

Anglo-Castilian trade in the later middle ages (Manchester, 1978). P. Nightingale, *A medieval mercantile community. The Grocers' Company and the politics and trade of London 1000–1485* (New Haven, 1995), says a little about purchase of spices. On credit see J. Kermode, 'Money and credit in the fifteenth century: some lessons from Yorkshire', *Business History Review*, 65 (1991), 475–501.

AGRICULTURAL TECHNIQUES AND PRODUCTIVITY

Agricultural techniques are much studied through the organization of fields, the most thorough work being A.R.H. Baker and R.A. Butlin, *Studies of field systems in the British Isles* (Cambridge, 1973). More direct investigations of productivity are J.Z. Titow, *Winchester yields* (Cambridge, 1972); B.M.S. Campbell and M. Overton (eds.), *Land, labour and livestock: historical studies in European agricultural productivity* (Manchester, 1991); B.M.S. Campbell and M. Overton, 'A new perspective on medieval and early modern agriculture: six centuries of Norfolk farming, c.1250–c.1850', *P. and P.*, 141 (1993), 38–105. For livestock, R. Trow-Smith, *A history of British livestock husbandry to 1700* (London, 1957); M. Stephenson, 'Wool yields in the medieval economy', *Ec.H.R.*, 2nd ser., 41 (1988), 368–91. The use of animal-power is revealed in J. Langdon, *Horses, oxen and technological innovation* (Cambridge, 1986). The resources of woods and pastures are discussed in O. Rackham, *Trees and woodlands in the British landscape* (London, 1976); J.R. Birrell, 'Common rights in the medieval forest: disputes and conflicts in the thirteenth century', *P. and P.*, 117 (1987), 22–49. On technology in general, G. Astill and J. Langdon (eds.), *Medieval farming and technology. The impact of agricultural change in northwestern Europe* (Leiden, 1997); R. Holt, *The mills of medieval England* (Oxford, 1988).

Fluctuations caused by the weather are discussed in W. Abel, *Agricultural fluctuations in Europe* (London, 1980); H.H. Lamb, *Climate, present, past and future* (London, 1977); M.L. Parry, *Climatic change, agriculture and settlement* (Folkestone, 1978); W.C. Jordan, *The Great Famine. Northern Europe in the early fourteenth century* (Princeton, 1996).

For agricultural history in general, H.E. Hallam (ed.), *The agrarian history of England and Wales*, vol. II, 1042–1348 (Cambridge, 1988) and E. Miller (ed.), *The agrarian history of England and Wales*, vol. III, 1348–1500 (Cambridge, 1991).

WAGES AND PRICES

W.H. Beveridge, 'Wages in the Winchester manors', *Ec.H.R.*, 7 (1936), 22–43 and 'Westminster wages in the manorial era', *Ec.H.R.*, 2nd ser., 8 (1955), 18–35, laid the foundation for the modern study of wage-rates. On prices of wool, T.H. Lloyd, *The movement of wool prices in medieval England* (Ec.H.R., Supplement, 6, 1973). On movements in both wages and prices, D.L. Farmer, 'Prices and wages', in *The agrarian history of England and Wales*, vols. II and III (see above); D.L. Farmer, 'Crop yields, prices and wages in medieval England', *Studies in Medieval and Renaissance History*, 6 (1983), 117–55; E.H. Phelps-Brown and S.V. Hopkins, *A perspective on wages and prices* (London, 1981). On the labour laws, S.A.C. Penn and C. Dyer, 'Wages and earnings in late medieval England: evidence from the enforcement of the labour laws', *Ec.H.R.*, 2nd ser., 43 (1990), 356–76; J. Hatcher, 'England in the aftermath of the Black Death', *P. and P.*, 144 (1994), 3–35.

Some historians stress monetary influences on prices: J. Day, *The medieval market economy* (Oxford, 1987); N.J. Mayhew, 'Money and prices in England from Henry II to Edward III', *Ag.H.R.*, 35 (1987), 121–32.

POPULATION AND POVERTY

On the population before 1348 Postan and his allies (see first section above) have defended a view that dangerously high levels led to a decline soon after 1300. For the contrary view see B.F. Harvey, 'The population trend in England between 1300 and 1348', *T.R.H.S.*, 5th ser., 16 (1966), 23–42. After 1348 mortality is emphasized by R.S. Gottfried, *Epidemic disease in fifteenth-century England* (Leicester, 1978): and by J. Hatcher, *Plague, population and the English economy 1348–1530* (London, 1977), and fertility by Goldberg and Poos, and by R.M. Smith, in Astill and Grant (eds.), *Countryside of medieval England*. For a partisan (pro-mortality) view, M. Bailey, 'Demographic decline in late medieval England: some thoughts on recent research', *Ec.H.R.*, 49 (1996), 1–19. For a radical perspective on demography and peasant society, Z. Razi, 'The myth of the immutable English family', *P. and P.*, 140 (1993), 3–44.

Most works on poverty stress the paupers' role as receivers of charity, for example M. Mollat, *The poor in the middle ages* (New Haven, Conn., 1986); M. Rubin, *Charity and community in medieval Cambridge* (Cambridge, 1987). It is seen from the recipients' point of view in B. Geremek, *The margins of society in late medieval Paris* (Cambridge, 1987).

Hospitals, almshouses and fraternities attract much attention: P.H. Cullum, *Cremetts and corrodies: care of the poor and sick at St Leonard's Hospital, York, in the middle ages* (Borthwick Paper, 79, 1991); N. Orme and M. Webster, *The English hospital, 1070–1570* (New Haven and London, 1995); C. Rawcliffe, *The hospitals of medieval Norwich* (Norwich, 1995); B.R. McRee, 'Charity and gild solidarity in late medieval England', *Journal of British Studies*, 32 (1993), 195–225; a special issue of the journal *Continuity and Change*, 3 (1988), deals with a number of issues relating to charity; the *Journal of British Studies*, 33 (1994) is also a special issue devoted to the theme of community in which charity and social security figure prominently.

INDEX

accounts, household, 1, 49–50, 60, 64,
68–9, 74–5, 77, 78–9, 92–7, 108, 210,
283–4; manorial, 27–8, 34–5, 68, 92,
128, 261, 308
Acton, Suffolk, 54
agriculture, 2, 7–8, 22–3, 28, 35, 37–43,
67–9, 101–2, 108, 110–18, 127–31,
143–5, 148–50, 166, 171–2, 185–6,
211–14, 221, 223, 231, 258–73, 289–95
Alciston, Sussex, 151
ale, 8, 38, 55–8, 64–8, 90, 94, 97, 114–15,
132, 133, 135, 146, 149, 153–4,
156–160, 172–3, 183, 196–8, 209, 210,
216, 220, 221, 224, 226, 244, 248,
249–50, 253, 270, 294–5, 297, 298,
308–9, 311; see also artisans, brewers
All Souls College, see Oxford
almshouses, see hospitals
Alnwick, Northumberland, 73
Alrewas, Staffordshire, 157, 174, 176, 179,
180
Alwerd, family of, 288
animals, 3, 28, 38, 76, 91, 101–2, 114–17,
128–31, 135, 144–5, 148–9, 155–6, 158,
166, 181, 185, 189, 221, 261, 289, 295,
298; see also cattle, deer, dogs, horses,
pigs, rabbits, sheep
Appleby, Sir Edmund, 76
Appleby Magna, Leicestershire, 76
apprentices, 23–4, 208, 212, 220, 231–3,
298
Aquinas, Thomas, 236
Arles, archbishop of, 67
arms and armour, 53, 76–7, 174, 206,
280–1
artisans and craftsmen, 2, 7, 11, 14–15, 20,
22, 24–5, 88, 105, 132–3, 166, 172,
195–6, 203–6, 208–9, 213, 214, 219–24,
226–7, 232–3, 234, 246, 254, 269, 276,
294, 295–6, 299, 300, 306–11; bakers,
13, 156, 197–9, 229; barbers, 206;
bowmakers, 132; brewers, 133, 156,
158–9, 197–9, 295, 298; butchers, 59,
156–7, 159, 191, 195, 197–9, 276, 298;
cappers, 196; carpenters, 32, 132, 167,
196, 220, 225–7, 230, 304; cartwrights,
132; cobblers, cordwainers, shoe-
makers, 13, 68, 172, 221, 222, 223;
cooks, 197–8; coopers, 132; cutlers, 8;
dyers, 13, 24, 79; fishermen, 132–3,
146, 172, 223; fishmongers, 197, 199;
fletchers, 132; founders, 195; fullers,
24, 79, 250; gardeners, 64, 198; glass-
makers, 132; glovers, 195; hoopers,
196; hosiers, 195; ironmongers, 13;
masons, 196, 216, 220, 225–7; millers,
11; miners, 132–3, 145; pewterers, 299;
potters, 8, 132–3, 174, 299; slaters,
170–2, 230; smiths, 11, 13, 14, 132,
172, 225; spinners, 132, 145, 222;
spurriers, 219; stringers, 195; tailors,
13, 195, 203; tanners, 172; thatchers,
215; turners, 132; weavers, 8, 13, 14,
24, 79, 145–6, 203–4, 212, 222, 224,
250; wheelers, 132
Arundel, earl of, Richard Fitzalan, 92
Arundel, Thomas, see Ely, bishop of
Ashby St Ledgers, Northamptonshire, 71
assarting and internal colonization, 37, 39,
41, 110, 119, 125, 131, 260, 266, 280,
287, 288, 291
attitudes to consumption, 7, 8, 19, 35,
50–5, 61, 67–9, 81, 83, 86–99, 105–6,
108, 146, 176–7, 199, 202, 275–6,
285–7, 311; to poverty, 23, 25, 54, 99,
234–40, 224–6, 249–54, 255–7, 284,
312–14; to social change, 16–17, 87–9,
145, 219, 221, 238–9, 276; to work, 23,
146, 213, 221–5, 231–3, 292, 305–6,
309–11

259, 285, 286
Winner and waster, 87, 89, 90
Wisbech, Cambridgeshire, 292, 312
Witney, Oxfordshire, 12–13
Wivenhoe, Essex, 59, 72
women, 3, 25, 44, 50, 71–3, 114–18, 120,
132–3, 145, 153–4, 168, 175–7, 192,
196, 211–14, 222, 229–30, 232, 237,
239, 243, 245–6, 250, 254–6, 294–5,
304–6
Wontley, in Bishop's Cleeve,
Gloucestershire, 110, 148
Woodford, Northamptonshire, 65
Woodmancote, in Bishop's Cleeve,
Gloucestershire, 110, 148
Woodstock, Thomas of, *see* Gloucester,
duke of
Worcester, 203, 251, 252–3
Worcester, bishops of, 36, 68, 100, 110,
182, 241; Thomas Bourgchier, bishop
of, 78; John Carpenter, bishop of, 241
Worcester Cathedral Priory, 68, 72, 125,

240, 253
Worcestershire, 72, 111, 112, 124, 153, 154,
156, 157, 161, 170, 177, 182, 266, 268,
288, 300
Writtle, Essex, 100, 230, 247, 256
Wye, river, 72

Yardington, Thomas, 149–50
yardlanders, 114–17, 119–20, 130, 134, 136,
142, 148–9, 154, 171, 177, 184, 186,
269, 288
yeoman, 2, 15–16, 20, 22–3, 31, 32, 51, 65,
98, 108, 142, 144, 173, 214, 282
York, 192, 195, 200, 203, 205, 213, 230–1,
305, 311, 316; St Leonard's hospital at,
242
York, archbishop of, 90
York, duke of, 31, 72, 74
Yorkshire, 37, 57, 80, 81, 125, 127, 154, 155,
161, 166, 175, 184, 266, 282, 283, 300,
314
youth, *see* children

Cambridge Medieval Textbooks

Already published

Germany in the High Middle Ages c. 1050–1200
HORST FUHRMANN

The Hundred Years War
England and France at War c. 1300–c. 1450
CHRISTOPHER ALLMAND

Standards of Living in the Later Middle Ages:
Social Change in England, c. 1200–1520
CHRISTOPHER DYER

Magic in the Middle Ages
RICHARD KIECKHEFER

The Papacy 1073–1198: Continuity and Innovation
I. S. ROBINSON

Medieval Wales
DAVID WALKER

England in the Reign of Edward III
SCOTT L. WAUGH

The Norman Kingdom of Sicily
DONALD MATTHEW

Political Thought in Europe 1250–1450
ANTONY BLACK

The Church in Western Europe from the Tenth
to the Early Twelfth Century
GERD TELLENBACH
Translated by Timothy Reuter

The Medieval Spains
BERNARD F. REILLY

England in the Thirteenth Century
ALAN HARDING

Monastic and Religious Orders in Britain 1000–1300
JANET BURTON

Religion and Devotion in Europe c. 1215–c. 1515
R. N. SWANSON

Printed in the United States
72820LV00003B/85